"A deeply layered and insightful book . . . [This] lyrical account presents the obscene inhumanity of slavery while celebrating the humanity of its victims. . . . While it may not be traditional history, it is certainly great history. *All That She Carried* is a broad and bold reflection on American history, African American resilience, and the human capacity for love and perseverance in the face of soul-crushing madness."

—*The Washington Post*

"A remarkable book, striking a delicate balance between two seemingly incommensurate approaches: Miles's fidelity to her archival material, as she coaxes out facts grounded in the evidence; and her conjectures about this singular object, as she uses what is known about other enslaved women's lives to suppose what could have been."

—JENNIFER SZALAI, *The New York Times*

"[A] powerful history of women and slavery."

—*The New Yorker*

"*All That She Carried* is a master class in the use of context in historical writing. Stymied by a lack of records, Miles thinks around the sack from every available angle. . . . Through her interpretation, the humble things in the sack take on evergreater meaning, its very survival seems magical, and Rose's gift starts to feel momentous in scale."

—REBECCA ONION, *Slate*

"[A] deeply and lovingly researched account . . . But even as a historian's creed dictates that corroborated facts are the most important ones, Miles honors the women with not only the scant facts she could gather, but also with belief that the story Ruth told was true. To bolster that belief and to fill in the gaps of the record, Miles relies on narratives from the formerly enslaved, primarily those of women, to illustrate what life was like for Black women and girls such as Rose and Ashley. . . . Miles' book gets as close as any document can to explaining why the sack remains so powerful. It contains great misery, but it is also a testament to the power of story, witness and unyielding love."

—*Atlanta Journal-Constitution*

"[An] extraordinary story . . . Unique and unforgettable, this volume is also a critique of the importance of archives and those who are routinely left out, to the detriment of us all."

—*Ms.*

"[The] sparkling tale of an embroidered bag from 1921. On its surface, Ashley's sack is an intimate family heirloom. In Miles's artful hands, though, the object is transformed—an embodied memoir of Black women traveling from slavery to freedom, South to North, carrying relics and hopes as they seek new lives."

—*Oprahdaily.com*

"Miles compels us to consider how objects hold a certain metaphysical space where memories and emotions meet, making them valuable and transformative sites for scholarly focus. . . . *All That She Carried* is the epitome of an artifactual Black women's history, one which begins with a cloth sack but ends with the bodies that held it."

—*Chicago Review of Books*

"With skillful writing, the author carefully explores South Carolina's history of economic dependence on slavery, and discusses the efforts of enslaved people to obtain sustenance and clothing and maintain family connections. Drawing on scant genealogical records and letters from people who were formerly enslaved, as well as research on ornamentation, Miles creates a moving account of three women whose stories might have otherwise been lost to history. Readers interested in often-overlooked lives and experiences, and anyone who cherishes a handcrafted heirloom, will enjoy this fascinating book."

—*Library Journal* (starred review)

"What container can hold so big a thing as love? In what small, silent objects can loss be stored, and passed on, screams of pain, and yet, somehow, too, hushed whispers of solace? In *All That She Carried*, the peerless Tiya Miles confronts both the staggering anguish and atrocity of American slavery and the still more staggering courage and beauty of the lives she chronicles. A history told with brilliance and tenderness and fearlessness."

—JILL LEPORE, author of
These Truths: A History of the United States

"*All That She Carried* is a brilliant exercise in historical excavation and recovery, a successful strike against the traditional archives' erasure of the lives of enslaved African-American women. With creativity, determination, and great insight, Miles illuminates the lives of women who suffered much, but never forgot the importance of love and family."

—ANNETTE GORDON-REED, author of
The Hemingses of Monticello

"Tiya Miles is a gentle genius. The histories she writes are as deeply feeling as they are brilliantly researched and her writing is both elegant and tender. *All That She Carried* is a gorgeous book and a model for how to read as well as feel the precious artifacts of Black women's lives."

—IMANI PERRY, author of *Breathe: A Letter to My Sons*

"*All That She Carried* is a moving literary and visual experience about love between a mother and daughter and about many women descendants down through the years. Above all it is Miles's lyrical story, written in her signature penetrating prose, about the power of objects and memory, as well as human endurance, in the history of slavery. Ashley's sack carries us into another world as it reveals our own. The book is nothing short of a revelation."

—DAVID W. BLIGHT, Yale University, author of the Pulitzer Prize-winning *Frederick Douglass: Prophet of Freedom*

"Tiya Miles has written a beautiful book about the tragic materiality of black women's lives across three generations, through slavery and freedom. She also allows readers to witness the historian's craft; how she carefully reconstructs marginalized and forgotten lives from and beyond unyielding and indifferent archives. This book is for anyone interested in learning about black people's centrality to American history."

—STEPHANIE JONES-ROGERS, author of *They Were Her Property*

"We live in a world that undervalues, ignores, and erases the work and the humanity of Black women. Ashley's Sack, as it is known, with its short and simple message of intergenerational love, becomes a portal through which Tiya Miles views and reimagines the inner lives of Black women. She excavates the history of Black women who face insurmountable odds and invent a language that can travel across time. She unearths how Black women fashion for their daughters sacks and words that will carry them into uncertain futures. *All That She Carried* is a stunning work of history and humanism, and Tiya Miles is one of our most eloquent chroniclers of the African American experience."

— MICHAEL ERIC DYSON, author of
Long Time Coming: Reckoning with Race in America

"Tiya Miles uses the tools of her trade to tend to Black people, to Black mothers and daughters, to our wounds, to collective Black love and loss. This book demonstrates Miles' signature genius in its rare balance of both rigor and care."

— BRITTNEY COOPER, author of *Eloquent Rage: A Black Feminist Discovers Her Superpower*

"Only a brilliant storyteller like Tiya Miles could get Ashley's sack to speak across the generations. This story, about an enslaved girl's simple cotton bag and its few embroidered lines, encourages us to pick up our treasured family keepsakes and recognize the love that they contain. Blending urgency, imagination, and poetic prose, *All That She Carried* is a masterpiece work of African American women's history that reveals what it takes to survive and even thrive. Read this book and then pass it on to someone you love — it is a fitting tribute to Ashley, her mother Rose, and all those foremothers who endured."

— MARTHA S. JONES, author of *Vanguard: How Black Women Broke Barriers, Won the Vote and Insisted on Equality for All*

ALL
THAT
SHE
CARRIED

My great grandmother Rose
mother of Ashley gave her this sack when
she was sold at age 9 in South Carolina
it held a tattered dress 3 handfulls of
pecans a braid of Roses hair. Told her

It be filled with my Love always

she never saw her again

Ashley is my grandmother

Ruth Middleton
1921

ALL

THAT

SHE

CARRIED

The Journey of Ashley's Sack,

a Black Family Keepsake

TIYA MILES

RANDOM HOUSE

NEW YORK

Published in the United States by Random House,
an imprint and division of Penguin Random House LLC, New York.

RANDOM HOUSE and the HOUSE colophon are registered trademarks
of Penguin Random House LLC.

Originally published in hardcover in the United States by Random House,
an imprint and division of Penguin Random House LLC, in 2021.

Permissions Acknowledgments can be found on page 373.

Library of Congress Cataloging-in-Publication Data

Names: Miles, Tiya, 1970–author.
Title: All that she carried: the journey of Ashley's sack,
a black family keepsake / Tiya Miles.
Other titles: Journey of Ashley's sack, a black family keepsake
Description: New York: Random House, 2021. | Includes index.
Identifiers: LCCN 2020051688 (print) | LCCN 2020051689 (ebook) |
ISBN 9781984855015 (trade paperback) | ISBN 9781984855008 (ebook)
Subjects: LCSH: Women slaves—South Carolina—Biography. | Ashley
(Enslaved person in South Carolina) | Mothers and daughters. | Women slaves—
Southern States—Social conditions—19th century. | Slaves—Southern States—
Family relationships—History—19th century. | Middleton, Ruth Jones,
1903–1942—Family. | African American women—Biography. | African American
women—Family relationships. | Memory—United States.
Classification: LCC E445.S7 M55 2021 (print) | LCC E445.S7 (ebook) |
DDC 306.3/620820975—dc23
LC record available at https://lccn.loc.gov/2020051688
LC ebook record available at https://lccn.loc.gov/2020051689

Printed in the United States of America on acid-free paper

randomhousebooks.com

6 8 9 7

Book design by Jo Anne Metsch

To my Grandmother Alice, Grandmother Lillian,
Grandmother Cornelia, Grandma Bertha,
Great-grandmother Ida Belle, Great-grandmother Rachael,
Great-grandmother Missouri,
Great-grandmother Anna Christian, Great-aunt Margaret,
and to all of the greats and grandmothers
whose handiwork made our survival possible

Love and empathy, together, lead to justice.

—JONATHAN L. WALTON,
A Lens of Love, 2018

Fear, too, is crucial to love.

—DIANE ACKERMAN,
A Natural History of Love, 1994

CONTENTS

PROLOGUE:
EMERGENCY PACKS

I think we should make emergency packs—grab and
run packs—in case we need to get out of here in a hurry.
—OCTAVIA E. BUTLER, *Parable of the Sower*, 1993

ROSE WAS IN EXISTENTIAL DISTRESS THAT FATEFUL
winter when her would-be earthly master, Robert Martin, passed
away. The place: coastal South Carolina; the year: 1852. We do
not know Rose's family name, or the place of *her* birth, or the
year of *her* death. Such is the case with the vast majority of African and Indigenous American women who were bought, sold,
and exploited by the hundreds of thousands. But we can be sure
that Rose faced the deep kind of trouble that no one in our present time knows and only an enslaved woman has seen. Rose
knew that she or her little girl, Ashley, could be next on the auction block, the cold device enslavers turned to when their finances faltered.

Ripping families apart was a common practice in a society
structured by—and, indeed, dependent on—the legalized captivity of people deemed inferior. And sale could not have been
the end of Rose's worries or the worst of her fears. She must have
dreaded what could occur during this relocation and after: the

physical cruelty, sexual assault, malnourishment, mental splintering, and even death that was the lot of so many young women deemed slaves. Rose and Ashley's life together, already encased by swales of suffering, could be torn asunder in a matter of moments with the stroke of a pen. Their lives apart portended even worse without the bonds of family. Rose adored this daughter and desperately sought to keep her safe. But what could safety possibly mean in a place, at a time, when a girl not yet ten years old could be lawfully caged and bartered? What would Rose do to protect her child? What *could* she do as an unfree woman with no social standing, political power, economic means, or cultural currency positioned in the trenches of unpredictable and insurmountable difficulty?

The kind of fix Rose was in—life-threatening and soul-stealing—was one that Black women like her had continually encountered over more than two centuries of life in America. It was a fix articulated by the few enslaved women who managed to escape and tell their stories in the nineteenth century and, later, by Black women thinkers and artists who drew sustenance from the writings of these cultural ancestors in the generations that followed, including our own. How does a person treated like chattel express and enact a human ethic? What does an individual who is deeply devalued insist upon as her set of values? How does a woman demeaned and cowed face the abyss and still give love? Rose's actions, outlined in a single and unusual text and barely preserved for history, give us a sense. When the auction block loomed on her little family's horizon, Rose gathered all of her resources—material, emotional, and spiritual—and packed an emergency kit for the future. She gave that bag to her daughter, Ashley, who carried it and passed it down across the generations.

Rose possessed inner strength and creativity even as calamity struck. Saving another's life meant acting despite despair, and she dreamed up means of survival as well as spiritual sustenance.[1] Surely Rose felt that what she did was far too little, much too late. Surely she feared that a battered bag would not matter enough in the end. But Rose pressed on, matching the mettle of an entrenched slave society with a glimmering will of her own. And although we cannot know exactly how events unfolded, we can conclude that Rose's gift *did* affect her descendants' lives, no matter how inconsequential her act of packing may have felt in the moment. For, three generations later, a great-granddaughter of hers, Ruth Middleton, created a remarkable "written" record attesting to Rose's deed. Ruth's chronicle is evidence of a long-term effect that Rose herself would never see: her female line would continue against all odds, and her will to love would be carried forward.

Rose couldn't know how things would turn out, but she held fast to a vision. She saw her daughter alive and provided for her into the future, a radical imagining for a Black mother in the 1850s. Rose's daughter, Ashley, realized that vision by surviving, and her great-granddaughter, Ruth, preserved their history by stitching sentences onto the surface of the sack. In the third decade of the twenty-first century, we face our own societal demons, equal in some respects to the system of slavery that would finally be slayed. The world feels dark to us, just as it must have for Rose, and like Rose, we can't know what will happen. We think it a fantasy that we might rescue our children's futures, or revive our democratic principles, or redeem our damaged earth. In our moment of bleak extremity, Black women of the past can be our teachers. Who better to show us how to act when hope for the future is under threat than a mother like Rose—or an entire caste of enslaved, brave women who were nothing and had nothing by the dominant standards of their time yet managed to save whom

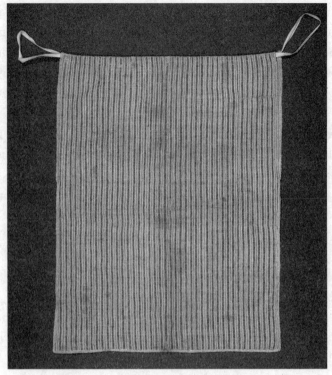

Embroidered work bag. Unknown maker, England or
United States, 1753, wool, linen, silk, and cotton, 1960.1123,
bequest of Henry Francis du Pont, courtesy of Winterthur Museum.

and what they loved? Rose and her long line of descendants realized that salvation depended on bearing up to the weight and promise of their baggage. We should, too.

Just as Rose and Ashley found on their forced journeys through slavery's landscape, there is no safe place of escape left for us. The walls of the world are closing in. We need to get out of here in a hurry. We need to get out of these frames of mind and states of emotion that elevate mastery over compassion, division over connection, and greed over care, separating us one from another and locking us in. Our only options in this predicament, this state of political and planetary emergency, are to act as first responders or die not trying. We are the ancestors of our descendants. They are the generations we've made. With a "radical hope" for their survival, what will we pack into their sacks?[2]

ALL
THAT
SHE
CARRIED

LOVE'S PRACTITIONERS

In African American life black women have been love's practitioners.

—bell hooks, *Salvation: Black People and Love*, 2001

WE FORGET THAT LOVE IS REVOLUTIONARY. THE WORD, cute and overused in American culture, can feel devoid of spirit, a dead letter suitable only for easy exchange on social media platforms. But love does carry profound meanings. It indicates the radical realignment of social life. To love is to turn away from the prioritization of the ego or even one's particular party or tribe, to give of oneself for another, to transfigure the narrow "I" into the expansive "you" or "we." This four-letter word asks of us, then, one of the most difficult tasks in life: decentering the self for the good of another. This is a task for which we need exemplars, especially in our divisive times. Here in these pages, we take up a quiet story of transformative love lived and told by ordinary African American women—Rose, Ashley, and Ruth—whose lives spanned the nineteenth and twentieth centuries, slavery and freedom, the South and the North. Their love story is one of sacrifice, suffering, lament, and the rescue of a tested but resilient family lineage.

By loving, Rose refused to accept the tenets of her time: that people could be treated as property, that wealth was a greater value than honor, that some lives had no worth beyond capital and gain. Hers is just one telling example of refusal from the collective experience of enslaved Black women, who practiced love and preserved life when all hope seemed lost. Even when she relinquished her daughter to the slave trade against her will, Rose insisted on love. Despite and during their separation, Rose's value of love prevailed. The emotional bond between mother and daughter held longevity and elasticity, traversing the final decade of chattel slavery, the chaos of the Civil War, and the red dawn of emancipation before finding new expression in the early twentieth century just as a baby girl, the fifth generation of Rose's lineage, Ashley's great-granddaughter, was born.

Just as remarkable as this story of women who dared to insist on love is how we have come to know about it. Rose's testament, as told by Ruth, is preserved on an antique sack that once held grain or seeds. Traces of the abused and adored, the devalued and the salvaged, the lost and the found accrue in this one-of-a-kind object. A mother bears the sacrifice of her daughter; a daughter carries on amid unspeakable loss; a descendant heaves the harrowing tale into the twentieth century; and we have the chance to be the better for its arrival here on our doorstep. Through the medium of the sack, we glimpse the visionary fortitude of enslaved Black mothers, the miraculous love Black women bore for kin, the insistence on radical humanization that Black women carried for the nation, and the immeasurable value of material culture to the histories of the marginalized. Although Black women have been treated like "the mules of the world," in the words of writer Zora Neale Hurston, this sack bears them up as at times exemplifying, to borrow Abraham Lincoln's phrase on the precipice of the Civil War, the "better angels of our nature."[1]

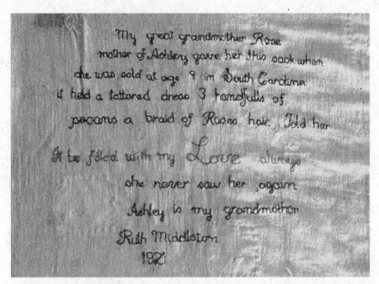

Ruth Middleton's embroidery on Ashley's sack, a gift from Rose.
Courtesy of the Middleton Place Foundation.

Ruth Middleton, a lineal descendant of Rose, embroidered the lines that follow on what Ruth identified as the original cotton sack Rose packed.

My great grandmother Rose

mother of Ashley gave her this sack when

she was sold at age 9 in South Carolina

it held a tattered dress 3 handfulls of

pecans a braid of Roses hair. Told her

It be filled with my Love always

she never saw her again

Ashley is my grandmother

Ruth Middleton

1921

With these words a granddaughter, mother, sewer, and story-teller imbued a piece of fabric with all the drama and pathos of ancient tapestries depicting the deeds of queens and goddesses. She preserved the memory of her foremothers and also venerated these women, shaping their image for the next generations. Without Ruth, there would be no record. Without her record, there would be no history. Ruth's act of creation mirrored that of her great-grandmother Rose. Through her embroidery, Ruth ensured that the valiance of discounted women would be recalled and embraced as a treasured inheritance.

The stained antique fabric once grasped in Ruth Middleton's hands now hangs in an underground case at the Smithsonian National Museum of African American History and Culture (NMAAHC), in Washington, D.C. The artifact, which is on loan from its current institutional owner, the Middleton Place Foundation in Charleston, South Carolina, immediately takes hold of those who view it. Ruth's intellectual work of interpreting Rose and Ashley's story and her handiwork in stitching it onto the sack in color produce a composite object of arresting visual and emotional impact. A testament to the national past fashioned of many thinning threads, it has an effect subtler yet more moving than the stone monuments built for pro-slavery statesmen and Confederate generals that have been widely contested in recent years. Those memorials, erected to bury a nation's sin, were made to be larger than life to command a presence in national memory. At the same time, though, Confederate monuments undermined the aspirational principles of America's founding: freedom, equality, and democracy. Ashley's sack makes no such pretense to vainglory. It does not have to. A quiet assertion of the right to life, liberty, and beauty even for those at the bottom, the sack stands in eloquent defense of the country's ideals by indicting its failures.

The sack crystallizes the drama of a region and a nation torn apart by the moral crisis of human sale and forced separation. But it also possesses a quality so tangibly intimate and personal that it filters a light of remembrance on the viewer's own familial bonds, leading any of us to ask what things our own families possess that connect us to our past and to wonder what we might gain from the contemplation of that connection. Such is the capacious nature of Ashley's sack that it can call hearts to attention while also speaking to local, regional, and national histories. Although the bag's material contents have long been lost, its essential provision—love of a mother for her daughter—still remains. Every turn in the sack's use—from its packing in the 1850s, to its tending across the dawn of a century, to its embroidering in the 1920s—reveals a family endowment that stands as an alternative to the callous capitalism bred in slavery. In the face of the base commercialization of their own bodies, these Black kinswomen cared for one another, preserving the next generations by provisioning their perseverance and remembering the past generations who defended their right to life. As the women in Rose's lineage carried the sack through the decades, the sack itself bore memories of bondage and bravery, genius and generosity, longevity and love.

STORY CLOTHS

My own grandmother's voice travels across warm breezes on a hilly side street in Cincinnati, Ohio. I am nine years old, or twelve and a half, or twenty-one.

"Lord only knows what we woulda done if she hadn't saved that cow."

Grandmother has told this story countless times to me, her

rapt audience of one, and to other women relatives in private moments over the years. Her dark eyes peer at me with the light of love behind her oversized men's glasses, the sort that come cheapest with her Medicare plan. She does not need glamour or fanfare. The red brick porch of the Craftsman cottage is her stage. She sits on her lounger with the metal frame, its pillows changed out many times and now mismatched in shape and pattern. Her skin is the honey of bees' combs, soft as crepe and just as creased. Her hair is a wreath of pressed cotton, once black, now white. A sleeveless, pale blue shift drapes to her calves, exposing ankles swollen from a lifetime of domestic labor in others' homes and agricultural labor on others' farms. She leans back and folds her hands across the broad moon of her belly, which birthed six babies in Mississippi and seven more in Ohio. In the summertime, she keeps a cool drink on the ledge of the porch wall—lemonade or sun tea sealed in a Mason jar. She reaches for the cooling liquid, wets her lips, and continues. She is my first storyteller, the one who tends me when I am sick, the one who bakes my favorite rice pudding. She is my beloved.

"If it wasn't for my sister Margaret," my grandmother preaches, "we woulda had nothin' left."

This was the defining story of my grandmother's childhood in Mississippi. It told of a fragile family and a brave Black girl. My maternal grandmother, Alice Aliene, was born in Lee County to a mother much younger than her father. Her father, Price, was tall as an oak, with bark-dark skin. He had "eyes like an eagle's," to hear my grandmother tell it, which she claimed he got from a "half-Indian parent." Price had been born into slavery's last days. He told my grandmother, and she told me, that he had been sold away from his mother. Maybe this is why the 1870 federal census lists Price as an eight-year-old alone, with no guardian or family.

My grandmother's mother, Ida Belle, was the yin to Price's yang, youthful, light-skinned, with long raven hair "swinging down her back." This mother, romanticized in the adoration of my grandmother's words, had somehow come from means. Ida Belle had been born in St. Louis; she could read and write; she could figure with numbers. Ida Belle's father was white and un-named in my grandmother's stories. Ida Belle's mother had had no choice about this intimacy. "When those white men wanted to go with you," my grandmother explained to me, "you went." Ida Belle had a bit of money, a set of gold-edged plates (now in my mother's display case), and even twenty-five acres of land in her possession. Price, Ida Belle, and their splitting-the-seams farm family of nine were getting by in rural Mississippi, the state that had harbored the worst forms of torturous, Cotton Belt slavery and would later see the gruesome murders of three civil rights workers in 1964's Freedom Summer. They farmed 165 acres, produced between 25 and 30 bales of cotton per year, and made around $100 to $125 per bale. They had "plenty to eat" back in the 1920s, my grandmother said, and lived "comfortable" on their land. She remembered their white house with the big hallway, long porch with a double swing, "fifteen to twenty head of cows," glossy green vegetable garden, and fruit cobblers cooling in the kitchen.

And then the family fell into debt, owing someone around fifty or sixty dollars. White men came from town, riding on horses. They appeared armed with papers that they insisted Price must sign. This was a trap. While Ida Belle could have read the contract, Price had never been educated. My grand-mother inserts this detail into the story as if it might have made a difference, as if Ida Belle might have marched down to that road in a long skirt and flour-sack apron, ferreted out the secret intention, and prevented the family's financial downfall. But I know after twenty-five years of studying Black women's history, and my grandmother must have known from experience as she told me the story back then, that a Black woman was better off hidden than smart when white men came calling in pre–civil rights Mississippi. "I remember seeing her standing on the porch crying," my grandmother said of her mother. Price signed the documents with his X. Weeks later, the men returned, claiming that Price had relinquished the farm. Who knows what the black marks on those papers really conveyed? The truth became irrelevant the moment those men returned with guns.

My grandmother's words pick up speed and seem to chase each other now as she tells the story, or maybe it is my memory that blurs the details. All is panic. Who runs to hide? Who stands by as witness? Price argues with the men. Ida Belle flies to locate her young ones. The children cower. The dogs warn. The family evacuates as alarm evolves into knowing fear.

They were being evicted by the Law of the South, which is to say by white supremacist whimsy. They had little time to think or plan, to collect and pack their necessities. They grabbed at dishes, blankets, clothing but lost all of their wealth, which was the land itself, the farmhouse, and the livestock. The men took the family's cows, which had belonged to Ida Belle. "I never will forget them, in the wagon with the horses, going on down the road," my grandmother told me. But my grandmother's sister Margaret, she was shrewd and she was quick. While commotion raged at the front door, Margaret slipped out the back, fetched a cow from the pasture, and led it over to the farm of Old Man Rose. He helped them, later allowing the family to rent one of his houses. My grandmother never mentioned his race.[2]

That cow was the only thing of significant value rescued from my ancestors' farm besides their lives. The expulsion drove my grandmother's family into poverty. This poverty, this pressure, this unrelenting fear of loss would later push my grandmother to marry young and migrate, out of the jaws of the Jim Crow South and into the teeth of the segregated North. But the act of strength and daring shown by Margaret that day enriched them in spirit despite their woes. This is how I remember my grandmother telling it. My great-aunt Margaret, only a teen, saved the day. And my grandmother wrapped the moment up in a silk sleeve of artful story.

I never had the chance to meet this dauntless aunt. I have never even glimpsed a picture of her. But I had seen and touched and admired the work of her hands, a connection just as powerful. My grandmother kept a quilt in her bedroom that Margaret had stitched sometime after the ouster. The quilt bears an appliqué fan design: rose and mint-colored circles and ovals alternating with a regularity broken only by shifts in shade. The backing has cobalt and powder-blue polka dots on a vanilla-cream background that brings to mind the sweet smells of an ice cream parlor. Margaret had folded a blue-dot border onto the edges of the appliqué side, mixing the mild pastel fans with an altogether different feel that smacked of modernist dots and splotches. She imposed what did not fit onto her visual canvas, the mark of a creative soul as well as a rebel. This girl, whom I would never know except through stories handed down, was both a maker and a savior. She is remembered in family lore in a way that reflects regional history tinged by archetypal myth.

I inherited my great-aunt's quilt when my grandmother passed away, more than fifteen years ago. The quilt was for my grandmother, and is for me, a treasured textile. It seems to have absorbed into its fibers the intangible essence of a past time. When I gaze at the vibrant colors of this quilt (including stains of an ancestor's blood), I see my grandmother as a girl and

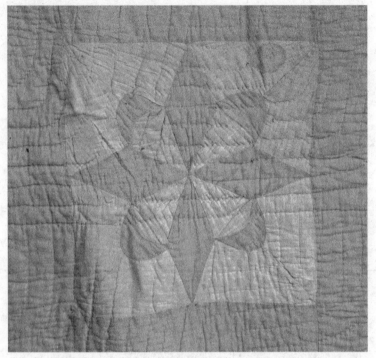

Great-aunt Margaret Stribling's quilt, close-up, ca. 1920s–1940s, Mississippi. Photograph by Tobi Hollander, 2018.

imagine the faces of her kin. I feel each syllable of that many-eyed monster, Mississippi—a place where heat, terror, and love intertwined. The story of Margaret saving the cow fused with the quilt's material. The most traumatic event of my grand-mother's childhood is embedded in it. The history of Africans in America is brutal, but we have made art out of pain, sustaining our spirits with sunbursts of beauty, teaching ourselves how to rise the next day.

I was born in the 1970s, a chaotic time to be sure, but more hopeful by bounds than the 1920s, when my grandmother and her sisters were young. I never knew enslavement firsthand, never experienced legal segregation, yet I savor the story of Margaret, her cow, and her quilt now more than ever. This fabric and the tale I associate with it have blanketed and anchored me, a reminder of dignity preserved, and of the hope in our dire times that something necessary for the preservation and elevation of life might, in the end, be saved.

There are myriad lessons in the story of the cow. What strikes me upon this telling, as I also ponder Ashley's sack, is the emphasis on girls and women, acts of rescue, and the salvaging of vital things that hold the deep meanings of our lives. This family story is about the resourcefulness of women and girls, even the most marginalized and maligned of them. It illustrates how the overburdened of the world can persist through unanticipated hardship. And this story suggests how instructive memories of perseverance from the past can be, especially when fastened to things that serve as aids of recall and connection.

I link the eviction to the quilt because of the heroine they have in common. In the case of Ashley's sack, the attachment is even more material. That story from the past is sewn directly onto the fabric. As the oft-quoted scholar of U.S. women's history Laurel Thatcher Ulrich recounts in her book *The Age of Homespun*, folks in the eighteenth and nineteenth centuries sometimes affixed stories to objects, tucking fragments of paper about origins or events from the times into woven baskets, or pinning information about an object's owner onto the heels of woolen stockings, or even painting wordy descriptions onto wooden chests of drawers. This impulse to preserve past knowledge by hitching narrative explanation to items exhibits what Ulrich calls the "mnemonic power of goods."[3] Things become bearers of memory and information, especially when enhanced by stories that expand their capacity to carry meaning.[4] And if those things are textiles, stories about women's lives seem to adhere with special tenacity, even as fabrics, because of their vul-

nerability to deterioration and frequent lack of attribution to a
maker, have been among the last kinds of materials that historians look to in order to understand what has occurred, how, and
why.

My attachment to an ancestral quilt tethers me to the breathtaking weight of the African American past. Certainly, my own
history is partly what drew me toward the sack, inspiring a wish to
know the women behind the object and explore more deeply
traditions of African American craft and family bequeathal. This
is a feeling I'm sure to share with other women (and men) of
Black, southern, rural, or crafting heritages. Many of us have felt
in our lives the allure of the cloth as a twining cord connecting
us to history.[5] Some save and repair hand-me-down table linens.
Others hunt the flea market aisles for vintage fabrics. A few of us
learn the skills of traditional sewing and quilting to reproduce the
experience and art of our foremothers. The past seems to reach
out to us through these fabrics and the practices of making them
that have survived over time. Gathered up like crisp ends of a
cotton sheet fresh from the washing, past and present seem to
meet above the fold. We feel a sense of contact with the women
who preceded us. We wonder if gaining knowledge about their
lives can shine new perspective on our own. And as we discover
the lives of these women from a time so different from ours, we
enhance our ability to peer across other differences—of race and
culture, class and status, ability and disability, youth and age. In
this intermediate space where the fold of the fabric forms, we
glimpse not only our foremothers' lives but also our foremothers'
allies and adversaries. We begin to see the makeup of all their
intersecting worlds and appreciate a larger swath of interwoven
experience. We notice a shift from the self to the other, from
personal and family history to local, national, and even global
history. This dawning awareness leads us to trace all of the inter-

twined threads, to appreciate that there is one earth and one humankind, one social fabric of many folds in dire need of mending.

It may not be coincidence that we feel this expansion of self in the quaint attic rooms or antiques shops where we ponder the fibers that remain. An essential medium of social messaging, fabric announced information (often about social status), triggered memory (of events and people), and even bestowed protective magic (through embedded sacred material and shared belief). Before word processors, the printing press, and wood-pulp paper, cloth fashioned by women makers preserved the "mythohistories" of entire groups. Noblewomen spun thread on gold and silver spindles, fashioning tapestries with grand visual narration. In ancient Greece, Europe, and the Mediterranean, cloth did the work of retaining stories of distant kin, as women "recorded the deeds and/or myths of their clans in their weaving." These tapestries, laden with messages of historical events and mythological symbolism, bore a critical record-keeping and cultural function as "story cloths."[6] While few ancient women had the luxury of twining their thread on golden spindles, the tradition of the story cloth of yore continues in the pieced quilts and cotton windowpane coverlets, embroidery samplers and crocheted afghans that we hand down through families with stories attached.

Though early women's history can be elusive, women need not "conjure a history for ourselves," says the archaeologist Elizabeth Wayland Barber. We do not have to magically pull our collective past out of thin air. "Very little of the ancient literary record was devoted to women," Barber continues. "Here among the textiles, on the other hand, we can find some of the hard evidence we need."[7] Similarly, in her essay "African-American Women's Quilting," the historian Elsa Barkley Brown insists that if we "follow the cultural guides which African-American women have left us," we will "understand their world."[8] Barber, a specialist in the ancient past, and Brown, a scholar of the recent past, agree on this: our foremothers wove spiritual beliefs, cultural values, and historical knowledge into their flax, woolen, silk, and cotton webs. The work of their hands can lead us back to their histories and serve as guide rails as we grope through the difficult past. Here I attempt, alongside you, an unpredictable expedition into the lives of Black women during slavery, Reconstruction, and Jim Crow segregation, locating them in the contexts of their dynamic social worlds by tracing the threads of a story cloth. I seek to uncover the story of an enigmatic object and its makers; to explore the historical meanings of things in Black women's lives, Black lives, and women's lives; and to stitch into our cultural memory the chief values Rose upheld: love, hope, and salvation.

ASHLEY'S SACK AS ARCHIVE

As multiple things rolled into one, Ashley's sack is an extraordinary artifact of the cultural and craft productions of African American women. Nothing else quite like it has yet been uncovered in the trunks, closets, or museum storage rooms of the North, South, or West. And the sack is more than an artifact. It is an archive of its own, a collection of disparate materials and messages. It is at once a container, carrier, textile, art piece, and record of past events.[9] As with any archive, we cannot presume that this sack bears straightforward, unassailable facts. Using the object responsibly as a source for historical inquiry means asking questions of it and, as uncomfortable as it might feel, maintaining a willingness to poke holes into it. Placing this artifact in conversation with other sources and considering its various historical contexts can help us test its reliability in the service of historical understanding as well as the search for "symbolic truths" that transcend hard evidence and speak to the intangible meanings of our collective human lives.[10]

Taking care with a singular and mostly undocumented object calls for a cautious process of interpreting inadequate records, interrupting my own narrative at times to bare its reconstructive elements, and unraveling some commonly held story lines—about the sack, the South, and even this country—in order to loosely weave others.[11] While these pages will offer grounded interpretations based on evidence, comparison, and context, they will also accommodate supposition and imagination, recognizing that there are a great many things about the past that we cannot know for certain, especially with regard to populations whose lives were mostly underrecorded or misunderstood. In this joint research, reading, and writing endeavor, Black feminist historical methods are usable hands-on tools. Among these approaches is a determined archival practice modeled by the historian Marisa Fuentes, who acknowledges the "violence" and "distortion" of traditional archives while refusing to abandon enslaved Black women to that discursive abyss. Employing methods of dogged documentary collection and analysis, Fuentes probes the records of slave owners, slave sellers, and slave jailers in Barbados looking for traces of Black women and following those clues across the historical and geographical terrain like bread crumbs. With fabric as her metaphor, Fuentes terms her archival strategy reading "along the bias grain." It is an approach that I apply throughout this exploration, but most prominently in the second chapter, where I embark on a search for Rose.[12]

I also adapt the writing practice beautifully captured by cultural theorist Saidiya Hartman as "narrating the time of slavery as our present." Hartman advocates incorporating a sense of the present moment and its failures to secure full freedom for Black people into our historical interpretations of slavery, as a means of illuminating "the intimacy of our experience with the lives of the dead." Writers "narrating counter-histories of slavery" and present-day inheritors of the legacy of slavery carry a responsibility not to forget our close ties to these lives, Hartman insists. Because archives do not faithfully reveal or honor the enslaved, tending this intimacy with the dead necessitates new methods, including a trans-temporal consciousness and use of restrained imagination.[13]

I take up Hartman's notion of past and present abutment, of imaginative license, and of recognizing the persistence of archival gaps. In select moments where I encounter archival deficit, I imagine onto the page the figures of Rose, Ashley, and Ruth. At other times, I take an opposite approach of marking their absence in the record, so that we remain aware of how the real conditions of their lives precipitated not only physical and psychological trauma but also archival diminishment. My way of linking past and present and, indeed, the future into this exploration is to make my best effort to bring these women vividly into our minds while linking their circumstances and hard-won wisdom to great urgencies of our present moment, such as the federal mistreatment of migrant children, the cultural neglect of African American heirlooms, the political betrayal of democratic principles, the economic cleavage of rich from poor, and the global shadow of an existential threat—for these women, chattel bondage; for us, climate change—that demands long-term, big-picture, cooperative response.

Finally, I practice a third approach in this work that is more expertly applied by art historians and archaeologists. In addition to stretching historical documents, bending time, and imagining alternative realities into and alongside archival fissures, I ask that we seek out the actual material—the *things* enslaved people touched, made, used, and carried—in order to understand the past. As Caribbean studies scholar Michel-Rolph Trouillot has trenchantly expressed it, referring to the basic material foundation of all life and, hence, inquiry: "The materiality of this first moment is so obvious that some of us take it for granted. . . . History begins with bodies and artifacts."[14] We, too, will begin with an artifact fashioned by hand and pressed against bodies long buried. Our journey with Black women's things in this book runs in a threaded loop, from Ruth's time, to Rose's era, to Ashley's moment, and back again. The past stays with us, wrapped inside our storied quilts, packed into our cotton bags, and written upon our memories. Past is present is passed on.

MAKING LOVE

Aptly called a "revelation" by a museum interpreter at the Middleton Place plantation, Ashley's sack illuminates the contours of enslaved Black women's experiences, the emotional imperatives of their existences, the things they required to survive, and what they valued enough to pass down.[15] For without their possessions, Black women, like any other people, could not sustain or express their lives. Although it may seem counterintuitive at first, attention to material things, especially ones elaborated by words or pictures, opens a route to accessing intangible feelings and desires that can evade the documentary record.[16] Humans are composite beings, made of matter and infused with spirit. We have always collected, created, and surrounded ourselves with material objects in order to express that inner ineffability. "The things we interact with are an inescapable part of who we are," as one historian of the environment has put it, and hence things become our "fellow travelers" in this life.[17] The physical traces left behind therefore allow us to glimpse what our fore-bears found worthy of making and keeping, and what, by impli-cation, they held dear.

What did Rose value enough to save, pack, and carry? How did she turn her vision of what mattered in life into action? The things Rose gathered for her daughter, according to the memory of her great-granddaughter, indicate her thoughts and guiding principles. She sought to immediately address a hierarchy of needs: food, clothing, shelter, identity through lineage, and, most centrally, an affirmation of worthiness. The wise values up-held by Rose reverberate across the testimony of African Ameri-can women from the slavery era. Rose's kit was, by all evidences, one of a kind, but she shared with other women in her condition a vision for survival that required both material and emotional resources. Rose supported Ashley's life through the collection and storage of stuff: a dress, nuts, a lock of hair, and the cotton tote itself—things shaped by the intermingling of southern na-ture and southern cultures. Rose then sealed those items, ren-dering them sacred, with the force of an emotional promise: a mother's enduring love.

The inscription on Ashley's bag contains a list that is nothing less than a prescription for survival. It allows us to appreciate what women in bondage deemed essential, what they were ca-pable of getting their hands on, and what they were determined to salvage. We save first that which we value most. Rose was de-termined to rescue her daughter. She understood, as did other Black women with their backs against a wall of entrenched de-humanization and impoverishment, that survival for future gen-erations meant fusing whatever one had together, the material and the emotional: *making* love.[18] The work of Rose's hands, as captured by her great-granddaughter's words, illuminates the importance of materiality as well as emotionality to Black women's survival strategies.

You can sense by now that this is not a traditional history. It leans toward evocation rather than argumentation and is rather more meditation than monograph. As science fiction writer Ursula Le Guin has previously said about the novel, a work of history could be conceptualized as a sack. "A book holds words," Le Guin explains. "Words hold things. They bear meanings."[19] This book bears meanings about the burdens of being human in an inhumane world; about the treasures, traumas, and capacities we inherit and carry; and about the means we have at our disposal for recalling and acknowledging the assembled wisdom of ancestral women. Chapter 1 introduces Ruth as the intellect behind the cloth record and sets the stage of colonial South Carolina, the place Ruth names as the scene of the crime. Chapter 2 confronts the devaluation of women like Rose in the records of American slavery and asks how we can recover the ignored and dispossessed. Chapter 3 ponders Rose's act of packing and discovers how her deliberate movement and carefully selected items were a claim for motherly love and familial continuity. Chapter 4 examines the dress Rose packed, exploring the things enslaved women cherished and unveiling how they used personal objects like clothing to protect dignity and reinforce relational ties. Chapter 5 explores the emotional world of the slave mother against the backdrop of the auction block, which hoisted Charleston and the South Carolina interior to heights of untoward luxury. Chapter 6 uncovers a survival culture rooted in nature, including the pecans inherited by Ashley after sale set her adrift. Chapter 7 follows the sack bearers after the Civil War, exploring women's stories of trauma and healing as exemplified by Ruth's embroidery. The Conclusion weighs the value of things, including textiles and sacks, to African American history and American imaginings of the future.

Beyond the trinity of Rose, Ruth, and Ashley, a circle of Black women writers and storytellers will emerge in these pages. Some, like Harriet Jacobs and Elizabeth Keckley, may be familiar as authors of classic slave narratives assigned in college classrooms; others, like Louisa Picquet, Eliza Potter, Melnea Cass, and Mamie Garvin Fields, are lesser-known figures with equally revealing stories. Harriet Jacobs, a survivor of slavery in North Carolina who executed a painstaking plan to free herself and her children, is the author of one of the most analytically sophisticated slave narratives in the genre. Elizabeth Keckley, an enslaved woman from Virginia taken to North Carolina and St. Louis by her owners, was a dressmaker for First Lady Mary Todd Lincoln and an autobiographical writer of the Civil War years. Louisa Picquet lived a harrowing existence of serial sexual abuse in several states. Nevertheless, Picquet persisted in loving the family torn from her in slavery, as well as the children that she conceived with her enslavers. She told her story in print form to purchase her mother's freedom. Eliza Potter, a self-professed fine artist of hairdressing and lay historian, plied her craft as a free Black woman in Cincinnati and points south while publishing a tell-all memoir about her wealthy slaveholding clients. Melnea Cass, a community organizer and women's club leader in Boston, had moved north with her family during the first wave of the Great Migration and contributed to the shaping of a mutually supportive and politically conscious Black urban community. South Carolinian Mamie Garvin Fields taught school, co-founded a club for Black women in Charleston, and published a memoir with her granddaughters that exemplifies, in full-length book form, the relationships between telling, hearing, and preserving Black family stories.[20]

Each of these authors professed a deep and committed love for their own families, for captive Black people, and for the principle of ethical action rooted in relationship. Together, these women and many others whose voices emerge in slave narratives, interviews, and letters create a chorus of corroboration for Rose, Ashley, and Ruth's tale, which illuminates separation, survival, and love as core features of Black women's experience.[21] Because formerly enslaved women regularly veiled the worst of their trials and the most private of their feelings, especially regarding the sexual atrocities that the tyranny of slavery encouraged, we will also turn for emotional context to contemporary Black women writers, whose literary representations in fiction and poetry approach an affective realm beyond the reach of historical accounts.[22] The women leading our way in these pages are the lineal ancestors of families whose migration spans from South to North, cultural ancestors of a Black racial family rocked by the hardships of history, and national ancestors of a broader American family whose social, economic, and political roots are buried in the mire of slavery. And as much as we are one human family that knows the feel of growing dread and shattered hope, they are the emotional ancestors of us all.

While working on this manuscript, I often turned to colleagues who regularly sew and presented my tangled knot of questions. To one of them, a close friend who makes her own wardrobe, studies prison garb, and writes about family relations as fabric, I put a query that arose as I contemplated Ruth's embroidery: "In sewing, is there a name for the space between the stitches?" My friend considered this for a beat before answering no and leaving me to settle for my own gangly phrasing.[23] The story of Ashley's sack that I endeavor to tell in these pages bares its thin spots and holes while simultaneously showing how material objects can help us to assemble rich histories of the marginalized. This book follows an odyssey set in motion by one Black woman whose ideals and actions, as recalled by her great-granddaughter, shaped a family's perseverance against the odds. It is a cautionary tale about the personal pain and collective price exacted when a society devalues what is precious. And it is an invitation for those who would honor histories of the lost to embrace the spaces between the stitches.

RUTH'S RECORD

My great-grandmama told my grandmama the part she lived through that my grandmama didn't live through and my grandmama told my mama what they both lived through and my mama told me what they all lived through and we were suppose to pass it down like that from generation to generation so we'd never forget.

—GAYL JONES, *Corregidora*, 1975

Then I found the slave lists. There were bundles of them, in thick sheaves, each sheaf containing a stack. When a rice planter handed out shoes, he wrote down the names of who got them. To pay taxes, he made an inventory of his human property. If he bought fabric so people could make clothes, he noted how many yards were given to each person. When a woman gave birth, the date and name of the child appeared.

—EDWARD BALL, *Slaves in the Family*, 1998

AS A YOUNG WOMAN WITH MODEST MEANS AND FEW prospects, Ruth Middleton transformed her life by moving north. Taking a leap into the unknown as a Black woman in the 1910s required tremendous courage. Ruth was still a teenager at the time, living in Columbia, South Carolina, and laboring as a domestic. She may have already met her future fiancé, Arthur Middleton, a South Carolinian from Camden and a tiremaker by trade.[1] And she would have known from what she heard and saw, and perhaps from incidents in her own life, that the South was still a dangerous place for African Americans at the start of the new century. The first generations to be born to freedom found few job opportunities beyond the agricultural work their forebears had done, risked indebtedness in the sharecropping system, and faced public humiliation as well as unpredictable violence in everyday life. Perhaps Ruth and Arthur evaluated their situation and determined that only drastic change would better it. For they, like so many other African Americans fed up with the dusty prejudice of the South, packed their retinue of things and traveled northward seeking safety and opportunity.

Ruth and Arthur made this move amid the uncertainty of World War I and a deadly flu epidemic, joining what historians have called the first wave of the Great Migration, which would, by the 1970s, reshape the demography and political landscape of the entire United States. African Americans, who had predominantly lived in the rural South, relocated in the hundreds of thousands to the urban South, urban Midwest, urban West, and urban North in search of physical security and economic opportunity. Half a million of these travelers relocated to northern cities in the period when Ruth uprooted herself, between 1914 and 1920. They pulled up stakes, packed their bags, and left behind all they knew and many whom they loved.[2] Those who departed must have faced tough decisions about which items they could afford to bring along on the journey and which things they would give away or abandon. Practical objects like skillets and skirts, cherished things like handmade quilts, and valuable items like tools and books might each have been scrutinized, weighed, and considered. We have no inventory of a great migration of things that accompanied African Americans northward and westward. Ruth Middleton's case stands as a precious exception.

When Ruth arrived in Philadelphia around the year 1918, she brought along the cotton sack that Rose had prepared for Ashley. Ruth's attachment to the textile reflects an important aspect of women's historical experience with things. While free men have historically owned and passed down "real" property (especially in the form of land), women have typically had only "movable" property (like furniture and linens—and, if the women in question were slaveholders, people) at their disposal. Although American women possessed a limited form of property, they used that property intentionally to "assert identities, build alliances, and weave family bonds torn by marriage, death, or migration."[3] A New England–born white woman in the colonial era, for example, cherished a passed-down painted chest not only for its function but also for the ways in which the object connected her to her women forebears, reinforcing a sense of belonging not to male ancestors but to a line of women. Ruth Middleton, who would take her husband's name upon marriage, as was the American legal custom, also took her foremother's sack as she traveled north. And one day, when she was herself on the verge of motherhood, Ruth decided to annotate it.

Ruth's fabric testament to Black love and women's perseverance did not—perhaps could not—exist in any historical archive. Though necessary to the work of uncovering the past, archives are nevertheless limited and misleading storehouses of information. While at times imposing and formal enough as to seem all-encompassing in their brick, glass, and steel structures, archives only include records that survived accident, were viewed as important in their time or in some subsequent period, and were deemed worthy of preservation. These records were originally created by fallible people rather like you and me, who could err in their jottings, hold vexed feelings they sometimes transmitted onto the page, or consciously or unconsciously misconstrue events they witnessed. Even in their most organized form, archived records are mere scraps of accounts of previous happenings, "rags of realities" that we painstakingly stitch together in order to picture past societies.[4]

Even when compared with the motley rags that make up the archives of history, the nineteenth-century seed sack that we are exploring together here appears particularly threadbare. Ruth's embroidery is the only definitive primary source detailing the fate of Rose and Ashley.[5] In addition, read in a certain mood, Ruth's verse on the bag can feel more like poetry than reportage. Slight on facts and specifics, the embroidered text states only three names (Rose, Ruth, and Ashley), one place (South Carolina), and one date (1921). None of the sources that scholars typically use to reconstruct histories of slavery directly address this object. No plantation supply log exists that tells of the sack's manufacture or acquisition. No mistress's handwritten letter describes an interaction with Rose. No formal bill of sale lists a buyer of Ashley. No published slave narrative describes this family and their travails. The bag dates back to the 1840s or 1850s, but the writing was added in the 1920s. And perhaps most glaringly—and, for the historian, most alarmingly—we have only one person's word that events took place as described and that the bag was packed with the listed items.

Ruth Middleton, that one person, probably rendered the details as she recalled them. While we can presume that she told the truth as she knew it, Ruth's version of events was formed, like any other, through the lenses of memory and narrative desire— what she consciously or unconsciously wanted this family story to mean. There is no reason to think that Ruth wrote this story as fiction, given the form she chose (amateur embroidery on a personal object with no commercial value at the time) as well as the first-person voice she used. The intimate, possessive, and immediate tone of the line "Ashley is my grandmother" suggests that Ruth knew this relative and remembered her.[6] The tale she stitched for private use was by no indications imagined, and by all reckoning, it was *true* to Ruth. Still, as a vehicle of historical recovery, memory is at least as fallible as paper records. It is possible, even likely, that Ruth mistook, mis-recalled, or rearranged aspects of her emotional family account. We all do this when drawing out and thinking through memory, a malleable store of information "retrieved even as it is refashioned."[7]

Nevertheless, with steady hands we can thread the eye of this needle and ask what Ruth's record can tell us about Black women, Black families, women crafters, and Black material, as well as social, worlds. By doing so, we refuse to give up on those many people of the past who did not—could not—leave behind troves of documents. To abandon these individuals, the "archivally unknown" who fell through the cracks of class, race, and position, would consign them to a "second death" by permitting their erasure from history.[8] It would also mean turning our faces away from fuller, if unwelcome, truths about our country and ourselves. Ruth's account, subjective and incomplete as it may be, stands as a baseline rebuttal to the reams of slaveholder documents that categorized people as objects. Her list of a dress, a braid, pecans, and whispered love accounts for the things that sustained life, rather than rendering lives as things. If Ruth's text did nothing else but replace the "slave list" of our cultural script with Rose's shimmering inventory, it would be enough. Yet Ruth's cloth chronicle does much more. By recovering, for history, Rose, her life conditions, and her act of love, Ruth sets the record straight.

THE DAZZLING SACK CLOTH

The sack Ruth Middleton embroidered in the 1920s is resplendent with "the power of simultaneous pain and hope."[9] It evidences a persistent Black matriline, a continuation of radical vision that should have been impossible, given the logic and enforcement of American enslavement. What had begun as a mother's prescient act of provision during those dim years of captivity became "symbolic armor" for the family over time, representing women's faith in the continuity of kinship, the protection to be found in the promise of love, and the defense of what was most certainly a sacred memory in the face of a national culture of Black parody and debasement well into the twentieth century.[10] As a thing fashioned and preserved by generations of African American women, as a woven and embroidered textile that has weathered slavery and the passage of time, this sack itself can claim a stunning survival story. The twists and turns of the bag's rediscovery and renewal also reveal contemporary racial dynamics obliquely reflective of power relations in play during Rose's, Ashley's, and Ruth's lives and times. When we recognize the value of objects to human identity and to African Americans in particular, as a historically demeaned group forced into captivity and lives of scarcity, it is frustrating, even infuriating, to trace the trajectory of Ashley's sack that landed it in the collection of a former plantation. How could a priceless object like this wind up in the inventory of a restored estate once maintained by an enslaved labor force and still partly overseen by descendants of its original owners?

The answer is fit for an episode of PBS's *Antiques Roadshow*.[11] In 2007, after having been lost for decades and presumably unknown outside of the original family, the sack Rose had packed reemerged. A white woman discovered the bag in a bin of old fabrics at an outdoor flea market near Nashville, Tennessee. In order to supplement her family's income, the shopper, a mother of three, routinely bought items and resold them on eBay. She might have done the same with the discolored sack had she not absorbed a few of the words on its surface. Realizing that "she had stumbled upon a precious object," the shopper offered the vendor twenty dollars for the sack and a bundle of other cloths. How much might the sack be worth? She followed the clues on the sack, noted Ruth Middleton's signature, conducted an Internet search, and contacted an appraiser. The search led her to Middleton Place, once the home of the famously wealthy Charleston slaveholders Henry Middleton and Mary Williams Middleton and now a nonprofit foundation. After a series of conversations with foundation staffers, a dream about the women whose names were on the sack, and perhaps reflection on being the mother of her own nine-year-old daughter, the flea market shopper donated the bag to Middleton Place in exchange for a lifetime membership and a very small sum.[12] "I happened to field the initial call from the donor and hear her description of the sack and how she found it in a rummage sale," Tracey Todd, the president and CEO of the Middleton Place Foundation, said. "And I'll never forget, after several weeks and numerous calls, the feeling when she decided to donate it to MPF. We knew it would be one of the most important artifacts owned by the Foundation."[13]

The Tennessee shopper's incredible find is an inspiring example of what historians have called "dazzling things" that "sometimes show up in ordinary places."[14] Like many flea market collectors, she had a keen eye for the rare possibilities of things categorized as rubbish. Her perception was matched months later by the duo of Middleton Place curators who took on the task of interpreting the donated sack. Although the remarkable textile belonging to an enslaved girl named Ashley bore only ten lines of embroidered text, the many layers of the sack's makeup—material, historical, and emotional—had myriad stories to tell. Who had manufactured it? Who were the people named on it? Why had this family been torn apart? And how had the bag survived for more than a century in the shadows? Pinning down specifics about the object's origins would take three years, and research is ongoing more than a decade later at Middleton Place and at museums and universities around the country.[15]

Mary Edna Sullivan, a textile specialist, and her senior colleague at the time, Barbara Doyle, a handwriting enthusiast, scrutinized the now long-empty bag. Sullivan chose the name for the object, emphasizing Ashley's role in the family. The curators' description reads like this:

RUTH MIDDLETON (DATES UNKNOWN)
Ashley's Sack
Charleston, SC
Ca. 1850, sack; 1921, needlework
Plain-weave cotton ground; cotton lock stitch fabrication; three strand-cotton embroidery floss, back-stitch embroidery
H. 29 11/16 x W. 15 3/4 inches
Sacks made of plain-weave cotton, like this example, were manufactured for flour, seeds and other food staples beginning in the late 1840s with the invention of the industrial sewing machine. Unlike stitching by hand, the double locking chain stitch produced by the machine made a seam strong enough to hold heavy contents. Constructed in the same way, Ashley's sack had seen much use by the time Ruth Middleton added her inscription; the numerous worn spots had been reinforced with rectangles of cloth carefully hand-sewn in place.

Searches through surviving Middleton family probate rec-
ords from the late-eighteenth and nineteenth centuries have
revealed at least nine enslaved women named Rose; however,
no Ashley has come to light.[16]

The curatorial team had pinned down dates and details of
the bag's construction, but their probe of plantation records led
to inconclusive findings about its origins, and the women behind the names on the sack remained out of reach. The foundation's gaining possession of the artifact had been, like the rescue
of the textile itself, a flash of luck.

The mysterious sack had only recently been placed on display in the reception hall of the Middleton Place manor home
when curators for the NMAAHC embarked on a southern tour
in search of objects for their collections. It was 2009, and the
new museum had not yet been built on the National Mall, when
Middleton Place curators showed the Smithsonian curators the
salvaged sack. The Smithsonian obtained the object on a long-
term loan from the Middleton Place Foundation, which main-
tains ownership. This sack, an artifact with a cat's nine lives, was
preserved for history through a serendipitous series of nearly
missed connections and occurrences.[17] Smithsonian curator
Mary Elliott explained that the fabric has been dated to the
1850s and is presumed to trace back to the Ashley River area of
South Carolina but not directly to the Middleton Place plantation. Tracey Todd acknowledged as much: "We treasured the
sack because of its story and its interpretive value, much more
than any specific connection to the Middletons of Middleton
Place. We always took the position that a direct link may or may
not exist."[18]

The Middleton Place Foundation possesses the sack because
of an assumed link between Ruth Middleton and the wealthy

Charleston family. And perhaps there is a genealogical link, as the anthropologist Mark Auslander has suggested, between Ruth's husband, Arthur Middleton, and an enslaved person at Middleton Place.[19] Because of the shared name, the sack went on display in the library of the restored guest wing (or "flanker") of the Middleton Place plantation, a national historic landmark and popular southern tourist attraction. Awash in bronze brick and greenery, Middleton Place calls to mind grand manor homes in the English countryside of Jane Austen novels. It is a place replete with pink azaleas blooming along stone pathways and silvery Spanish moss draping from sprawling oaks. The supple bends of the Ashley River ribbon the edge of the property. Dirt paths lead to stone ruins and delicate reflecting ponds shaped like butterfly wings—ponds that enslaved people dug by hand out of steaming, mosquito-thick mud banks. These pools are among the many luxuries exorbitant wealth bought in Charleston, one of this country's richest towns in the era of the American Revolution, due to the rice and cotton profits of legalized slavery.

While the butterfly pools rippled outside, the cotton sack hung inside was an open rebuke to slavery's harms. The textile was displayed at the plantation from 2007 to 2010 before making a debut in New York City, which had itself been a slaveholding hub on par with Charleston in eighteenth-century colonial America. In New York, unfree people of African and Indigenous descent were routinely traded and held in the households and businesses of entrepreneurial merchant elites. At the New York Winter Antiques Show in 2011, *Grandeur Preserved: Masterworks Presented by Historic Charleston Foundation*, the less than grand cotton sack drew long looks and torrents of tears.[20] Upon its return to the Charleston plantation, the sack went on display again until it was selected in 2015 for the col-

The butterfly-wing-shaped reflecting pools at Middleton Place plantation, hand-dug by enslaved people, border the main house grounds and the Ashley River. Photograph by Tiya Miles.

lections of the Smithsonian. On loan from Middleton Place, the sack went into storage and was later unveiled among a host of other treasures at the NMAAHC's grand opening in the autumn of 2016.[21]

This object was a marvel despite its lack of physical luster. It moved the emotions of viewers; so many of them succumbed to sobs that Middleton Place curator Mary Edna Sullivan fell into the habit of handing out tissues beside the display.[22] The powerful pull of the sack lay in the way it personalized and also materialized every parent's and child's worst fear, telling an intimate account of one family's separation and survival through direct language and an approachable, familiar medium. As the Civil War historian Stephen Berry succinctly put it in a conversation we once had about the sack: "It is the world's shortest slave narrative, stripped down to its essence, sent back to us through time like a message in a bottle."[23]

The allure of the sack existed in its form as well as its story: the seeming simplicity of a utilitarian object; in its function: the protection of a vulnerable child; and in its elaboration: the neatly stitched words of a hobbyist's needle. This bag elicited a sense of sentimentalism like no other object at Middleton Place or a high-culture antiques show, and certainly not in the archival documents chronicling slavery from the perspective of enslavers. The sack seemed, in fact, to possess a kind of purity—of original intention, expression, and form—that made it both mesmerizing and distinctive.[24]

But this textile does more than reflect its viewers' submerged worries and innate sympathies. It stands in for a series of facts that are common knowledge but are not often consciously examined or fully absorbed: the brutality of American slavery, the ugliness of lovely places like the Lowcountry South, the invisible hand of planter authoritarianism, and the triumph that is Black love. Ashley's sack is not so simple as it seems, nor so saccharine. This object that barely survived the one hundred plus years since its original manufacture and transport across urban, rural, state, and regional lines is complex, forceful, resplendently symbolic, and a dramatic form of synecdoche—a part standing in for the whole.

The textile was exhibited for years inside a plantation house, exposed to the scrutiny and projected feelings of mainly white tourists. In a coincidence that makes this chain of events even more uncanny, the small sum that the Middleton Place Foundation exchanged for the sack, not accounting for inflation, nearly matches the price of Ashley's ascribed value in Robert Martin's estate inventory of 1852: $300. How would Rose have taken the news of this unexpected outcome? What would Ashley have felt at the sight of her survival pack on display? What would Ruth Middleton say if she knew who now possesses her hand-sewn story of slavery's emotional toll? The irony here might feel like tragedy, or even betrayal, to these women. This heirloom, passed down by Black women through the last generations of midnight slavery and first generations of twilight freedom, traveled all the way north to Philadelphia only to be sent down south again, right back to the unholy city where its story most likely began. From the moment the bag departed from the Black Middleton family in the mid- to late 1900s, most of its caretakers and interpreters have been white. Shouldn't we be uncomfortable with this chain of possession, with a contemporary market in Black heritage items and the "circulation of slavery relics in modern-day museums"?[25]

The complicating dynamics of race in processes of museum collecting, philanthropy, and stewardship become, like all the phases of this artifact's rich history, part of the story of the sack. The same is true in a consideration of the fabric work of the legendary African American quilter Harriet Powers, who did not want to part with her intricate quilt that relayed Bible stories through cut and sewn pictures. As a formerly enslaved woman in rural Georgia struggling alongside her husband to acquire and hold on to a parcel of land for the livelihood of their family, Powers reluctantly sold what was possibly her first full-sized picture quilt to a white collector and artist, Jennie Smith, around 1890. Powers was disinclined to part with this quilt and did so only at her husband's urging, due to their financial distress. When Powers delivered the quilt to Smith by way of an oxcart, she held the "precious burden in her lap encased in a clean flour sack, which was still enveloped in a crocus sack."[26]

It is not through Powers's intentional will that her quilts wound up on display in two of the country's most renowned museums: the Smithsonian National Museum of American History (which owns the Bible quilt) and the Boston Museum of Fine Arts (which owns what is referred to as the Pictorial quilt, featuring Bible stories as well as local events). At the same time, it was the desire to possess Powers's art and experience the romance of what it represented (about racial difference, gender, and religious faith) on the part of wealthy and connected white women that protected those pieces for posterity. And Powers did maintain influence over future interpretations of her art by carefully relating her own artistic intentions orally. Collector Jennie Smith, herself an artist and teacher, recorded minute translations of each visual square, certainly told to her by Powers. A New England minister who received Powers's second quilt as a gift from a group of white women at Atlanta University (now Clark Atlanta University) wrote down Powers's account of each picture in sentences that hold a hint of her speech and on index cards that mimic her quilt block form. To further the understanding of her work and preserve her interpretations of it, Harriet Powers left keys to her quilts. We can think of Ruth as having done something similar with her inscription on the sack, a key to the story of her foremothers. Like Powers, Ruth conveyed meanings through words attached to her creation and, while never intending to share that work with the world during her lifetime, left a bountiful gift.[27] Her words turn the key in the lock of history's door.

Ashley's sack was touched by many hands as it wove its way through two centuries to finally appear before us. It was likely produced in a cotton factory in the 1850s. It served the utilitarian purpose of carrying seeds or raw foodstuff for who knows how many before it came into Rose's possession. Rose packed the bag with items from her environment, things that had been grown, harvested, or sewn by different individuals. Ashley

This undated portrait of master quilter Harriet Powers accompanied her transcribed oral description of the squares on the Pictorial quilt when it was acquired by the Museum of Fine Arts, Boston. Note the detail of the artist's scalloped apron embellished with the sunburst or starburst shapes that are also found on her surviving quilts. Photograph courtesy of the Museum of Fine Arts, Boston.

Harriet Powers described her quilt squares to purchasers, who wrote her intended meanings down. This quilt key transcribed on paper cards, together with a portrait of the artist, accompanied Powers's quilt featuring Bible scenes and local events when it was acquired by the Museum of Fine Arts, Boston, in the mid-1970s. The quilt had been owned by the family of the Reverend Charles Cuthbert Hall, who received it as a gift in 1898 and displayed it in the family's summer house in Westport Point, Massachusetts. Photograph courtesy of the Museum of Fine Arts, Boston.

received the bag from her mother and may have shared its contents with others, allowing them to press their fingers into the tensile fibers. She then made it all the way to freedom with that sack as her companion and managed to pass the item down to her daughter and granddaughter. Ruth embellished the bag with thread, stitching it tightly to its story, before passing away and passing it on. Unknown strangers in Pennsylvania and Tennessee (and perhaps places in between) shifted the sack from box to vehicle and into a flea market booth. A shopper discovered it, paid a merchant for it, took the fabric bag in hand, and forwarded it on to Middleton Place. Foundation board members received the textile and promised to steward it. Curators tended, inspected, and preserved it. Scholars researched, analyzed, and wrote about it. And now this item, having passed through countless fingers and imaginations (including yours and mine), hangs on the wall in a grand national institution. Saving this sack so that it could arrive at a point where we can together reflect on its meanings has required an all-hands-on-deck ethos despite the complications of racial politics. The sack still carries a burden of layered power relations, but it also contains within its preservation history a model for repurposing that past and for regenerating relationships as we engage in work of shared purpose across racial and regional lines. This is surely the same inclusive value needed to carry us forward in the challenging decades and centuries ahead.

Rather than being anomalous in its former display in a plantation house parlor or its current display by the cultural arm of a federal government that once condoned slavery, perhaps Ashley's cotton sack is exactly where it should be housed at our precise moment in time. Perhaps Mary Edna Sullivan, in naming the object, intuited that there was something productive in the abutment of the words "Ashley" and "sack," a sound or a sense when the syllables rubbed against each other on a breath. Sack of ashes, sacrifice, circle of fire, funeral pyre. It is not a far stream-of-consciousness stretch to arrive at sackcloth, a coarse textile woven of goats' hair used by those in the Old Testament to express contrition for their sins. Perhaps the Middleton Place plantation wore Ashley's fabric like a sackcloth, a quiet testament to its founders' wrongs of the past. And now the nation bears witness to this sackcloth in its virtual temple of public learning, the Smithsonian Institution, on the National Mall. The suffering and persistence of Black people, and of Indigenous people, made this country possible, shaping its cartographic boundaries, social structures, wealth distribution, founding documents, and everyday interactions in profound ways that can still be traced.

The sack Ruth embroidered in the 1920s is evidence of a Black matriline with staying power, a triumph that should have been impossible, given the conditions and logic of slavery that intended the loss of ties between mother and child. Rose, Ashley, and Ruth Middleton lived hard lives, chased by outsized threats and immediate terrors that many of us can barely imagine. "The sack," the historian Heather Williams has written, "was a repository for their memories of vulnerability and grief." But the object also contained within it inspiration for social renewal, when, "in a new generation, Ruth Middleton embroidered an inscription that carried the story beyond the immediate family" in its ultimate preservation and public display.[28]

WHITE RICE, BLACK BODIES

Considering the physical object itself, what it is made of, who has touched it, and who has in turn been touched by it is a fitting starting point for considering the journey of this sack. But

Ruth's record offers another way into the story. Her threaded annotation pins the pivotal event of Ashley's sale to a location and a time period, placing a dramatic change in the circumstances of this family within a larger geographical and temporal context: the elite American Southeast prior to the Civil War. The scene of the crime—the sale of a child away from her mother—was shaped by the environmental, economic, political, and social conditions that precipitated it. That is, the history of a particular place spanning nearly two centuries made the trade of a small Black girl not only possible but probable. There is a prologue to Ruth's family story that traces back to colonial South Carolina, the darling of coastal planters, and its bustling, bedazzling seaport city: Charleston.[29] Restarting our story then and there grounds the unfolding drama of the sack and its carriers in the historical evolution of Lowcountry slave society.

If the old cotton sack is a synecdoche for American slavery, Charleston represents the same for the eighteenth- and early-nineteenth-century South during the long reign of rice and the bright rise of cotton, staple crops dependent on rich, abundant land and cheap, plentiful labor. Over a few short decades, people rendered as things by law became fundamental to the establishment of this colony and metropolis. As Angelina Grimké, a pampered daughter of South Carolina, explained in her anti-slavery appeal to Christian women in 1836: "Slavery in America reduces a man to a *thing*, a 'chattel personal,' robs him of all his rights as a *human being*, fetters both his body and mind, and protects the *master* in the most unnatural and unreasonable power."[30] Here in Grimké's homeland, the horror of this inhumane transfiguration was submerged and sequestered in local culture. Charleston, South Carolina, was a place of startling contrasts and distorted reality. A pre-twentieth-century twilight zone, it was also "the South."[31]

Carolina was one of the oldest colonial settlements in the southern American mainland, and by the early 1700s, it had become the Blackest, the richest, and the most unequal.[32] The ancestors of the Middleton family, on whose estate Ruth Middleton's sack would wind up, contributed to this transformation of what had been Indigenous territory. When Edward and Arthur Middleton arrived in Carolina in 1678 and 1679 (successively), they surfed at the leading edge of an immigration tsunami. Their family hailed from London by way of Barbados, a small, sun-drenched island in the English West Indies (now the Lesser Antilles) where planters had built the richest colonial society in the whole of North America, based on "sugar and slaves."[33] Two decades after Puritans shaped their imagined Christian haven in Massachusetts (in the 1620s) and the first enslaved Africans were traded for food on the coast of Virginia (in 1619), English colonists landed on Barbados, where they attempted to grow tobacco and cotton before seizing on sugar as a core crop. With the support of investors back in England, early-arriving families with means acquired land and cheap labor, including the English and Irish poor who were also arriving in the 1630s and 1640s. Slavery was an early feature of Barbadian life. The first Englishman to arrive on the island brought Indigenous American as well as African slaves along with him.[34] As the decades passed and the wealth and authority of the planter class grew, Barbadians preferred readily available and easily replaceable African slaves to Indigenous slaves and time-limited European indentured servants, whose numbers in the fields began to fall. An increasingly African labor force grew cane and processed sugar, a luxury commodity in the west European market. By the 1680s, Barbadians had the largest, most comprehensive, most lucrative slave society in all of the English colonies, and their financial success in sugar depended wholly and "existentially"

on the degradation of human beings. This was "the most system-
atically violent, brutal and racially inhumane society of modernity," as a leading Barbadian historian has put it.[35]

Among English slaving colonies in America, Barbados was
first, and Barbados was ruthless.[36] The system, practice, and
logic of slavery seeped into the very bones of island residents.
Wealthy and middle-class English Barbadians legalized and
tightly controlled the theft of labor from people they deemed
unworthy of better lives. Violence was a key tool to extract this
labor from unwilling, unfree darker-skinned people. By the time
of Barbados's initial growth in the 1630s and 1640s, justification
for the racial debasement of dark-skinned Africans was already
present in English thought, stemming from associations between darkness and sin rooted in religious belief, and between
darkness and ugliness stemming from ethnocentric ideals of
beauty, as well as from cultural stereotypes about African barbarity.[37] Anti-Black racism had not yet formed in whole cloth. The
knot of associated negative meanings that was "Blackness," a biological racial essence viewed as immutable, heritable, and de-
terminative, would take two more centuries to tighten and fully
mature into the zealous arguments of nineteenth-century scientific racism and the vehement policies of twentieth-century
American Jim Crow. But the degraded racial categories called
"Negro" or "Indian" had already developed enough by the mid-
1600s to propel the targeting of darker and culturally different
people for opportunistic, economically driven maltreatment.
Through the production, sale, and expansion of sugar on the
backs of the mostly colored unfree, the English elite in Barbados and their financial investors in London found the golden
formula that would not only launch this island into new economic heights but also inspire the founding and phenomenon
of Carolina.

Barbados was a small island with an economy based on agriculture and the stolen muscle power necessary to fuel it. Eventually, and especially as the wealthiest planters consolidated landholdings, arable land hit its natural limits. Anxieties about a shrinking land base and recent changes in colonial governance pushed many of the island's planter elites to retire to England in the 1680s. Meanwhile, in London, a group of eight noblemen, most of whom had no Barbadian ties, obtained a charter from King Charles II for a massive tract of land on the southeastern coast of mainland North America. The "True and Absolute Lords Proprietors of Carolina," as King Charles II loftily deemed them in 1663, held a royal decree that gave them total control over a vast territory that would later be divided into North Carolina, South Carolina, and Georgia. As capitalist investors, the lords proprietors aimed to generate wealth out of this new domain. The majority of the proprietors would never personally set foot on American soil, but they could attract industrious colonists who would. Barbadians, a pretested set of settlers who knew how to build wealth and desired more land for their plantations, were a proprietor's dream population.[38]

From the bounty granted by King Charles (Carolina's namesake), the lords proprietors apportioned, sold, and rented lands fanning far out from the coastline. Among the early takers were men who envisioned a familiar model of Caribbean plantation society that employed extreme brutality (whippings, mutilations, caging, executions) to keep an enslaved labor force in the fields.[39] Joining them were artisans and indentured servants hoping to make new beginnings. Numbered among the lords proprietors, Barbadian planter Sir John Colleton organized the first mass-immigration wave from the island to the mainland. In 1670, two hundred Barbadians sailed across the Caribbean Sea and then farther north, to the coast of Carolina. Some 150 of these were Anglo elites with a "desire to resemble genteel land-owners in the Old World, perhaps those from a lost age of paternal relations between lord and retainer."[40] The wealthy among the immigrants towed along their lifeblood of unfree labor: European indentured servants bound to them and captive African people owned by them. Even some farmers of middling means and a few working-class Englishmen arrived in Carolina with one or two enslaved Blacks in these early years.[41]

By relocating to Carolina from Barbados, as well as Bermuda and England, in the late 1600s, the original English immigrants scored economically not once but thrice. Through a practice known as "headright," initiated by the proprietors to settle the colony more quickly, land assigned to a recipient increased by 150 acres a "head," or per family member, which for these calculations included any servant or slave the grantee imported.[42] Unfree people in Carolina made their masters richer in land just by virtue of being forcibly transported there. Planters and farmers who attained land began with a foundation of wealth that rocketed once their servants and slaves began to work the lush soil to produce crops. The lords proprietors achieved their aim of attracting colonists to Carolina with lures of land and the promise that "every freeman of Carolina shall have absolute power and authority over his Negro Slaves, of what opinion or religion soever," as professed in the Fundamental Constitutions of the colony, penned by philosopher John Locke and Lord Proprietor Anthony Ashley Cooper, First Earl of Shaftesbury.[43]

The founding lords and their sponsored planter elites envisioned an agricultural treasure land, and the settlement in Carolina was set on a course to mirror Barbados, England's most lucrative colony in the 1600s.[44] By the late 1670s, Edward and Arthur Middleton and other younger sons of Barbados planters set out for Carolina to tap new fortunes in a place where the

A map of the province of South Carolina showing all the rivers, creeks, bays, inlets, islands, roads, marshes, ferries, bridges, swamps, parishes, churches, towns, townships, and county, parish, district, and provincial lines, as well as inland navigation, soundings, and time of high water on the seacoast. Note the enslaved, partially clothed African figure carrying a burden, and the nobly rendered, feather-bedecked Indigenous man grasping a weapon. Native and Black people were integral to economic development in the colony of Carolina, and later the colony and then the state of South Carolina. The placement of these figures on either side of two hearty white male colonists suggests, further, that actual American Indian and African-descended populations, as well as racialized ideological notions about them, framed the existence and persistence of the settlement. Drawn and published in 1773, London. Library of Congress.

climate was similarly tropical and land was seemingly plentiful. The wealthy arrivals from Barbados brought along their sensibility of race- and class-based human subjection, of quick riches, aristocratic affectations, and English gentry mannerisms bent to the excesses of fantasy-island culture.[45] Like their owners, many of the first enslaved people in Carolina were Caribbean, having been transported from the islands with colonists or purchased later through a thriving English intercolonial trade in people of African descent.[46]

The Middleton family succeeded royally in South Carolina, along the lines of the Barbadian model. Edward Middleton's son, Arthur Middleton, would later become a prominent political leader. In the 1720s, Arthur Middleton was among Carolina's several Barbadian-born governors. Arthur's son Henry Middleton would join another influential Carolina planter family when he wed Mary Williams, whose dowry included the house and land that became Middleton Place, the present-day national landmark. Henry Middleton was a South Carolina rice magnate whose lands totaled fifty thousand acres worked by eight hundred enslaved Blacks.[47] With the founding of Carolina, "slavery, Barbados style," had come to mainland North America.[48]

Back on Barbados, English colonists had not been compelled to deal much with local Indigenous people. The Carib Indians of the region tended to populate the westerly islands of the Lesser Antilles, like St. Christopher, where in 1629 the English had banded with the French to attack and kill Carib residents seeking to defend their home.[49] The lack of a large Native population on Barbados meant less resistance to European settlement, which was partly why the English had selected the island as their first major West Indian enterprise. The Indigenous enslaved whom Anglo-Barbadians (and Anglo-Bermudians) acquired tended to come from other places, including Virginia,

New England, and later Carolina, following colonial wars for territory that led to the death and capture of thousands of Pequots, Wampanoags, Narragansetts, and many more.[50] In contrast to Barbados, Carolina was widely populated and regularly traversed by scores of small Indigenous nations, which would prove to be both a problem and an opportunity for the English.

When Carolina's first Europeans settled west of the Ashley River in 1670, they squatted in an area occupied by the Kiawahs, Santees, Sewees, and several other communities of Indigenous people. The colonists then moved slightly southward and westward to the slipper of a peninsula tucked between the Ashley and Cooper rivers (named for Anthony Ashley Cooper). The colonists called this peninsula Charles Towne in honor of their king. But to secure the land beyond the writ of a distant monarch, they would have to contend with the more than twenty Native societies in the general vicinity—including the Cheraws, Cherokees, Congarees, Catawbas, Kussoes, Muskogees, Pedees, Santees, Savannahs (also known as Shawnees), Stonos, Sugerees, Waccamaws, Waterees, Waxhaws, and Yamasees, whose villages spanned the coast as well as the interior.[51]

Seeing the advantage of commercial engagement, some among the English newcomers quickly commenced a brisk trade with Native people along the coast and inland. This trade, in which settlers exchanged finished English goods (like metal pots, guns, blankets, and beads) for animal hides (especially deerskins) that would be shipped back to England, as well as for Indian captives (taken by Native people from other tribes), helped to stabilize the colony in its infancy.[52] It also eventually weakened Native groups who were drawn more tightly into the colonial orbit and came to rely on trade goods and the political and territorial advantage that being well positioned in the trade could afford them in relation to other Native nations. Taking advantage of this disruption, Carolina Indian traders would supply a precious "commodity" planters desired: human beings.

As Indigenous groups did business with the English, they had shifting degrees of power in trade largely dictated by their location on the landscape, the size of their population, and the strength or weakness of their alliance with the English. The Catawbas, for instance, were a sizable community settled in the riverine interior where piedmont plains and hillsides converged. By the early 1700s they had become influential middlemen between South Carolina and Virginia traders and other Native groups, due to their large size and their strategic location on a geographical and cultural border.[53] But the Catawbas were drawn into the center of a volatile trade that they could not control. Doing business with the English (who, it is important to remember, stockpiled and distributed firearms) became a means of political and economic survival for Native groups, yet it was not a reliable enterprise. The English shifted allegiances, sometimes subjecting peoples with whom they had once traded, like the Westos and the Yamasees, to personal attacks and military assaults. Those who traded heavily with the English became more subject to the colony's demands, such as capturing and returning fugitive African slaves and providing higher numbers of Indigenous captives taken in intertribal raids. In 1719, local elites in the Carolina assembly, including convention president Arthur Middleton, the son of Edward Middleton, a member of a wealthy mercantile family who arrived from London by way of Barbados, revolted against proprietor rule by gaining control of the militia, choosing their own governor, and then petitioning for the Crown's approval. As the proprietors' authority gave way to a colony run by planters, efforts on the part of government officials to rein in English traders diminished.[54]

In addition to trading *with* Native people, Carolina settlers increasingly traded *for* them, purchasing American Indians captured in conflicts between Native groups that the English themselves often spurred in order to produce slaves.[55] The settlers' appetite for cheap and plentiful labor was reinforced by Native people's growing desire for English goods. Carolina men accepted slaves from any quarter, and Native men captured Indigenous people from other communities to acquire goods or in payment of debts accrued in trade. In 1675, just five years after the colony had been established, colonists were purchasing Native captives from the Sewees and other proximal tribes. Local colonial officials functioned in cahoots with the Indigenous traders turned slavers, who sponsored attacks on Native groups, such as the Kussoes, who refused to vow allegiance to the colony, and looked the other way as English slave hunters surged into the Gulf Coast and parts of Spanish Florida in order to capture hundreds of Native people living in Catholic mission communities. Native bands who had once been trading partners of the English or who had no relations at all with the English could find themselves the victims of slave raids carried out by armed Englishmen or armed Indigenous enemies who had themselves become slave hunters to enter or sustain a trade relationship with the English.[56]

Such was this whirlwind of multidirectional atrocities that approximately thirty to fifty thousand Indigenous people (poor documentation means the numbers cannot be exact) were captured or purchased by English colonists and their Native allies in the North American South before 1720. In Carolina during the lords proprietors' era, 25 percent of enslaved people were Indigenous. By the second decade of the eighteenth century, Carolina had surpassed New England as the largest Indian slaving area, and many of the Native nations that had been present upon the arrival of the English were depleted, enslaved, or on the run. The Catawbas became a culturally composite community in part composed of survivors from smaller nations. Native men of fighting age captured in this storm of slaving were most often killed; women and, especially, children remained, consigned to generations of suffering. Snatched from their villages of origin and circles of kin, these women and youngsters (often orphaned) were cast onto rice and indigo fields alongside Africans collared from West and central Africa and the Caribbean islands.[57]

African captivity and Native captivity were endemic to Carolina, despite Enlightenment-era rhetoric that romanticized notions of an American "noble savage."[58] By the 1680s, a decade into their experiment on the Carolina coast, English immigrants had developed a secondary use for the Indigenous enslaved. Because local Native people remained too close to their home villages for the comfort of enslavers who feared escape and rebellion, wily traders carted Indian slaves out of the colony to Virginia, selling them in exchange for Black slaves, white servants, and even cattle.[59] We might wonder which of these forcibly separated Indigenous families had a mother like Rose with a daughter like Ashley who carried their story into the future.

Arriving at the determination that stealing large numbers of Indigenous people could harm trade relations and coming to prefer the use of readily available Africans as slaves, South Carolina settlers exercised self-imposed limits, decreasing their practice of Native enslavement over time and outlawing it by the mid-1700s. As the white settler population grew and the Native population decreased, due to disease, slave raids, and warfare with colonists, English settlers gained greater dominion over the landscape and began to enlist Indigenous people as Black slave-catchers and to position weakened Native towns as spatial barriers to African escape.[60] Carolinians could import tens of thousands of Africans for less trouble than it took to continue enslaving rebellious American Indians, who were cheaper, to be sure, but more susceptible to transatlantic diseases (like the deadly and prevalent yellow fever), to which some Africans had already been exposed and, therefore had immunity.[61]

Over these same years, Carolina settlers inched toward the discovery of a profitable staple crop that the people they owned could raise and process. Colonial revelations about what would grow best where often depended on the knowledge of other groups, such as the Indigenous people of the Powhatan Confederacy, who were growing tobacco long before the Virginians of Jamestown arrived in 1607. On this low-lying land of Carolina everywhere permeated by water and marsh, the fortune-making miracle crop would turn out to be the rice plant. After experimenting with growing rice on higher, inland ground with the labor of white servants and enslaved people of color, South Carolina planters realized, in the mid-1700s, that the tidal flow of water from rivers and wetlands made an ideal environment for coastal rice cultivation. They learned how to reproduce their Barbadian Eden, as "irrigated rice was, here, what sugar was to the West Indies: a lucrative staple on the profits of which planters built a wealthy and leisured provincial culture." When planters learned that indigo would flourish in the fallow periods of the rice plant's growing cycle, they cultivated the plants in tandem. Both rice and indigo turned out to be jackpot crops, sought in local markets (for human diets and textile dye) as well as around the world.[62]

Early into this coastal experiment, European émigrés of different ethnicities discovered the economic promise of Carolina. Anglo-Bahamians and Irish sojourners soon joined the Barbadian transplants. French Protestants (called Huguenots) journeyed from France, as did French Acadians from Nova Scotia, Canada. Large numbers of Jewish immigrants traveled from the Iberian Peninsula (Spain, Portugal, and Andorra) to take advantage of the colony's legal protection of religious freedom, as did western Europeans from Germany, Holland, Switzerland, and Scotland. No matter their varied spoken languages, religious affiliations (nearly all attended Protestant churches at first), or cultural practices, these founding Carolina families shared the opportunity to obtain land, own slaves of color, and thereby build heritable wealth.[63] By the 1760s, the Lowcountry South, a ricing zone that included South Carolina and Georgia, stood as the "richest region in North America."[64] A century later, that aristocratic planter elite, joined by upper-class planter-merchants, still maintained outsized economic and political influence. As one Union soldier describing Charleston after the city's bombardment during the Civil War reflected: "The state was ruled by a clique, composed of wealthy men, of ancient name, who secured privileges and prerogatives for themselves at the expense of the people."[65]

Rice, the Carolina planters' fixation, "remained the coastline's distinctive crop" for generations, fattening the colony with rich returns until the abolition of slavery in 1865 undercut a key factor of this success: unpaid skilled workers.[66] For rice was also a labor-intensive crop, dependent upon smart engineering and meticulous management at certain times of the plant's growth cycle. To ensure enough water to nourish the plant and at the same time ward off destructive flooding, planters required canals, dams, water gates, muscles, and minds to control the direction, intensity, and timing of the tide's flow. Their solution was to increase the enslaved labor force through African importation, including from the cultures of the Windward Coast or the Grain Coast (such as Sierra Leone), of people who were experienced in rice agriculture.[67] Following the alluring example of

Barbadian sugar, elite Carolinians built their colony through the tragic alchemy of "white rice and black bodies."[68] And their principal port city, Charleston, was equally characterized by troubling contrasts, as a "brittle, gay, and showy society, compounded of old-world elegance and frontier boisterousness, [that] echoed the Barbados atmosphere of a century before."[69]

Charleston was a cradle on the slip of the coast, tucked into the tender crook where the Ashley and the Cooper met. Rocked

Mary Elizabeth Hartt, a white student in South Carolina, created this award-winning map sampler made of silk on silk, chenille, and paint on silk in 1820. She worked her sampler at Steele Creek Female School under the direction of Miss Dorcas J. Alexander. This sampler is part of the "Bethel Group," comprising needlework made in schools affiliated with Bethel Presbyterian Church in York District, South Carolina. Collection of the Museum of Early Southern Decorative Arts, Old Salem Museum & Gardens. Given in memory of Nell Rankin Spratt and Bess White Rankin.

by Atlantic breezes, the world's grand trading channel tainted by the cast-off bodies of unloved human cargo, the city fed its glistening life for nearly two centuries on the strange black fruits of this bitter sea. Here, on unpaved streets stinking of trash and saltwater, lay a city of extreme contrasts, a town of crepe myrtles and unchecked cruelty, a place of diamonds and dung.[70] Fondly called "the Holy City"* because of its openness to religious diversity and stately churches with visible spires on every cobblestoned street corner, Charleston was actually the opposite.[71] For Charlestonians chose to worship the idols of rice and cotton, plants that may as well have been spun from gold. And it was here, within a jewel box town that doubled as a prison house, that a determined woman named Rose envisioned the impossible: a future life filled with love for her unfree daughter of African descent. We would not know the names of Rose or Ashley, or where to begin a search for them in the wild country of Carolina slavery, were it not for Ruth's embroidery, rendered, with a painful irony, on a slave-grown cotton textile manufactured with a "double locking chain stitch."

---

* "The Holy City" is a fairly long-standing nickname for Charleston. The term likely dates back to the late 1800s just prior to the city's cultural renaissance of the early 1900s, when a history professor, Yates Snowden, and a local author, John Bennett, were exchanging letters comparing Charleston and Boston. The recurring suppositions are that the name developed (1) because a church steeple can be seen from every sidewalk of the old city and (2) because Carolina's first government created by the lords proprietors did not exclude colonists on the basis of religion.

SEARCHING FOR ROSE

With this scant accounting we must write her history.
—MARISA J. FUENTES, *Dispossessed Lives:*
Enslaved Women, Violence, and the Archive, 2016

Relying on so spotty a record requires caution. Still, even its
absences speak.

—JILL LEPORE, *These Truths:*
A History of the United States, 2018

THE LACK OF INFORMATION ABOUT RUTH MIDDLETON'S
ancestor Rose is enough to stop the heart. But as difficult as it
will be for us to identify Rose with the use of historical records,
images, maps, the Internet, and freedom of movement at our
disposal, it would have been exponentially harder for Rose and
Ashley to reunite once they had been split apart by sale. Yet
throughout the course of their separate lives, mother and daughter did not forsake each other. Nor did their descendant Ruth
consign a vanished ancestor to anonymity. Rose vowed to always
love Ashley and pressed that promise into the sack. Ashley passed
that promise down, along with the object and the story of its origins. Ruth reinforced their bond by stitching their story onto the
bag. Despite the external devaluation of their family ties, evi-
denced by forced sale and absence in the formal written record,
these women valued one another as kin and understood the

transcendent worth of lineage. To bear proper witness to this testimony, to glean what this family's tale can yield, and to count their story in the annals of history that would tend to exclude it, we will follow Ruth's lead. Just as Ruth's chronicle on the sack emphasizes individual women, a location, a single event, and the materials Rose packed, we will endeavor to augment these details of Ruth's record, to confirm her account of southern transgression, and to write her foremothers' history.

Who was Rose? This question, while beguilingly straightforward, is mired in the obfuscations of the historical archive. As a leading historian of South Carolina, gender, and the Civil War South has put it: "Historical visibility is everywhere related to social power."[1] It is a madness, if not an irony, that unlocking the history of unfree people depends on the materials of their legal owners, who held the lion's share of visibility in their time and ours. Captive takers' papers and government records are often the only written accounting of enslaved people who could not escape and survive to tell their own stories. The wealthier and more influential the slaveholder, the more likely it is that plantation and estate records were kept and preserved over centuries in private offices and, later, research repositories.

As the richest U.S. colony for a span of time prior to the Revolutionary War and a nexus of economic growth into the nineteenth century, South Carolina has more than its share of these tainted but crucial, documents. The records are thin and flaked, yellowed and faded into pale lunar shades, tattered around the edges. They exist in the hundreds and thousands of pages, neatly filed in folders or compiled in heavy, aged books, leather-bound and massive. They are kept in tucked-away places: the official archives of the state, special collections of libraries, city deed offices, plantation attics, and the private files of personal homes. This makes information about the people whose lives are recorded there difficult and sometimes impossible to uncover, save how they appear as property tallied, as dependents receiving food and fabric rations, as laborers carrying out all the tasks necessary to sustain the southern way of life: from cooper to cook, servant to midwife, carpenter to blacksmith, boatman to field hand. To find Rose, we must fish for her in this wild current of records, casting out the widest, most delicate net. To find Rose, we must drag for her, combing the rivers of South Carolina, intent on a mission of historical rescue. This mission is similar to, but not the same as, the one Ruth Middleton undertook when she set her needle upon the cloth to stitch Rose's name into memory. We search because we must remember. We seek because we need to find. We are "duty bound," as Alice Walker writes, "to carry the ancestors."[2] But first we have to track them in the documentary briar patch of the past.

A ROSE BY ANY OTHER NAME

Charleston was once and is still Carolina's emerald city, a crown jewel on the southeastern Atlantic coastline. On the foundation of slave-grown rice, the earliest Lowcountry planters here secured economic, racial, social, and cultural prominence and maintained that status for generations that followed. In the early decades of the 1800s, around the time when Rose was born, tourism to Charleston was already a popular pastime. Visitors eagerly tarried in this sparkling city. The scenes these travelers recounted in diaries and letters usually included unfree people like Rose in the frame, a recognition, if unconscious, of the fundamental and compelled role that African Americans played in building and maintaining this exclusive society. Harriet Martineau, a British writer on an American tour in the 1830s, fell into

Rosetta, ca. 1855–80. Unknown artist, ambrotype. Pictured here may be one of the many enslaved Roses in Charleston or South Carolina at large. Image courtesy of the Gibbes Museum of Art.

blissful reverie over the Charleston cityscape despite her anti-slavery views. From the top of a church steeple opposite the guardhouse where soldiers kept watch for slaves out of line, Martineau gazed out at the glistening rooftops, rivers, and bay.

> The city was spread beneath us in a fanlike form in streets converging towards the harbor. The heat and moisture of the climate give to the buildings the hue of age, so as to leave nothing of the American air of spruceness in the aspect of the place. The sandy streets, the groups of mulattoes, the women with turbaned heads, surmounted with water-pots and baskets of fruit; the small panes of the house win-

dows; the yucca bristling in the gardens below us, and the hot haze through which we saw the blue main and its islands, all looked so oriental as to strike us with wonder.[3]

To hear Martineau tell it, Charleston was a kaleidoscope for the senses foreign in nature, awash, as it was, in aged splendor and "exotic" color, courtesy of enslaved people—from the fruit they grew, to the plants they tended, to the textiles wrapped around their heads. The very sediment that upheld the chapel where Martineau took in the view would not have existed without slave labor. To make way for the city, the colony's early planter elites first had to make land in the early 1700s, filling in the swampy sod that permeated the subtropical peninsula. They commanded the people they owned or rented to carry out this dirty work. Through the eighteenth and nineteenth centuries, residents reclaimed over half of what would become the city's land base from wetlands. The urban plan called for the use of soil to engineer elite areas, while the streets of outlying neighborhoods to the north frequented by poor whites and poor Blacks were filled with "cheap organic" materials, including garbage and animal carcasses.[4] The aristocratic hierarchy of South Carolina society was rendered concrete in the built environment of Charleston, where ornate mansions lined the lanes inside the boundaries of the old walls, and neighborhoods in outlying districts were identifiable by the stench of their filth-filled streets.

The ground on which lovely Charleston stands is literally and figuratively unstable. And the records of its slaveholding past are just as slippery and unforthcoming about the nature of the muck that lies beneath. So how, in this seaport city built of sagging infill, do we go about finding one unfree woman? The particular Rose recalled to memory by Ruth Middleton's looping stitch may have been given this name by a mother or a caretaker. She could have been called Rose, a flower of Old English derivation, by one of the people who owned her. She may have garnered the nickname Rose because she loved summer blossoms. She may have borne a rose-shaped scar on the tender skin of her back. And she was not alone, this woman named Rose, whose naming remains, whose parents remain, whose origins remain a mystery. She rises from the documents of South Carolina slavery along with many others who bear the same name, a sorrowful garden of captured Roses.

Rose was not an uncommon name in plantation office record books; it recurred again and again in the unfree population of antebellum South Carolina. Many plantations across the state claimed one or more Roses among their holdings. A search of paper and digitized records of South Carolina slaveholders' wills, estate inventories, property transactions, and the household textile distribution indexes referred to by archivists as "blanket books" yielded just shy of two hundred women (198) named Rose (including derivations of the name: Roze, Rosie, Rosetta, and Rozella).[5] "Rose" appears alongside enslaved people carrying names for days of the week and seasons of the year, in the West African tradition, such as Monday, November, and Autumn. She appears as a small girl, as a woman in her childbearing years, as an elderly grandmother called "Old Rose."[6]

The records of the extended Middleton family's nineteen main properties kept between 1738 and 1865, for instance, list sixteen Roses, beginning in the year 1776, ranging in monetary value from $0 (indicating an aged person who can no longer work) to $225. Precious little is recorded about these women and girls beyond their age and pecuniary worth. The first Rose to appear in the Middleton family's record is twenty-two years old and resides at Middle Place with seventy-nine other captive people sometime in the 1700s. Another Rose is a child at Middleton

Place between 1742 and 1787 whose cash value is listed as £25; this child is named in a family grouping replete with poetic botanical associations: a father named Winter, who worked as a gardener; a mother named Flora, who worked as a washer; and two siblings, including a baby brother marked at £8. The only Rose in the Middleton records with any identifying feature beyond age and monetary value is Rose of 1854, kept at their plantation called Horse Savanna among ninety-four other enslaved people, where she labored as "a nurse for the children." On Henry Middleton's Weehaw Plantation, where he kept meticulous annual records of slaves' births, deaths, tasks, rations, allowances, and blanket distribution in a journal titled "Weehaw People," another skilled nurse named Rose labored without recompense.[7]

The Middletons' neighbors, the Drayton family, also possessed at least one enslaved Rose. Drayton Hall, built around 1738, is a Palladian palace of a plantation home that still stands on the Ashley River, not far from Middleton Place. The Drayton "List for Negro Clothes and Blankets" from 1860 details each unfree person who received a fabric ration on the "country" estate as well as the mansion in "town." The women enslaved by the Drayton family in the city received a wider array of fabric varieties, like calico and flannel—for the purpose, it would seem, of keeping up the appearance of Drayton wealth in the eyes of their Charleston neighbors. Outfitting one's slaves well was an extravagance that gained more notice in the urban milieu than in the more sparsely populated rural landscape, where individual plantation estates extended for hundreds of acres. A single Rose on a textile list worked in the country for the Draytons and, in 1860, received five and a half yards of cloth, barely enough for two dresses.[8]

The stinginess of these Ashley River planter records stings.

They illuminate just how little enslaved women mattered to those who inscribed their names on these lists. Of all the Roses who appeared on these cold, monotonous inventories, only one I encountered carried the faintest outline of a story, but for the most awful of reasons. In 1853, Barnett H. Brown submitted a court claim to the state of South Carolina. He was seeking compensation for his "slave Rose," who had been "executed for murder." Who was *this* Rose, also called Rosanna in alternate records? Was she guilty of the crime for which her life was taken? And what would lead an enslaved Black woman to kill?

The most sensational and hence best-documented example of a comparable crime comes to us from the state of Missouri, where, in 1855, a nineteen-year-old woman murdered a man many years her senior. Celia, like most enslaved women, had no surname on record when she clubbed her owner, Robert Newsom, to death. Then she burned his body in the fireplace of her cabin and paid his grandson to sweep up and help dispose of the ashes. Celia's was a crime of passion and a cry of pain. Newsom had been raping her for approximately five years, since his purchase of her when he was sixty and she fourteen. It is probable that Celia's sexual initiation was violent and certain that her life under Robert Newsom's tyranny was unbearable. When Celia found a Black man she loved and glimpsed the possibilities of chosen intimacy and family, she begged Newsom's relatives to help her, pleaded with him to cease assaulting her, and finally lashed out to end the abuse. As a result of this desperate act of self-defense, Celia was tried, found guilty, and executed by the state of Missouri.

Only a few curt lines remain about *this* condemned Rose/ Rosanna, who might also have killed and is named in the South

Carolina records. The man seeking to recoup her monetary value and the functionaries of the South Carolina Legislature, which was disproportionately made up of slaveholders, were not interested in the facts of her case. The loss of "Rosanna the property of B. H. Brown" through execution was a cost the state was willing to underwrite. In 1855, the treasury office paid Brown $200 to cover the "value" of Rosanna's spent life.[9] So many Roses grew in the "reaper's garden" of South Carolina.[10] Each of them had a priceless life hidden within or buried beneath the indifferent record books of slavery. Each of them has an instructive tale about value judgments and misjudgments begging to be recalled and placed before our witness.

The life of every enslaved Rose shines with its own worth and brilliance, even as their lives taken together illuminate a sense of a larger whole, a society in which it was commonplace to both capture women and name them for flowers, and where, despite deep-seated cruelty, an African American people took root. Among these many Roses, how do we find and faithfully tell even one of their life stories? Here is where a surviving artifact tied to the word of a descendant saves the venture, encouraging us to pay respects to all of the Roses in slavery's garden and, at the same time, gather up a particular one. The oral story Ruth recorded helps us to identify the bias grain, or tensile give, in the traditional archive, the place where the records can be stretched to reveal still more.[11]

Ruth's Rose carried with her an identifying feature: her love for a child named Ashley. It was for lack of finding an Ashley along with a Rose in their records that led curators at Middleton Place to strike a sentence from their early catalog entry on Ashley's sack. Whereas at first the text had read, "Searches through

This Drayton Hall "blanket list," 1860, is one among many in
South Carolina that includes a woman named Rose.
Addlestone Library, College of Charleston. Photograph by Tiya Miles.

surviving Middleton family probate records from the late-
eighteenth and nineteenth centuries have revealed at least nine
enslaved women named Rose," that sentence was deleted before
the artifact was put on display.[12] Middleton family records included no enslaved girl named Ashley, which led curators to

doubt the likelihood of the Middletons having owned this Rose. They chose to delete the line referring to Roses on the Middleton premises in an abundance of caution. The curators did not want to give the false impression that the existence of several Roses meant that one of these was Ruth Middleton's ancestor. The presence of Ashley is an arrow pointing to Rose. A Rose without an Ashley, while precious, is likely not this particular woman. While Rose is a recurring name among enslaved women and girls in South Carolina, Ashley is a rarity. A search of the same documents that revealed nearly two hundred Roses produced only three Ashleys owned by residents of the colony, then the state. The name Ashley becomes more than an arrow in this sparse documentary environment; it is an arrow illumined with strings of lights.

One Ashley among these records, the legal property of Archibald Conturien McDonald of Sumter County, appears in his will of 1838. No Rose is inventoried in McDonald's rural estate, however. A second Ashley emerges from that same decade, belonging to a woman named Judith H. Wilson. Following her move to Bourdeaux, France, in 1836, Wilson sold Ashley to John E. Bonneau, a wealthy planter whose central estate was located in St. John's Berkeley Parish, up the Cooper River from Charleston. Bonneau bought Ashley in a $400 lot with two other enslaved people, Sappho and Abraham. All three are described as "Mullatto." While their relationship to one another goes undisclosed, we can guess that they may represent a family grouping. No woman named Rose appears here. Because enslaved people drew little attention from record keepers until property changed hands or someone died, we do not get another chance to trace this second Ashley's story until John Bonneau's death in 1849. But John Bonneau's estate inventory of 1849, which lists more than ninety enslaved people, including a woman with a disability, blindness, valued at $0, fails to make note of Ashley. Neither does she appear in his will. This Ashley may have been sold or freed in the decade between her purchase and Bonneau's death.

In 1850, Eliza M. Bonneau, John's executor, sold his plantation villa in St. John's Berkeley Parish with no Ashley listed in the property valuation. Five years later, when Bonneau heirs Peter and Martha Bonneau sold thirty enslaved people hailing from the estate, Ashley still does not appear. But this time, a woman named Rose does. It seems that John Bonneau had, at some point during his last years of life, owned an Ashley *and* a Rose.[13] The sale of Bonneau's Rose following his death as part of the redistribution of his estate was a shared trauma for many enslaved people. The earthly demise of a master often meant separation from home and family for those enslaved. But this Rose and Ashley's story is unlikely to be that of Ruth Middleton's ancestors. This Ashley appears on the scene too early to be the grandmother of Ruth, a woman born at the turn of the twentieth century. And if this Ashley had been a daughter of Rose, they would more than likely have both appeared in Bonneau's legal papers when Judith Wilson, Ashley's former owner, moved away. Finally, this Ashley was sold to John Bonneau more than a decade before Ruth's ancestor Rose gifted a sack to Ashley. In the marshes and swamps of St. John's Berkeley Parish, this Ashley and this Rose may have toiled together, sung together, watched in tandem the rise of the sun, but their personal story, so far as we know, lies buried with the boggy estate of John E. Bonneau.[14]

Sometimes our third try carries the charm. The Ashley whose name is caught next in the documentary net is a girl inventoried as part and parcel of Milberry Place Plantation, the country estate of one Robert Martin, "late of the city of Charleston."

Ashley is listed among one hundred unfree people in the inventory of Martin's enslaved property taken in the year 1853. Her attributed value of $300, in comparison to that of other women listed at $500 and $600 in the cotton boom decade of the 1850s, suggests that she may have been a younger or relatively unskilled worker. Robert Martin's rural plantation, named after his "beloved wife," Milberry Serena Daniel Martin, was located in the Barnwell District of South Carolina, approximately one hundred miles northwest of coastal Charleston. Here Martin directed his manager to direct his drivers to direct his slaves to plant and harvest short-staple cotton, a hearty, stout-flowering variety of the plant that grew more readily in the interior than the sea island cotton that had brought so much wealth to Lowcountry planters. No woman named Rose appears on the list of the Martin family's country slaves, who are seamlessly followed in the record by mules (also listed with personal pet names and valuations), and then by horses, calves, and hogs, followed by blacksmith and carpentry tools. But like many of his wealthy fellows in the planter class, Robert Martin had acquired more than one slave-run estate. He kept a plantation in the countryside, where most of his wealth was consolidated in the capital of enslaved bodies and was, at the same time, being produced by the labor of those bodies and minds. In addition, Martin possessed a manor house in Charleston, where he could oversee business dealings and keep his family properly situated in the social rituals of urbane society. Martin's house in town was inventoried in a separate appraisal upon his death. Here, he owned pricey china, fashionable carriages, a pair of horses, one cow, stocks and bonds in numerous companies, and seven enslaved men and women, one whose name was Rose.[15]

This Rose, listed with the value of $700 beside her name,

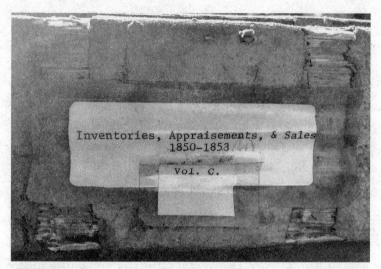

This "Inventories, Appraisements & Sales" volume in the South Carolina Department of Archives and History, in Columbia, contains an Ashley and a Rose listed as the property of Robert Martin. Photograph by Tiya Miles.

was the most expensive woman on Martin's urban estate. She must have been in her prime age of life. She may have been highly skilled. However much we hate to confront it, she may have been priced at this amount because of her sexual appeal to white men. She could have been valued for any one or all three of these qualities in the slaveholding household of Robert and Milberry, but she certainly was prized for more than these qualities by those she loved. This Rose is also the one most likely among the existing South Carolina records to be the mother of Ashley. Circumstantial evidence in the documents points directly to this woman. She is the only Rose in the surviving and searchable slaveholder records of South Carolina who is shown as owned at the precise time (the 1840s through 1850s, when sacks like the one Rose packed were being manufactured) by the same person who held a girl named Ashley.[16]

ALL THE FORMS OF BUSINESS

This person who owned the two of them, Robert Martin, was described by a judge of the district court as "a man of experience, and sagacity, and acquainted with all the forms of business."[17] Indeed, Martin was a successful planter by the time of his death; shortly thereafter, in 1853, his inventoried estates, confidently entered as "True and Perfect" by the attorneys, listed Ashley as well as Rose among his property holdings. Robert Martin got his start, however, in lowlier ranks, as a peddler of common necessities. He made his place as a merchant and businessman rather than by inheriting a spot in the landed gentry of Charleston's first aristocratic families, like the Middletons. He was, in the language that nineteenth-century narratives love, a self-made man.

Born in South Carolina in 1791 to Irish immigrants, Martin ran a dry goods store on King Street, the hub (then and now) of commercial Charleston, in the 1810s. By 1827, he was operating a grocery at two locations. He may even have been involved in transporting goods between the city and countryside, an enterprise that eager traders took up as inland cotton plantations became more plentiful. A few years later, he had made the leap into the professional financial class, working as a "factor," a handsomely paid accountant and broker, in a concern called Robert Martin & Co. If he already owned an enslaved person while working as a grocer, he would have increased his human holdings on a factor's salary, as much for the sake of appearances at his townhome as for the smooth operation of the business, since Charleston was a place where owning others signaled one's status more than any other accoutrement.[18]

The 1820s and 1830s were heady years for Martin, as he began to expand his entrepreneurial portfolio and to play at the buying and selling of slaves. In 1828, he married Milberry Serena Daniel, the daughter of a wealthy farmer in Kershaw District, in the interior of the state. Hailing from the White Oak plantation, Milberry Serena had grown up with greater means than her husband. Milberry's father owned eight enslaved men, women, and children when he passed away in 1828. In his will, he left one of these, a girl named Leana, to Milberry. By the spring of 1829, Milberry had inherited from the White Oak estate and taken with her to Charleston a piano, a bureau, two feather beds, sundry furniture, and, we can surmise, Leana.[19]

The timing of this marriage benefited Robert as well as Milberry. He gained a measure of social status and "movable" property, and she gained an urban seat and a husband with ambitions. Robert continued to operate as a merchant and a factor, now on the action-filled wharf, where he could more efficiently broker rice and cotton trades for product coming in by water. His brokerage company had evolved into a partnership with three other men. Martin hustled to expand his financial profile and professional influence in this period, when the remnant record of his slave trading begins. In 1824, Martin, exhibiting no scruples about relocating children, sold "a certain Negro boy, slave named Cesar, warranted sober, sound, honest and no runaway" for $230. A man named Fortune was the next to be off-loaded; in 1825, he went for the sum of $200. In 1831, Martin sold "a negro woman about 28 years of age named Silvia and her son Robert" for $575. By that same year, he had successfully worked his way into the professional circles of Charleston's upper echelons, accepting the job of financial representative with power of attorney for William Aiken, Jr., a future governor of the state (in 1844–46) and the owner of seven hundred enslaved people.[20]

Though still not a planter himself, Martin was a successful cotton-trade middleman, handling the finances of old-money clients in the city. His aspiration to join this class showed in his

Searching for Rose 73

addition to Charleston's elaborate architecture. Around the year 1834, Martin commissioned a stately brick Georgian mansion at 16 Charlotte Street, on the north side of town. A few years later, in 1839, he drew up an exacting last will and testament. In it, he predicted and ordered monetary dispersals and withhold-ings for various possible twists of fate in the lives of his heirs (the children's deaths, his daughters' marriages, his wife's remar-riage, his daughters' husbands' remarriages, should the daugh-ters die after receiving their inheritance, and so on). Martin named his "beloved wife Milberry Serena Martin" his executor, and bequeathed to her "my House and Lot in Charlotte Street in which I reside with all its Appurtenances, furniture, house servants together with all the rest and residue of my estate of every kind." Martin also directed his wife to liquidate much of his estate upon his death so that she could pay out "as fast as money for that purpose can be realized" $20,000 to every one of their children (nearly $500,000 each in today's value) as income upon their twenty-first birthdays.[21]

By the late 1830s and early 1840s, Martin had come up in the world. He was a man gainfully employed in the field of "commerce," according to the 1840 federal census, living at home with his wife, four white children, and eight enslaved people. The 1840s is probably the period when he acquired a young woman named Rose, who was listed among his Charlotte Street holdings a decade later. In 1843, Martin began buying tracts of land upstate in the town of Aiken and in the Erwinton community near the town of Barnwell, both in the Barnwell District. In 1845, he purchased an entire lot of slaves in Barn-well: Amy, Mingo, July, Lovy, Dinah, Leah, Cornelia, and a child, Reuben—presumably, to work that land. In 1846, Martin acquired twenty-five hundred contiguous acres along the Savan-nah River and pieced it together with additional parcels to en-

Robert Martin House, 16 Charlotte Street, Charleston, South Carolina, 1933. The brick wall and ironwork that surround the property are visible in this photograph. Historic American Buildings Survey, HABS SC-150.

large what had become his rural estate. By 1849, apparently flush with cash, he paid $30,000 to purchase bonds on a mortgage for a Pee Dee River plantation in Richfield, South Carolina, and the enslaved people on it. Martin continued to work as a factor in partnership on the Charleston wharf, but by 1852 he had taken on a second, higher status. Having parlayed profits from sales and brokering into landed wealth, the dream of many a free southern man, he was now a planter.[22]

Martin proudly identified as "planter" rather than "factor" in the 1852 Charleston City Directory. In so doing, he joined the ranks of a second wave of wealthy Carolina planters, men who had missed the original aristocratic rice coast boom but breezed into luxury on the snowy-white sails of latter-day cotton. Martin was comfortably rich by an antebellum southern measure, plenty affluent, but not ensconced in a princely life of old rice money, palatial estates, many thousands of acres, and hundreds of unfree people to work them. He was wealthy and influential but not quite important enough to leave a trove of personal papers that would be carefully curated over the years. For this reason, we know less about the African Americans he owned than about people enslaved on the famous Middleton or Ball plantations. Still, Martin occupied a respectable rung near the top of Charleston society.

He and his wife were focused on building and maintaining wealth, as was the tendency of slaveholders with roots in the middle class, and a legal trail marks their many transactions in land and people.[23] During the decade or more in which Robert Martin rose to the ranks of factor and planter, he and Milberry lived in elegant comfort and saw their two eldest daughters, Ellen and Henrietta, marry into Charleston upper-crust families, the Aikens and the Meanses, respectively. Henrietta's merger with one of Charleston's older established families, the Meanses, became the primary vehicle through which the Martins' papers have been preserved in the collection of the South Carolina Historical Society.[24] Martin died with a small fortune to bestow upon his heirs, made up of owned people, animals of husbandry, land, houses, a hotel near the new intrastate railroad in Aiken, furnishings, and stocks. Because he had risen high enough for his property to have been cataloged in detail and, later, for his house to have been photographed for the Historic American Building Survey in 1927, we can gather an inkling of how everyday life unfolded for Rose and her enslaved fellows behind the walls of his Charleston estate.[25]

In the 1830s, the prized lots south of Broad Street were already occupied by the ornate second homes of rice planters. Martin had no choice but to build farther north, in a neighborhood called the Neck because of its elongated shape above the harbor. Because it had not been the first choice of white planter families, the Neck was a neighborhood of racial and class diversity, a place where the rich and the poor spied each other across the narrow streets. Here in relatively close proximity in the interior of the coastal city, lived working-class whites, free people of color, and a subset of enslaved people who were permitted to live on their own, hire themselves out, and pay wages back to their owners.[26] But even in this unusual enclave, monied men like Robert Martin found ways to set themselves apart. They purchased corner lots on higher ground with robust sea breezes, installing water-control systems that flushed their waste downhill to their poorer and colored neighbors, and surrounded their large parcels with stout brick walls, in keeping with an earlier Charleston architectural practice. These men erected virtual country estates inside the northern part of the city, creating a Charlestonian architectural form known as the "plantation-style suburban villa." Rather than mimicking the slender, sideways orientation of Charleston's oldest planter homes in the "single house" style by the bay, the suburban villa strutted out, broad and brash, toward the street. These homes, built from the 1830s through the 1850s, were wide and open-armed, with verandahs facing forward, grand exterior entry staircases, and rows of elegant pillars making for a dramatic curbside presence. They mimicked the look of eighteenth-century plantation mansions, bringing the country into the city and declaring the owners' desired, and at times realized, planter status.[27]

Robert Martin's suburban villa, built around 1834, was a classically Georgian-style mansion with Greek Revival elements. It featured a "triple tiered piazza entered by divided curving stairs." The structure revealed, according to the art historian Maurie McInnis, "the importance [Martin] placed on entertaining" and "his preference for bold architectural details . . . indicated by the heavy Tuscan columns below and fluted Doric ones above that support the piazza." Like other merchants and planters who built on the Neck, Martin "devoted considerable attention to elaborate and extensive gardens."[28] His was a walled compound completely surrounded by red brick and wrought iron, softened only by the lush green of the subtropical foliage. What felt luxuriant and safe for Robert, Milberry, and their children, however, would surely have been bleak and imposing to their captive human "chattels" like Rose.[29]

We know so much about Martin from his records and the imposing house he built. Historians follow paper trails. Since Rose left none, it is easy to let her fade into the margins of this record-driven chapter, to let the Martins take center stage in our time as in their own. There is a centrifugal pull, in reconstructing enslaved lives, toward telling the stories of their owners primarily or instead. This is a default we must resist—but how? Not one record in the Martin family papers describes Rose or the life she lived. Her cares and her kindnesses, fears and frailties, fade behind a wall of silence. Can we scale it?

Let us turn to Harriet Jacobs for guidance in imagining. Jacobs masterminded her family's escape from North Carolina to New York. From her room in the home of an employer in upstate New York in the 1850s, Jacobs penned a penetrating memoir of social critique. Hers was the first autobiography by a Black woman to reveal the insidious culture of sexual harassment and assault in slavery as well as to confront the gender double standard between white women and Black women in Victorian society, which always categorized Black women as impure. She expressed, pointedly, that those who have not experienced legalized bondage can never know "what it is to be a slave; to be entirely unprotected by law or custom; to have the laws reduce you to the condition of a chattel, entirely subject to the will of another." We cannot enter the consciousness of a girl born into slavery who matures to give birth into slavery and can have no reasonable hope of rescue.[30] We cannot know Rose, but we can draw on the resources at our disposal—documents, cityscapes, architectural records and the built environment she inhabited, slave narratives, and Ruth's inscription on the sack—to picture the woman she might have been and summon the shape of her daily life.

PAINED BY THE RETROSPECT

Today the brick walls of Charleston seem picturesque, luxuriously fringed by palmetto fronds, burnt-orange trumpet vines, and snow-white gardenias hot with perfume. We admire the Old World intricacy of this storied city while taking photos of Charleston's famous iron gates. We see the tall, striking walls as elaborate garden boxes resplendent here as nowhere else in the nation. We gaze with longing glances at the seeming romance of another age, lapped by gentle waves and bathed in sunlight. But in the early and middle 1800s, when Rose likely lived in this city, these walls were barrier fences. The urban estates inside functioned like prisons, with every white person a virtual warden. The walls could double as weapons, too, when spangled on their upper ledges with sharp barbs of broken bottles placed at the master's direction. Elaborately worked wrought-iron gates adjoined the thick segments of brick, spiked in their decorative aspect like knives and swords. To Charleston's elite slaveholding residents, like Ralph Izard of Meeting Street, these weaponized walls bestowed "an air of comfort to the premises." The walls represented social order, the proper structuring of life, in which certain classes of people (white, Black, free, slave, men, women) and different types of activities (business versus domestic affairs) were kept to their appointed places. Comfort and structure for the owners meant danger and chaos for the enslaved. Walls barricading family homes from the sight lines of the streets prevented freedom of movement, escape, and revolt by enslaved people and, more subtly but just as ominously, veiled the sights and sounds of physical and sexual abuse. The romantic walls of Charleston, as an art historian of the city put it, "forced slaves to focus on the master's world."[31]

The palisaded Georgian villa at 16 Charlotte Street, where Rose lived and labored for the Martins, now houses a legal firm. Behind the main structure, a "brick two-story dependency" is shrouded by a net of vines. This was the kitchen and slave quarters back in the mid-1800s, the shadow space of the grand estate where Rose might have spent much of her time.[32] Imagine Rose, dressed in a plain frock of cotton or linsey-woolsey, perhaps in a

Miles Brewton House fence with mounted spikes, 27 King Street, Charleston. The spikes were added to the plain ironwork fence after Denmark Vesey's rebellion plot of 1822. Photograph by Tiya Miles; information from William P. Baldwin, ed., *Ornamental Ironwork of Charleston* (Charleston: History Press, 2007), 95.

The Charleston suburban villa of Robert and Milberry Serena Martin and their family, built in the 1840s, is now the site of a law office. Photograph by Tiya Miles, 2018.

shade of blue or gray or a printed calico, covered in front by a simple apron. She wears a square of fabric around her head to catch the sweat in the southern heat and, perhaps, to enjoy a flash of some preferred pattern or color. This was a style, as New England schoolteacher Emily Burke said of enslaved women in the nearby coastal city of Savannah, Georgia, in the 1840s, that fashioned a "headdress" out of "a sort of turban, made by folding a cotton handkerchief in that peculiar kind of way known only to themselves."[33] Beneath Rose's brightly colored head wrap, she thinks thoughts we cannot conjure, perhaps about a parent long lost, or a God on high, or ancestral spirits who could protect a downtrodden people.

Rose's waking hours must have revolved around the Martins. This family held power of breath over Rose, power to overwork and extort her, to make her tend to the private needs of their feelings and bodies. Rose was subject to them, directed by force of law and custom to carry out, as Harriet Jacobs baldly put it, their "will in all things."[34] She might also have been a prop to her owners, another sign, like their double parlors and fine furnishings kept within it, of their solidified wealth and membership in the planter class.[35] During the short hours when Rose was not carrying out commands, she probably slept in the stifling brick kitchen house, on a pallet or a bare stretch of floor. Rose may have had her own family members on this compound, Black, or Native, or mixed-race people with whom she was intimate. We cannot access this part of her life, however. The kinship bonds of a slave were often of little consequence to enslavers and therefore unnoticed in the record.

We will never know, for instance, based on the inventory taken after Robert Martin's death, whether any of these enslaved residents were related, if they supported one another or rivaled one another for status, if they chose to spend time in the evening talking together, or saw the same cloud shapes in the sky on an overcast Sunday afternoon. Cicero, the highest-valued enslaved person on these Charleston premises and listed at $1,000, would have possessed special skills for life in the city. Perhaps he was a head man in the house, a butler and a carriage driver, outfitted in the formal livery of suit jacket and brass buttons as a display of the white family's wealth. Jack and David, listed at $800 each, may have been mechanics, coppersmiths, or wheelwrights who kept things running about the place and could be hired out by the Martins to bring in extra cash. Sophia, valued less than most adults on the list at $300, likely performed basic cleaning, maid-in-waiting services, and domestic maintenance tasks. Other enslaved women who worked at the house at various times but may not have been captured by this specific document would have contributed to keeping the home clean and orderly. James, valued at only $100, must have been a child. The elderly woman valued at $100, who did not even warrant a recording of her name, may have been a nanny to the children or light task worker at the house. Rose, whose name on the list is preceded by a spare "ditto" symbol, indicating that she, too, was enslaved, was the counterpart of Cicero among unfree women in the household, valued the highest. Rose's monetary estimation of over $500 suggests that she was talented in some manner that slaveholders appreciated, perhaps as a seamstress (the only artisanal craft that measurably elevated enslaved women's ascribed "worth") or as a cook.[36]

Rose likely knew the fundamentals of sewing, a critical skill for enslaved women. She was unlikely, however, to have been a mantua-maker (to use the term preferred in Charleston for an accomplished dressmaker). If a seamstress, she would have stitched clothing for others enslaved at the Charlotte Street house or on the Martins' country estate, mended clothing for her owner's family, and repaired torn or frayed sheets, blankets, quilts, and tablecloths in heavy use.[37] If a cook, she would have spent her days bending and sweating over iron kettles at the open fireplace in the kitchen behind the big house and trudging several long blocks to market for ingredients and then bearing them all back again.

If the Martins saw fit to subdivide Rose's efforts and sell her labor, they might have hired her out to white associates or free people of color in the city (some of whom owned and rented enslaved people) and then pocketed the income. In order to walk the mucky streets crowded with other Black workers, Rose would have worn a required badge of copper or tin reading "SERVANT" or "HOUSE SERVANT." These tags were meant to differentiate Blacks with permission from owners to chase errands,

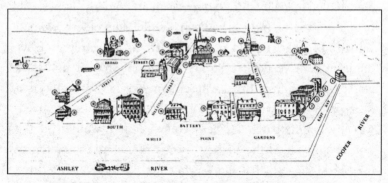

"Bird's-Eye View of Charleston, 1850." From Erskine Clarke, *Wrestlin' Jacob: A Portrait of Religion in Antebellum Georgia and the Carolina Low Country* (Tuscaloosa: University of Alabama Press, 2000).

hawk fruit, or work the wharves as hired-out slaves from those who lacked it, in a city where, as one British traveler put it, "the whole of the working population are Negroes . . . all the servants, the carmen and porters, all the people who [sell] at the stalls in Market, and most of the Journeymen in trades."[38] The city guardsmen who patrolled the movements of enslaved people looked for undocumented victims to jail. An enslaved person without a badge (also required for free people of color for a short period of time, as well as for resident dogs)* or present on the streets after curfew faced police harassment and capture, jailing, and carceral torture in the city's fortress-like Work House.[39]

Rose's purpose, in the minds of her owners, was to serve liqueur and season meat, ease aches and sooth discomforts, embody value and increase wealth—in short, to sustain *their* lives and livelihood while relinquishing her own. She would also have been an intimate, a caretaker as well as a dependent, which made the nature of this relationship between owned and owner enmeshed and corrupt. Why did the Martins, professors of the Christian faith and congregants of the Episcopal Church, treat a member of their household as if she belonged to a demoted category of the human?[40] How were they able to maintain a bifurcated view of their world, one in which they could possess a person, steal her labor, rely on her ministrations daily, and still think themselves upstanding members of society?

* Charleston is the only American city that required slaveholders to purchase badges. These badges, meant to be worn visibly on the body, displayed an enslaved person's occupation and announced the master's permission for that person to be mobile for the named work and even to live in a separate, independent household while carrying out the work. Example occupations found on preserved badges include servant, mechanic, porter, and huckster (seller of fruit). In 1840–50, the city of Charleston regularly sold some 3,700 to 4,100 badges per year to enslavers who wished to hire out the people they owned.

By the time Rose was subject to the Martins' authority, in the early 1800s, South Carolinians of the upper classes had long adopted a frame of mind, often referred to as "paternalism," that allowed them to feel that slaveholding was morally right and even benevolent. Inspired by their cultural roots in European feudalism, in which lords and serfs related on unequal but accepted terms, elites believed in the correctness of a hierarchical social structure that they understood as being not only natural but also ordained by God. To them, the world was strictly ordered, with a proper place for everyone in it: a select few at the top would dominate and take responsibility for a vast mass of dependents below. In this eighteenth-century paternalistic vision of a stable, organized society bolstered by an early-nineteenth-century Christian revivalism, landholding white men maintained the right to control those beneath them in status, even and especially loved ones within the household.

The refined men, or fathers, at the heads of these estates eschewed the outright brutality of previous generations of patriarchs, preferring to enact their will through the pull of mutual obligation and emotional manipulation, as well as by bestowing perks in exchange for desired behavior. Their method for exacting compliance often devolved, however, into psychological or physical punishment.[41] In cities with infrastructural support for slaveholder dominance, an owner could tell himself he was kind to his owned man while "send[ing] him to the jail with orders to have him whipped so many times a day for a certain number of days," as Emily Burke put it in a letter.[42] Just as God reigned over his creation with the carrot of heaven and the stick of hell, the white male father figure governed the dependent inhabitants of his household. In addition to being culturally familiar to the many South Carolina elites who borrowed the cultural practices of British high society, the ethos of paternalism legitimized slavery by suggesting that the slave order was organic and right.

White women, white children, Black and Indigenous enslaved people, free people of color, and even white men without independent financial means were therefore subject to the direction of well-heeled men at the top of the social ladder in Charleston and the Lowcountry South. Elite white women benefited from this social structure even as they paid a dear price to live within it. Trading autonomy for bodily protection, personal comforts, and elevation to the respected pedestal of southern "lady," wealthy white women often consented to this order through silent acquiescence and active reinforcement of racial lines.[43] During her ten years in Savannah and on nearby plantations, Emily Burke recounted a series of abuses carried out by women slaveholders. She described, for instance, the beating death of a twelve-year-old Black boy who fell asleep while caring for a white baby, thereby allowing his face to touch the child's. The mistress, "enraged" when happening upon the boy dozing with the infant in arms, "gave him such a beating as he deserved at such an outrage." A few weeks passed before the boy died, and, as Burke reported, "by his death his master lost five hundred dollars."[44]

Enslaved women saw through this contradictory social arrangement that allowed white enslavers to claim beneficence, decrying in oral and written narratives the emotional cruelties and physical acts of violence encouraged by a system in which a subset of the population dictated the terms of most others' lives. Harriet Jacobs described southern slave society as "a curse to the whites as well as to the blacks. It makes the white fathers cruel and sensual; the sons violent and licentious; it contaminates the daughters, and it makes the wives wretched. And as for the colored race, it needs an abler pen than mine to describe the extremity of their sufferings, the depth of their degradation."[45] Rose may have agreed with Harriet about the interpersonal rot endemic in a society built on slavery. Rose may have thought a great many things about her condition and the state of her social world that we cannot quite access.

At a distance of nearly two hundred years, we can recognize, though, that Rose had a mind of her own, whether or not she masked those views when interacting with her owners. We can see that she was smart and sensitive to the needs of others. She was also resourceful, with an admirable ability to acquire things and address problems. She was, beyond that, courageous, given her willingness to engage in activities that could have resulted in harsh punishment. All of this is apparent in Rose's actions as recorded by Ruth on the sack and hinted at, perhaps and in part, by the high valuation assigned to her in the Martins' estate papers. Even her owners and their legal proxies seemed to attest to Rose's talents, though they did so in the language of market value.

With no protection of the law, no recompense or regard, no permissible route to fulfillment of her own inner purpose, this Rose in our imagination strips the sheets and scrubs the floorboards, sews the hems of the slaves' work pants and fastens the back of the mistress's corset, stirs the soup in the silver tureen or empties the urine from the porcelain pot rotten with the stench of an enslaver's waste. As one of two young adult Black women in the household, Rose would have had to juggle these and manifold other demanding duties, serving as a Jill of most trades. She may have washed china and silver salt spoons, cleansed wool blankets and cotton sheeting, dusted tables and writing desks, polished banisters and railings, buffed floors and beaten carpets, laundered and ironed an array of apparel, and made food spills, mud stains, and bodily accidents fade from all of these surfaces, day in and day out. She would have served cups of tea and plates of cake, presenting heavy, ornate trays and whisking them away again. If she also worked as a waiting maid or a children's "nurse," she would have helped her mistress to bathe in water that she had hauled and warmed at the fire and then to dress in taffeta that rustled like the sound of paper money fanned out. She may have tended to the feeding and toileting, watching and chasing, and fresh-air gathering of the four Martin children—two boys and two girls—living in the house in 1840.[46] She may have gazed at those pampered little ones and hoped for, and feared for, a child of her own. When Rose did become pregnant, she stood at the cusp of a transformation that would reorient her world of captivity. She would gain someone to love fiercely but under the constant shadow of loss that was the lot of the person deemed chattel slave.

Rose entered motherhood in the 1840s, probably 1844. This date is measured by Ashley's age (nine) at the time of her sale as inscribed on the sack paired with the year (1852–53) that both women entered the documentary record in Martin's estate inventory, an owner's death being a time common in the lives of the enslaved when familial separations occurred. Rose was probably twenty-six in 1844, young in our day, but no babe in the woods of America's nineteenth-century South. She was old enough by more than a decade to have been exposed, in Charleston or elsewhere (for we do not know where she was born), to the sexual travails enslaved Black women regularly faced in a culture where rape was never considered a crime against their persons.[47] No record reveals the paternity of the child, Ashley, who probably was not Rose's first, given that enslaved Black girls usually had a first child at age nineteen.[48]

Martin's household included two enslaved males between the ages of ten and twenty-three and one enslaved man between twenty-four and thirty-five in the 1840s. Any of them might have fathered a baby with Rose. One of them, too, may have been Rose's husband, though this is unlikely. Enslaved Black women in Charleston were less frequently wedded than free women of color and white women, due to the necessity of obtaining an owner's permission, the lack of legal recognition for conjugal unions between unfree individuals, and the frequent forced separation of couples. Robert Martin could also have fathered Rose's child, a reality we cannot ignore, especially when peering into the shadow spaces of the slaveholding home, where decades of scholarship have proven sexual predation a common occurrence. Rose may have felt similarly to Harriet Jacobs, who wrote obliquely of her master's sexual abuse: "I cannot tell how much I suffered in the presence of these wrongs, nor how I am still pained by the retrospect."[49]

Censuses scheduled a decade apart notating Black members of the Martins' Charleston residence do not allow us to pinpoint Ashley's paternity or her birth date within the decade of the 1840s. We can surmise, though, that by the time of Robert Martin's death, in December 1852, Ashley had been transferred to his cotton plantation, since her name surfaces on the plantation's separate estate inventory. It was common practice for planters in South Carolina to move enslaved people around their properties without compunction, in service of labor needs, or as an act of punishment, or as a means of psychological control. Martin may have shifted Ashley or any of his town slaves to the country as it suited his or his wife's inclinations. We can imagine a situation in which Milberry Martin may have sorely wished to see a brown baby girl born into her Charleston townhome (around the same year as her own youngest daughter and namesake was also born) swiftly relocated.

While this is supposition in this specific case, primary and secondary evidence back up a picture of vindictive behavior on the part of mistresses whose husbands strayed with female slaves. In all likelihood, Rose was separated from her daughter when Ashley was younger than nine, but Rose may have been sent to the Martins' cotton plantation to work for short stints. It was typical for the Charleston elite to spend the winter social season in town, reside on their plantations during warmer months, and vacation in the hills, mountains, and cities farther north during the sweltering summertime. They would have brought along close domestic staff on whom they depended, and these enslaved personal servants likely also had familial or social ties on plantations in the country.[50] The Martins probably took Rose — a valued servant, given her price — to Milberry Place Plantation for seasonal jaunts. Perhaps Rose had chances to watch over Ashley there, giving the girl hearth-baked bread or salvaged strips of pretty ribbon, and wishing she possessed the power to free her child from the invisible prison that she knew with a painful intimacy, and that would, with time, slam shut unyielding bars between them.

The odds that a mother and daughter separated by slavery would ever find each other again were scant. The odds that we have identified Ruth's great-grandmother Rose among the records and buildings of South Carolina are surer but not absolute. In that hazy space between "probably" and "certainly" lies a discomfiting gap. Our desire to know falls headlong into the holes of the record. It is a worthwhile practice, then, to learn the language absences speak and build the skill of valuing what has previously been voided. For here, in the space of loss and longing that the enslaved knew too well, we can choose an "abundant" approach to history, resisting the default in which historical gaps feed contemporary forgetfulness.[51]

Who was Rose? We know at least this: Rose refused to submit to the lie that said she had no right to love her daughter. Instead, she claimed her child, sought to shield Ashley, and provided a priceless inheritance, which she folded into a sack. Rose's radical stance, obfuscated in the archives, reveals to us the potential force of human will against the odds. How did an enslaved woman continue to "make generations," birthing and bringing up babies in the face of impossible exigencies?[52] How did a maligned population with no logical reason for hope carry on to keep the country's faith in the possibility of equality? Even in its faint outlines dredged from the antebellum Charleston muck, Rose's story begins to show the ways.

PACKING THE SACK

In the diaspora, most black people's relationship to love has been shaped by the trauma of abandonment.

　　　—bell hooks, *Salvation: Black People and Love*, 2001

The captive person developed, time and again, certain ethical and sentimental features that tied her and him *across* the landscape to others, often sold from hand to hand, of the same and different blood in a common fabric of memory and inspiration. We might choose to call this connectedness "family."

　　　—HORTENSE SPILLERS, "Mama's Baby, Papa's Maybe: An American Grammar Book," 1987

WHEN DID ROSE KNOW? DID A SENSE OF DREAD descend on her in the Charlotte Street manor house when she learned, through the wails of Milberry Martin or the murmurs of Cicero, Jack, or David, that Robert Martin, the man who owned her, had breathed his last? Did a shadow fall across her mind on the day of his interment in Magnolia Cemetery, a burying ground for Charleston's elite?[1] Did Rose's thoughts whirl wildly to her daughter, situated far away at remote Milberry Place Plantation? Did she think about how hard it was to raise a child to nine years old, the age before which many unfree children died of sickness?[2] Did she begin, at that moment, a countdown to the inevitable? Did she plan, in that instant, to fight back with love?

A condition described as "brain disease" had taken the life of Robert Martin, as assessed by a Dr. Bellinger and recorded by a city clerk, between December 12 and 18 of the year 1852.[3] Martin died within two decades of his ascent to the planter elite. His demise would have grave consequences not only for his family but also for the Black families he and Milberry owned, whose fate was tied up with the lives of their captors. When an owner died and his or her estate was reorganized, liquidated, or apportioned out to heirs, enslaved people suffered. Like ancient slaves for whom burial alongside precious goods with deceased pharaohs and priestly chiefs was customary, modern slaves of the American South in the mid-nineteenth century could expect a kind of death with their masters' earthly departures. They were made dead to one another through quick sales and forced separations that could lead to relocation deep within the cotton South. Wise to these realities, Rose would certainly have wondered what fresh evils Robert Martin's passing portended for those she knew and loved.

Surely Rose had witnessed the coffles of forlorn men, women, and children, gliding like ghosts to and from the Old Exchange Building, which served as an outdoor slave mall. These dark human trains of the shackled and surveilled moved across southern roads with increasing frequency in the 1830s, 1840s, and 1850s as cotton plantations spread westward. White men on horseback with whips and guns guarded the valuable cargo. Along the way, these middlemen of the domestic trade took sexual advantage of vulnerable girls and women, vended people to eager buyers, and transported the suits of new clothes that the prisoners would be forced to wear once they reached the selling floor of a market flying the customary red flag that advertised the peculiar nature of its merchandise.[4] A formerly enslaved man from Tennessee who had been sold four times across three states described the dreaded coffle: "We had to travel a good deal of the distance on foot. . . . The women, they put them in the wagon and carried them, but the men had to walk . . . and you could see the women crying about their babies and children they had left."[5] Some unwilling migrants who came through Charleston, strangers to Rose from distant parts, would have lugged grimy "tow sacks" on backs welted like wounded trees.[6] In the surge of forced migration that delivered tens of thousands from the Upper South and the coastal zone to the interior southwest stretching from Alabama to Missouri during the post-1820s cotton boom, enslaved people carried these rough-hewn bags to their next places of incarceration. As one formerly enslaved man from Virginia remembered: "They sold slaves here and everywhere. I've seen droves of Negroes brought in here on foot going South to be sold. Each one of them had an old tow sack on his back with everything he's got in it."[7] Perhaps Rose had traveled in a coffle herself before falling into Robert and Milberry's possession. At the very least, she would have heard of this bipedal transit system and been familiar with the sights, smells, and sounds of its cruelties.

Is this how Rose seized upon the thought of the bag? Did she picture herself or her daughter marching in melancholy step to the sound of chains clinking across the Carolina swamps and pine forests like so many others? Or did Rose prepare her bundle weeks or months in advance, in expectation of emergency? Considering Rose's consciousness, her tangle of thoughts and knots of emotion in the winter of 1852, leads us into the unmapped territory of the slave mother's mind. What was this place like, the inner psychic universe of mothers to the unfree-born? Where were the borders of this place? What were its dominant seasons

"Edward Stone's Coffle Gang." From J. Winston Coleman, *Slavery Times in Kentucky* (Chapel Hill: University of North Carolina Press, 1940). Note the sacks carried by the enslaved women in the middle of this group of people being marched to a place of sale. Schomburg Center for Research in Black Culture, New York Public Library, https://digitalcollections.nypl.org/items/510d47dc-9fb2-a3d9-e040-e00a18064a99.

and colors? Did it ever see the warm touch of a sun? Survivors and witnesses of slavery tell us that if we were able to enter that land, we would find ourselves wading through desert sands of "grief and dread."[8]

Here, in this country of grief where the danger of separation loomed so large, we can imagine that residents always kept a bag packed, whether physically or psychically. When Rose prepped an emergency kit for her daughter, she packed for persistence in the face of "incapacitating uncertainty," the common lot of un-free people then—and, increasingly, of many people in our present moment of extreme political and climate disruption.[9] Rose would have known this state of instability as the only con-stant in her life. Yet she found the inner strength to meet a mea-sureless threat with thoughtful action.[10] In this determination to act, Rose represents a population that "exercised a degree of courage and will to survive that startles the imagination even

"Slave Trader, Sold to Tennessee." From Lewis Miller, *Sketchbook of Landscapes in the State of Virginia, 1853–1867*. Note the enslaved men carrying sacks on a stick and over the back toward the front of the line. Courtesy of the Abby Aldrich Rockefeller Folk Art Museum, Colonial Williamsburg Foundation, Williamsburg, Virginia; slide 84-896c.

now," in the words of the Black feminist theorist Hortense Spillers.[11] Out of the shadows Rose would emerge, bearing the sack as a lifeline and staking a claim for her family's continuance amid and despite unrelenting change.

A SADDER LOVE

We know, from the words they have left behind in narratives and letters, that slave mothers lived in a shadowland of constant, scathingly rational fear. This state of being bred a special brand of resourcefulness. Harriet Jacobs, who had a child with a wealthy white man, "Mr. Sands," from her North Carolina town, as a form of self-protection from the sexual predation of her owner, "Dr. Flint," tells us and her nineteenth-century readers that motherhood brought with it "a mixture of love and pain." "[From the moment] my children were first laid in my arms," Jacobs disclosed, "there I had watched over them, each day with a deeper and sadder love." Jacobs was so distraught that her infant son existed as movable property with no surname to speak of that she prayed for the newborn's premature death. But when her son actually became ill, she desperately sought a reprieve from God, begging for the child to be spared. "Alas what mockery it is for a slave mother to try to pray back her dying child to life!" Jacobs bemoaned. "Death is better than slavery." After Jacobs gave birth to a daughter fathered by Sands, she expressed even greater dismay: "When they told me my new-born babe was a girl, my heart was heavier than it had ever been before. Slavery is terrible for men; but it is far more terrible for women. Superadded to the burden common to all, they have wrongs, and sufferings, and mortifications peculiarly their own."

To save her children from plantation slavery, a fate promised by Flint since she had refused concubinage, Jacobs ran away. She hid in the attic crawl space of her free grandmother's attached shed, meanwhile convincing the father of her children to buy them in the hope of securing their freedom. Jacobs remained in her hiding place for nearly seven years. The space was barely larger than a coffin. Jacobs could not even stand at full height within it. But she could thwart her master's efforts to control her life, and she could watch over her children through a hole she'd bored in the attic wall. Outwitting her owner, Jacobs made it north to Philadelphia, then New York, and, after a series of twists, aided her children's release from the family of their father. Her wily plan to secure her family's freedom proved successful, and her story is a stunning example of the creative extremes to which enslaved mothers went to fight a system that corrupted the bonds of kinship. But Harriet Jacobs was lucky. Even brilliant escape plots usually failed. The South was a society organized around controlling Black movement, and the North and Midwest were enlisted, by federal law, to aid in the capture of runaways.[12]

The specific variety of fear that drove Harriet Jacobs to heights of acuity, cunning, and self-sacrifice bloomed like invasive algae among slave mothers. From the scraps of documentary evidence attesting to their desperate acts, we learn that "the enslaved mother spent her entire life fearing the separation, sale, beatings, and deaths of her children."[13] Knowing the likelihood that their offspring would be torn from them, unfree Black mothers went to extreme lengths to prevent the ruin of what the character Sethe in Toni Morrison's novel *Beloved* called their "best things," at the hands of another.[14] Enslavers were legendary among the unfree for selling children while a parent slept or carried out an assigned errand. Upon suspecting or hearing about the coming sale of their children, Black women screamed and cried, fell to their knees and begged, ran with their babes into the woods to try to hide them, endured kicks and lashing whips as they clung to their little ones on the precipice between trader's bid and master's handshake. Enslaved mothers planned and plotted to avoid such wrenching pain to themselves and untold peril to their offspring.

One formerly enslaved man from North Carolina, Moses Grandy, recalled how his mother had lost multiple children to death or sale before he, the youngest, was born: "I remember well my mother often hid us all in the woods, to prevent master selling us."[15] Another mother struck awe into members of her enslaved community when she escaped to live in the woods for two to four years with her children. "She had been cruelly treated and run away with her children . . . seeking shelter under the ground. There another child was born to her," a formerly enslaved woman from Alabama recounted.[16] Fannie, an enslaved mother in Tennessee whose story we will learn more about in the next chapter, threatened to kill her infant rather than be separated from the child. Fannie's older daughter, Puss, recalled that her mother and father had been hired out to Memphis. When the master ordered Fannie to leave her baby behind, Puss reported: "At this, ma took the baby by its feet, a foot in each hand, and with the baby's head swinging downward, she vowed to smash its brains out before she'd leave it. Tears were streaming down her face . . . and everyone knew that she meant every word." After this breathtaking threat of an infanticide that she knew would decrease her owners' wealth, Fannie was permitted to take her baby when her owner sent her to work in the city.[17]

Other enslaved mothers were not so fortunate as Fannie, if "fortunate" is ever a word safely used in conjunction with slavery. Rescuing one's child could mean, as in the case of Margaret Garner, who killed her toddler daughter when the slave catcher pounded at the door to retake them, a present death in exchange for the dream of an afterlife of freedom.[18] And enslaved mothers did not go psychologically unscathed by the violence and separations that daily confronted them. One woman who had been enslaved in Virginia remembered, simply: "My mother nearly died when they sold my sister."[19] At times, mothers perceived frightening or beating their children as forms of protection and rescue. Lewis Hayden, who would become a key abolitionist organizer in Boston following his escape from slavery in Kentucky, recalled his mother's mental distress and the fear she instilled in him. Hayden describes his mother as a woman of "high spirit . . .

part Indian" with "long, straight black hair." His mother attempted suicide multiple times and would fall into fits, during which she fixated on the children from whom she had been separated. Jailed for her unpredictable and dangerous behavior, Hayden's mother was released once and went immediately to find her seven-year-old son. "She sprung and caught my arms, and seemed going to break them," Hayden recollected. She "then said, 'I'll *fix* you so they'll never get to you!' I screamed, for I thought she was going to kill me; they came in and took me away."[20] One formerly enslaved woman painfully recalled how her mother beat her in the same sadistic way that her mother had been abused by whites. "She would make me thank her for whipping me. . . . That was the way they wanted her to do in slavery."[21] Fannie, who swore to kill her own infant rather than be separated from the child, threatened her older daughter, Puss: "I'll kill you, gal, if you don't stand up for youself." Puss was both terrified and in awe of this mother, whom she described as a "demon" and a "captain," with smarts "as quick as a flash of lightning."[22] The scars Black mothers bore and sometimes inflicted on their children as a reaction to and defense against captivity were prominent topographical features of the shadowland.[23]

Mothers schemed silently and sometimes with the aid of others to "rescue their families, and especially their daughters" in the best ways they knew how.[24] Black mothers cherished and feared for their sons, just as their sons adored them. There is no question of this in the emotionally wrought stories of parting described by men who had been sold from their mothers as boys in slavery. When Charles Whiteside was ninety-three, he still remembered viscerally the day his mother was sold in Tennessee, and the "something fierce [that] burned in his heart when he saw the planters who had come to buy, pushing her and looking into her mouth as though she were a horse."[25] But daughters, "ties to life" who could also create new life that accrued to the credit side of an owner's balance sheets, were exposed in ways routine and systematic, sexual as well as physical and psychological.[26] Because of their value as producers of pleasure and of labor (in the form of staple crops as well as slave babies), unfree daughters suffered the most intimate of horrors and humiliations.[27] Enslaved mothers knew that daughters required special protection, creatively fierce defenses that circumvented the laws and customs of a slaving society. So Black women prayed and appealed to forces both divine and terrestrial and, when they had the social connections and the means, "made a special habit of buying and manumitting their daughters."[28]

When enslaved mothers could not prevent the theft of daughters, they pursued reunion against the odds of missing information and crushing distance. A rare letter written or dictated by an enslaved woman in North Carolina gives us a glimpse into these desperate reunification efforts prior to the end of the Civil War, when, according to a South Carolina Freedmen's Bureau agent, "every mother [seemed to be] in search of her children."[29] Writing in 1857, a woman named Vilet wrote to her former mistress seeking knowledge about the whereabouts of her daughter. Vilet had changed hands at least three times over the course of nearly eleven months while being sold from North Carolina to Georgia. At her final place of captivity, Vilet was owned by a man who had held her for four years and, she disclosed in the missive, "says that he will keep me til death Siperates us." The language Vilet attributes to her new owner, "a man by the name of Lester," rings with the uncanny trills of wedding vows in a context dark with sexual exploitation. Despite—or perhaps because of—her trials, Vilet is writing her former mistress, Patsey Patterson, to achieve an end. She adopts a tone both respectful and affectionate, calling her mistress "My Loving Miss Patsy" and mentioning times the two spent together as "play mate[s]" (likely childhood years when Vilet acted as a servant and companion to Patsey). Vilet's letter meanders as she tells her "Dear Mistress" how desirous she is of seeing her, as well as the mistress's mother. Vilet expresses her longing to see her own mother and inquires after others who had not been sold. Then Vilet fishtails into her last and central point, the clear intention of this purposeful letter. "I wish to [k]now what has Ever become of my Presus little girl," Vilet pleads. "I left her in goldsborough with Mr. Walker. . . . I do wish to see her very much and Boss [her current owner] Says he wishes to [k]now whether he will Sell her."[30]

Vilet's report about this separation makes it appear as though she had some choice in leaving her child behind, when the account she opens her letter with suggests the opposite—that she had suffered a harrowing chain of exchange among traders and owners after being sold by her mistress, with her daughter likely taken along the way. Her precious girl, the last Vilet knew, was slated to go to the sister of an unnamed trader who had handled them. Now that she was situated with an enslaver who intended to keep her (for reasons we should question), Vilet sought information and help from the mistress who had known her at the "Long Loved home." Vilet had managed to convince her current owner to buy the girl, through, we can guess, a sacrifice related to her condition. Vilet's is one of the few letters in existence attesting to the feelings and strategies of enslaved women in real time rather than in retrospect. The sentimental language of the letter was likely intended to draw Vilet's former mistress into a sympathetic act. This letter stands alone in the historical record, as perhaps "Presus little girl" stood alone in her new place of servitude. The archive contains no indication of how this story ends. Vilet's love for this particular child was hers alone, as was the pain of losing her, but she shared with other unfree mothers the determination to save a daughter and the ever-present sense of mourning when efforts failed.[31]

Did Rose devise similarly inventive methods in an attempt to rescue Ashley?[32] Did she set in motion elaborate escape or purchase schemes before the day of final parting? Enslaved people who were hired out sometimes saved earned funds to purchase their own freedom or the freedom of a loved one. However, such efforts required years of overwork while putting aside small amounts from earnings of typically less than a dollar a day, the majority of which went to one's owner. In addition, bids to purchase freedom sometimes ended in the enslaved person being betrayed or defrauded.[33]

Even if Rose was hired out and could save enough to buy Ashley for the price of $300, where could she have sent a lone Black child for protection? Rose would have had to earn at least $1,000 in order to free her child and herself in hope of having a life together. This price was astronomical and nearly impossible for a woman like Rose to raise in the 1850s, and, even if she could get the money, the successful negotiation of manumission was not guaranteed. South Carolina had regulated manumission since 1800 and had tightened those regulations in 1820 such that an owner had to seek approval from the state legislature in order to free a slave. Among the relatively few Black women in Charleston who did achieve freedom for themselves and their daughters after 1800, associations with white men, often sex partners and fathers of the enslaved, facilitated that outcome.[34] If Rose could not purchase liberty, would she have tried to escape on foot with a nine-year-old? Most unfree people did not have opportunity to run, and very few of those who tried would ever make it to freedom. Long-term escapes were extremely hazardous and, therefore rare in a society where unfree people were intensively surveilled, policed, and punished. As one historian of slavery and capitalism concluded: "The number of enslaved migrants who made it from the depths of the cotton and sugar frontiers all the way to the free states probably numbered under a thousand during all the years of slavery. That amounts to one-tenth of 1 percent of all forced migrants."[35]

Ruth's stitched record does not address whether Rose ever attempted to buy or take her family's freedom. What we do know from the sewn account is that Rose responded with a practical tactic driven by a sense of higher purpose. She gathered items to provide for her daughter's basic needs in the temporary time of the present and the possible time of the future. By sustaining her daughter's life in the now, she forged a pathway for Ashley's longer-term survival. And setting her daughter down that path was a projection of continuation, both for Ashley herself and for the kin from whence Rose came. In packing the sack, Rose rescued not only a single beloved girl but also the persistence of a family.

Rose's packing highlights an essential element of enslaved women's experience. Black women were creators, constantly *making* the slate of things necessary to sustain the life of the family, "one of the supreme social achievements of African-Americans under conditions of enslavement." These made things included clothing, brooms, quilts, meals, medicines, and an array of mementos, like buttons and beads, that might one day be pressed into the palm of a parting loved one's hand. Black women fashioned and gathered these things into emotional nets that affirmed their love for self and others, channeling visions of perseverance through the work of their thoughts and hands, often at their own risk.[36] As Alice Walker illuminated decades ago in stories and essays, Black women of past generations poured their souls and creative energies into the things they made and the plants they grew. Searching for our mothers' things, the gardens and garments of their eras, can yield a sense not only of their experience but also of their strategies for surviving the shadowland, while "bind[ing] blood-relations in a network of feeling, of continuity."[37]

One day when Rose cast her gaze about the Martins' brick kitchen in the city, or perhaps their plantation storehouse in the country, she decided she would repurpose a sack as a parachute. It would tie together mother and child while gently lowering that child down to a new and dangerous patch of ground. We can imagine her sable fingers drawing open the lip of the sack, see her staring into a bottomless well of trepidations. Was the sack empty when Rose first grabbed it for this purpose? Or was it in use as a storage container for seeds or nuts, like the handfuls of pecans Ruth said it would later carry? Perhaps Rose had to turn the cotton bag upside down, scattering husks, shells, or debris in order to make room to refill it. Picture her by a candle's light. She holds the rough cloth in rougher hands. She tucks a dress around the nuts, then lifts a knife. In one swift slice, she harvests a braid, laying claim to the very body that her deceased master and living mistress would have called their property. As we watch her hands fall away from her hair, we know that one more thing has yet to be packed. "My love," Rose whispers in our mind's ear, cinching the sack shut.

OBJECTS EMPOWERED

As Rose packed the cotton seed sack with things and words, she drew on all of her resources. The specific mix of items enclosed may have been unique to Rose, but the logic of the need to pre-

Miles Brewton House, back stairs, n.d.
By Alice Ravenel Huger Smith (American,
1876–1958). This photograph of an unnamed
Black servant at the rear of a Charleston
manor house may help us picture Rose in
similar environs. Image courtesy of the
Gibbes Museum of Art.

pare was shared by her fellow enslaved. Others also packed a bag
or had a bag packed for them, in frenzied moments of departure. When one girl of around eleven who had already lost her
mother and sister ran into the woods to avoid her own relocation, it was her aunt who explained that she must go with the
new owner and, the speaker recalled, "tied my clothes up in a
bundle."[38] Jane Clark was raised in the home of her maternal
grandmother until, at age six or seven, Jane was "taken in payment of a debt." The girl was hired out and labored "with two
other children, to bring water a long distance from a spring for
culinary purposes for all on the plantation." As a young woman,
Jane became a cook back on her owner's farm. There she experienced multiple whippings and "scenes of severity" that made
her "determined to escape or die in the attempt." While keeping
a close eye on her master and mistress's daily routine, Jane
packed two pillowcases with "such things as she could take with
her." She "dropped her bundles out of the window" while her
owners sipped their tea, and fled "carrying both bundles on her
head." Jane made good her escape to New York after months on
the run, with the aid of her enslaved brother as well as white and
Black helpers on the "underground railway."[39]

Like these women, and they like her, Rose took a planful step. She packed a bag to aid in an unpredictable journey. It is rare that we get to peer inside one of the hastily prepared bundles that sold or escaping enslaved people grasped in times of sudden change. Rose's bag, enhanced by her great-granddaughter's inscription, allows us an illuminating visibility. Each item Rose packed for so significant a parting was both essential and versatile. The tattered dress, listed first, could protect a body from exposure and shield an enslaved girl's inner dignity. What is more, a different item of clothing, such as a dress an individual had not yet worn, could also function as a costume, altering that person's external identity and thereby aiding escape. (This is why many accounts of enslaved people who took their own freedom include cross-gender dressing or wearing someone else's clothes.) The dress Rose packed also had another potential function, as fabric stored wealth, especially for women, who used cloth as currency or a trade good.[40] Although Rose seems to have packed a shredded dress most valuable for its personal meaning, she must also have recognized that Ashley could repurpose the fabric or trade it. Next Rose packed pecans, a concentrated energy source and a specialty food in the 1850s Lowcountry that Ashley could have eaten to stave off hunger or bartered for another necessity. Rose also tucked a lock of her own hair into the bag, the most unusual element of her care package. While hair seems at first a whimsy in an emergency bag such as this, it may be the most potent item, symbolically and even spiritually, that Rose packed that day. For hair may offer a glimpse into Rose's beliefs about spirit power, transcendent connection, and the importance of carrying on a sense of lineage.

Rose's packing priorities—clothing, food, and a token of memory—mirrored the material agendas of other enslaved people as reflected in letters, narratives, and plantation store ledgers. Her packing also revealed a collective hierarchy of human need. Food was included. Clothing was there. Only physical shelter was missing. Or was it? The sack itself, over two feet long and more than one foot wide, notably large enough for a young child to partially crawl into, could have served as a tented covering, a pillow, a blanket, or a sleeping bag along the road of Ashley's forced journey. And more than this, Rose transferred another kind of protective structure through her parting words. The emotional shelter of love eternal would travel with Ashley inside the sack. Fitted to a range of needs—physical, emotional, and spiritual—Rose's kit was ingenious.

A gift is never given without anticipation—indeed, expectation—of the recipient's response. The giver predicts and hopes for a desired reaction, as small as a thank-you note or as large as a promise of marriage. Sometimes this aspect of gift giving can take manipulative forms and poison the well of right relations. Examples are plentiful in the records of slavery—when, for instance, enslavers parceled out extra food on Christmas Day or bestowed "gay" gifts of cloth to mandate enslaved people's gratitude and mold their behavior. When we give, we often want, or even demand, something in return. What did Rose demand of her daughter, in their last meeting on this earth? What did Rose hope her bestowal of food, clothing, and shelter would give rise to? Rose had a vision for her daughter after the amputation of sale; she held out a hope for Ashley's survival. Although a disintegrating dress could not endure for long, and three handfuls of nuts might be devoured in one hungry sitting, Rose communicated a message through this special collection of things. Ashley could carry on in the light of love and connection. With the sack as her lifeline, she could persist.

Rose may have understood her movements to matter on more than one plane of being. Just as she drew on inner strength to withstand this trauma, she may have called on spiritual help to sanctify her emergency pack. Extrapolating from interviews with Black residents of coastal South Carolina and Georgia, one anthropologist who has worked closely with the sack has suggested that Rose's packing instantiated a spiritual ritual, given that the bag resembled "regional medicinal bundles." And Rose, he has indicated, quoting contemporary interviewees, may have been "doing something with, a blessing, something sacred, the way a rootworker would." In this interpretation, the sack, once packed, became animated with a protective spirit through Rose's ministrations and, especially, through the lock of her hair, which could hold special purpose in the religious practices of the enslaved.[41]

The little sacks known as conjure bags populated enslaved people's daily lives across the U.S. South, the Caribbean islands, and Latin America. Red flannel was a favorite color for these magical packets, which were often sealed with string and then worn around the neck or waist or buried near a person's dwelling.[42] Manufacturing conjure bags fell under the purview of conjurers or rootworkers, spiritual practitioners in a Black folk tradition that borrowed from African religious beliefs, particularly the Kongo culture of central Africa.[43] While many enslaved Blacks accepted the Christian faith of the dominant slaveholding society in the late eighteenth and nineteenth centuries, others rejected Christianity and upheld African-based beliefs. The majority of enslaved people engaged in religious conviction and ritual that interwove Euro-American and African traditions of faith to greater and lesser extents, praying to a Christian God or Islam's Allah, singing biblically inspired spirituals and retelling Bible stories, while also fearing witches and turning to rootworkers in times of need.[44] We know from the reports of formerly enslaved people, most famously Frederick Douglass, that medicinal and spiritual specialists produced roots stored in folded cloth or fabric bags to protect recipients from sale and beatings. The Bakongo version of these conjure bags are known as *minkisi*, while the American varieties are often referred to as gris-gris bags, hands, or mojos.[45]

Knowledgeable, respected, and also feared, people accepted as conjurers in enslaved Black communities possessed special skills and responsibilities. Their craft involved divining information and influencing social relations through rituals that drew on the "spiritual empowerment of . . . objects."[46] Adherents of this faith believed that rootworkers' packets carried magical properties to act in the world—to heal, protect, harm, or ferret out information. While there is no evidence to suggest that Rose was herself a rootworker with unique spiritual powers recognized by a community, the bag she packed does bear resemblances to items used in this magical system. Conjure bags were made of cloth. They typically included an object personal to the recipient (the person being helped or harmed)—such as a swatch from an item of clothing or, especially, a cutting of hair. The bags included natural elements like roots or vines, animal body parts, and particularly dirt from graveyards (often called "goofer dust"), which was thought to facilitate connection with ancestors. In Brazil, these African-inspired conjure bags, called *mandingas*, contained the kinds of natural elements described above as well as handwritten notes; in Islamic-influenced African regions, gris-gris bags also contained scraps of paper with writing.[47] Among Bakongo believers, these bags could include terrestrial elements viewed as "medicines," including "chalk, nuts, plants, soil, stones, and charcoal."[48] The items pressed into a conjure bag took on spiritual power through the ritual work of the maker, who called on the aid of external spirits or invigorated things inside the bag by eliciting the spirits within them.

Words, either written or spoken, were an element of the con-jurer's practice that invigorated the conjure packet. Through ritual, the bag could come alive, in a sense, to do its intended work.

Perhaps Rose hoped that her bag would act as a protective charm for Ashley, or as an aggressive charm against Ashley's traders or new owners. According to Ruth's sewn record, the sack enclosed hair, clothing, a natural element (pecans), and even spoken words. Or maybe Rose was suspicious of African-inspired magic and trusted in prayer to a Christian God. It is possible, too, that she believed in aspects of both faith traditions and doubly endowed the sack, speaking to the object itself or praying for its recipient as she completed her solemn task. We do not require a firm grasp on Rose's religion in order to see her packing as an act of power meant to stymie the slaver's theft of her daughter's life and identity. Rose made an evocative thing on the day she packed the cotton sack, a thing full of potency and intention. Through the work of both heart and hands, Rose rebutted the tyranny of slavery with the force of spirit material-ized.

BINDING TIES

Of all the things packed into Rose's "artful composition," hair is the most symbolically compelling.[49] A reading of the sack as a protective spirit bag would suggest that a braid of Rose's hair was meant to enliven it with Rose's spirit. Certainly, the braid must have been meant to capture and concretize a tactile memory of Rose for her daughter, functioning like a snapshot that Ashley could hold in her hands. For Rose, the associations attached to a braid may also have been similar to the tattered dress, as an example of the care that Black women could take with themselves even as masters and mistresses sought to disparage and control them. For hair, like the clothing we will explore in the next chapter, was an arena of personal struggle with political implications for the owned and their owners.

Black women took special care with their hair when they managed to steal time from their manual labor, but this proved an infinitely challenging task. Curly hair is more vulnerable than straight hair to the stresses caused by sun, water, sweat, and grooming, making the tight spiraling curls common to many African Americans especially delicate and fragile. Caring for this hair type requires patience, even as the flexibility of Black hair has long inspired creativity and versatility. In the central and West African regions from which enslaved Blacks were taken, community members prized intricate hairstyles formed of braids and twined tresses, which rose to the height of an art form. Black women in slavery, however, lacked the leisure time for hairdressing and did not possess the implements (picks and wide-toothed combs) best suited for grooming their particular texture of hair. They, as well as Black men, sometimes used wooden implements with metal teeth intended for carding wool (separating and elongating the fibers) on their own heads, due to a lack of grooming tools. After "combing" their hair with a carder or their fingers, Black women often wove it into cornrows braided flat against the scalp in arresting designs or into plaits that extended out from the scalp or hung to various lengths. As an alternative to braided styles, they frequently separated locks of hair into sections and wrapped each section with string or twine to keep the hair untangled or to extend their corkscrew curls into straighter tendrils.[50]

Black women covered their heads with handkerchiefs or bandannas during long days out in the fields or inside hot kitchen houses. These head coverings protected the hair from dirt and exposure and often preserved the hairdressing preparations that the women had created for themselves or that had been styled for them by others on their lone day free from forced work. On Sundays, before attending church or clandestine parties, enslaved women changed out of their everyday head coverings for distinctively arranged head wraps and sometimes revealed their hair untwined and loosened.[51] The African American practice of oiling the hair with grease to moisturize and further protect it (curly hair dries out more rapidly; hence the avoidance of daily washing in most Black people's hair-care routines in our time) may have been borrowed from local Native Americans. According to the travel accounts of European explorers who observed them, members of Indigenous nations in the Southeast regularly "shined" their hair with bear grease.[52] Hairdressing was for many unfree African Americans a communal endeavor that brought women (and men) together as they helped one another to comb, braid, twist, or shave their hair. The sense of sociability and mutual support around hair-care activities continued past slavery into the barbershop and the beauty parlor, fixtures in Black communities even today.[53]

While enslaved Black women took pride in caring for their hair when they could seize the opportunity, they also faced punishment for having hair that white slaveholders found too similar to their own in texture, length, or style. Hair on "Black" heads that seemed "white" according to a Eurocentric standard threatened to blur the exaggerated lines between the races that buttressed a hierarchical slave society. The cultural associations of hair with erotic beauty and certain types and arrangements of hair with European feminine ideals also influenced the likelihood that longer, straighter hair on Black women would attract sexual interest across the color line. Evidence culled from slaves' narratives and testimony, white women's diaries and letters, and descriptions of the increasing mixed-race population that emerged in early and antebellum American society points over-whelmingly to a pattern of interracial sex (often, but not always, coerced or forced) between white men and Black women of any hair type. But Black women with hair approximating a white feminine ideal and the lighter skin tone that often accompanied this characteristic were particularly sought after by white men and deemed dangerous by white women.[54]

In numerous narratives and accounts of their experiences in slavery, African American women and their male relatives revisit the trauma of hair shaved or cut in acts of slaveholder retribu-tion. Harriet Jacobs, we will recall, suffered the sexual predation of her master but chose intimacy with another white man in order to ward off her owner. When her owner discovered that Harriet was soon to have a second child with this sexual rival, he lashed out to exert control and deface her allure. "He rushed from the house, and returned with a pair of shears," Jacobs re-lates. "I had a fine head of hair; and he often railed about my pride of arranging it nicely. He cut every hair close to my head, storming and swearing all the time. I replied to some of his abuse, and he struck me."[55]

Louisa Picquet experienced captivity in South Carolina, Ala-bama, and Louisiana, sold each time to a new man with plans to hold her in sexual slavery. After gaining her freedom in the 1860s through the will of her deceased final owner, she moved to Cincinnati. One of Picquet's owners attempted to pay her for sexual favors and left her physically scarred when she refused; he also, in retribution, kept her hair short. "Mr. Cook had my hair cut off," Louisa explained, while telling the story of her sale and the auctioneer's comment about her "good quality" hair, which was still visible despite the lack of length. "My hair grew fast, and look so much better than Mr. Cook's daughter, and he fancy I had better hair than his daughter, and so he had it cut off to make a difference."[56]

In a devastating account told by an enslaved witness, a woman named Charlotte lost her life through her captor's gruesome act of hair punishment. Charlotte "had real long hair and they cut one side of her hair off and left the other side long." After being whipped, Charlotte was "jerked . . . by the hair" through a barbed-wire fence and never regained consciousness.[57] Like so many acts of horrific violence that we are witnessing through the eyes of the enslaved in these pages, the teller of this story did not know why Charlotte had been singled out for such cruel treatment. Given her shorn head and the manner of her murder, sexual jealousy or sexual exposure was probably the cause.

In Harriet's and Louisa's accounts, white male owners used the shears as weapons to separate and demean Black women. In most cases recalled by formerly enslaved people in interviews and narratives, however, it was the white mistress who directed that punishing blow, striking out against Black women whom they feared would attract white men in the family, or already had. One Black woman, the biracial daughter of a planter's son, was commanded not to refer to her own hair as hair. Instead, her female owner, stressing racial difference, insisted: "Don't say hair, say 'wool.'" A formerly enslaved man described the fate of his grandmother, who possessed hair that was "fine as silk and hung down below her waist." Due to the jealousy on the part of the mistress who observed attentions the master paid to this woman, the mistress ordered a whipping and hair shaving. "From that day on," this interviewee remembered, "my grandma had to wear her hair shaved to the scalp." Another "pretty mulatto girl" whose hair was "long black [and] straight" was purchased by a judge and brought back to his home. There, the judge's wife "got the scissors and cropped that gal's head to the skull."[58] As a signifier of past sexual relations between white men and enslaved women, long, straighter hair on Black children was also targeted by mistresses. One formerly enslaved woman, in describing how masters would impregnate the cooks in their households, remembered: "Sometimes the cook's children favored him so much that the wife would be mean to them and make him sell them. If they had nice long hair she would cut it off and wouldn't let them wear it long like the white children."[59]

Hair was a medium through which captors and captives fought for corporeal as well as psychological control. Since slaveholders claimed the right, by law, to the bodies of the people they owned, they sometimes sought to demonstrate that right by dictating hair length. By caring for and claiming their hair as a part of their own bodies that they should have the right to treat as they wished, enslaved Black women like Rose rejected this unjust authority and invasion of bodily privacy. Rose took this sense of self-possession even further when deciding to part with a braid of her hair, a piece of herself, by choice. When Rose clipped one of her braids for Ashley, she was passing on proof of the kind of self-regard, self-care, and mutual aid that sustained life in captivity and even sometimes brought to beleaguered souls moments of pleasure in bodily adornment.[60]

By giving a gift that had once been a part of her own body, Rose also bestowed a potent reminder of her presence in Ashley's life. For hair could function as a token of memory and social connection across the distances the slave trade created. In one such example, a formerly enslaved man in Texas wrote to his sister in Virginia after the siblings and their mother had been separated. The letter writer, Hawkins Williams, begged for a piece of his niece's hair to remember her by: "Please send me some of Julia's hair whom I left a baby in the cradle when I was torn away from you—I know that she is a young lady now, but I hope she will not deny her affectionate uncle this request."[61] Through the medium of her braid, Rose may have wanted to synthesize nearness and convey to her daughter a lasting memory of their emotional connection. She might have used her hair to materialize the mournful yet bracing sentiment expressed by another enslaved mother, Phebe of North Carolina, on the eve of her master's move out of the state:

> My dear daughter—I have for some time had hope of seeing you once more in this world, but now that hope is entirely gone forever. I expect to start next month for Alabama, on the Mississippi River. . . . If we never meet in this world, I hope we shall meet in heaven where we shall part no more. Although we are absent in body, we can be present in spirit. Then let us pray for each other, and try to hold out faithful to the end. Farewell my dear child. . . . Farewell my dear child.[62]

Phebe would leave behind not only Amy, the daughter she addressed in this letter, but also another daughter, who was pregnant and could not travel, as well as several grandchildren. Amy would probably have treasured a braid of Phebe's hair if she sent one and if, in fact, the desperate letter ever reached her. Hair carries with it a meaningful, even mystical, valence that Phebe's Amy and Rose's Ashley would have felt, as it exists in an odd in-between space that defies biological or cultural categorization. Hair on the head is both dead and alive, part of a body but not a body part, and hair transgresses social space by extending out from a person's form. Hair also resists decay, giving it the strange quality of time arrested. Hair fibers may have therefore been experienced as a special kind of material that represented the life of the giver.[63]

White Victorians of Rose's and Ashley's era also thought that hair could bind together disjoined persons. Widespread cultural practices of the 1800s and early 1900s show that many people saw hair as a tie between loved ones separated even by the distance of death. Hairwork, the craft of fashioning hair into objects such as jewelry, buttons, or wreaths, was a product and exemplar of a nineteenth-century ethos of sentimentalism. In a custom that reached its height of popularity between the 1850s and the 1890s, members of the white upper and middle classes bestowed and saved locks of hair in remembrance of a deceased loved one or as an expression of a romantic relationship. Artists fashioned innumerable strange and wonderful trinkets out of human hair: necklaces and bracelets woven of hair with clasps made of gold and precious stones; lockets and brooches featuring miniature painted scenes in which hair was pressed in to provide color variation and texture; rings, earrings, and watch chains inset with woven hair; framed embroidery with hair used as thread. Lovers exchanged paintings of one another's eyes adorned with hair strands and set into rings or lockets.[64] Mourning jewelry (as well as wreaths fashioned of hair of the deceased and dried flowers) was the most popular use of an art form crafted to heighten and display emotion. Wearing or keeping safe the hair of a departed loved one "physically manifested that grief," providing a constant material reminder of the emotions attached to that person (including the pain of loss).[65] For members of Victorian society, hair was a sentimental material that functioned as an emotional tie or thread; the association makes sense, given that hair is itself a natural fiber with properties akin to wool and the special quality of belonging to a specific human body.

Like other fashion accoutrements of middle- and upper-class

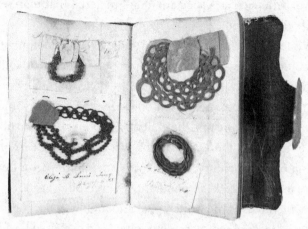

Hairwork album of Etta Smith, 1858–1924. "This meticulously kept hairwork album, created by Etta Smith of Gaysport, Pennsylvania, from 1858 to 1924, exemplifies the intimate and sentimental nature of Victorian hair collection and display. Arranged in braids and wreaths, each labeled with the name of the person from whom it was snipped (sometimes posthumously), each of the 90 tresses serves as a quiet testimonial to friendship and family." From *75 Stories, 75 Years: Documenting the Lives of American Women at the Schlesinger Library*, exhibition, 2018. Photograph by Kevin Grady/Harvard Radcliffe Institute. Courtesy of the Schlesinger Library, Harvard Radcliffe Institute.

American society in the nineteenth century, elaborate hairwork was intended for white wearers. A Charleston art reviewer, when describing the Victorian-era craft in retrospect in the 1940s, pointed out how "the hair of the living . . . was used in romance and fashion" and "advertised to be more desirable than jewels and more becoming, in contrast to a delicate white skin."[66] White women of means, already trained in embroidery as one of the cultured "feminine" arts, were the most common creators of hairwork, and they crafted their pieces as private keepsakes and for interpersonal exchanges, rather than for the marketplace. Wealthier individuals could hire members of a new class of artisans, also mostly women, able to craft locks of a customer's loved one's hair into elaborate "fancywork" pieces. While African Americans did become hairwork artists and merchants in the 1800s and participated in Victorian cultural practices, one historian suggests they may have viewed detached pieces of hair differently than did white Victorians in the period—as evidence that a child lost to the slave trade was still alive. In this case, hair functioned as a signifier of hope rather than as a memento of death.[67]

Hair, then, was proof for Victorians that separation is not necessarily final. Division would, in fact, be impossible, because each of us is deeply connected to the other, and hair, again, is the evidence. "Hair is the thread that binds us to our ancestors across time," says the award-winning fiber artist Sonya Clark, referring to our contemporary experience with the material. Clark uses human hair in the re-fabrication of common objects (such as violin strings) and re-creates the elaborate stylings of contemporary African American braidwork in silk on canvas.[68] In addition to viewing hairdressing as "the primordial fiber art," Clark sees hair as a special material laden with cross-cultural and trans-historical meaning. "Hair is power," she says. "Note the Samson myth, Rastafarian dreadlocks, and Angela Davis's Afro in the 1960s. Hair grows approximately 5 inches a year and measures our lives like Lachesis of the Three Fates in Greek mythology. A carrier of DNA, hair is the essence of identity. Deep within each strand, the vestiges of our roots and histories resound." Working within an African diasporic tradition of visual art, Clark sees hair as a way of "know[ing] our ancestors," in keeping with a Yoruba belief that self-knowledge flows from ancestral connection. As a genetic carrier tracing back through discrete family lines all the way to the origins of humanity, hair is, in this way of thinking, a tie between present (and future) life and the near and far past.[69] A braid of Rose's hair, then, may have been a token of deep familial lineage, a reminder that Ashley belonged not only to a long line of African ancestors but also to the greater human family. Hair, in this way of reckoning, parallels the work of history by binding individuals to one another across vast time periods and story lines.

Eliza Potter, a Black hairdresser in the 1850s, when Ashley was still enslaved in South Carolina, understood the race, gender, and class dynamics that made care of the hair so important to women. Born free in New York, Potter labored as a domestic servant, then briefly married. She traveled to Canada, Ohio, New York, England, France, and across the southern states while working as a hairstylist. She helped an enslaved man escape from prison in Kentucky because she believed in a higher standard than U.S. slave law, one she called "the bar of God." Early in her career, Eliza traveled with a family, as their employee, to Paris, where she learned to speak French, visited the Palace of Versailles, and began working for a countess. There she learned the "fine arts" of flower-making, dressmaking, and hairdressing. Of these crafts, Eliza proclaimed, "Nothing but hair-dressing pleased my fancy for any length of time." She returned to the States with a "talent in hair-dressing" in the French style that attracted wealthy white clients.[70] In the early 1850s, she took up residence in Cincinnati and traveled to Kentucky, Louisiana, and Mississippi to craft hairstyles for southern belles. Potter's services to the white elite and aspiring middle classes were in demand in mid-century as she styled hair for soirees and weddings while keeping a minute record of the rich and famous. Her tell-all account published in 1859 included frank revelations about slaveholding society while detailing her labor as both a hairstylist and a chronicler of events.

Back in Cincinnati, Eliza Potter lived comfortably on the border of a respectable white neighborhood downtown, where she opened her home to formerly enslaved women and trained apprentice hairdressers.[71] She saw herself as a tradesperson and craftswoman "dependent on the public for a livelihood."[72] In the long tradition of Black women who serviced the personal needs of whites, Eliza Potter closely watched and listened to her clients. Her memoir, described as a "graphic narrative" and a "bestseller" by reviewers in 1859, reveals her to be an astute observer with a journalistic eye and ear.[73] Eliza claimed of her own talent for peering beyond the pretense of performance: "I have seen so much of human nature in my humble position that I can, by looking at a man or woman, tell what they are." With her penetrating gaze, Potter took note of American ladies desiring to marry titled European men who returned their interest only to recoup lost fortunes, wealthy husbands who doted on their wives in public and abused them behind closed doors, and the trickery of a vacationing coastal lady who pretended to help an enslaved girl obtain her freedom, then sold her.[74]

Eliza Potter inserted herself into the historical record. Her ability to notice and notate events stemmed from her sharp mind and the access she gained to the intimate spaces of people's lives. As she declares in her "Author's Appeal" at the start of her book:

> The physician writes his diary, and doubtless his means of discovering the hidden mysteries of life are great. The clergyman, whose calling inspires the deepest of confidence . . . sends forth his diary to an eager world, and other innumerable chroniclers of fireside life have existed; but the hairdresser will yield rivalship to none in this regard. . . . She will tell her story in simpler language; but it will be none the less truthful, none the less strange.

While Potter declares her narrative style simple, she also claims the value of her intellectual work, refusing to "yield rivalship," by which she means relinquishing her writerly authority to those who have more education or higher class standing. Later in the book, she refers to herself as a "historian" outright.[75] We might say that in Eliza Potter's memoir, hairdressing and historical writing are activities requiring equivalent skill in the interpretation of social life. Indeed, hair seems to hold an associational kinship with history, as both enwrap deep human lineages. Hair is a tether between persons, as the Victorians felt, and also a genetic tie to the past, as we now know. The symbolism of both meanings converge in Rose's decision to pack her hair. In bestowing a braid upon Ashley, Rose passed on a piece of herself while transmitting a cosmic continuity that slavery could not sunder. Her gift might remind Ashley that she belonged—to a Black family that persevered through racial animus and a human family that had once not known it.

With her package of clothing, nuts, and hair carefully wrapped and stowed away, Rose may have turned her thoughts to delivery. Did she seek help in identifying Ashley's whereabouts, the way Vilet did when in search of her precious girl in Georgia? Did Rose attempt to send the bundle out to Milberry Place Plantation by way of another person the Martins owned? Enslaved women who sought freedom for themselves or their children consistently looked to allies for aid. We know this from the testimony of slave narratives, where ordinary Black men and women and white women and men answer calls for help, and through the documented experiences of formerly enslaved women in Charleston who depended on alliances in order to gain freedom.[76]

The notion of a mother tracking her child with assistance in order to bestow a gift is not unheard of in the annals of slavery.

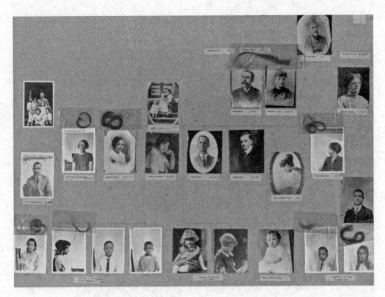

Chart F-2, Caroline Bond Day Genealogical Chart. African American anthropologist Caroline Bond Day interviewed mixed-race Black families and created detailed charts featuring photographs and hair cuttings for her master's thesis, A *Study of Some Negro-White Families*, 1932. Day's thesis underscores both the individuality of hair and the ways hair connects family lines. She wrote, "It is doubtful two people are ever seen with hair that is exactly alike," even as she traced "the inheritance of hair form." Peabody Museum of Archaeology and Ethnology, Harvard University, PM 993-21-10/100160.1.132.

In a moving story, an enslaved woman named Winnie Martin had received several beads from her mother. Winnie was sold away with her daughter for having a sexual relationship with a white man and forced to separate from her young son, John Sella Martin. In a determined search for her son, Winnie managed to enlist "a coloured man from the country, who had brought in a load of cotton." When the man found the boy, holed up in a gambling hotel with his new owner in Georgia, he handed the child "a rag of cotton cloth, tied all about with a string." Later, as an adult, John remembered this earth-shattering moment from his boyhood: "I opened it, and found some blue glass beads—beads given to my mother by her mother as a keepsake when she died. I knew by that token that he was a messenger from my mother. . . . I had often heard her say that nothing would make her part from these beads."[77] Winnie had found an ingenious and courageous way to comfort her child through material items that would always remind him of her love and his familial lineage.

Rose may have sought allies, too, in delivering her emergency pack. Did she suspect that Ashley had been transported into the city center, where Charleston traders did a hefty turn in the scarred flesh and blood goods of the slave trade? Did she search the side streets of Charleston, risking arrest by the armed city guard? Or was Ashley much closer to Rose on the eve of her sale than she had been in months or years prior? The inscription sewn into the sack indicates that Rose bestowed the bag in person. Perhaps Ashley had been collected from the rural estate and deposited at the Charlotte Street house for a brief time prior to her relocation. If Milberry Martin had Ashley moved to the brick villa, Rose may have found an opportunity to seize a private word with her there. Rose would have acted during the night,* a time of sanctuary to the enslaved when textiles were fashioned, rude quarters were made habitable, extra vittles were stewed in the pots, and escape plots were planned and executed.[78] Perhaps, in the darkness during the spring or summer of 1853,† Rose pulled her own precious girl into the corner of the

---

* Often a source of fear because of what opaqueness hides, night has also been an aid to fugitives and a cloak for secret, resistant activities. Darkness carried with it a special kind of buffer that might at times have felt like a source of power to the enslaved. Defining oneself as "part of the night" could also have been experienced as a kind of "kinship" with nature by the captured and the hunted.

† The sale of an enslaved person could take place at any time, depending on the needs or whims of the owners. Still, the market had cycles, as did the growing of

yard, cradled the child against her, and smoothed down her dusty, plaited hair.[79] What we know of this moment, though, we must take from the only record, Ruth Middleton's chronicle from family memory. According to Ruth, Rose spoke to her child in those parting minutes when she handed over the dingy cotton bundle. Rose may have believed these to be her last words on the eve of a parting that could have the same effect as a death.[80] If so, we might dwell on the notion that the sack was a kind of living will, an expression of what Rose intended for her daughter to do in the case of relentless limbo: carry on with the armor of love.

How did little Ashley feel upon receipt of this weighty inheritance? Perhaps she reacted like the young John Martin did when the man dispatched by his mother gave him the "rag of cotton cloth" filled with beads. "I trembled all over," John recounted in his memoir, so shaken was he to have been lost to his family, then suddenly found. If Ashley trembled, if she sobbed into Rose's encircling arms, she might also have grasped the lifeline her mother extended that night. Rose had created a vision of life in and among the thickets of fear and packed that picture into the sack. The maternal bond exhibited by Rose was stronger for being hard-won.[81] Enslaved mothers like Rose battled the hounds for their children, using whatever means they could. And, in so doing, they wrestled not only to rescue individual offspring but also to save Black family lines.[82]

When did Rose know? We must presume that Rose always knew that she would birth a motherless child. For this was the root of

crops. The typical season for slave sales was September through May. Many sales took place in autumn, following a summer season during which traders collected the "goods."

slavery: theft of the maternal. Since the inauguration of the transatlantic slave trade in the late 1400s, through the acceleration of the American domestic slave trade in the early 1800s, and still today, Africans and people of African descent have borne a crisis of mother loss. The memoirist and cultural theorist Saidiya Hartman captured this profound historical state when she traveled to Ghana in search of her African roots. Her numbing insight arrived at on the journey became the organizing idea of a breathtaking travel narrative. "Lose your mother," Hartman found in her book of the same title, was the forced imperative of the slave trade and a raw truth of African American experience.[83] We are a people suffering from the loss of a motherland, a mother tongue, and a mother's knowledge of our new names. It might even be said that the search for true belonging and the quest for relational repair lie deep at the heart of the modern Black psyche. In the face of devastating mother loss, our ancestors' answer was mother love: a graspingly fierce, imperfect insistence on making and tending generations.[84] An affirmation of Black life embedded in love and stashed in a sack is, after all, what Rose was packing for.

ROSE'S INVENTORY

Viz Wine @ 7, 700, Furniture in late residence Charlotte st. 4,820, China and Glassware 200[,] 2 Carriages & Harness 400, 1 pr Horses 150[,] 1 Cow 100[,] 1 slave Cicero 1,000[,] 1 slave Sophia 300, 1 slave James 100, 1 slave Jack 800, 1 [ditto sign] Rose 700[,] 1 [ditto sign] David 800, 1 [ditto sign] Old Woman 100, Silver plat[e] 2,500 . . .[1]

—ROBERT MARTIN, property appraisement, 1853

It held a tattered dress[,] 3 handfulls of pecans[,] a braid of Roses hair.

—RUTH MIDDLETON, sack embroidery, 1921

WE HAVE IN ASHLEY'S SACK A NEARLY UNPARALLELED opportunity for insight into the lives of enslaved women. In the bag Rose packed and the description Ruth appended, we see an index of treasures. In contrast to the blatant devaluation of en-slaved people *as* people evident in slave owners' property lists, the slave woman's inventory, a countercompilation, points us to the deep worth of Black female humanity as well as to the role of things in defending enslaved people's dignity as humans and as women. We find, in the single line that composes Ruth's itemization, a parry to the planter's belittlement. This chapter will pause to dwell on the idea that one of Rose's packed items—a dress—offers a case study of the kinds of things Black women prized.

The list of "things" Robert Martin left behind when he died unwinds across time like a measuring tape. We can deduce that Martin esteemed fine wine, fancy furnishings, and the ornate silver article that is the last thing on the list before it turns to a detailed accounting of mortgages and investment bonds. We can discern from this document that the Martins traveled about in carriages roughly equal to the cost of two Black children, and that people held as property at 16 Charlotte Street did not stand out from objects in the eyes of the financial appraisers.[2] Like many enslaved people who overheard what they were "worth" in the parlor of the big house or the marketplace of the auction house, Rose likely had a sense of her assigned value as judged by her owners.[3] But what of Rose's own list of things? What might it tell us about *her* scale of values?

We lack estate records for enslaved people.[4] Nevertheless, we can gather from their firsthand accounts, personal letters, and post–Civil War testimony that possessions were just as valuable to the enslaved as they were to enslavers—and perhaps even more so. Though crushingly poor, enslaved people did attain property, mainly through working around the clock in moments the master did not claim. During that "off" time on evenings or Sundays or after their assigned tasks had been completed on the Lowcountry rice estates, enslaved people grew food or made objects that could be traded for other things or sold for cash. They also sometimes worked for hire, receiving a portion of the pay (as approved by their owners), and with this they could buy items. Once enslaved people acquired things, they struggled not to lose those things to theft or sudden relocation. As one prize-winning legal historian has noted, enslaved people often thought first about the safety of their families and next about the safekeeping of their things.[5] One Virginia woman, when facing the impending sale of herself and a child after already losing one son, wrote sorrowfully to her husband in 1852: "Myself and other child is for sale also. . . . My things is in several places . . . and if I should be sold I don't know what will become of them."[6] As this rare letter indicates and slave narratives amply demonstrate: Black people held in bondage lamented not only the loss of kin but also the loss of cherished things that could be counted among life's companions.

Enslaved people undertook feats of great imagination, courage, and grit to acquire the materials needed to sustain and cushion their existence. Making things, receiving things, having and using things of their own had immediate purpose as well as deep symbolism. For unfree people, things could soften an unrelenting daily routine, as practical items like shoes, quilts, and drinking cups protected against the elements and diminished deprivation. Having things also undermined the logic of slavery in a society in which it was formally illegal for "property" to own property. As possessors of stuff, Black people demonstrated their personhood, reflecting dignity inwardly to themselves and outwardly to others. Possessing things inspired pride and challenged the belief that Black people were unworthy of property's privileges.[7] As a formerly enslaved woman from Mississippi insisted: "Lord, chile, if they had two dishes, four plates, a cup and a saucer, they thought they had something; then somebody might give'm a table, and maybe a homemade safe; and they thought they was the smartest things in the world."[8] Having possessions was a salve that reinforced a sense of self-worth in a society that demeaned Black people by equating them with objects.

Yet, so many things that enslaved Blacks made or acquired would eventually be lost, stolen, confiscated, or left behind due to the interstate slave trade that dominated Black experience in the first half of the nineteenth century.[9] When speaking of her aunt in an interview in 1929 or 1930, a formerly enslaved woman from Tennessee paused to retrieve a special object: "I am gonna show you something that my auntie made, and she was gonna make me one, but they took her away. She used to make everything. My auntie done it. She was gonna make me a spread, too, to go over all my bed, but the white folks took her away." As the speaker caressed the bedspread her aunt had made, she brought to mind the pain of that long-ago separation. Her repetition of the moment of her aunt's sale speaks to trauma, indicating the impact of this loss many decades after the Civil War. The speaker cherished the work of her aunt's hand. She refused to sell the textile, even amid economic deprivation and the onset of the Great Depression when "everything has been so tight." She said about the coverlet: "A white woman told me the other day if I would carry this to the capitol I would get something for it. I am gonna keep this as long as I live, because my aunt made it."[10] In the view of this speaker, the bedspread had already "gotten something" more valuable than money: a feeling of closeness with the aunt who had been snatched away. As an adult, this formerly enslaved woman became a quilter, entreating her children to make bed coverings alongside her, perhaps with the hope that a special one among these textiles, too, would one day enfold memories.

For generations of Black people dispossessed of their freedom, belongings held a deep emotional valence, representing not only dreams but also ties to the people *with* whom one belonged by choice, as opposed to those *to* whom one belonged by force. In this way, things linked kin together, materializing family members' devotion even across insurmountable distance.[11] In contrast to the Martins, who legally owned her, Rose owned very little. But Rose's list of things to pack, as recorded by Ruth on Ashley's sack, indicates where Rose placed her emotional investments. Some of the items Rose packed, like the pecans, might have been chosen in part for potential exchange value. But the list includes no prices or equivalencies; the items are not recalled as if they were ever intended for trade. These things were more meaningful to Rose, as understood by her descendant, for their symbolic, rather than their commercial, value. In silent rebuke of the emotionally bankrupt inventory of the slaveholder, Rose prized things that reaffirmed relational ties.

THE LANGUAGE OF DRESS

A "tattered" dress appears first in Ruth's embroidered catalog. This placement should give the object weight for us. It hints that the dress was the first thing packed, or the first thing recalled, or the main thing highlighted in this family's separation saga. The list and its order presages, perhaps, a personal trait of Ruth the sewer, who, as we will later see, gained public notice for her stylish attire in Philadelphia. Whether or not Rose packed the dress first, it is clear from the list that Rose thought immediately about the problem of clothing Ashley. Rose knew, as did many women ensnared by slavery, that apparel is simultaneously material and social. By providing Ashley with a dress, worn and frayed as it may have been, Rose insisted on Ashley's right to bodily protection and feminine dignity, while also emphasizing the relationship between them. A tattered dress was a thousand things to Rose and her figurative sisters in slavery: protection, honor, artistry, memory, and connection. In our hands and imaginations, a garment like the dress Rose gave Ashley might index social-relational worlds crosscut by the intricate weaves of race, gender, and status.

Dress made by an unidentified enslaved woman or women. Collection of the Smithsonian National Museum of African American History and Culture, gift of the Black Fashion Museum, founded by Lois K. Alexander-Lane.

Across the sweep of human history and vast differences in climate and culture, people have clothed their bodies to reflect complex relationships among them.[12] Wearers adopted select apparel to transmit social messages through color, pattern, texture, fiber type, and the particular flourishes of skilled workwomanship.[13] How one dresses is a form of social communication in a complex field of relational power plays. In the U.S. South, dress "became a language" in which enslavers and enslaved were fluent.[14] The relationship between these two groups was fundamentally based on a power differential that authorized one to control the other, and visible distinctions emphasized that critical line of difference. The categorization of "Negroes" as a race fit for slavery (and also of "Indians" previously) already relied on a shorthand of visual cues. It was easier to set aside a class of people as inferiors if they shared readily identifiable characteristics: the skin color, hair texture, and facial features that became the building blocks of race. Fabric, an additional layer on top of these features, signified who owned others or who could be owned. Slaveholders sought to materialize and dramatize the debasement of enslavement, covering captive brown-skinned bodies in coarse fabrics dyed in drab colors and marked by simple prints. Masters and mistresses attempted to dictate what fabrics and styles their workers could don, for the express purpose of highlighting the wearers' low status. States that systematized and codified slavery even wrote clothing bans into legislation called sumptuary laws.

South Carolina legislators passed the colony's first slave law, "An Act for the Better Ordering of Slaves," in 1690, stipulating first and foremost that "in his Majesty's plantations in America, slavery has been introduced and allowed, and the people commonly called negroes, Indians, mulattoes and mustizoes, have been deemed absolute slaves." The law required, among other stipulations, that no slave could leave the owner's premises without a ticket and promised that owners would be reimbursed in case of the state's execution of human property. By 1735 lawmakers had added restrictions about clothing expenditure to the slave code. Section 26 specified the boundaries of permissible slave dress in detail:

> Whereas, many of the slaves in this Province wear clothes much above the condition of slaves, for the procuring whereof they use sinister and evil methods . . . no owner or proprietor of any negro slave or other slave whatsoever (except livery men or boys) shall permit or suffer such negro or other slave to have or wear any sort of apparel whatsoever,

finer, other, or of greater value, than negro cloth, duffelds, coarse kearsies, osnabrigs, blue linnen, checked linnen or coarse garlix or calicoes, checked cottons or scotch plaids, garlix or calico under the pain of forfeiting all and every such apparel and garment that any person shall commit his negro or other slave to have or wear.[15]

Clothing, as South Carolina's oligarchic rulers knew, was deeply political, bespeaking moral values, social standing, and social allowances.[16] But Black captives were acquiring access to materials and garments far above their station just decades into Carolina's experiment with slavery. Unfree people, especially women, were getting ahold of fine fabrics primarily through long-term liaisons with white men. Women as well as men also purchased fabric and premade articles on the informal or underground market of one-to-one exchanges and pawnshops.[17] They shopped for items that they felt might distinguish them using money earned through the extra work of hiring themselves out beyond the hours required on-site by their masters.

Black people's means of accessing this clothing, the South Carolina sumptuary law accused, was "sinister and evil." This barely veiled language pointed to the suspicion that Blacks were engaging in theft as well as sexual misconduct to acquire fine clothing. For Charleston was an urban milieu, similar to New Orleans, where elite white men were known to have relatively flagrant and orchestrated erotic dalliances with unfree women of color, sometimes through coercion or force, other times through a subtle arrangement of material exchange, and, often, through a complex set of motivations and interactions that combined these elements and more. In this glamorous seaside colonial city, enslaved women could outshine free white women in appearance and apparel, despite the statute outlawing their donning of fancy dress. This was also true for Charleston's neighboring coastal city, Savannah, where, according to long-term visitor Emily Burke, it was still difficult to distinguish who was and was not enslaved in the antebellum period. "As a general thing the slaves in the city wear good clothing," Burke observed. "Many even dress extravagantly and decorate their persons with a great deal of costly jewelry. . . . I have seen ladies in the streets with such light complexions and dressed so elegantly that when told they were Negroes I could not willingly credit the assertion." This New England schoolteacher's comment suggests that dress, like skin color, was key to identifying southern status. Enslaved people in urban areas realized this and took advantage of their relatively greater access and mobility. Later, when Emily Burke visited in the home of a planter and encountered an elderly enslaved woman "flitting about to get a peep at the newcomer" while "dressed in a coarse osnaburg gown," Burke professed herself to be "a little amused." Observing Black people, and particularly women, attired in accord with her expectation of their subjugated status seems to have relieved Burke's social anxiety.[18]

As Burke's confusion and discomfort indicates, clothing was a contested arena in southern society. Dress marked not only status but also, as one prominent Civil War historian has pointedly put it, the *stability* of that status.[19] Fluctuations in who had access to which fabrics and in who was permitted to wear certain articles of dress portended societal disruption. While some slaveholders bent the law to allow favored unfree people to acquire nice clothing and some enslaved men and women provided such items for themselves against their owners' permission, other whites vehemently protested Blacks' adoption of high fashion and ridiculed what they saw as copycat clothing styles. In 1772, a European traveler bunking with a monied planter in Charleston published a letter in *The South-Carolina Gazette* castigating the mannerisms of urban Blacks. While he found enslaved people in the countryside to be appropriately matched to their apparel, "clad suitable to their Condition, contented, sober, modest, [h]umble, civil and obliging," he judged Charleston slaves to be "the very Reverse—abandonedly unmannerly, insolent, and shameless—and many of the female slave[s] by [f]ar more elegantly dressed, than the Generality of women." This caustic observer, who signed his accusations anonymously as "The Stranger," blamed Black women, who, he had heard from his planter friends, "prostrate their Bodies to all Persons that will offer them a Penny." He also condemned the cohabitation of white men, "as Husband, with Negro Women . . . to whom any person is a welcome Bed-fellow."[20]

It is not untrue that in the eighteenth and nineteenth centuries, enslaved women sometimes directed the attention of their free white sex partners toward items of apparel that were otherwise denied them. As the memoirs of Black women tell us, however, sexual ties that might enable better material conditions came at great physical and emotional cost. We might also see Black women's encasement of their bodies in layers of silk and chintz as "defensive costume," a means of fending off verbal as well as physical assault. To dress above their station was to call upon the sartorial security of the white lady, who, clad in laces, wires, and ruffles, kept her body private, kept unwanted others at a measured distance, and signaled the hidden resource of familial status that could be leveraged for her defense. The silent and secret emotional toll paid by enslaved women to obtain elegant dress went unnoticed by those in the white upper class who stereotyped them all as lascivious "black Strumpet[s]."[21]

Why, this European "Stranger" demanded, were slave women cloaked in "splendor" and traipsing about the open streets? Where were the "Magistrates, Constables, and Watchmen" charged with policing them? Those same Blacks who dressed in finery, gambled, drank, and cursed aloud in the open of what the traveler thought should be a crystalline white city posed an insidious, closeted threat to the colonies. "What Dependence can we have," the stranger demanded of his readers, on Blacks who would behave so outrageously? The answer: none. Captive Blacks and American Indians could not be counted on to willingly maintain a status quo in which boots trampled upon their backs. And one can scarcely imagine a more precarious position than being dependent on a class of people with every reason to detest you. Enslavers feared that unfree people dressing above their station and thereby expressing, as well as feeling, a sense of equality with their betters was a step along the road to outright rebellion. South Carolina would have to tame and cage enslaved people in order to extract full-scale servility, relying on tools as subtle as "the language of clothes" and as brutal as the Work House, where corporal punishment was imposed.

Colonial lawmakers passed the 1735 statute on slave dress in order to hold the garment line of social hierarchy. Certain cloths were for certain people, just as bathrooms and water fountains would be two centuries later, in the Jim Crow era. A new law on slave dress in South Carolina would not appear until 1814, when Charleston city leaders passed an ordinance prohibiting owners from bringing slaves "in irons" or "insufficiently clothed" into public view. The ruling elite apparently feared sartorial feast as well as famine, disallowing fancy dress and then, decades later, when a paternalist ethos had solidified, discouraging an outward display of cruelty. But subjugation through dress persisted.[22]

In order to obey the law and satisfy their own cost-saving impulses, enslavers like Robert Martin could call on a variety of providers for textiles made expressly for the enslaved population. Producing subpar apparel for millions of unfree African Americans was big business. British textile manufacturers were the earliest suppliers of such fabrics in the 1700s, soon followed by New England companies, dominated by those in Massachusetts and Rhode Island in the early and mid-1800s, and then joined by southern textile producers.[23] The cloth for human bodies treated like chattel was purposefully substandard, made of poor-quality fibers roughly and efficiently woven. Certain types of fabric fitting this description became associated with slave dress and were increasingly sought for that purpose: osnaburg (an unfinished German linen), linsey-woolsey (a coarse linen or sometimes cotton-and-wool combination), homespun (home- or plantation-made fabric), and, to a certain extent, calico (plain-weave cotton prints) and hemp. Most often, these fabrics intended to clothe the enslaved were left white in color, dyed blue or gray, or woven with blue and white stripes or checks. The general sameness of these tones and prints, meant to set a people apart, shares a similarity with prison garb as well as with forced hooding. Uniformity served to broadcast their wearers' subjugation, obscure individuality, and suppress expression of cultural identities through dress.[24]

Manufacturers, sellers, and buyers described this special category of low-grade fabric as "Negro cloth" (sometimes referred to as "Niger," "Plantation," or "Slave" cloth).[25] Negro cloth was not one specific textile. It was, instead, a motley category including any kind of fabric possessing characteristics (cheapness, coarseness, dullness) meant to publicly identify and demean the wearer. While all manner of white working-class and poor people wore clothing made of affordable fabrics like linsey-woolsey, they sought out the best grade of the category they could afford and would not deign to wear fabric marketed as Negro cloth.

Enslavers in South Carolina and elsewhere, however, took pains to acquire it, a virtual brand unto itself that conveyed the opposite of luxury. As New England's textile-manufacturing industry surged in the industrial revolution, this fabric became more readily available. Planters ordered Negro cloth directly from American companies, particularly from mills in Lowell, Massachusetts, that were weaving cotton produced by the unfree people it would clothe and from the Peace Dale Manufacturing Company in Rhode Island, as well as from local distributors who advertised in the same newspapers that carried an abundance of notices for "runaway" slaves.[26]

Negro cloth produced a counterintuitive doubling effect, making those forced to wear it highly visible in society as abject inferiors and at the same time perfectly invisible as social actors of any consequence.[27] A free white person, no matter his or her station, could pass through a novel city or an unfamiliar plantation, take in the scene at a glance, and know how the various residents were to be treated, based on the fabric, cut, style, and

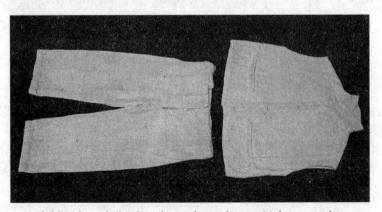

Child's "slave cloth" sleeveless jacket and pants. Unknown maker, Louisiana, 1850s. Cotton; hand-spun and hand-woven. From the Collections of Shadows-on-the-Teche, a Site of the National Trust for Historic Preservation, New Iberia, Louisiana.

condition of their apparel. For in addition to being made of rough cloth, slave dress was rudely cut, without attention to fit or fashion. Women wore plain shifts (long, loose, straight dresses) with petticoats (loose undergarments). Sometimes enslaved people received a pair of shoes or a coat. It was not uncommon for enslaved children—both boys and girls—to be clothed in apparel resembling a loose shirt called a "slip." One English journalist visiting a South Carolina rice plantation described a young girl wearing a shapeless "sort of sack" as her clothing.[28] Although Negro cloth was made of rough-hewn, sturdy fibers, it disintegrated quickly under the conditions of hard daily use in a subtropical climate such as the coastal Southeast, leaving enslaved people in near rags much of the year.[29]

Clothing was usually distributed by owners or plantation managers once or twice annually. Summer and winter apparel varied by household but usually included just one or two whole suits of dress for the season or the fabric required to sew them. Louisa Picquet, who never gave up on finding her mother, despite decades of separation through sale, detailed the inadequate clothing worn by those in bondage. She remembered: "In the summer-time we never wore but two-pieces—only the one under, and the blue homespun over. It is a striped cloth they make in Georgia just for the colored people."[30] One woman enslaved in Tennessee similarly recounted in an interview, "We went barefooted 'til Christmas. . . . In the Spring, they would buy brown domestic and make underclothes out of that and you would have two dresses. Some of the mean ones just had white gingham dresses and they would be so narrow that they would split them sometimes." A man interviewed in the early 1900s described the apparel of boys and girls on the plantation where he was enslaved: "Boys until they got up large enough to work wore little slips. We called them shirts; they'd sew it up like a sack and cut a hole in the neck for your head to go through. . . . There wasn't much difference in the dress of girls and boys. The women wore theirs straight, too, they called them sacks. . . . Sometimes it would fit and sometimes it wouldn't."[31] In addition to being uncomfortable, ill-fitting, and woefully inadequate to protect the wearer against the elements, these shapeless shirts worn by girls and boys alike deemphasized gender in a larger society in which perceived differences between boyhood and girlhood, manhood and womanhood were stridently marked and observed.[32]

Eliza Potter, the free Black hairdresser who traveled through the Midwest and the South arranging the coiffure of wealthy white ladies (and taking detailed notes), addressed the hypocrisy of New Orleans slaveholders who made the "greatest show" of appearing at the opera in fine fashion yet kept their enslaved workers raggedly dressed. "Some of the slaves have no hats on, and others are scarcely half clad, and that of the coarse stuff that goods are packed in," Potter charged. Outside Natchez, Mississippi, she described "slaves badly treated, half clothed, half fed, and misused in every way." Potter concluded of her southern sojourn: "The cruelty there was more than I could bear."[33] Substandard clothing (cheap, scratchy, shapeless, thin, and poorly cut) kept an enslaved woman in her place, both in the eyes of others and, it was hoped by owners, in her own mind. Particularly in a society as image-conscious as Charleston, ragged, unartful apparel struck a great contrast to the silks, cashmeres, jewels, furs, feathers, and fabric finery of the planter elite. The impoverished, disheveled appearance of these Black wearers contributed to a public "proof" of their innately inferior status.

White observers recirculated this sense of proven deficiency as captured by dress. Frederick Law Olmsted, a landscape architect and author from New England, wrote these lines, difficult to read for their degree of insult, about Black women he observed on a trip through South Carolina and Georgia in the 1850s:

> The women struck their hoes as if they were strong, and well able to engage in muscular labor. The expression of their faces was generally repulsive, and their tout ensemble anything but agreeable to the eye. The dress of most of them was uncouth and cumbrous, dirty and ragged; reefed up, as I have once before described, at the hips.[34]

To Olmsted, the Black woman was a masculinized figure, made grotesque as much by her unflattering, indecent attire as by her physical strength. Among white women observers, even Harriet Martineau, a staunch abolitionist from Great Britain, fell prey to the negative stereotyping such costuming could elicit. While visiting a string of plantations across the South in the 1830s, Martineau was overcome with aversion. "There is something inexpressibly disgusting," she confessed, "in the sight of a slave woman in the field. . . . In her preeminently ugly costume, the long, scanty, dirty woolen garment, with the shabby large bonnet at the back of her head, the perspiration streaming down her dull face, the heavy tread of the splay foot, the slovenly air with which she guides her plough, a more hideous object cannot well be conceived." For Martineau, the enslaved woman's degrading apparel fused with her posture of defeminizing work and racialized physical features to create a monstrous body. Ugliness and manliness, as materialized through dress, became part of the Black woman's perceived essential nature.[35]

Unfree people resented the stingy rationing of coarse and stigmatizing clothing and at times informed their owners of their discontent, declaring certain shipments of Negro cloth worse than others and even refusing to accept particular fabrics. Because nineteenth-century enslavers often strove to cajole their owned people into higher work production before forcing them through violence, these appeals sometimes worked.[36] Records of exchanges between planters and New England manufacturers reveal slave owners reporting the distaste of their workers for some fabrics and their relative preference for others. All of this negotiation occurred, however, on a charged, uneven field of action in which enslaved people could attempt to influence owner behavior but could never enforce outcomes. Slaveholders—women as well as men—held the ultimate controls of the pocketbook and the chastening rod and did not hesitate to use them.

In an example of manipulative prowess, one New Orleans mistress attempted to bribe the women she owned into having more children (hence begetting more slave property). Her tactic is preserved in a letter to a dry goods merchant, whom she entreated: "I must request the favor of you to add 28 yards of cheap calico. . . . Please let it be gay. I have always given a dress of such to every woman after . . . she has a young child. . . . They do much better being encouraged a little." Another white female owner had an enslaved woman named Charlotte physically punished and then sought to diminish this act of cruelty by directing the abused woman to "look cheerful, and be good and friendly with her" and then lending Charlotte a "silk dress" to wear on Sunday. Charlotte was an aunt of Elizabeth Keckley, the future dressmaker of a First Lady; Keckley described the incident and called her aunt's mistress "severe with her slaves in some respects." Since this mistress had only "one silk dress in the world, silk not being so plenty in those days," as Keckley re-counted, and since the mistress found herself with a social occa-sion to attend that same week, she had to request her own dress back from her slave, a turning of the tables that Charlotte must have taken some degree of satisfaction in.[37]

Enslaved people were keenly aware of these psychological tricks—of clothing meant to demean the wearer and gifts in-tended to extort labor as well as to ensure loyalty. The fortunate few who escaped slavery and wrote autobiographies of life be-hind the southern lines often reflected on their hatred of slave dress and the social work it performed. These writers knew ex-actly what was at stake: that slave clothing was a uniform of infe-riority, a method for simultaneously enforcing bodily deprivation and social degradation. As Harriet Jacobs angrily recalled about her "scanty wardrobe" as a preteen: "I have a vivid recollection of the linsey-woolsey dress given me every winter by Mrs. Flint. How I hated it! It was one of the badges of slavery."[38]

Elizabeth Keckley was hired out by her owner in 1850s St. Louis, and her skills as a dressmaker so inspired clients that one of them loaned her the funds to purchase her freedom as well as her son's. Keckley relocated with her son, who had been con-ceived through the sexual assault of a white man, to Washing-ton, D.C., where she sewed delicate garments for high-ranking political wives. Mary Todd Lincoln, spouse to President Abra-ham Lincoln, was Keckley's most devoted (and emotionally de-pendent) client. Keckley's thoughtful memoir of her years in captivity and in Washington reveals the power dynamics of slav-ery poignantly recalled, as well as a perspective on national pol-itics. Keckley remembered that when she was called upon, at the age of four, to tend her mistress's baby, she was relocated to the main house from the "rude cabin" where her mother re-sided, and her wardrobe improved to "simple attire" that "was a short dress and a little white apron." With this Keckley also recorded a memory of her first "lash[ing]," a severe beating suffered for not knowing how to properly pick up the infant. Enslaved children, Keckley learned at a tender age, were trained in their work by means of punishment and insult. Her uniform, even "improved," set her apart as a person worthy of such abuse.[39]

Louisa Picquet knew slave dress and harsh treatment intimately. Born near Columbia, South Carolina, to a fifteen-year-old enslaved girl named Elizabeth and their master, John Randolph, Louisa was soon relocated. Randolph sold the enslaved mother and daughter because Louisa looked too much like another infant in the household, the half-sibling born to Randolph and his wife. Louisa's pale skin color and straight hair, as we have previously seen, were signs of the sexual indiscretions that haunted numerous enslaving families, especially the white mistresses within them. Under a new regime of control in Mobile, Alabama, Louisa's mother suffered sexual exploitation by their second master, Mr. Cook, who serially impregnated her. This master then eyed the teenaged Louisa, inaugurating a true story of generations of enslaved women preyed upon by the same man that would inspire the plot of Gayl Jones's terrifying novel *Corregidora*.[40]

After gaining her freedom and moving to Cincinnati, decades later, when her third owner (who had purchased her from Cook) died, Louisa painfully recalled that her assigned dress in slavery was "very thin" and "low-neck'd." When Picquet's second master, Mr. Cook, had whipped her with a cowhide lash for refusing to appear in his room and succumb to his barely disguised sexual demands, he had gained easy access to her thirteen-year-old body through the skimpy material of her slave uniform. Picquet described the marks his assault left on her, repeating, in a pained haze of remembrance, "I was dressed so thin." This thinness of enslaved women's clothing, the grossly inadequate coverage that violated societal norms for their gender in the nineteenth century, is another feature that set their apparel apart, not just as Black people but also, and especially, as women. In a vicious cycle of mistreatment and slander, Black women's revealing dress became evidence of their hypersexuality in the attestations of slaveholders and travelers.[41] Rose would have recognized, too, the difference a dress could make to a girl always in danger of bodily exposure and abuse, and hence prioritized giving a dress, perhaps the only extra change of clothing she had, to Ashley.

In contrast to the costume of the unfree woman, the lady of cultivation must never be caught improperly attired, warned Emily Thornwell, the author of *The Lady's Guide to Perfect Gentility in Manner, Dress, and Conversation*, published in 1856 in Louisa Picquet's city of newfound freedom, Cincinnati. Thornwell was referring to white women, but she did not say so, since Black women were already imagined by the author and her readership as existing outside of the category "lady." "Disorder of a lady's toilet . . . the result of negligence or slovenliness" was, Thornwell declared, "unpardonable." Neither "great heat of weather" nor "cold and rainy weather" will "permit us to go in slippers, or with our legs and arms bare, or to take nonchalant and improper attitudes," she intoned, as these behaviors were "an error of persons of a low class."[42] Enslaved Black women could not hope to approximate these gendered standards of propriety. Scant dress, as well as hard labor in hot environs that necessitated the hiking up of skirts, were conditions of their forced servitude that led to grossly unfair charges of immodesty and sexual immorality.[43]

Enslaved women found the clothing forced upon them insulting to their dignity. Worse, enslaved women were themselves tasked with the taxing, monotonous labor of making plantation textiles by hand. While some planters ordered ready-made cloth for their human property, most preferred the cost savings that came from directing slaves to produce their own necessities.[44] Enslaved women were crucial spokes in the wheel of slave apparel and plantation cloth production. Most would have known how to do the basic spinning, weaving, and sewing required to keep a slave quarters population in clothing and coverings, as a part of, or sometimes as a secret supplement to, fabric and apparel rations. On one Alabama plantation, nursing mothers were commanded to weave in order to produce immediate benefit for their owner while they breastfed. The formerly enslaved man whose boyhood job it had been to ferry the product of their labor to the big house called it "nursling thread." On plantations with greater enslaved populations and production capacity, Black women were put to work in weaving or loom houses, designated exterior structures where they spun thread on spinning wheels and wove cloth on looms.

Some women worked in both hands-on and managerial capacities as head weavers. The fabric they made would later be sewn into clothing for their families and others on the estates. In interview after interview, formerly enslaved women and men remembered their female relatives making fabric and clothing into the night and vividly recalled the sound of the looms. Ida Adkins, in North Carolina, recollected: "Mammy worked in the weaving room. I can see her now setting at the weaving machine and hear the pedals going plop, plop." One man remembered: "My mother would spin. She would make our clothes. She would take the cotton and card it, then she would weave that, and after that it would come to cloth; then she would take that and put it in the loom and weave it. My mother done all the washing and ironing and cooking and work in the field, too." This speaker also shared the memory of "seeing my old mother spinning with tears running down her cheeks, crying about her brother who was sold and carried to Arkansas." How often, we might wonder, was the cloth produced on plantation looms interwoven with sorrow? The same man quoted previously about sack-like clothing recalled: "My mother worked in the field. . . . The women had to work in the field and spin four cuts before they went to bed." A woman called Vergy remembered doing textile work as a child, a common occurrence: "I had my five cuts a day to make, just like the old folks. . . . I had to pull the thread like this, and pull it over the loom like this, and then cord it. It was real work, I tell you. . . . Yes, it was really work." Vergy's mother also worked at the loom, and Vergy recalled how "Mammy just kept on weaving" as her mistress sent for the master to whip Vergy's mother for some petty offense. Ellen Cragin, in Arkansas, remembered her mother working "so long and so often that once she went to sleep at the loom." Ellen's mother was awakened by a beating meted out by the owner's son, who had once been nursed at her breast.[45]

Slave owners noted Black women's textile production on large estates. Eliza Lucas Pinckney, an agriculturalist and entrepreneur, whose family had emigrated from the Caribbean island of Antigua to Charleston in the early 1700s, attested to enslaved women's excellence in spinning and weaving. Pinckney managed her family's plantation on the Cooper River during her father's absence, while he served in the British military and as lieutenant governor of Antigua, a slaving and sugar colony. Eliza Pinckney is credited with the widespread adoption of indigo cultivation in South Carolina. She had her enslaved people experiment with seeds her father sent from the island. In a letter to her father in 1746, Pinckney wrote about cloth production on their

American estate: "The sensible Negro woman and hundreds of others learned well to spin, and excellent cloth has been always woven in the low country of Carolina."[46] Enslaved cloth-makers were also experienced with natural dyes like the indigo that owners made them grow for profit, as well as dyes from varieties of tree bark collected in the woods. Black women's unpaid labor produced much of the fabric needed to supply the plantations where they lived and worked, contributing to the sense of "self"-sufficiency that masters of these rural fiefdoms often sought. But even under authoritarian conditions, Black women's textile production exceeded their owners' ability to control their creativity and inner feeling. Many children of weavers recalled the skill, artistry, and pride Black women put into their handmade fabrics. Susie King, from Arkansas, fondly recalled her "good mother" who wove some and dyed all the cloth. Susie herself became a fabric craftswoman, telling an interviewer, "I loved to weave, all them bright colors, blue and red and green and yellow."[47]

Rudimentary spinning and weaving was viewed by slaveholding society as necessary but low-level work fit for Black women.[48] Only a small subset of enslaved women received advanced training in sewing, piecing cloth, and even embroidery, often from mother figures but also from practitioners to whom they were informally apprenticed. In 1775, South Carolina planter Ralph Izard is said to have contracted with a townswoman named Martha Chubb to train eight enslaved girls in spinning and weaving.[49] Elizabeth Keckley learned needlecraft from her mother, whose mistress, Mrs. Burwell, "was a hard task-master," assigning her mother "so much work to do in making clothes, etc., for the family, besides the slaves."[50] Elizabeth learned at her worn-out mother's knee the skill of making, measuring, cutting, and assembling fabric that would later become her livelihood. As a child, she was put to work knitting socks while minding the baby on whose behalf she had received her first beating.

Black seamstresses produced the majority of garments enslaved people wore, either from fabric made on-site or from imported low-grade cloth. They also created domestic textiles like coverlets and quilts. On the largest estates, Black women were directed to spin fiber into thread, weave thread into cloth, and produce — in cramped, hot quarters — badges of slavery.[51] Their callused hands crafted the slave uniform their children and fellow captives would wear, along with the finer patterned quilts the slave-owner family members would drape across their polished mahogany bedsteads. Theirs was a "hidden world of . . . enslaved artisans whose skills with spindle, loom, and sewing needle were an integral part of the antebellum South."[52]

RAIMENT ROLLED IN BLOOD

Even as enslaved women bent beneath the relentless burden of the spinning wheel, they took up the symbolism of clothing. In a proxy war of warp and weft, enslaved people fought back on plantations and farms, as well as in cosmopolitan cities like Charleston, by creatively mixing materials to fashion clothes that defied their station. They sabotaged attempts at sartorial control by their owners as well as lawmakers, knowingly and deliberately.[53] Black men and women often dreamed of obtaining new clothing and footwear. Soft clothes and well-fitting shoes that honored their bodies challenged the notion that they were a subset of the species deserving to be dressed in rags and sacks. When enslaved people had the means, they often set their sights on cloth and apparel that signaled their essential worth. Ledger books from stores operating on plantations indicate how enslaved people spent their scarce funds. Slaveholders housed these stores on their premises because they'd realized that unfree people sought material pleasures, and they wanted to capture this population's meager income while discouraging attempts to acquire things from afar.

Unfree people whose spending has been traced in plantation store records across Virginia, the Carolinas, and Georgia spent most of their rarely obtained dollars on "Cloth, Clothing, Sewing Supplies, [and] Handkerchiefs," which made up 64.6 percent of their purchases across six surviving account books. Food, the second-largest category of spending in these ledgers, captured only 14.6 percent of enslaved people's money by comparison. When enslaved women could not purchase new clothing, they sometimes surreptitiously took swaths of fabric, ribbons, buttons, and even fully made dresses from their mistresses, at times radically altering the garments to avoid detection. Black women transformed these bolts of hard-won cloth into masterpieces of cut and color that earned them back an ability to signify their sense of self-worth and community value through dress.[54]

By hook or by crook, through theft, trade, or sometimes purchase, enslaved women acquired colorful fabric and fanciful trimmings. They sacrificed nights, time most often set aside for familial caretaking, cabin maintenance, and extra work that might earn them money, to engage in the labor of producing clothing for themselves. They created striking outfits with specially procured cloth, Negro cloth at their disposal, and homespun they wove themselves. One man formerly enslaved in North Carolina described the harsh treatment of his mother, "whose mistress did not provide her with clothes." Determined to create her own wardrobe, his mother acquired a wheel with the help of her husband and spun "in the night" in her cabin.

The mistress, seeking to commandeer all of the woman's work time, confined her to the plantation spinning house twelve hours a day. In response, the son recalled, his mother "would then go home, and, fixing her wheel in a place made in the floor to prevent its making a noise, she would spin for herself, in order that she might be decently clad."[55] Through a degree of self-motivated work that is difficult to conceive of, Black women fashioned their wardrobes and expressed creative imagination, ornamentation, and personal style. They risked punishment to wear these self-designed dresses at religious and social gatherings with their families and community on Sundays, often a day off from labor, and at secret evening revelries that took place in the woods at plantation borders. Relying on natural items to finish and embellish their clothing, enslaved women used vines and tree limbs to replicate the full-bodied look of the iconic southern hoopskirt, which symbolized femininity and luxurious excess in the 1850s and 1860s.[56] Notably, the hoop also created "protected space" around the wearer, a symbolic shield for their bodies.[57] Celebration, pleasure, and joy of the body in snatches of time beneath the moon's clarifying light returned enslaved women to themselves.

Black girls also experienced newfound pleasure when dressed in keeping with the gender norms of their times. One girl, whose mother was sold away when she was six, later remembered being purchased and moved to Mississippi, where a kindly mistress (a recurring character type in many slave narratives, as is the cruel mistress) took pity on her. After professing the girl to be a "Po' little thing . . . a little motherless child," this new mistress "got some domestic and some calico and made . . . a dress and some drawers." The woman who had been that girl recalled many decades later: "I was never dressed so fine in my life. . . . I went out in the woods where there was lots of cedars thick around and . . . pulled up my dress and just looked and danced and danced." Due to the vividness of her description, we can almost see this parentless girl dancing alone in the forest, the skirt of her dress playfully lifted so that she could admire the fabric. Whatever her new owner's motives, the pride and pleasure the girl felt at being clean and dressed with care inspired a sublime moment.[58]

Black women also fought daily battles for their dignity in more dramatic ways. A few were bold enough to tear the clothing right off of their mistresses' backs, acting on resentment as well as self-defense. A girl enslaved in Tennessee, nicknamed "Puss" by her mother, Fannie, watched her mistress hit Fannie with a stick for unknown reasons. In the absence of the master of the household, "Ma struck back and a fight followed. . . . The thought seemed to race into my mother's mind to tear mistress' clothing off her body. . . . She caught hold, pulled, ripped and tore. Poor mistress was nearly naked when the storekeeper got to them and pulled ma off." When the master returned, he promised to have Fannie "whipped by law"; the mistress proclaimed that Fannie would be knocked down "like a beef." Fannie was hired out after this incident and returned a year later wearing "new clothes, and a pair of beautiful earrings," a vision of triumph to her daughter made real through the symbol of dress. Puss "decided to follow [her] mother's example." "I intended to fight," she recalled many years later, "and if I couldn't fight, I'd kick; and if I couldn't kick, I'd bite."[59]

Black women also took advantage of the disruption of the Civil War to rifle through plantation chests and put on the dresses of their mistresses, "want[ing] to give their exhilaration the shape of their own form."[60] And after the war, the notion of freedom included the right to be properly clothed. Elizabeth Keckley recounted an example of this desire to wear respectable clothes in association with a free life. Soon after the Civil War ended, Keckley encountered a woman on the street who had migrated from her former plantation to Washington, D.C. Bent at the spine with old age, the woman confided to Keckley that she had hoped to receive a "shife" (shift dress) from Mrs. Lincoln while there in the nation's capital. While Keckley interpreted this expectation as a remnant of slavery in which the master or mistress distributed clothing rations, the garment may also have represented a bid for respectability and the protection of modesty that the speaker believed should come as part of the package of freedom.[61]

With such transformative rewards to the psyche and spirit, it is no wonder that Black women took risky measures to shake off the stain of Negro cloth and shapeless tunics. Even in the most frightful circumstances, they hunted for items of clothing and clung to the pieces they acquired with fierce protectiveness. Louisa Picquet, whose second owner had beaten her for evading his sexual advances, took the risk of accepting six half dollars from him, although she recognized this as a bribe. Her master was drunk at the time, so Louisa convinced herself that he would forget about the money and the implied expectation of an erotic exchange. Why would she behave so recklessly? Louisa had never touched so much money before, and she knew what she would do with it: purchase a special dress. This garment would be nothing like her thin, drab, inadequate covering. "I had seen a flowered muslin dress in the store several times," she recalled. "And I take a fancy to it; I thought it look beautiful. It was perfectly white, with a little pink leaf all over it." The full skirt of the dress captured her imagination, as did the soft white cloth. Picquet, who was herself light enough to pass for white but would never know those privileges due to her birth to a slave mother, may have longed for the protective powers that perfect whiteness seemed to bestow upon some women. This fine white dress graced with a springtime motif of flowers seemed interlaced with goodness, dignity, and purity. Louisa wanted to feel these qualities attached to her person in a way that verified her inner worth. She took her master's money, inciting his ire when she did not later return to his room as ordered. Cook exacted severe punishment for Louisa Picquet's disobedience, whipping her naked body and leaving a tangle of scars on her flesh, one of which, she disclosed, she would take to the grave.[62]

Louisa's decision reveals to us just how much enslaved women valued the chance to care for themselves, to restore their feminine honor in an era that prized gentility and modesty, through dress. Not long after this encounter, Picquet's owner sold her to a third man, nearly fifty years old and also seeking sexual prey. On the auction block beneath the roving eyes of this known species of vulture, Louisa begged for a chance to retrieve her special muslin dress, tucked away, we can imagine, in a holding room where people were kept pre-sale. But Louisa would be separated from the white dress that had restored some portion of her autonomy and dignity, as well as from her mother, who sobbed and prayed when a "gentleman" bid Louisa's price up to $1,500. Very few enslaved people were purchased for an amount that high, which would today be nearly equivalent to $38,900. Young, attractive women—many, but not all, mixed race and pale of skin—fetched these astronomical prices because of their intended use as sexual servants called "fancies." When hairdresser Eliza Potter traveled down the Ohio River, she commented on this trade in girls with "beauty enough to arouse *the base lust of some Southern buyer*." These innocents, Potter felt, were "doomed" to "*ignominy*."[63] Perhaps Louisa did feel doomed. John Williams, Louisa's new owner, denied her wish to recover the white muslin gown, promising to supply her "plenty of nice dresses." Louisa's last thought of the dress that she had risked so much for was wrapped up in sadness at parting from her family. She hoped that perhaps her mother would find the frock, reuse the material to clothe Louisa's baby brother, and have something beautiful to remember her by.[64]

On the steamboat ride to New Orleans, Louisa learned how she would be forced to procure the promised "nice dresses." Her owner explained "what he had bought [her] for," then swore that if she did as told, he would provide her with niceties, but if she refused him, he would "whip [her] almost to death." Williams kept Louisa as his "housekeeper" and sex slave in New Orleans until freeing her upon his death, twenty years later. Supported by limited proceeds from the sale of Williams's furniture, Louisa went north to Cincinnati, where she married a Black minister also born to an enslaved woman and her master, and published an account of her life in slavery to raise money to free her mother.[65]

Even as Louisa Picquet was desperate to retain her muslin dress, Elizabeth Keckley worried over her wardrobe in North Carolina. Separated from her mother when their master decided to send Elizabeth to his eldest son, young Mr. Burwell, she wrote a letter that circles round and round clothing. In it, she asks her mother, still enslaved in Virginia, to "tell Aunt Bella that I was very much obliged to her for the present; I have been so particular with it that I have only worn it once." She frets over "not know[ing] whether my frock was clean or dirty." And before concluding, she begs her mother for a dress, desiring, perhaps, another item touched by a loved one's hands. "I wish you would send me a pretty frock this summer," Elizabeth writes, asking for the garment to be relayed through the chain of people who owned and managed her family. She signed the missive, "Farewell, darling mother. Your affectionate daughter, Elizabeth Keckley." Keckley could write, a rare skill, and yet literacy could not save her from the cruelty of a system that devalued her as a person.[66]

In this note that Elizabeth knew would be read by slaveholders, she told her mother about a dress she had been gifted, a dress she wanted, and a dress she was sewing ("the body and sleeves to make, and only one hour every night to work on it") but not about her "griefs and misfortunes," revealed years later in her narrative, that could "fill ten pages." Keckley did not disclose the "torture" she had suffered under the reign of Burwell, a Presbyterian minister, and his vindictive wife. Intent upon having her strong will broken, the minister placed her in the household and under the authority of Mr. Bingham, "the village schoolmaster," a "hard, cruel man." When the schoolmaster coolly declared, for no reason Elizabeth could fathom, "I am going to whip you . . . take down your dress this instant," she refused, attempting to protect her privacy as "a woman in full development" ordered to disrobe before a man who had promised to assault her. She recounts in her narrative how she "resisted with all [her] strength" while the schoolmaster "succeeded in binding [her] hands and tearing [her]dress from [her] back." Our review of this scene will close here, before the worst of Elizabeth's sufferings, which she chose to keep from the mother who could not protect her. The ripped raiment and torn pride that Elizabeth bore were scars she carried alone.[67]

We do not know if that summer frock Elizabeth Keckley requested ever arrived, only that she was surely seeking a different, deeper kind of cover when she asked her mother for a dress. We do know that Elizabeth would develop her mother's knack for the craft; years later, she proudly reported: "I had acquired something of a reputation as a dress-maker." Talking of dresses, making dresses, and donning the self-defense of dresses was a balm for enslaved women's sufferings, sorrows, and sullied

The Keckley Quilt (1862–80). This quilt is thought to have been made by Elizabeth Keckley from silk scraps of Mary Todd Lincoln's dresses. Sprays of flowers, eagles, and baskets of fruit frame a blue-and-yellow mosaic design, with a richly textured eagle in flight in the center. The word LIBERTY is spelled in gold letters below the eagle. According to quilt historian Ricky Clark, quilt collector and quilt historian Ruth Finley attributed this quilt, which she then owned, to Elizabeth Keckley in a 1954 lecture titled "Quilts." Finley said this quilt "pieced of Mrs. Lincoln's dresses" was "a personal gift from Mrs. Keckley to Mrs. Lincoln, who used it as a counterpane on her bed at the White House. As such—a personal gift—Mary Lincoln took it with her when she left after her husband's assassination—left with Lizzie Keckley to companion her shattered health and broken life." Image courtesy of the Kent State University Museum; photograph by Joanne Arnett.

dreams. Their decorous apparel, sewn by hands intent on surviving "the lowest yet," was raiment rolled in blood.[68]

Amid the gloom of slavery, women like Rose and girls like Ashley recaptured the beauty of color and shape that brought pleasure and dignity to their lives. But the initiative Black women took in their dress angered some white slaveholding women, who recognized the silent affront to their authority. In Charleston, a woman named Silla "was only allowed to wear such dresses as her mistress described," according to the formerly enslaved man Sam Aleckson, who depicted her in his autobiography. But Silla was "fond of dress" and had access to material provided by an enslaved brother. Silla, also a devout Methodist, labored secretly at night to sew "a beautiful dress made in the latest style, a rich mantilla, and a bonnet that was not inexpensive." With the permission of their owners, unfree people could choose among a range of Christian services on Sunday morning: Episcopalian, Anglican, Congregational, Catholic, Presbyterian, Baptist, Lutheran, and more. Those in Jewish households may have attended Beth Elohim Synagogue with their owners on Saturdays. Enslavers who believed in a paternalistic approach to chattel bondage thought religion could be employed to temper the behavior of their slaves while at the same time allowing these owners to demonstrate proper kindness and guidance. The Methodist meeting, which permitted a greater degree of expressiveness in worship, was popular with enslaved people in early- and mid-nineteenth-century Charleston.[69]

However, Silla's mistress only allowed the people she owned to attend her house of worship. Silla broke two rules when she glided into the Methodist church looking so fine that Sunday morning. She returned to the mistress's house late after the church service and tried to sneak in undetected in her lovely suit of clothes. But Charleston's walled estates were built for surveillance and containment, and the mistress, Octavia, had taken "her seat on the piazza which commanded a full view of the servants' entrance." She spied Silla and meted out immediate punishment, ordering Silla to set a fire and sacrifice her bonnet to it. The symbolic significance of the burning bonnet would not have been lost on either woman, as the bonnet was an "important" accessory, Emily Thornwell lectured in *The Lady's Guide*, "characterizing a lady's appearance." Octavia had never permitted Silla to wear a bonnet, forcing the enslaved maid to instead "have her head tied with a bandanna," a tag of servitude that the iconic Aunt Jemima character would famously wear less than a century later. Octavia concluded this vindictive spectacle with a command: "Go and take off those horrid things and never let me see you in them again." Silla's silent message of corporeal possession and personal expression had communicated clearly. Her mistress attempted to kill such dangerous inclinations and the self-worth—indeed, self-ownership—they signaled.[70]

Where they could not exert complete control, slaveholding mistresses such as Octavia disparaged Black women's fashion as outlandish because of its bright colors, contrasting patterns, and whimsical embellishments made of natural elements like gourds, cranberries, or animal horns. Fanny Kemble, a British actress who married into a family of wealthy rice planters on the Georgia coast, ridiculed the women on her new estate, noting: "Their Sabbath toilet really presents the most ludicrous combination of incongruities that you can conceive—frills, flounces, ribbons; combs stuck in their wooly heads . . . , finery, every color of the rainbow . . . chintzes with sprawling patterns . . . ; beads, bugles, flaring sashes, and, above all, little fanciful aprons."[71] Mary Boykin Chesnut, a South Carolina plantation mistress and senator's wife whose diary is a classic text for the study of elite white women's experiences in the Civil War South, did the same. Chesnut opined upon the garish state of slave women's dress, praising their drab everyday-wear in comparison to their personal Sunday concoctions: "The maids here dress in linsey-woolsey gowns and white aprons in the winter—and in summer, blue homespun. These deep blue dresses and white turbans and aprons are picturesque and nice looking. On Sundays their finery is excessive and grotesque. I mean their holiday, church, and outdoor getup."[72]

That mistresses saw Black women's independent designs as crude reflected an investment in the social hierarchy of dress. For surely Kemble and Chesnut realized that Black women were speaking out through these flamboyant outfits, expressing their right to personal worth as well as an aesthetic taste influenced by their African homelands. Black women's sartorial rebellion ripped through the cloth cages imposed by their owners. Rose may have hoped to capture some of this spirit when she put a dress in the sack for Ashley. From the tattered scraps of old dresses, from the shards of slavery's separations, Black women continued to care for themselves and others.

We have spoken of many dresses, but Rose had only one to give. Perhaps that single dress had been laundered over and over again, like the "little dress" saved by one formerly enslaved woman for a lifetime. Labeled "my little breeder" by her mistress but beloved by her mother, this woman, unnamed in an interview, wore the dress as a girl when her father died on a Civil War battlefield. For the speaker and her mother, both, that dress was entwined with the memory of him. After the woman's father was gone, her mother washed the dress weekly, until finally passing away. As the new caretaker of her childhood garment, the woman chose not to sew a visible rip she saw in the lace. This blemish reminded the woman of "going to her mother" in the dress as a child, the physical motion that had caused the original tear. "My mother been dead 44 years," the woman said to an interviewer after living many decades in freedom. "It gives me pleasure to look at this little dress."[73] The aged garment that had at first carried a memory of a deceased father now also bore a tie to her absent mother.

The torn dress Rose possessed and then gave to her daughter was probably made of coarse cotton or the linen-woolen blend characteristic of Negro cloth. If Rose was hired out by her own-

Printed floral skirt worn by Lucy Lee Shirley as a child. Collection of the Smithsonian National Museum of African American History and Culture, gift of the Black Fashion Museum, founded by Lois K. Alexander-Lane.

ers and permitted to retain a fraction of her income, she may have had the chance to purchase a fabric she favored. It is a guess more than fair, given the proficiency of enslaved women with the needle, that Rose sewed this garment for herself years before that fateful winter. Perhaps she had worn it over time, imparting to it a singular scent that only her child might recognize. And maybe there was another significance interwoven into the cloth that Rose was determined to pass down. We know from the stories of enslaved women that special items of apparel were not acquired without sacrifice.

"A tattered dress is a thousand things," my friend who sews her own wardrobe told me when I shared the words stitched onto the sack with her.[74] I think we sense this to be true of our own aged dresses that morph into many meanings and memories of intimate ties: a hope of happiness for the grandchild who marries in this same satin gown; a parent's loving look of pride frozen into a pink tulle tutu; a slave mother's final embrace, arms outstretched, then empty. This dress belonging first to Rose and then to Ashley—a fabric scar, a second skin, a shield— was a sign of women's lives frayed by slavery but nevertheless resplendent with beauty.

THE AUCTION BLOCK

I am going to tell you unwelcome truths, but I mean to speak those *truths in love.*

— ANGELINA GRIMKÉ, *Appeal to the Christian Women of the South,* 1836

Every day shows how many mansions were in this hell.

— HARRIET MARTINEAU, *Retrospect of Western Travel,* 1838

The auction block underwrote the purchase of pianos, wedding dresses, the education of slaveholding women and men, tours of Europe, northern vacations, the purchase of vacation homes, gifts to white children, marriage presents, and the maintenance of the slave society of the South.

— THAVOLIA GLYMPH, *The Women's Fight: The Civil War's Battles for Home, Freedom, and Nation,* 2020

HOW DID WE ARRIVE HERE, WITH THE MEMORY OF a tattered dress and yet another Black mother's daughter on an auction block? How did South Carolina become a place where the sale of a colored child was not only possible but probable? The answer lies in the willingness of an entire society to bend its shape around a set of power relations that structured human exploitation along racial lines for financial gain. While vending Black people to underwrite material pleasures, South Carolina sold its soul. As we explored in a previous chapter, by the onset of the American Revolution, Charleston had built a culture of luxurious living and conspicuous wealth from slave-produced rice profits.

Unlike in Jamestown, Virginia, or the younger Savannah, Georgia, enslaved African people had been present in South Carolina since the colony's fledgling first year and made up most of the population by 1710. By 1820, the pattern of a Black majority had spread into the interior "middle country" of the state, where cotton planters joined the ricing elite in rampant slave-holding and political power grabbing. This demographic imbalance set Carolina apart from all other colonies and states.[1] The sizable Black population, shaped by the international slave trade, as well as the natural increase in Black families, fueled agricultural production and the frenzied exchanges of Black people for cash, mortgages, and bonds. Society here was shaped and supported by "the most undemocratic political structure in the Union."[2] South Carolina's history, punctuated by the sale of little children, might be read as a cautionary tale about how a self-centered ruling class could rely on racial prejudice in the service of unchecked capitalism and to the detriment of moral character.

Charleston's tolerance for racial exploitation was fully on display. Visitors commented on the contrast between white opulence and Black diminishment that fed and was sustained by a culture of human sale. Adam Hodgson, a British businessman, was dumbstruck by Charleston's extremes during a tour of North America in 1819. He exclaimed in his travelogue published a few years later: "The real plague-spot of Charleston is its slave population; and the mixture of gaiety and splendor, with misery and degradation, is too incongruous not to arrest the attention even of the superficial. It reminded me of the delicate pink peach-blossoms which surround the black hovels of the slaves on the plantations." Harriet Martineau drew similar conclusions after her 1834 visit, commenting in an unveiled critique: "Charleston is the place to see those contrasting scenes of human life brought under the eye which moralists gather together for the purpose of impressing the imagination." Martineau then described a "slave market" into which she was "plunge[d]" while strolling about the streets. She observed Black mothers with babies, as well as children alone, being hawked by the "restless, jocose zeal of the auctioneer who counted the bids." After watching a boy of eight or nine who "shrunk" in "helplessness and shame" when ordered to stand on the auction block, Martineau "entered a number of fine houses" where she was "presented with flowers and entertained with lively talk." This contrast, to Martineau, was abominable. "If there be a scene which might stagger the faith of the spirit of Christianity itself," she declared, "if there be an experience which might overthrow its serenity, it is the transition from the slavemarket to the abodes of the slavemasters, bright with sunshine, and gay with flowers, courtesies, and mirth." Both Hodgson and Martineau captured Charleston as a city characterized by flowers fertilized by the ugly practice of human captivity. In this socially sanctioned split between the sellers and the salable, Martineau charged, "All intercourse lost its innocence."[3]

MANSIONS IN HELL

Charleston was, indeed, no innocent. As a pivotal international port, Charleston both received hundreds of thousands of Africans and Afro-Caribbeans and dispatched Indigenous slaves to the West Indies. Charleston became, at the same time, a redistribution center for internal slave sales among American colonies and, later, states. Following the United States prohibition of the international importation of slaves that took effect in 1808, Charleston continued as a "hub of human trafficking," attracting sellers and buyers from the southern interior. Slaveholders from the border states of Virginia, Maryland, and Delaware were losing productivity on depleted lands, so they sold masses of enslaved people through Charleston to the newly seized lands of the Deep South, wrested from Cherokee, Creek, Choctaw, Chickasaw, Natchez, and other Indigenous people in the throes of federal Indian removal from the 1810s through the 1840s. From the early 1700s through the mid-1800s, Charleston was a primary slave trade portal, eventually losing ground to New Orleans and Richmond, Virginia, in domestic trafficking numbers in the nineteenth century, but consistently ranking among the top few sites of human import and export.[4]

The presence of enslaved Indigenous people and, increasingly, enslaved Africans, fueled a roaring economy and shaped the flamboyant local identity of the Lowcountry super-rich. In wealth, manners, and reputation for high-minded sociality along

"Slave Sale, Charleston, South Carolina. From a sketch by Eyre Crowe," *Illustrated London News* (November 29, 1856), collected in vol. 29, July–December 1856 (London: William Little, [1857]), 555.

the lines of English gentry, Charlestonians surpassed all other southern city dwellers. By the early 1800s, Charleston slaveholders possessed 82 percent of the city's wealth, and most loans in South Carolina were secured with slaves as collateral.[5] Charlestonians rolled in financial returns from interests in slave production, slave sales and mortgages, and cotton land speculation to the west. They flaunted their glamorous lifestyle, too, erecting manor homes like Robert Martin's, swaddling themselves in imported textiles, draping their wives and daughters in jewelry, and likening their society to ancient Greece and Rome.[6]

Charleston had reached its economic apex prior to the American Revolution. War damage and fluctuations in the financial markets (especially a decrease in cotton prices in 1819 and a national financial panic in 1837) disrupted the city's so-called golden age of the 1700s.[7] This downward turn in the early 1800s was the period in which Rose was probably born. But decades after this decline, the town still glowed with the bronzed patina of old money. Fanny Kemble, the English actress married into a Georgia planter family, first visited Charleston in 1838 and marveled at the town's elegant aspect:

> The appearance of the city is highly picturesque, a word which can apply to none other of the American towns; and although the place is certainly pervaded with an air of decay, it is a genteel infirmity, as might be that of a distressed elderly gentlewoman. It has none of the smug mercantile primness of the Northern cities, but a look of state, as of quondam wealth and importance, a little gone down in the world, yet remembering still its former dignity.[8]

New England writer Frederick Law Olmsted commented similarly, if less loquaciously, about his visit in the 1850s:

"Charleston, more than any town at the North, has the character of an old town, where careful government and the influence
of social organization has long been in operation." The "careful
government" to which Olmsted referred, as well as the "social
organization," operated in tandem to keep enslaved people subject to the will of wealthy white overlords.[9]

By the 1850s, after Rose had given birth to Ashley, Carolina
was once again scaling the heights of slave-produced profit.
Money flowed into planters' pockets and merchants' coffers not
only from rice but also from cotton, the crop that had spurred
the industrial revolution in England. After Eli Whitney's invention of a machine that revolutionized the efficient separation of
the fiber from the seed in 1793, cotton production and profits
had soared. As mentioned in chapter 2, planters along the southeastern coast had begun cultivating a silky, long-grain variety of
the plant called sea island cotton in the 1790s. Would-be planters like Martin who were not aristocracy but hoping to become
wealthy enough to join the old coastal clans' social set moved
inland in greater numbers during the first decades of the 1800s
to raise short-staple cotton, the basic stuff of the lion's share of
global textile production.[10]

Slavery continued to underwrite the wealth of this place, and
most free white residents discounted the immorality of it by insisting that Black people were inferior and therefore destined to
serve others. They told themselves that this unequal system actually bettered the lives of the enslaved. Abolitionist Angelina
Grimké described the internal contradiction of slave society in
an 1829 diary entry. After tracing the travails of a Black boy,
John, who had run away because of a whipping threatened by
her own brother, Grimké sharply observed: "O, who can paint
the horrors of slavery & yet so hard is the natural heart that I am
continually told that their situation is very good, much better

than that of their owners." When Grimké "pled the case of humanity" in defense of the fearful boy, she elicited her brother's rage.[11] But gain built on suffering produced an excess of risk, a reality white Charlestonians keenly felt, betraying their actual understanding of tense racial relations. Here, the glitz was shadowed by what Harriet Martineau called a "moral gloom." This gloom "oppress[ed] the spirit of the stranger" in Charleston and fomented the discomfort of residents who were "never content" in a "society . . . composed of two classes, which entertain a mortal dread of each other."[12]

The presence of a mistreated and commodified Black majority fed anxiety among white elites, who built an elaborate apparatus of surveillance and punishment between the late 1700s and early 1800s to cauterize resistance and ensure compliance. The only way to compel submission was through force—the force of physical violence, the force of psychological threat, the force of intimidating brick, stone, and iron environments. Charleston constructed an "architecture of racial control" made up of private homes surrounded by high walls, as we have seen, and municipal watchtowers and workhouses.[13] City officials fostered a pseudo-militarization of public space consisting of a hired slave patrol that harassed Black people who were out on the streets without written passes or after curfew or who failed to display the "slave badges" required by law for unfree people hired out by their owners to work for others in the city. Following a thwarted rebellion organized by formerly enslaved carpenter Denmark Vesey in 1822, city leaders ordered the construction of a military-grade arsenal stocked with weaponry and manned by soldiers (where the Citadel military college campus stands today).[14] This is the intimidating infrastructure that Frederick Law Olmsted would make special note of in his travelogue, highlighting the "frequent drumming . . . the citadel, the guard-house . . . the

The Charleston Work House jail. Image published by S. T. Souder, 263 King Street (between 1870 and 1890?). Library of Congress.

frequent parades of militia . . . and especially the numerous armed police, which is under military discipline."[15]

Charleston also fine-tuned government-run programs of torture, which slave owners could access for a price. By the early 1800s, the city had institutionalized the violent correction of unfree people in a local holding facility known as the Work House. The development of the Work House as a notorious site of slave punishment, known to city residents, country planters, and abolitionists in the North, had occurred gradually over time. Built in 1738 on the outskirts of the city and originally intended to house impoverished white people who would work for their keep, as well as white elderly and disabled people, the Charleston Work House later took on a punitive and racial cast. In the mid-1700s, so-called criminals and people with illnesses were consigned to the Work House alongside the "worthy" poor, as the facility served various functions.[16] When white residents complained about the mixed cohabitation of whites, Blacks, the needy, and criminal detainees there, the city funded a separate building on the extensive existing four-acre lot at the intersection of Magazine and Queen streets for the "confinement and correction" of "fugitive seamen, runaway slaves, vagrants, and disorderly people." In piecemeal fashion, the city was creating what amounted to a multipurpose social services and imprisonment campus. In 1768, this new facility, located on the same large lot as the home for the poor and elderly and a hospital, was used to incarcerate accused criminals of all races. The criminal corrections facility, which became known by the same name as the whole complex—the Work House— was destroyed in 1780 in a Revolutionary War battle, leading city officials to temporarily rent a sugar factory for the housing and punishment of criminals. By 1783 a rebuilt structure in the original workhouse complex was holding an inmate population skewed toward enslaved Black people. Revamped city management in 1839 tightened operations such that the Work House operated primarily as a punishment center for slaves but still functioned as a punitive facility for miscreants of any race picked up by the city guard. Here, the major objective would be the "correcting of slaves," and the warden's first duty was to oversee whippings.[17] Enslavers in the city and on surrounding rural estates, such as Middleton Place, could send owned people who displeased them to this facility and relieve themselves of meting out messy corporal punishment. Work House wardens whipped and flayed unfree people for a charge, based on set prices.[18]

As the holdover name announced, forced work was an integral part of the punishment package. Inmates were made to perform hard labor under the threat of still more whipping. City planners innovated in order to make punishment pay bigger dividends. Starting in 1825, wardens at the Work House directed enslaved inmates to power a massive milling wheel. Women and men marched on the treadmill that turned the mill for nearly eight hours a day, with breaks of only a few minutes each, whips tearing at their backs, faced with the constant risk that their limbs might get caught in the metal spokes and ripped from them. On the wheel, enslaved people cracked whole ears of corn, which the city then sold.[19] Charleston earned doubly from the suffering of enslaved people: fees collected from owners and profits procured for milled corn. Meanwhile, planters and urban dwellers called this system of punishment "being sent for a little sugar."[20] The childlike euphemism obfuscated the cruelty and perhaps even sadism while hearkening back to the temporary period when the Work House had been housed in a sugar factory after the previous building burned down. This was southern gothic horror made real, reflecting an inner commitment to blind profiteering at Charleston's civic and moral core.[21]

Carolina rice and cotton elites carried the banner of an American brand of authoritarianism that we like to forget ever existed. Despite the principles of equality and liberty espoused by the American Revolution, South Carolinians—or, at least, the ones who wrote laws and wielded whips—reestablished a long-held "norm of inequality" even as northern states intro-

Old Charleston Jail, north side. This dilapidated structure is now a tourist attraction and the purported location of ghost sightings. Photograph by Michael Rivera via Wikimedia Commons, 2019.

duced gradual emancipation laws and mid-Atlantic states loosened manumission requirements. Slavery was just too lucrative for powerful Carolinians to relinquish. The norm of inequality, influenced by English aristocratic roots and undergirded by slavery, penetrated electoral politics in the state, where only privileged white men had formal influence.

From their seat of economic power in Charleston and political authority in Columbia (which succeeded Charleston as capital in 1786), Carolina "planter-politicians" presided over the most undemocratic society ever sustained in this country, a society where patriarchal ideology fueled oligarchy, the rule of a few wealthy men from old, aristocratic families. Here, super-rich slaveholders "monopolized not only state but also local offices." They controlled the bodies of slaves and wives, as well as all posts in the governor's mansion and statehouse. They directed elections and government operations to the extent that South Carolina became "the only state in the Union that did not have a two-party system or popular elections for the presidency, the governor, and a host of state and local offices." Instead, candidates for key offices (including presidential electors) were appointed by the state legislature, which was dominated by planters, due to large minimum land requirements, and, in the case of state representatives, minimum slave property requirements.[22] South Carolina was, as many historians and commentators have pointed out, an exaggerated version of the undemocratic slaveholding South and typified its ambition to maintain an extreme gap between the (all-white) haves and the (mostly colored) have-nots in the right to life, liberty, and enjoyment. In that gap lay the fate of thousands of Black children, whose existences, and the quality of all the days of their young lives, would be deemed expendable.

SAYING HER NAME

Except that she will wind up sold, a victim of the auction block, Ashley's lyrical name is nearly all we know about her. Ashley (an uncommon name for enslaved people in the Carolinas and for women of any race in eighteenth- and nineteenth-century America) was usually reserved for Anglo men like Anthony Ashley Cooper, the lord proprietor who championed English settlement in Carolina and became the namesake of the two rivers that formed Charleston's peninsular arch.[23] Might Rose's daughter have been named for a river that was named for a man whose venture inaugurated Carolina slavery? And who would bestow such a name on an enslaved baby girl in the decades before the Civil War?

Enslavers tended to name their human property in ways that reaffirmed their own status and authority while simultaneously demeaning the people named. The result was a denial of enslaved people's surnames, a slew of personal names that were the shortened form of European names (like Beck, Harry, or Jenny), names more fitting for household pets (like Hero, Cupid, or Captain), and names reminiscent of classical figures (like Dido, Caesar, or Venus). The excision of surnames had the effect of rhetorically severing Black family lines, erasing rights of natal belonging, and denying maturity in adulthood. The bestowal of diminutive nicknames or cutesy pet names belittled recipients as perpetual children or domesticated animals rather than recognizing them as the subjects who would mature into their own lives. Enslavers also appreciated, perhaps, their own sardonic wit in naming people with little social power after characters with great cultural recognition. Every time a master or mistress called upon "Hercules," "Samson," or "Prince," they rubbed enslaved people's noses in the shame of their assigned inferiority.[24]

In subtle and sometimes secret opposition, kin to unfree children also gave babies names. These affectionate appellations were sometimes known as "basket names." Parents bestowed honor names after family members, both living and dead. Loved ones called children by names derived from African languages (like Affy, Quanimo, or Mingo), or by names for the day or season when a child was born, or for meaningful places. Although the precision of "day names" (that is, a practice in which a person born on a certain day, such as Friday, was called some derivation of Pheba or Phoebe) and of seasonal names (children called September, for instance, if born in that month) was fading by the nineteenth century, the names themselves continued to be popular (in that a baby born in winter might be called Autumn). These Black cultural practices of naming stood against the names of "contempt" chosen by enslavers, and are revealed by the many individuals named Monday, April, November, February, July, May, Autumn, and Winter in the records of South Carolina planters.[25] Though it wasn't as common as using day names and seasonal names, Black relatives also named children after places, like Boston, Africa, or Paris.[26] Calling a child Ashley after a nearby river would parallel this practice. Still, we know nothing conclusive. Rose's Ashley may have been named by the Martins to reflect her lowly status as a child for whom the English name Ashley was humorously ill-fitting, or Ashley may well have carried a place-name given by a loved one of African descent. Such were the complex cultural filaments of what, borrowing from Harriet Jacobs, we might call the "tangled skeins" of slavery.[27]

From her unusual name, we gather not only the complexity of Ashley's cultural context but also the greater circumstantial evidence indicating that she was born in the vicinity and environs of Charleston.[28] But as a form of legal "movable property," Ashley could and would be transported far from the place of her birth. The Ashley whose name appears in Robert Martin's estate inventory would spend most of her life in the South Carolina interior, more than a hundred miles distant from the coast. As a young child, Ashley was likely separated from her mother, Rose, and installed on the Martins' cotton estate, Milberry Place Plantation, in the "middle country" district of Barnwell, South Carolina. The estate inventory of 1853, our single source for Ashley's location, lists owned people on the premises by family groupings.[29] The word "family," though, takes multiple shapes and forms, especially in the stained documents of slavery.

The use of the term "one family" as an organizing schema on the Martins' slave register reflects as much or more about slaveholder conceptions and priorities (such as how to measure "increases among their slaves and allocate rations") as it does about enslaved people's notions of kin.[30] This list may have reflected biological ties among the Black residents at Milberry as perceived by the Martins or their estate manager, and these biological links might have been first compelled by the Martins through arranged, but legally unrecognized, slave "marriages" and coerced sexual relations (crudely referred to by some owners as "breeding"). Or "one family" could have reflected unrelated individuals assigned to reside together in the slave cabins of the quarters. It may also—or alternatively—have reflected clusters of close-knit people called kin by one another, whether biological or socio-emotional (as in adopted family or "fictive kin"). We cannot conclude from this record that enslaved family units were actual or sustained on the Milberry plantation, nor can we assume that strong family units and prolonged family ties were impossible there. Some plantation owners did structure or encourage the formation and enlargement of intact family units, while others routinely or sporadically separated Black family members through sale.

Robert Martin's financial records indicate that he sold people singly, but he also may have recognized, and to a certain extent preserved, African American family groupings. Ashley is included in this line on the Martin estate inventory: "Toney 100, Vinney 50, Mary 500, Emma 500, Ashley 300, Levy 250— —one family 1700." It is plausible that Toney and Vinney were elderly grandparents to Mary, Emma, Ashley, and Levy, given the low monetary values ascribed by the auditor.[31] At $500 each, Mary and Emma would have been young women in their prime, likely appointed to labor in the cotton fields. Ashley and Levy's values, set at $300 and $250, suggest that they were children old enough to perform discrete tasks but too young for heavy cotton-picking quotas. Was Rose once part of this unit—daughter to Toney and Vinney, sister to Mary and Emma, and mother to Ashley—plucked from there to serve in the Charleston manor house? Or did Robert Martin purchase her expressly for use in the urban mansion, due to her youth, pleasing appearance, or domestic skills with the needle or cookpot? If Rose was procured for service in the city, and if she gave birth to Ashley in Charleston, her daughter may have been transplanted to the country estate and lodged with other enslaved family members. Ashley could have been biologically related to those listed with her as "one family" or linked through relations of care that made kin out of blood strangers. If Ashley was born in Charleston and taken from Rose at an early age, she would have been far from her birth mother when absorbed into Toney and Vinney's clan, and she would have lost an extended circle of care when placed on the auction block following Robert Martin's death.

An auction block was a real thing. We sometimes forget this.

Stone auction block. Collection of the Smithsonian National Museum of African American History and Culture, partial gift of Mr. and Mrs. Sean P. Guy. This artifact, from Hagerstown, Maryland, was on display beside Ashley's sack at the time of this writing.

We allow the physicality of a rock worn smooth by time and the press of bare, stolen feet to slip from our awareness. But these mundane things—a concrete block, a wooden set, a hollow stump—were props for the ritual dehumanization of a people. Much like the "uniform" of Negro cloth, the auction block set a group apart in order to lower their social status and justify their contemptuous treatment. The rock or stump functioned like a department store window where "the human-commodity is put on display," raised up and set apart.[32] The auction block's structuring presence made one thing clear: if you were someone who could be treated to the indignity of sale, then you were barely a person at all. The Black men, women, and children framed as separate and rendered as passive became seeable, touchable, and testable by any buyer with the means to enter the market. And those buyers looked to purchase not only Black people but also an idea of themselves as richer, more powerful, more virile, and kinder.[33] With the promise of irresistible pecuniary payoffs and psychological dividends, first-time buyers and experienced collectors invested small fortunes to acquire slaves. By the early 1800s, these transactions had grown into an industry complete with traders, investors, accountants, warehouses, private showrooms, and painted company shingles dangling outside the slave mart door.

In the decades before the Civil War, cotton agriculture underwent changes that thrust hundreds of thousands of African Americans onto auction blocks. Technological innovation (the cotton gin) sped up processing potential and introduced new and brutal forms of punishment (like whippings in the cotton rows for slower pace of movement). And as the price of cotton spiked in these decades (with a plunge in the late 1830s and 1840s followed by recovery), easy credit circulated through local networks, national banks, and foreign entities for the purchase of the one thing that kept the whole raucous venture rolling: Black people in pain.[34]

From the perspective of a Black family made more vulnerable by the growth of the cotton industry, the 1850s would have been a terrible time for an owner to die, potentially thrusting the family members into the market. This decade marked the height

of westward-bound cotton frenzy and spikes in the capital value
of slaves. If a master or mistress saw reversals of health or fortune
at this moment, Black families would, more likely than not, suf-
fer the heartbreak of separation. In the years just before the Civil
War, more than two million unfree women, men, and children
were yanked from their home places and thrown into a whirling
market that landed them elsewhere in their states or across state
lines.[35] Ashley was one of them.

Most traffic in the domestic slave trade was heading westward
into the fertile lands of interior South Carolina and Georgia, Alabama, Mississippi, Louisiana, Arkansas, and Missouri, made plentiful as a result of violent Indigenous expulsion. Enslaved people
sent "down the river" toward the Mississippi Delta would face a
kind of slavery much worse, if such a thing can be imagined, than
the variety they had suffered in the established eastern rice and
tobacco zones. In these southwestern "frontier" lands where newcomers to the slaveholding classes sought fortunes in cotton, the
established customs of eastern formality and restraint, such as
they were, fell away. Landholders tried to squeeze more labor out
of their owned humans with as little additional financial input as
possible. The urban context of Charleston, while characterized
by surveillance and the threat of state-sponsored punishment,
had at least imposed expectations of social acceptability. As slavery moved west, living quarters were more squalid; food rations
were smaller and less varied; "free" time was reduced; and violent corrections increased. When cotton fetched astronomical
prices and credit flowed like water, white owners looked upon
Black workers as crop-producing, slave-baby-birthing, wealth-
making machines, denying them even the modest allowances or
concessions that had been customary along the coastline.

The middle zone of South Carolina, between the coast and

the mountainous piedmont region near the Georgia border, lay in the direct path of slavery's expansion and had provided the first spaces of new white-owner and Black-slave settlement. These had been the homelands of the Cherokee and Creek nations, whose grounds spanned Carolina, Georgia, and Alabama prior to the pressured signing of treaties in the 1820s and the passage of the Indian Removal Act under President Andrew Jackson in 1830. Rice did not thrive here; nor did sea island cotton. Short-staple cotton became the lucrative mass crop. The Savannah and Edisto rivers, together with a net of swift streams and stagnant swamps, cut through this flat land, forested with pines and poplars.[36] A traveler passing through the Barnwell District, where Robert Martin owned land, in 1843 glumly described "the forest of gigantic long-leaved pine" that possessed "a beauty & even sublimity which is rarely surpassed" but lamented that the trees were being exposed to "useless & unprofitable destruction." Many of these pine trees, on tracts disparaged as "pine barren" by landowning settlers, would be felled by the edge of the blade and the bulk of enslaved people's muscle amid sweltering summer heat.[37]

This was the future Ashley faced in inland South Carolina, along with the other captives on the Martins' premises. Following Robert Martin's passing, Milberry Serena Martin began liquidating the family estate "for the purpose of Partition," as required by the terms of her late husband's will as well as lawsuits brought against the estate by his former business colleague.[38] She sold her namesake plantation in Barnwell (the 2,951-acre estate was later recovered and occupied by her son Robert Martin, Jr.), as well as a hotel and several land lots in the railroad town of Aiken, located in the Barnwell District. She also sold various lots in Charleston and along the wharf to several buyers, including the city of Charleston, her son-in-law Joseph Aiken, and the slave trader Thomas Gadsden.[39] It was this virtual big tent sale, a whirling dervish of court appearances and property transactions presided over by Milberry Martin, that sealed the fate of the people she owned.

Ashley, at just nine years old, must have been gathered up in this squall of the Martin household transformation, after which her mother, Rose, was lost to her. But what can this kind of senseless, existential break have meant for a real, living child? It is nearly impossible for many of us to fathom. Elizabeth Keckley, who eventually purchased her freedom through sewing, recalled childhood emotions upon the division of her family that we cannot adequately convey. "The announcement fell upon the little circle in that rude-log cabin like a thunderbolt," Keckley remembered when recounting the separation from her father, who was being moved west by his owner. "The shadow eclipsed the sunshine, and love brought despair. The parting was eternal. . . . We who are crushed to earth with heavy chains, who travel a weary, rugged, thorny road, groping through midnight darkness on earth, earn our right to enjoy the sunshine in the great hereafter."[40]

Being yanked by shaking limb into the void of parental separation was "crushing" for the young Elizabeth Keckley. After experiencing it, and in recalling the hollow moment, Keckley's mind sought solace in the relief of death. It is possible that forced separation of the still living was worse in its toll on the spirit than actual death, which at least allows for psychological closure.[41] Memories of being sold away burned holes into the psyches of unfree children. They could recount the chilling details of these episodes—the sights, smells, and feelings of terror—long into elderhood. For Louisa Picquet, the enslaved woman from South Carolina who moved to Ohio after her owner freed her upon his death, the moment of her sale away from her mother and brother never faded in intensity. When asked by an interviewer, "It seems like a dream, don't it?," Picquet replied, "No; it seems fresh in my memory when I think of it—no longer than yesterday. Mother was right on her knees, with hands up, prayin' to the Lord for me. . . . I often thought her prayers followed me, for I never could forget her."[42]

The only kind of love an enslaved child could know was laced with despair, and this they learned early from their parents. Fanny Kemble, the English actress who married into a Georgia planter family, also noticed how loss colored enslaved people's affect. "I have observed this pathetic expression of countenance in them, a mixture of sadness and fear," Kemble penned. "The involuntary exhibition of the two feelings, which I suppose must be the predominant experience of their whole lives, regret and apprehension, not the less heavy, either of them, for being, in some degree, vague and indefinite—a sense of incalculable past loss and injury, and a dread of incalculable future loss and injury."[43] Children held captive to slavery suspected that loss and inordinate grief would come for them in ways they could not predict. These little children, like their mothers, dwelled in a state of crushing uncertainty. They overheard parents, grandparents, and adoptive loved ones fretting and fearing visits from body snatchers whose actions were legal. Starting around the age of ten, when the thin veneer of maturity dawns, a child began to understand what she was to slave society: "a person with a price."[44]

Finding herself on the auction block of the private parlor or public street, a child strove to withstand assaults to bodily privacy and human dignity. But this was impossible for children—boys as well as girls—as they heard themselves and people like them, including loved ones, referred to by animalistic and pejorative names: "bucks," "wenches," "breeders," or "fancies." For

Black women and girls, this virulent form of degradation meant routine exposure to violation, as shoppers touched the private parts of women's bodies and had license to take them behind curtains or into private rooms to "inspect" the "goods" more closely. Buyers also had the option to take women off-site for trial-period test runs, even as the traders who procured, stored, polished, and displayed enslaved girls and women had access to their captive bodies at all points along the way of the chain of sale.[45]

Ashley would be here, among these girls and women auctioned as things even as they were subject to the most human of bodily abuses. She may have been transferred to other hands inside a private home in the country or sold to a trader who would transport her miles west on foot. But it is more likely that Ashley suffered examination and sale in the city of Charleston, a two-to-three-day journey from Milberry Place.[46] Hawkers and purveyors of people in Charleston conducted sales on the street outside of the Old Exchange Building (or Customs House) until 1856, when a city code required them to move indoors for the sake of propriety. This regulation led to the establishment in 1859 of Ryan's Mart, an enclosed slave sale showroom with jail-like pens out back (preserved today as the Old Slave Mart Museum on Chalmers Street).[47] Adam Hodgson, the English traveler, was one witness among several to describe the sight of a Charleston slave auction:

> Turning from a fashionable promenade, enlivened by gay parties and glittering equipages, I came suddenly in sight of at least 80 or 100 Negroes sitting on a large heap of paving stones. . . . Several merchants and planters were walking about, examining the unhappy creatures who were to be offered for sale. A poor woman, apparently about 29 years of

age, with a child at her breast, her two little boys, from four
to six years old, and her little girl, about eight, composed *the
first lot*.[48]

At the end of his lengthy description, which continues beyond
this heartbreaking moment, Hodgson castigates the domestic
trade in people.

Ashley was not alone in this grueling passage on the block,
but, even surrounded by others who shared her circumstances,
she must have been emotionally isolated. We might picture her
clutching a grimy cotton sack with all her mother had to give
stowed away inside its folds. She might even have used that
swath of cloth as a shield from probing stares, like a teenaged
girl named Adeline, also sold in South Carolina, on the steps of
the Columbia courthouse. Described by an eyewitness as possessing a "pleasing countenance" and holding a "light-colored,
blue eyed, curly-silked-haried [*sic*] child," Adeline was dressed
in a hooded cloak, which she struggled to keep in place over her
head and infant son. The auctioneer, intent on moving the sale
of a girl "only 18 years old, and already . . . [with] a child" along,
repeatedly drew down the hood to highlight Adeline's attrac-
tions. Vulnerable and terrified under the glare of lust and greed,
Adeline waged a silent contest with the auctioneer to maintain
her cover. Ashley's sack, versatile in its material makeup, could
also have been used like a curtain, a means of creating physical
and psychological distance between a girl and her purveyor.[49]
Even on the stage of the auction block, the things enslaved people could sometimes carry brought a measure of self-protection.

How could Ashley preserve an oversized sack amid the unrelenting conditions of sale and transport? The observations of on-
lookers and testimony of formerly enslaved people tell us that
some were able to safeguard small tokens of past lives that

"helped them to remember: a pair of gloves worn by a dead mother; a small blanket, split with a sister," in the words of one prominent historian of slavery.[50] For Louisa Picquet, whose story we only began to learn in a previous chapter, the moment of sale at the auction block and the years of separation from her mother were marked by the presences and absences of physical tokens. We may recall her treasured white muslin dress. In the auction room, a "gentleman buyer" was offered the opportunity to "strip" Louisa for closer inspection. He purchased her for $1,500, while a Texan bought Louisa's mother and brother. She wanted to recover the garment, but "Mr. Williams," her new owner, refused. As Louisa watched her mother cry and pray for "the Lord to go with her only daughter, and protect [her]," Louisa's thoughts, disorganized by trauma, swam back to the muslin dress.

Louisa, a girl of around fourteen who had been shuttled from one sexual predator to another, reassured herself in the only way she knew how: by fixating on the white dress, still unstained by slavery, which she hoped her mother was saving to remember her by. During years of separation, Louisa's mother repeatedly attempted to contact her daughter, penning or dictating letters, some of which made it to New Orleans, though many got waylaid in a Texas post office. In a first letter that Louisa never received but learned about years later, her mother had enclosed "a ring also a button" for "my little grandchildren," the offspring of Louisa's concubinage to Williams.

Just as her daughter, Louisa, had wanted her to have the dress as a keepsake, Elizabeth sought to knit a connection with grandchildren she had never met through tokens of remembrance. Realizing that her daughter was installed as the "housekeeper" in Williams's home and may have had a degree of influence, Elizabeth begged Louisa to provide her with the small comforts of tea and sugar, and to convince Mr. Williams to buy her and her son so the family could be together. In a letter dated 1859, Louisa's mother relates a heartbreaking offer of what her master will take for her: "Col. Horton would let you have me for 1000 dol. or a woman that could fill my place. . . . I think you can change his Price by writing Kindly to him aske him in a kind manner to let you have me for less." The recognition of self as a commodity and the devaluation of one's worth is nearly unbearable in this passage. We feel, again, in this exchange between parent and child the unspeakability of slavery's humiliations and corrupted relationships. Worse, Louisa did not possess the wherewithal to help her desperate mother. Louisa's owner was not rich. He lived in a rented house and had borrowed money from his brother to buy her. "My feelings on this subject are in Expressible," Louisa's mother wrote in her appeal to be purchased. "I would giv this world to see you and my sweet little children."[51]

Louisa Picquet carried the memory of her mother with her through two decades of sexual slavery, during which time her master, with whom she had four children, threatened to kill her if she tried to escape. Louisa prayed that Williams would die, and eventually he did. But a master's death, though long desired, brought instability. Barely escaping Williams's brother's attempt to claim her, Louisa moved north and immediately launched a search for her mother. She took out an advertisement in the *Cincinnati Daily Gazette* newspaper, published her as-told-to memoir, delivered speeches across the region, and begged donations from churches and anti-slavery organizations. In the fall of 1860, Louisa succeeded in freeing her aged mother with the $900 she had raised. She learned, then, that her baby brother John's slips had indeed been made "of Louisa's pink dress bought with the half-dollars." The white muslin dress with the pink floral print had been taken up by her mother's hand

and refashioned for new use as a keeper of memories. Twined with a mother's love, the fabric of kinship sustained the wear and tear of slavery's assault.[52]

Ashley would not be like Louisa in finding and holding her mother again, but she did manage to hold on to an object as special as Louisa's dress. Ashley's sack—her emergency pack, her cloak, and cover, and shield of dignity—was also her memory stone in the trying times to come. She had in it an heirloom, property of her own, a thing nested with still more things and unfathomable uses. In her possession of this item, she shared a link not only with other enslaved people but also with American women regardless of race, since women rarely had rights to land until the twentieth century. "Movables formed the core of a female inheritance," wrote one eminent gender historian. "Women too used property to assert identities, build alliances, and reweave family bonds."[53]

Ashley carried the bag and, we can presume, most of its contents into the Carolina interior, where slaveholders (rice planters' sons, yeoman farmers, and new-money merchants seeking to make fortunes) were migrating from the coastline. There, in the uplands of Carolina and Georgia, planters and farmers started anew with land clearance and town-building projects, establishing plantations, mills, and eventually a railroad (in 1833) that would transport cotton back to the port city of Charleston. What began as a hinterland to coastal elites had exploded into a boom zone by the early 1800s.[54] Like the coastal world it grew out of, this society held slavery and agriculture at its center. The "Midlands," a swath of inland cotton plantations separated by vast acreages, was to be the place where Ashley matured and later had a family. Because her child and grandchild that we know of from the sack lived in Columbia, South Carolina, after the Civil War, we can assume that Ashley was sold to a plantation in the same region that also housed Milberry Place.[55] Her descendants lived in this inner zone of rural Cotton Belt South Carolina until the unpredictable wave of the first Great Migration carried Ruth Middleton northward to Philadelphia.

Ashley was sold not far from the world she had known as a young child. The fast-running rivers, the remaining stands of "magnificent" pines and the scarred soil where they used to grow, and the acres of ghostly white-blossomed cotton might have been hauntingly familiar.[56] She might have at first remained fairly close to her mother in terms of physical distance. But Rose may have been sold herself soon after Robert Martin's death. Between 1853 and 1857, a woman named Rose passed away in a Charleston slave pen owned by Thomas Gadsden, a man to whom Milberry Martin had sold land. Robert Martin himself had done business with Thomas Gadsden in the past, purchasing from him a woman named Betty and her four children in 1851.[57] It is not a stretch to wonder if, in a flurry of private property sales amid a regional slave-trade boom, Milberry Serena Martin requisitioned Rose into the hands of her family's associate, a known slave dealer.

The scenes of forced parting that shadow slave narratives are difficult for us to absorb as twenty-first-century readers. Vivid descriptions of fathers begging and mothers wailing as children cried out for rescue are almost too much for us to bear, even with the distance of time, which operates as our emotional shield. Although we might like to believe that slaveholders and slave traders strove to keep families intact, this was not universally, or even usually, the case. Children and teenagers, whose monetary values were boosted by youth and strength, were often sold singly between the peak years of the antebellum era. Because states like Louisiana and Alabama forbade the sale of individual children under ten, many more children than seems credible were listed as ten to twelve years of age in slave traders' business records.[58] In a culture devoid of moral values and in which they were financial assets, children like Ashley were hand-selected for victimization.

If we can hardly contend with the enormity of despair that characterized these thousands of partings, how would a child cope with the sudden loss of family? In our modern era, the experience of another class of severed children offers heart-wrenching insight. In 2018, the U.S. federal administration began arresting and incarcerating undocumented immigrants at the southern border. The policy called for detention of parents and children in different facilities—in many cases, in human cages—forcing their separation for weeks and months at a time. In some instances, our government deported parents while assigning children to foster care indefinitely. According to clinical psychologists who work with these children and research psychologists who assess collected data on their condition, separation severely impacts migrant youth, many of whom are members of families seeking political asylum from harm previously experienced in Latin American nations. The research, detailed in the American Psychological Association's public appeals to end this governmental policy, demonstrated an intensification of fear, a feeling of helplessness, and a sense of endangerment among these youths. Children taken away from their parents experienced increased symptoms of anxiety, depression, and post-traumatic stress disorder, enduring mental health effects "on par with beating and torture." The psychological well-being of these already fragile children shatters when they are deprived of parental care, requiring the understanding and intervention of behavioral health specialists and educators over a long term.[59]

As a girl born to live in perpetual captivity and then torn away from her mother a century and a half ago, Ashley shared, to a certain extent, the condition of a present-day migrant child seeking asylum. The state from which she came was one of extreme threat, and parental separation would only deepen her pain and terror. How could a child—how could so many children caught in the jaws of slavery's expansion—survive this ordeal of truncation? Where could a girl like Ashley turn for affirmation that life was worth living? We should not disillusion ourselves with the notion that full recovery was ever possible, or the idea that enslaved people did not carry psychic scars. But we can hope that in the wake of this severing, Ashley found in her mother's sack a kind of sanctuary.

"Told her," Ruth stitched onto the bag seventy years after the breach, "It be filled with my Love always. She never saw her again."

ASHLEY'S SEEDS

Real progress is growth. It must begin in the seed.
    —ANNA JULIA COOPER, *A Voice from the South,* 1892

For over 200 years we were told where to live and where to
work. We were given husbands, and we made children, and
all these things could be taken away from us. The only real
comfort came at the end of the day, when we took either the
food that we were given, or the food that we raised, or the
food that we had caught, and we put it in the pot, and we sat
with our own kind and talked and sang and ate.
    —RUTH GASKINS, *A Good Heart and a Light Hand: Ruth L.*
        Gaskins' Collection of Traditional Negro Recipes, 1968

Those who love us never leave us alone with our grief.
                —ALICE WALKER, Foreword, *Barracoon:*
                    The Story of the Last "Black Cargo," 2018

DID ASHLEY KNOW WHEN HER MOTHER WAS LOOSED
from the earth's moorings, carried off to some unknown realm
of spirit and light? Maybe she felt the shift inside her soul, the
way some sense that a storm is coming. But Rose, whose actions
demonstrate a planful nature, had not left her child to survive a
world of cold captivity alone. She must have believed that
whether she lived to see Ashley again or died before the two of

them could be reunited, the things she packed would aid and comfort her daughter for some time to come. Rose imagined Ashley, or even a multigenerational family line, continuing beyond the breach that occurred in 1853–54. Propelled by what Black feminist theorists Stanlie James and Abena Busia call a "visionary pragmatism," and in order to protect this radical vision of life sustained, Rose did something familiar to many mothers. She bundled extra food—and not just any food—into her care package.[1] The edible items she tucked inside bore out a dictum known to anyone enslaved: survival is rooted in the land.[2] Although Rose had no choice but to let Ashley go when their owners willed it, she released her child creatively provisioned with natural and cultural resources that seem to have made a difference—perhaps all the difference—in Ashley's capacity for resilience.

THREE HANDFULS OF PECANS

Rose left her daughter supplied with the basic things that might momentarily keep a small girl alive. Chief among these items, more fundamental than clothing or the physical cover that the sack itself might provide, was a bountiful serving of particularly nourishing and naturally preserved food. The unusual specificity of the phrase "three handfulls of pecans" comes to us through Ashley's story as stitched by Ruth onto the sack and captures a sense of sheer physicality in the act of measuring. We can imagine Rose in a kitchen testing the weight of the nuts in her hand, perhaps following a recipe she knew by heart, in Ashley's presence.[3] These words Ruth sewed connote the sense, too, of having been spoken aloud and repeated, even as the number three, perfectly exact and strangely parallel to our trinity of main-character women, seems to carry an echo. Rose's inclusion of a material that could serve as food or as seed suggests her awareness of nutritional necessity as well as future possibility. Seeds surely have secret lives unto themselves inside their husks, but to humans, their use points to a time beyond the present. We plant seeds with the hope, in the knowledge, that they will grow into something not yet existing in this world. The nuts Rose packed were useful things and also signs with more than one meaning. Even as they nourished Ashley physically and emotionally, they symbolized her ability to take root anew and to grow.

Here is a moment where we need to pull a thread in Ruth's inscription in order to loosen the weave. It is possible that Ruth misremembered the specific kind of nut Rose stored and that rather than pecans, Rose packed a more common nut, like chestnuts. If so, we might note that while distinct, the chestnut was similar to the pecan in terms of planting and culinary properties. If Rose did pack pecans specifically, as Ruth recorded, she could not have come by her private stash easily. In the 1850s, when Rose filled the sack, pecans were available in Charleston from only a few outlets. The harvested and cured nuts were delivered to the wharf by boat in barrels. They were a recent fixture in Charleston, too, having first arrived in 1832 from Texas. The natural habitat of the pecan was not the coastal Southeast but, rather, westerly riparian zones of Illinois, Louisiana, Texas, and northern Mexico. It was a delicacy deemed an "exotic import" in antebellum South Carolina, second in exoticism only to almonds.[4]

In Rose's day, access to pecans would have been limited in the Southeast. She would have obtained them from the wharf in the city, perhaps through bartering with another enslaved person but, more likely, at the direction of Milberry Serena Martin.

Pecans might have appeared on the Martins' dinner menu on an evening when they were hosting guests. In expensive Charleston restaurants of the 1840s and 1850s, chefs served pecans as delicacies in a pastry course that included fruit and other nuts. In comparison to the "exotic" pecan, harvested and cured hundreds of miles to the west, the American chestnut was more accessible, grown locally in the Carolinas.[5]

Pecans would have been all but out of reach for an enslaved mother in the Southeast whose worldly possessions consisted of not much more than a tattered dress. Though wild pecans were harvested in the southwestern and midwestern climes of the Mississippi River valley and its tributaries, in the 1850s pecan trees had not yet been widely cultivated or commercialized anywhere in the United States. The first pecan trees advertised for sale in Charleston did not appear in the print press until 1859.[6] By the 1860s, pecan trees were growing on Boone Hall Plantation, northeast of Charleston, but only because they had been carefully transplanted there. The owner, John Horlbeck, acquired cuttings from Louisiana and had them planted near the avenue of oaks that led to Boone Hall's grand entry. By the 1890s Horlbeck's grandson, who had enjoyed the plantation's nuts as a child, was pursuing the establishment of large pecan groves; his initiative helped turn the nut into a Lowcountry mainstay.[7]

Since she lived far to the east of their natural habitat, Rose would have had to be deliberate about getting her hands on so many of these delicacies. Even the idiosyncratic spelling of the word "handful" on the sack as "handfull" highlights Rose's feat of plenty (symbolically indicated by that extra *l*). Her access to this luxury food adds greater strength to the speculation that Rose worked in the Martin household as a cook. An image forms more readily now in our minds of Rose going marketing at the behest of the Martins while dressed in some checked or calico cloth, toting a basket on her head, in the custom of Black Charleston women, and returning from the crowded wharf with the basket full and a sack of pecans. Perhaps she had been instructed to use these nuts in some popular holiday dish, such as pecan-stuffed dates or fruitcakes.[8] We can imagine that she surreptitiously set aside a quantity as well, hoping to later provide a measure of secret pleasure for herself or loved ones.

It is likely not coincidence that Rose procured these pecans after Robert Martin's death, which occurred during winter's social season. Pecans can remain fresh for up to twelve months when stored in cool, dry places. And Ashley was "inventoried" less than a year after Martin passed away. The timing was right for Rose to have had these special nuts on hand, and access to the kitchen would have made it more possible for her to store them. Maybe these nuts were the first item Rose collected in the sack, with the dress, the braid, and her whispered feelings pressed in on top of them. Rose may even have bought pecans in the very bag we are tracing, which is of a type originally manufactured for agricultural use. For Rose, these salvaged nuts were among the ingredients of a recipe for survival. By choosing to pack pecans for her daughter, Rose bears a link to another enslaved craftsperson who made history through the work of his hands: the first recorded cultivator of the commercial pecan tree, known simply as Antoine.

METHODS OF FORCING

Just as they longed for a Black population who could be depended on to produce crops, goods, services, ideas, and more unfree people in the form of slave babies, southern plantation owners, who had been experimenting with agricultural innovation since the mid-1700s, wanted a pecan tree that could be counted on for consistency. By the early 1800s, elite agriculturalists were tinkering with grafting (or budding), trying to create an engineered pecan that would produce a consistent form, taste, and shell. This approach involved taking shoots ("scions" or "graftwoods") from the limbs of pecan trees producing ideal nuts and carefully merging them with branches of existing trees in desired locations, such as plantation acreage where they could be readily tended and harvested ("rootstocks").[9] The aim was for these hybrid trees to reliably produce the desired quality of nut—tasty, shapely, and easy to crack. The first experimenter credited with noteworthy results was Abner Landrum, a South Carolina plantation owner and physician already well known in his time for creating a method for glazing stoneware pottery without the use of lead. In the 1820s, Landrum made at least two attempts to graft pecans on his plantation in Edgefield, in the interior of the state. He explained his first unsuccessful trial as having been "made rather late in the season." He did better on the next occasion, reporting,"I have this summer budded some dozens of pecan on the common hickory nut, without a single failure as yet; and some of them are growing finely."[10] Landrum was proud of his efforts and detailed an account of his method in the trade serial *American Farmer*, so meticulously that he apologized for the length.[11]

The pecan tree had, up to this time, escaped the earnest attention of cultivators. This might have been a great first in southern agricultural history if Landrum's method had been taken up and replicated. Landrum's painstakingly recorded directions in *American Farmer* did not inspire followers, but his writing pulls back the curtain on a planter-scientist's mind-set. Landrum's account reveals an uncanny parallel between unconscious views of owning people and the domestication and commercialization of nature. Landrum sought to compel conformity and increase productivity through forced reproduction of his trees. We can presume he felt the same about his slaves, likely the ones tending his orchard. (An enslaved man named Dave Drake who worked in Landrum's industrial-scale pottery studio on loan from Landrum's nephew later became known for his distinctive craftsmanship. Drake's over-sized glazed pots, often signed and embellished with lively lines of poetry, are highly valued as collectibles today.)[12] In addition to the obvious point about the unpaid support staff sustaining an elite planter's innovations, enslaved people seem to have hovered in the back of Landrum's consciousness as he grafted trees. Landrum's descriptive language is stridently violent, as he discusses his "method of forcing" trees as an "amputat[ion]." Consider, as you read these next lines, the objects of Landrum's ministrations. Is he speaking of walnuts and pecans or of Black women, men, and children?

"It seems to be a prevalent opinion," Landrum protests, "that buds cannot be separated for any length of time, from the parent tree without ceasing to vegetate. I kept some cuts of the almond, peach, and apricot, nearly a month in moist earth, and budded them with success." The "wild plum," he continues, "will be found an excellent stock for an extensive tribe of delicious fruits." (Those who have read or will read Colson Whitehead's novel *The Underground Railroad* may shudder, as I did, at Landrum's reference to his plums, as this is the language a cruel enslaver uses in the novel to describe the Black women he owns and routinely assaults.)[13] This "art," Landrum insists, "enables us to collect from all quarters of the world (climate not forbidding) the most choice fruits, and plant them on stocks hardy and mature, capable of affording as much fruit in two or three years as the seed would yield in a dozen or more."

Abner Landrum speaks of fruit trees on the surface, but his

words referencing "tribes," "collect[ing] from all quarters," and "hardy" stock echo the transatlantic slave trade, which pillaged African peoples of various ethnicities, as well as the forced "breeding" of Black women and the separation of African American parents and children. Grafting, Landrum believed, could "produce a paradise of fruits and flowers" where "thorns and briars now grow," and those who accomplished this transformation were bound for "glory."[14] Landrum seemed to uphold the work of forcing new life and the planter's wish for order and productivity as nearly divine. His thoughts, in fact, lead us back to a needle we threaded in a previous chapter, in which elite white southern culture subscribed to a hierarchical order ordained by God with propertied white men at the apex.

It seems an irony, then, that it was not Landrum or some other wealthy planter-scientist who invented a successful pecan-grafting method that stuck. That innovation sprang from the hands of an enslaved man most of us have never heard of. In the 1840s, a Louisiana doctor tried to graft a pecan tree on Anita Plantation. When the merger did not take, he carried the cuttings (or perhaps sent an enslaved person to carry the cuttings) to his neighbor across the Mississippi River, the owner of the now-iconic Oak Alley Plantation. A man named Antoine enslaved at Oak Alley possessed considerable and unusual skills as a gardener. His owner passed the challenge of growing the cuttings on to Antoine. In the winter of 1846, Antoine hand-grafted 16 trees, which he extended into a healthy orchard of 110 trees.[15] Would that we could read a detailed account of Antoine's artisanal method in a nineteenth-century agricultural trade journal. Perhaps we would find, in language or technique originating from his experience as chattel, a difference in how he perceived or treated the trees.[16]

After Antoine's trees reached maturity, in the years following

CARRYING CAPACITY

Michelle May-Curry and Tiya Miles

This visual essay, "Carrying Capacity," draws on contemporary art by Black artists to read Ashley's sack not only as a historical object but also as a textile, a poem, and a work of art. As a textile, Ashley's sack reminds us of the many ways Black people have used the fiber arts to stitch together themes of family and ancestral ritual. As a written message for future readers, Ruth's and Rose's words are at once poetry and prayer. As an heirloom layered with carefully chosen, colorful embroidery, the sack itself finds echoes across the contemporary art landscape as artists turn and return to visions of inheritance and the natural world. That Ashley's sack still has the capacity to carry these multiple needs for viewers is further testament to Rose's ability to provide resources for a journey she could only imagine. So, too, do artists equip us with tools for the road ahead. They expand our perception of the sensorial environment that Rose, Ashley, and Ruth navigated and that we have inherited, an environment that is quickly changing before our eyes. They remind us to not only see but to touch, smell, and taste our way through these changes, as those before us have and those after us will.

SACKING

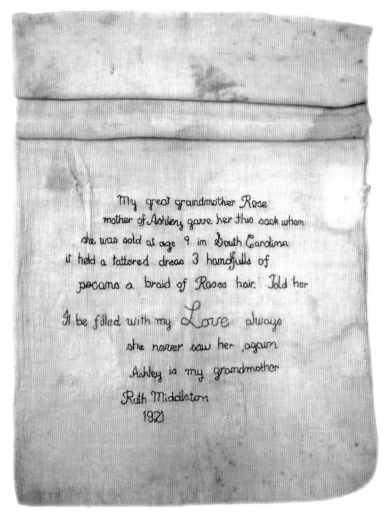

My great grandmother Rose
mother of Ashley gave her this sack when
she was sold at age 9 in South Carolina
it held a tattered dress 3 handfulls of
pecans a braid of Roses hair. Told her
It be filled with my Love always
she never saw her again
Ashley is my grandmother
Ruth Middleton
1921

Ashley's sack. Brown for the past, red for love, green for the future. Timeworn stains on fraying fibers (perhaps dirt, perhaps blood) frame words in the abstract shape of a heart. Ruth's stitchery on Rose's medium brought forward through time by Ashley invites contemplation of the fabric of family.

Kelly Taylor Mitchell, *Up River*. 2018. Letterpress on handmade paper with smells of peanut. Printed at Minnesota Center for Book Arts in 2018. Mitchell uses sensorial tools to reimagine rites and rituals of the African diaspora—poems with a scent memory, paper made of flax, milkweed, and abaca. What might Ashley's sack have smelled like?
KELLY TAYLOR MITCHELL

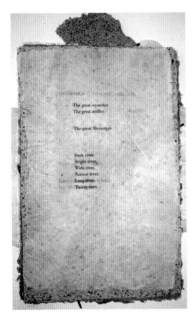

Letitia Huckaby, *Sugar and Spice (Suffrage Project)*. 2018. Huckaby uses a vintage cotton picking sack as a canvas for a pigment print of her daughter holding a sign saying, "Enough." The image is reminiscent of Norman Rockwell's *The Problem We All Live With*, which depicts Ruby Bridges on her first day of school. Like Ruth and Rose, Huckaby imprints the seed sack with her own family story.
LETITIA HUCKABY, PHOTOGRAPH BY
RYAN MICHALESKO

Quilts

Harriet Powers, Pictorial quilt. 1895–98. In this multicolored story quilt featuring biblical and climatic events, master quilter Powers depicts a cosmological vision of choice and consequence, all overseen by the Eye of God (pictured in the top row, square four, with Eve, the serpent, and Adam). Her textile, like embroiderer Ruth Middleton's, speaks simultaneously of kinship (the children of God, people, and animals) and distance (the acts of disobedience, selfishness, and greed that necessitate divine sacrifice).

Great-aunt Margaret's quilt with pink-and-green floral pattern and blue polka-dot backing and hem. Ca. 1920s–1940s, Mississippi. Margaret Stribling, a lay quilter, appears to have fashioned this covering out of mixed fabric remnants. While the quilt contains no words, it holds the memory of a family story of survival and persistence. African American women across a range of locations and experiences— and, indeed, American women of all backgrounds—used cloth to express artistic visions and familial bonds.

Letitia Huckaby, *Halle's Dress.* 2009. The patchwork layering of heirloom fabrics invokes a quilted aesthetic. A photographic print of the Huckabys' daughter, Halle Lujah, lines the hem, imprinting legacies of family directly onto the surface of the garment. Passed between hands, Rose's gift of a dress to her daughter prompts us to think about what touches, marks, and smells lingered on the garment well after their separation. LETITIA HUCKABY

Sanford Biggers, *Selah.* 2017. Abstract husk of an African sculpture with its arms raised in a position of prayer. The sculpture's name, *Selah*, comes from the Hebrew word appearing at the end of Bible passages, signaling a pause. In the cutting and readorning of geometric heirloom fabric patterns, Biggers asks viewers to pause to consider the patchwork history each quilt calls forth. Viewers of Ashley's sack are similarly called to pause and contemplate the many prayers breathed in Ashley's name, and the countless twin prayers unnamed.

MARIANNE BOESKY GALLERY, PHOTOGRAPH BY OBJECT STUDIES

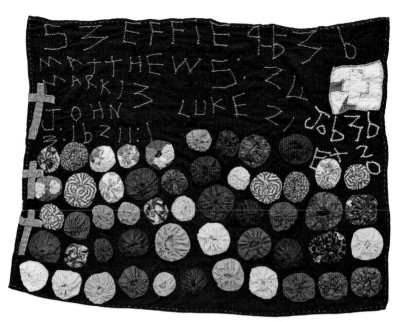

Rosie Lee Tompkins, *Untitled*. 2004. Fifty-two "yo-yos," or quilting appliqués that resemble small seed sacks, are assembled in free-form lines next to crosses to represent the age of the quilter, Rosie Lee Tompkins, born Effie Mae Martin. Tompkins, being a deeply religious woman, found power in numerology and combined Bible verses with other personal dates, such as her own birthday (9-6-36) or addresses. Because Tompkins imagined each cloth sack as its own colorful prayer, her improvisational quilt-making techniques remind us of Ruth's embroidery and Rose's quick assemblage for Ashley's journey.

HAIR

Deja Milany, *Undone*. 2020. Milany braids synthetic hair into burlap, a material often used for sacking, in a bending and uneven pattern. Like the fragile skeins that form the knit of kinship, the rows of braids leave trails of loosely falling curly hair in some places, while elsewhere tight plaits hang outside the frame. The versatility of the chosen fibers, burlap and hair, as carrying materials illuminate potential motivations behind Rose's gifts.

DEJA MILANY, PHOTOGRAPH BY
DARRYL DEANGELO TERRELL

Marianetta Porter, *Found.* 2015–16. Braided hair, letterpress printed paper. Poem reads "Found / In a bible / tucked discreetly / behind a nail / in the spine / a single braid / clipped from a child / sold off / to unknown traders." An unthinkable loss and a desire to remember similarly inspired Rose, and comforted Ashley on her journey.

MARIANETTA PORTER

Angela Hennessy, *Mourning Wreath.* 2017. Synthetic and human hair, artist's hair, found hair, 24K and imitation gold leaf on copper sheet, enamel paint, chain, steel frame, and cement base. The braid that once graced the sack Rose gave to Ashley prompts us to ask, How can hair tie the living to the dead? At the intersection of African and Victorian mourning rituals, Hennessy weaves a garland of synthetic and human hair, turning intricate braids into a portal to the ancestral realm. PHOTOGRAPH BY ANGELA HENNESSY

Sonya Clark, *Heritage Pearls.* 2010. In molding Black hair into jewelry, Clark values hair as one might value a pearl: precious, a gemstone to be inherited and bestowed from generation to generation. Far from a position of lack, hair is cast as an exquisite gift. So, too, was Ashley's sack an heirloom, passed down between generations, lost and found again amid other treasures, the hair inside a pearl in its own right.

SONYA CLARK, COLLECTION OF SUSAN CUMMINS

Sonya Clark, *Skein.* 2016. Clark wraps locks of human hair from an anonymous woman to resemble a skein of yarn. As curly hair is more vulnerable than straight hair to the stresses caused by sun, water, sweat, and grooming, the "dreading" or "locking" of hair is often done as a way of protecting and strengthening textured hair. Implied in the size of Clark's skein is the health of the hair used, as well as its ability to endure as a fiber material for the production of art, mirroring the care and endurance of Black family bonds in the midst of extreme stressors. SONYA CLARK

Michelle May-Curry is the project director of the Humanities for All initiative at the National Humanities Alliance and is a PhD candidate in American Culture at the University of Michigan. Her scholarly and curatorial work has appeared in two art exhibitions, in Detroit and Havana, Cuba, in partnership with the Carr Center and Carrie Mae Weems.

the Civil War, they produced plentiful nuts that sold for fifty to seventy-five dollars per barrel. Still, the plantation's new owners (the property had changed hands more than once) felled many of those trees to free the land for a more lucrative sugarcane crop. In 1876, the then owner of Oak Alley, Hubert Bonzano, exhibited nuts from Antoine's remaining trees at the Centennial Exposition, the world's fair held in Philadelphia and a showcase for inventors like Alexander Graham Bell. The nuts received a commendation from a Yale botanist and professor, who praised them for their "remarkably large size, tenderness of shell, and very special excellence." This singular notice bestowed a name on "the first vegetatively propagated pecan cultivar." It was called the "Centennial" and became the first pecan variety used in a commercial orchard, making Oak Alley the "birthplace of commercial pecan production." Antoine, who is but a shadow in the historical record, received no glory or remuneration for his botanical feat. Even the "mother tree" from which the first of Antoine's grafted shoots came has disappeared from the landscape. In 1890, a levee breach created a sudden sinkhole that carried "Mother Centennial" down into the bowels of the earth.[17]

The pecan trees grafted by an unfree man would lay the foundation for distribution and commercialization. After the Centennial was commercialized, though, the pecan industry was sluggish to develop. For the better part of the century, pecans were accessible to people mainly through foraging, trading, or purchasing the wild nuts. The tree escaped widespread cultivation and commercialization until the late 1800s and early 1900s, "much longer," the environmental historian James McWilliams contends, "than any other native edible plant." The pecan, he insists, "continued to stand tall on its own terms."[18] For this was a tree with an especially deep tap root invisible above the soil surface, a tree with unpredictable verve and a "strength that remains hidden from view."[19] The plant's durable root system, versatility, and fierce adaptability enabled it to thrive from Texas to Georgia, from Louisiana to Illinois, and to withstand the heavy foraging of human and non-human creatures as well as to resist attempts at domestication for decades. Pecan trees can live for hundreds of years, and their species "preceded hate," as geologist Lauret Savoy has profoundly observed about the American landscape writ large.[20]

Indeed, we might conceptualize the wild pecan as a deeply democratic type of tree. Indigenous people who have long collected, planted, and prepared pecans seem to have valued the tree in this fashion. Caddos of the southern plains tell a traditional story about a "mother to all the pecan trees." The old woman of the tale possessed all the pecan trees and horded the nuts in her home, stingily rationing them out to the people. Coyote, a trickster figure and a stranger to the village, kills the woman, "and ever since then the pecan trees have grown everywhere and belong to all of the people."[21] In the mid-1800s, the Cherokee Nation and the Chickasaw Nation passed legislation to ban the cutting down of pecan trees, followed by the Seminole Nation of Oklahoma, which in the 1920s fined perpetrators for "mutilating a pecan tree."[22]

We know that enslaved people and their descendants across the South loved the nuts that dropped from those trees. They may have enjoyed the pecan's unique earthy flavor, so influential now to a regional food culture that the pecan is the base for the "South's most popular pie" and the French-inflected pecan praline, a famous southern delicacy.[23] The pecan appears in all manner of Black southern recipes, both sweet and savory, from delicate wafers to turkey stuffing. We will return to food and ways of preparing it in due course. For now, let us dwell on the trees themselves. We can surmise, from Antoine's artisanal work as a horticulturist and from the unknown, unsung work of many other enslaved gardeners and foresters, that Black people also felt a fondness for pecans as trees. They may have recognized the tree's toughness in the face of assault, its adaptability to a range of habitats, and its tenacious ability to put down roots, no matter the quality of the soil. They may have looked to the wild pecan tree as an example of how to live long with steadfastness and dignity, even in inhospitable circumstances, and even when, as was the case with Antoine's Mother Centennial, a maternal anchor has been lost.

The lone surviving pecan tree from Antoine's originals, Oak Alley Plantation, Louisiana. Reproduced in Lenny Wells, *Pecan: America's Native Nut Tree* (Tuscaloosa: University of Alabama Press, 2017), 41.

"I used to know every pecan tree," Mary Yelling, the descendant of enslaved people, said about her hometown of Spring Hill, Alabama, in an oral history interview.[24] Might Ashley have said the same, or her daughter, or hers, of the wild pecan groves that would later spread across the South Carolina interior? Might she, with nuts in hand that also were seeds, have planted pecans in some secret spot near the Savannah River? Is it too far a stretch to see Ashley as a grafter, too, attaching the shoots of her new forced life onto the strong roots of memory that kept her lost mother close? Imagine Ashley: a long-term survivor like a wild pecan tree, fiercely resilient, roots holding fast to the ever-changing ground.

SURVIVAL FOODS

It took an online foray into the subculture of "prepper" communities for me to learn that "survival food" now refers to items that might be packed into an emergency kit in case of disaster.[25] The term has another meaning, though, one not entirely unrelated: the foods that enslaved people used to "sustain themselves" when they possessed few ingredients of high nutritional value.[26] How did enslaved people find, grow, and prepare the foods that kept them alive and even provided emotional comfort? How did nine-year-old Ashley maintain a diet? What did she manage to eat? And what did she think of the plants and animals that sustained her? Ashley began her journey to a new plantation with three handfuls of pecans. This is all we know. As with the dress, we must turn, then, to the accounts of other enslaved people to paint a composite picture of their foodways. Jane Clark, the woman we encountered in a previous chapter who escaped her owner's house with two packed pillowcases in tow, has a story that offers a view into an unfree child's experience of food, hunger, and cookery.[27]

Enslaved girls like Jane and Ashley often did not have enough to eat. They dwelled in a world of deprivation even as they were compelled, as children and then adults, to grow, harvest, prepare, or clear away food for their owners. Children, mostly girls, could face punishment for mishandling food preparation or presentation. At the same time, artful dishes prepared with skill for an owner could be a source of satisfaction and pride for the maker. When Jane was six, her work in the rural kitchen started on the lowest rung, and she carried water several times a day for the enslaved cook.[28] As Jane grew older and was called to the estate of her owner's heir, she would become that Black cook herself. Jane excelled in "culinary affairs," besting her older and more experienced cousin, Mary, in food preparation and cooking skills (leading to conflict between them). Perhaps she also excelled in the gardening that provided herbs and an array of vegetables for the master and mistress's table.

Jane's daily tasks began with rising early to feed the cows before building a fire and cooking the white family's breakfast over it with bulky cast-iron pots and pans. Southern kitchens in the 1800s were often "dangerous, smoky, and hot," with poor ventilation. The heavy labor was also exacting, as cooks wielded iron implements, gauged the heat and cooking times in imprecise open hearths, learned their owners' preferences, and sometimes worked with unfamiliar ingredients.[29] Jane suffered her "first whipping," one she described as "severe," for serving breakfast late one morning due to a slow-heating fire. For this, she was "flogged" five times by her master, as well as by her overseer. That is, Jane was beaten by two different men multiple times because the fire on which she cooked, for free and by force, did not heat fast enough. Her narrative recounts with remarkable restraint how she "became accustomed to scenes of severity" on that plantation.

Jane also became accustomed to scenes of lack. As a child, she had labored on a skeletal, protein-light diet consisting of a rationed "pint of corn meal . . . seasoned with salt, mixed with water and baked in the ashes." It is no wonder that enslaved children suffered health consequences from poor and insufficient diets. They sickened and died at high rates, particularly under the age of nine, as rations tended to increase when a child turned ten and could do more labor for their owners.[30] Years later, as a teen and young adult cook, Jane would have had greater access to foodstuffs, including the first chance at leftovers from the master and mistress's table. But the enslaved people around her, especially those at work in the fields, would have had rations low in variety and nutrition, greater in volume but similar in makeup to the hominy she had received as a child.[31] The fields of slavery in the nineteenth-century interior and westerly South made up a landscape of physical want.

On the coastal edges of South Carolina and Georgia, and during the first several generations of slavery's reign, unfree people had greater opportunity to round out and improve on their diets. Slaveholders in this Lowcountry region organized enslaved people's work by task, meaning that an owner or plantation manager typically made assignments based on age and expected capacity. Once a person completed her task (which, if she was strong and industrious, often took most but not all of the day), she could turn her energies and time toward personal matters, such as tending a vegetable garden, raising livestock, or piecing a strip quilt. Enslaved women farmed their own small patches of ground. Enslaved men regularly fished and hunted wild game, sometimes with firearms.[32] In addition to growing food on "provision plots" assigned by owners and overseers, enslaved women finagled ways to access their owners' rice stores.[33] Children growing up enslaved under the coastal task system fared better than their southern interior counterparts, as their parents were able to procure a wider variety of foods.[34] A formerly enslaved man from South Carolina described his diet to an interviewer: "The colored people were given their rations once a week, on Monday, they got corn, and a quart of molasses, and three pounds of bacon, and sometimes meat and peas. They had all the vegetables they wanted they grew them in the garden." Another man, formerly enslaved on a South Carolina plantation, reminisced about the tasty meals that could be made from a combination of rationed, grown, and foraged resources: molasses and pone bread for breakfast, roasted corn, string beans, hog jowls, bread with buttermilk, and blackberry cobbler.[35]

Surviving in the Lowcountry, though, also required caution around gathering food. Enslaved people were often forbidden to eat the rice they planted, weeded, harvested, winnowed, and pounded, but according to oral history, Black women fashioned a work-around through the canny use of their garments:

The women had to go down to the low, wet places to get the rice. To do that, they would hitch up their skirts and tie them. When they got ready to "fan" the rice that was dry enough, they used a wide fanner basket, and they kept their skirts knotted. I guess you can see what's coming. After pounding the rice to open the husks, they poured it into a flat basket made like a tray. Then they threw the rice up in the air to let the husks fly away. Each time it came back down, they "fanned" first one way and then the other, "some for you and some for we." What was "for we" fell into the knots and folds. The rest fell back onto the basket. When they got home, the women untied those big skirts and let their families' rice fall out.[36]

As the women threw rice into the air to separate the husks from the kernels, part of the intricate work of processing rice, they used their skirts as nets to catch some of the wayward rice as it fell back down into the baskets, then carried the rice caught in the "pockets" of their skirts to their cabins. Mamie Garvin Fields, a descendant of enslaved Carolinians who recounted this practice, noted that a cultural belief arose from it. Black girls were cautioned by elders never to "sweep at night" because they might overlook loose grains of rice in the darkness, thereby leaving behind evidence of forbidden food for an overseer or owner to discover.[37] Another technique for the collection of falling grains was, reportedly, to catch the overflow in too-large shoes while one worked.[38]

Sustenance depended on persistence in hostile circumstances, a knack for gathering and growing foods wild and farmed, and an art for turning (often limited) raw foodstuffs into comfort foods laden with flavor. The ability of inspired cooks to work this magic turned slave-quarter cabins into havens of communion, if only for a few hours at the close of the day. When Rose packed nuts into the sack, thereby coating them with the oils of her palms, she passed on to her daughter a source of life-keeping energy, as well as cultural associations with mealtimes spent in the company of others.

Enslaved cooks drew from African traditions, using plants carried on slave ships (as food for the human cargo and crew) and plants accidentally transported as seeds. Cooks were resourceful in combining these African elements with ingredients found in Native American dishes and the cast-off edibles of white enslavers, including African yams, black-eyed peas, and peanuts; Indigenous corn varieties, pumpkins, wild greens, and pecans; and European meats and spices. To season meals in their cabins, they added salt, the sweetness of molasses, and, when obtainable, remnant parts of the pig. Blacks and the American Indians enslaved with them in the earlier centuries created "fusions" of local foods for meals inside their cabins as well as for the big-house or farmhouse table. African Americans learned to bake cornbread out of corn ground into meal from Indigenous co-laborers and family members. They adjusted their selection of fresh greens, a long-established ingredient in their West African ancestral homelands, to include native greens preferred by Indigenous people. Indigenous Americans, in turn, traded food with enslaved Blacks and developed a fondness for black-eyed peas, an African legume transported on the slave ships. The culinary creativity of enslaved people of African and Indigenous American descent shaped an exquisite multicultural, multinational cuisine that forms the basis of modern southern regional foods.[39]

The ability to procure a diverse buffet from the land decreased as slavery pushed west into "frontier" lands recently taken from expelled Native Americans and not yet fully settled by Euro-Americans. Even as far east as central South Carolina where Ashley lived (the "backcountry" to wealthy planters along the coastline), the task system gave way to the gang system already employed in the tobacco zone of Virginia and Maryland, and the quality of life for enslaved people diminished. Slaveholders in the cotton-producing central South prodded Blacks to do more with less, trading individually assigned discrete tasks for pro-longed mass-organized gang labor. This consolidation of Black labor coincided with a plummeting quality of food as owners reduced rations, withheld costly meat products, and siphoned off time that could have been devoted to hunting, gardening, gathering, and cooking. Enslaved people in the Cotton Belt often labored while plagued by intense hunger.[40] By the 1850s, when Ashley was sold, Blacks in the cotton South had little time or autonomy to procure their own vegetables, fruits, grains, or meats, leaving them dependent on the regular rations of the enslavers, whose interest in them was financial. Seeking to clear as much profit as possible, slaveholders often limited food distribution to a level just above subsistence, reserving poor-quality ingredients, including food reserved for animal feed, like cowpeas (black-eyed peas) and sweet potatoes, for their captive labor force.[41] Their intent was to extract the maximum amount of labor while bestowing a minimal level of comfort.[42] The pleasures of satiation, contentment, and enjoyment derived from the fruits of one's work were withheld from unfree African Americans.

Enslaved people in the states farther to the west lived with a recalcitrant "caloric gap," a deficit between calorie intake and calorie need. The result of this gap was suffering. They "labored too much *and* ate too little," one environmental historian has contended, adding: "In the cotton belt, slaves were not just traded *like* livestock; they *were* livestock." This metaphor emphasizes that Black people performed heavy labor in place of large beasts and were compelled to shift from an omnivore's diet to a herbivore's diet.[43] The physical ache of hunger and physiological need for nutrition pushed the enslaved to desperate acts, which is why food was the most common item stolen on plantations, even though getting caught with the master's hog or a buttered biscuit might lead to harsh reprisals.[44]

Meager, corn-centric rations stuck in the memories of formerly enslaved people decades after the Civil War. At the same time that slaveholders withheld food to shrink budgets, they also deployed food as a weapon, dividing the enslaved population into stratified groups who received either more and relatively better foods (such as house servants and Black "slave drivers") or lesser foods (such as the mass of fieldworkers and their children).[45] Aware of the power of psychological incentive, slaveholders nudged the enslaved toward desired behaviors in exchange for greater quantities or selective kinds of foods and made a spectacle of bestowing food on special occasions.[46] The three-day Christmas holiday, a brief and eagerly anticipated respite for enslaved people, was often accompanied by master-class distributions of additional rations and sweets, such as "plum pudding, and gingerbread, apples, oranges, currants, and other fruits." As the daughter of a Lowcountry planter reminisced, seeming to fondly recall her family's largesse: "There was much feasting at Christmas, for a beef and several hogs were always killed and extra rations of sugar, coffee, molasses, and flour were given out, and great quantities of sweet potatoes."[47]

But most seasons were not Christmas. For the other 362 days of the year, enslaved people in the Cotton Belt consumed a monotonous, grain-heavy diet (with the ubiquitous corn sometimes replaced by sweet potatoes) unless they could enrich their meager rations with supplements they procured or skills they gained for adding flavor over the cookfire. A woman formerly enslaved in South Carolina recalled "coarse rations" of cornbread and molasses.[48] Another woman, this one from Georgia, complained that her "mean" mistress "never gave them anything but the coarsest foods" and only distributed "sour milk and stale bread."[49] Eliza Potter, the free Black woman who worked in wealthy white southern homes as a hairdresser, reacted in shock at the stinginess she witnessed among a family of New Orleans slaveholders: "I went out every morning to see the slaves at breakfast in the quarters, and to my astonishment, I did not see any of them have anything for the whole week but a pint cup of buttermilk and a slice of bread, those who could not take buttermilk, had a cup of coffee, made of browned corn, sweetened with molasses. I never saw meat of any kind given to them while I was there."[50]

Enslaved people's constant struggle to stay fed linked them closely to their environments. For them, wild and salvaged edibles—like pecans, as slavery moved westward—were life-lines.[51] Children on the plantations became accustomed to scavenging for food, and these quests to satiate appetites could sometimes turn into play. As the son of an enslaved seamstress in South Carolina remembered, he and the other children ran through the woods in the summertime collecting "grapes, mus-cadines, strawberries, chinquapins, hickory nuts, calamus root, slippery elmer (elm) bark, wild cherries, mulberries, and red and black haws." Another man from a South Carolina planta-tion recalled how the children ran through patches of plums and blackberries "hunting" for strawberries. But foraging for fla-vorful plants was not without risk. A third Carolinian recounted the memory of arising late one night from his "pallet on [the] floor, goin' out in [the] sugar can patch and gittin' a big stalk of [the] cane." The son of his owner caught him and meted out ten lashes in punishment, treating the abuse like a game. Although the strikes by the young white man against the Black boy were not "soft a-tall," the punished boy "didn't cry out on [the] night wind."[52] While performing her services among the elite in New Orleans, Eliza Potter became sickeningly aware of the penalty that could be incurred when hungry enslaved people helped themselves to the plantation's bounty: "Their slaves have noth-ing provided for them to eat, drink or wear; they work hard all the day, and at night they plunder what they can from some of the rich plantations. If they are not caught, they are smart; and if they are, they are punished."[53]

Ashley, along with those whose voices fill the pages of slave narratives and interviews, probably had to forage for food and risk correction for doing so, as her mother likely did to provide her with a cache of pecans. Under these unforgiving circumstances, the nuts must have felt like manna from heaven. Here was a way to beat back hunger's ache, at least for a spell, and to remember her mother, who had cared enough to plan for her sustenance. High in nutritional value, pecans would have been especially satisfying to a famished child. The "protein, fiber, healthy fats, nutrients, vitamins, and antioxidants" stored within these nuts turn them into miniature energy packets, points out one environmental historian. Robin Wall Kimmerer, a Potawatomi botanist, captures the special essence of pecans in language perhaps more resonant with Rose's and Ashley's sense of their circumstances. "They are designed to be food in the winter," Kimmerer writes about these nuts, "when you need fat and protein, heavy calories to keep you warm. They are safety for hard times, the embryo of survival."[54]

Across regions that now make up central-southern and midwestern landscapes (Louisiana, Alabama, Texas, Illinois) and northern Mexico, pecan groves overflowed with "a natural food resource so nutritious and so prolific" that ancient Indigenous peoples chose those areas as camping grounds.[55] Native Americans have gathered and prepared this food for thousands of years, traveling hundreds of miles to visit fruiting groves in season, planting trees from seed, and trading the nuts in a complex web of intercontinental exchange. Payaya people camped near the groves in the late 1600s through the early 1700s.[56] In the 1700s and 1800s, Comanches, Caddos, and Kickapoos sometimes settled close to pecan groves, fermented pecans into a drink used for ceremonial purposes, and ground pecans into a fine meal as an additive for breads, corn dishes, and meats.[57]

Comanches and Kiowas used ground pecan leaves and bark as medicines to treat ringworm and tuberculosis. Apaches near the Rio Grande and Cherokees along the Arkansas River (having relocated there during the period of federal Indian removal in the early 1800s) gathered and traded pecans.[58] Of course the word "pecan," like so many other American words in English, derives from a Native language (in the Algonquian linguistic family) and reveals a substrata of cultural exchange over centuries. Indigenous people used the term *pakan* for "hard-shelled nut." French settlers learned the word from Natchez people in Mississippi in the 1700s and spelled it *pacanes*.[59] From this we take our "pecan," which is pronounced differently in the South and the North, depending on which syllable is emphasized.*

In autumn, the fingering branches of the pecan tree spread and droop toward the ground, dropping showers of amber nuts beneath its canopy. The nuts are easily gathered and store well.[60] The same benefits that attracted Native peoples made this nut important to enslaved African Americans on plantations and

---

* I was reminded of this regional difference in pronunciation of the word "pecan" as PEE-can or pe-KAHN through an exchange on Facebook about my own pecan tree seedling. The seedling had its roots in an environmental history workshop during which I presented a previous version of this chapter. The environmental historian Ian Miller suggested that I contact the director of Harvard's Arnold Arboretum to see pecan trees and ask a specialist whether they could be started from the nut. My visit to the arboretum was scheduled for March 2020, just as COVID-19 was beginning to spread across the Northeast and our campus closed down. In the midst of this research setback, which paled in comparison to rising national anxiety about larger health and economic threats, arboretum director William "Ned" Friedman did a remarkable thing. He planted pecan seeds for me and dropped a pot off in front of my house weeks later, after they had germinated. As my seedling (nicknamed "my little pecan baby") soaked in the sun and grew, I shared a photograph on Facebook, which prompted discussion about the pecan's regional origins and whether it could survive in a backyard outside Boston. I also gained what felt like a pandemic pen pal in the arboretum's director. He wrote about our pecan seedlings and sent photographs marking the parts of the plant and illustrating its deep taproot.

First leaf. This close-up view of a pecan seedling, planted and labeled by the biologist and Arnold Professor of Organismic and Evolutionary Biology William Friedman, director of the Arnold Arboretum at Harvard University, shows the plant's unusually long root. Used by permission of William Friedman.

Beyond imagining. This pecan seedling was planted by William Friedman as an accompaniment to the writing of this chapter during the spring of 2020. He said about the process: "For me, there is something almost beyond imagining when watching a plant germinate and thinking of its potential. To think, these little one-inch seedlings will eventually tower a hundred feet in the air and live for centuries!" Photograph by William Friedman. Photograph and quotation used by permission.

farms in the nineteenth-century Cotton Belt, a population in desperate need of a food that was plentiful, free, portable, nutritious, and filling. The rich taste of the pecan, which endears it to bakers of cakes, pies, and cookies, would only have added to its allure for people deprived of sensory satisfactions.[61] Wild pecans sustained Indigenous Americans for millennia and African Americans for generations.

Perhaps in the immediate aftermath of her seizure for sale, Ashley searched inside her sack and found her mother's store of nuts. Perhaps the primal pang of hunger and the relief of satiation reminded the child that she felt and indeed was still alive. It is possible that in its inherent power to "cushion deprivation," this delicacy carried her through those first lonely hours.[62] We know from the testimony of formerly enslaved people that forging new kinship ties aided survival after forced relocation, and personal relationships were reinforced in and through the material realm. In addition to satisfying physiological needs, food forged social connections. If Ashley first saved herself by eating her mother's packed pecans, she may have begun to regather her spirit by sharing the food she possessed with others. Migrant children dislocated by sale slowly entered new circles of kin where a Black food culture reminiscent of Africa, influenced by Europe and reflective of Native America, succored cotton plantation communities.[63]

The loose, oblong nuts felt smooth in Ashley's palms, the sound of their jangle in the sack a soothing and muted music. Their sensual materiality—touch, sound, smell, and taste— must have been a balm for this girl, reminding her that she was loved despite being cast off, her own and every enslaved child's private apocalypse. On the dirt floor of some dark cabin, Ashley may have curled up with her sack, taking comfort from the food her mother had packed for the journey. Surely Ashley drew spiritual strength, as well as life-sustaining energy, from those three potent handfuls. Rose did not leave Ashley alone with her grief. In the cup of Ashley's hands, survival culture grew from seed, sprouting, blooming, and sustaining the next generations.

NEVER ALONE PECAN RECIPES

The foregoing pages have explored how African Americans survived enslavement through close relationship with their envi-

African American boy selling pecans by the road near Alma, Georgia, 1937. Library of Congress, Prints & Photographs Division, FSA/OWI Collection, LC-USF33-T01-002339-M2 (b&w film dup. neg.). LC-DIG-fsa-8a08065 (digital file from original neg.).

African American woman trading a sack of pecans for groceries in a general store, Jarreau, Louisiana, 1938. Library of Congress, Prints & Photographs Division, FSA/OWI Collection, LC-USF34-031759-D (b&w film neg.).

ronments in the planting, foraging, and preparing of food. And as Alice Walker's words at the top of this chapter promise, loved ones who have departed "never leave us alone with our grief." Together, these two notions suggest that the making and enjoyment of food is a mode of company and, indeed, comfort passed down and adapted to new needs and circumstances. Even when our ancestors are long gone, we hold their signature dishes in our memories and on our tables. In continuation of that cultural ethos of cooking and eating together that traditional chef Ruth Gaskins called "real comfort," and in honor of Ashley's nuts and Antoine's trees, we pause to collect recipes for sweet pecan treats from five historic Black cookbooks.[64]

PECAN PIE

Vertamae Smart-Grosvenor's recipe from when she was
cooking at Pee Wee's Slave Trade Kitchen; from her
Vibration Cooking, or The Travel Notes of a Geechee Girl

Boil 1 cup sugar with 1½ cups cane or corn syrup for about 3 minutes. Beat 3 eggs and slowly add the syrup mixture. Add lots of butter and vanilla and about 1½ cups coarsely broken pecan nuts. Turn into unbaked pie shell and bake about 40 minutes.

OLD REGIONAL RECIPES FOR
THANKSGIVING PIES: PECAN PIE

National Council of Negro Women,
The Historical Cookbook of the American Negro

½ cup sugar
1 cup dark corn syrup
3 eggs
4 tablespoons of butter
1 tablespoon vanilla
1 cup broken pecan nuts

Cook syrup and sugar until mixture thickens. Beat eggs; slowly add hot syrup to eggs, beating constantly. Add butter, vanilla and nuts. Pour into unbaked shells. Bake in preheated oven (450 degrees F.) for 10 minutes, reduce heat to 300 degrees F. for 35 minutes. When cooled serve with whipped cream.

PECAN CRISP COOKIES

Carolyn Quick Tillery,
The African-American Heritage Cookbook

1 cup butter

1½ cups dark brown sugar

2 eggs

2¼ cups all-purpose flour

1 teaspoon baking powder

¼ teaspoon salt

½ teaspoon baking soda

2 teaspoons vanilla extract

¼ teaspoon lemon extract

1 teaspoon ground cinnamon

1¼ cups finely chopped pecans

Preheat oven to 350 degrees F. Place butter in a bowl and beat until fluffy. Gradually add brown sugar, beating after each addition. Sift together flour, baking powder, salt, and baking soda; add to butter mixture and stir until well blended. Add extracts, cinnamon, and chopped pecans, stirring until blended. Drop by the teaspoonful onto a greased cookie sheet. Space about 2 inches apart and bake for 10 to 12 minutes or until golden. *2 dozen cookies.*

PECAN WAFERS

Ruth L. Gaskins' Collection of Traditional Negro Recipes

Do not make these in very hot or humid weather or they won't hold their shape.

½ cup shortening
1 cup brown sugar
2 eggs
4 tablespoons flour
½ cup chopped pecans
½ teaspoon salt
½ teaspoon maple extract

Preheat oven to 375 degrees. Cream shortening and sugar. Add eggs, one at a time, beating well after each addition. Stir in flour and blend well. Add nuts, salt and extract. Drop by teaspoons 5 inches apart on a greased and floured baking sheet. Spread out very thin with the back of a spoon. Bake for 8 minutes. Remove from cookie sheet immediately. Yield: 36 wafers.

NUT BUTTER BALLS

Edna Lewis, *In Pursuit of Flavor*

Nut Butter Balls are the cookies everybody likes and they're easy to make, too. [Lewis explains that she uses either pecans or walnuts but prefers pecans.] Makes about 4 dozen balls.

6 to 7 ounces pecans
2 cups unbleached all-purpose flour
1 cup (2 sticks) unsalted butter (softened)

¼ cup granulated sugar
Pinch salt
1 teaspoon almond extract
1 teaspoon vanilla
3 cups vanilla sugar[65]

Put the nuts through a nut grater and measure—you will need 1½ cups. Handle lightly so as not to pack down. Sift the flour once. Beat the butter and sugar together until the texture becomes creamy. Add the salt and flavorings and mix well again. Beat at a low speed, gradually adding the flour. When the flour has been mixed in, add the nuts and beat until the batter lightens and becomes a grayish color—about 4 minutes. Spoon the dough into a bowl, cover, and put in the refrigerator overnight to chill.

The next morning, preheat the oven to 400 degrees. Remove the bowl from the refrigerator and shape the dough into 1-inch balls, using a melon scoop. Place the balls on ungreased cookie sheets and bake for 12 minutes. Check the balls to be sure they are not browning. If they seem soft, let them bake for another minute or two, but do not let them brown or they will be dry. Take the balls from the oven and leave them on the cookie sheets for 5 minutes or more before removing them with a spatula to a wire rack. Let them cool about 15 minutes or more. Then roll them in the vanilla sugar and let them cool before storing them in a clean, dry tin.

Or perhaps, we might say, store them in a sack.[66]

THE BRIGHT UNSPOOLING

In the dark at the start of the world: Theseus wandered the labyrinth, dispersing behind him red thread from his beloved. It was only this bright unspooling that allowed him to find his way back, to follow the line that ran through the maze like a seam.

—NATALIE SHAPERO,
"The Nature of the Rows: Blanket," *Habitus*, 2017

It was as if I, with all my story-tellers gone, was now authorized to be one.

—FAITH RINGGOLD, *We Flew over the Bridge:
The Memoirs of Faith Ringgold*, 1995

IN THE 1920S WHEN RUTH MIDDLETON SEWED HER family's story, she stood as inheritor to mother loss and mother love. As a Black daughter just two generations removed from the slave trade, she bore a familial and, some would say, spiritual duty to mark the memory. Ruth fulfilled this sacred duty in a way that captures and mirrors the journey of her ancestors. Even as the words she inscribed tell a story, the open space on the surface of the material calls attention to the chapters we cannot know. Ruth's stitchery is concentrated toward the bottom of the sack and mostly achieves an even spacing of regular lines. But between line five, which marks the quoted speech to come with the words "Told her," and line seven, which reveals the lifelong separation of mother and daughter, a noticeable gap appears. It is as though the arrangement of words on the sack part in the middle, creating a physical space on the surface that echoes a hole in the historical record. So many African American ancestors seem to vanish, or at least to fade from transparent view, behind what genealogists sometimes call the wall of slavery. The same is true for Ashley, who appears in the blink of a paper eye and then disappears again until Ruth Middleton picks up the thread. How do we know that Ashley lived when the documented trail of her life goes dark after she is named in an 1853 property inventory? We learn of Ashley and her sack, of her survival and resilience, solely because a female descendant heard the story and held it close. Ashley's passing of the tale along to Ruth is the evidence of her perseverance.

A chronicler with a needle and cloth rather than a pen and paper, Ruth Middleton stood at the edge of history's gap, her sewn testimony the only bridge stretching back to her foremothers' experience. Although Ruth named Rose and Ashley as lineal ancestors, the thread connecting Ashley to Ruth in formal paperwork is even thinner than that connecting Rose to Ashley. A cavity opens between the 1850s and the 1920s, between an enslaved southern grandmother and her free northern granddaughter. Within that chasm a maze of cataclysmic events arises, more than enough for a lone person—or a narrative thread—to get lost in. The Civil War, Reconstruction, Jim Crow segregation, and the Great Migration proved epic in scale in the lives of African Americans as well as in the life of the country.

TRACING ASHLEY, ROSA,
AND RUTH IN SOUTH CAROLINA

After 1853, then, Ashley is visible to us only in the shadowy form of a girl, young mother, and old woman. Like four million others who had survived stolen lives and loves, she persevered as the Civil War sparked, burned, and smoldered. Given that her descendants were born in central South Carolina, it seems that Ashley remained there throughout her lifetime. After being sold, she may have changed her name or been assigned a new name by mandate of a subsequent master or mistress.[1] Such a change would not have been unusual for an enslaved person transferred into new ownership. If Ashley was around nine or ten at the time of her sale, she would have been nearly twenty by the end of the war. That prolonged conflict between Union and Confederate forces created hardships for enslaved people even as it bestowed the hope and promise of freedom. In early 1865, the battle returned to the state where the first shots had been fired at Fort Sumter nearly four years prior. Blacks as well as their owners in South Carolina experienced material deprivation, dislocation, and terrorization after William Tecumseh Sherman marched troops across rice and cotton lands, burning a path of destruction from the Georgia interior to the seaside and then turning his sights on Columbia. Following the upheaval of war, freedom for African Americans was "fragile," an uncertain condition of new "privileges" bound with "terrible disappointments."[2]

Even as both sides lay down their arms in the late spring of 1865, wartime tensions carried over into fraught questions about the reformation of southern governments, the place of former Confederates, and the status of freedmen and freedwomen. With former modes of governance and elite control in chaos,

South Carolina planters maneuvered to shore up their political power at the state and local levels, protect their landed property from the threat of federal confiscation, and regain control over a free but still subjugated Black workforce. Within one year of Robert E. Lee's surrender in Appomattox, Virginia, state leaders in Columbia, South Carolina, held a state constitutional convention (required by the federal government as a condition of capitulation). State representatives at the convention established a harsh set of new laws—known as Black codes—strictly limiting the actions of African Americans. These codes outlawed the right of Blacks to sell items of their own production without written permission of an employer or judge, gave every white man the right to apprehend and arrest a Black person accused of a misdemeanor, and mandated a workday that mirrored the long hours of slavery.[3]

The federal government under the leadership of President Andrew Johnson refused to confiscate Confederate property, resulting in southern elites' retaining or regaining much of their land, among the best soils in the South. Although the Freedmen's Bureau (a federal agency instituted to aid freedpeople's transition to independence) attempted to oversee labor contracts between formerly enslaved women and men and their employers (in many cases, former owners), the bureau had neither the staff, the budget, nor the enforcement capacity to do this work effectively. Unfair labor contracts with echoes of slavery (such as requirements for long workweeks and few breaks throughout the day, prohibitions against visiting and talking with fellow employees, and financial penalties for leaving the workplace without permission) became another means of planter control and freedpeople's subjugation. Armed groups of white men sprang up to enforce the new form of labor extraction just as slave patrols and the city guard in Charleston had monitored the movements of Blacks before the war. White vigilantes wielded violence as the primary tool of intimidation and social control, threatening, beating, and murdering Blacks with impunity to compel their labor. In the inland town of Edgefield, a group of Black men appealed to a Freedmen's Bureau agent in 1865, exclaiming, "There is no safety in our lives, we hear of men being found dead in different places we apply to you to help us."[4]

Without land of their own and compelled to do backbreaking labor at the behest of a white ruling class, freedpeople like Ashley were, in many ways in the immediate aftermath of the Civil War, just as much at the mercy of the planter elite as they had been before. After the 1866 election, a majority Republican Congress took the reins of Reconstruction (the federal plan to rebuild and remake society following the war) from the conservative president, Andrew Johnson. They aimed to protect the newly freed population through the imposition of federally designed districts and a federal military presence.

But it would be hard to roll back the powers the South Carolina elite had already grabbed immediately after the war. South Carolina's former slaveholders had worked their way back into local political power on the watch of a moderate provisional governor (Benjamin Franklin Perry) appointed by a "hands-off" president (Johnson). The planter elite saw their bid for control backed up by a surge of white vigilante violence. White men across social classes orchestrated and carried out acts of terror and retribution against Black individuals, families, and communities under the banner of discrete patrol groups, loosely formed "guerrilla" units, "armed bands on horseback," the Ku Klux Klan, and rifle clubs. Posses of men in support of white dominance and Black submission patrolled rural plantation areas to keep Black people working on the grounds of their current employers and prevent the ability of workers to move to different and preferred places of employment. After the passage of the Fifteenth Amendment guaranteed Black men the vote in 1870, armed supporters of the Democratic Party targeted Black voters (who largely supported the Republican Party of Abraham Lincoln), Republican organizers, and polling places across the South.[5]

While no place was safe for African Americans in post-emancipation South Carolina, the worst of these abuses took place in the rural interior stretches of the state where lucrative plantations were located. Even as late as the 1920s, South Carolina memoirist Mamie Garvin Fields (whose recollections about an ingenious way of fanning rice to catch loose grains we described in the preceding chapter) recounted visiting a plantation in an isolated pocket of South Carolina. There, in her words: "They still had slavery. S-L-A-V-E-R-Y."[6]

Mamie Garvin Fields had been born to a middle-class Black family of preachers, carpenters, and homemakers in South Carolina in the 1880s. She was, however, just two generations removed from racial captivity. Her grandparents had been enslaved in rural South Carolina, and her grandmother was lost to the family when their owner moved her to evade Sherman's incursion during the Civil War. Fields had become a teacher and community organizer by the time she made this observation. A respected member of her community, she had been asked by a medical doctor to accompany him on house calls as a cultural liaison of sorts. The doctor treated an isolated Black population engaged in farm work for wealthy townspeople as well as domestic work for local officials (such as the postmistress) at minimal pay. Fields observed that this Black community had been denied the privileges of freedom and purposefully separated from the outside world. Their former owner sequestered workers behind six locked gates, blocked their access to telephones, vehicles, and mail, kept them hungry on meager rations, and terrified them with threats of beating and jailing.[7]

The chaos of large-scale war, guerrilla assaults, and stringent restrictions on mobility legalized in Black codes surely touched the lives of Ashley and her circle of kin. Each tumultuous moment might have caused successive separations, across which it became even harder to maintain family ties. Tracing a solid line forward in time from Ashley in 1853 to Ruth in 1921 through documentary records proves impossible. And Ruth Middleton does not name her mother on the sack, resulting in a lost generation in our paper-and-cloth trail. Nevertheless, Ruth asserts her own place in this ancestral line, and Ruth herself does appear in a series of vital records, government documents, and newspaper announcements in the early to mid-1900s. Picking up the thread with Ruth, we can trace her birthplace and parentage and, from there, backstitch a path to the woman she called "my grandmother."

Ruth Middleton was born to Rose (also known as Rosa) Clifton Jones and Austin Jones in Columbia, South Carolina, around the year 1900 (various documents date her birth to 1897 and circa 1902). This would have made Rosa Jones Ashley's daughter or Austin Jones Ashley's son. Given the cultural tradition of naming children after loved ones, especially in this period, it seems more likely that Ashley gave birth to Rosa, naming the girl after her own lost mother, Rose.[8] If Rosa Clifton was born around 1880, as census records indicate, Ashley would have been in her mid-thirties at the time. By then Ashley had survived not only enslavement and familial separation but also wartime violence and the accompanying societal upheaval. She had seen Black men rise to state political office in South Carolina during the period of Reconstruction, but also the reconsolidation of white power, the hardening of legal segregation, and violent rebukes of Black political and economic advances by the end of the century. Ashley lived her life out in the cotton midlands of South Carolina, where she had been held captive as a girl. Her daughter Rosa was born in this same region during a terrifying moment that the esteemed historian John Hope Franklin has called the "long dark night" of African American history.[9]

After nearly ten years, federally enforced congressional reconstruction ended when a political compromise intended to reconcile the North and the South secured the presidency for Republican Rutherford B. Hayes. Following the withdrawal of federal troops from the South, rural areas became even deadlier for Black residents. Women were vulnerable to sexual assault by white men in the homes of their employers as well as their own homes, where members of the KKK and other vigilante groups sought to instill terror through physical intimidation and abuse. Black women, men, and children were beaten, raped, shot, lynched, and burned out of their homes as political strategy and as sport. Ashley may have been among the thousands of African Americans who abandoned the countryside for southern cities in the last decades of the 1800s, seeking greater safety from racist attacks prevalent in the relatively isolated woods and plantation lands, as well as better work conditions. Perhaps she brought her daughter Rosa with her to the capital city of Columbia and made a first home there with other relatives. Or maybe Rosa undertook the move on her own, hazarding the risk of leaving a familiar rural landscape and life behind.

Rosa Clifton Jones's trajectory reflected that of many Black women in the first generations born after slavery. Her experience, and theirs, points to the extraordinary nature of ordinary Black women's lives. Rosa and her peers lived between a "backdrop" of violence and a foreground of "banal racial prejudice" as they moved through public and private spaces that reaffirmed a separate and denigrated status for their race. Rosa made her living through household labor, as did 90 percent of African American women in 1900.[10] Domestic work was the primary form of employment open to them. In a large city like Columbia, Black women performed any number of household service jobs, including "general" domestic labor and the more specialized tasks of cooking and laundering. In 1909, a woman named Rosa appears in the Columbia city directory as a cook and the wife of Austin, a deliveryman. They shared a home with another man on Laurel Street. The couple likely lived there as boarders; working-class African Americans who had recently migrated to cities often shared living quarters to afford rents on low wages. A year later, when the 1910 census was taken, Rosa and Austin resided on the University of South Carolina campus, where they worked as "servants" and were raising a young family: daughter Ruth, age seven; son Claud, age two; and daughter Mary, age one.[11]

We know these things about Rosa Jones: she worked hard, had versatile skills, and managed to keep her children under one roof at least for a time. Rosa died in 1916, when Ruth was just about thirteen, following the death of Austin a few years prior.[12] Ruth may have inherited the heirloom sack not long after the census of 1910 was taken. And the story of the sack was conveyed to Ruth, it would seem, by Ashley herself. The narrative perspective that Ruth assumes in her embroidered inscription omits Rosa while highlighting Ashley, suggesting a close connection with this grandmother. Ruth's even stitches assert a strong possessive reference to Ashley, and, importantly, Ruth describes this relationship in the present tense, indicating current time. "Ashley *is*," Ruth sewed on the sack, "*my* grandmother."[13]

Along with the bag and whatever materials had been preserved inside its depths, Ruth inherited her grandmother's story of trauma and transcendence.

STORYTELLING, SEWING, AND HEALING

To tell the story of one's own life is to change that life, as telling is an action that can revise one's relationship to the past. Perhaps this is something a younger version of Ruth Middleton intuited as she listened to her grandmother Ashley speak of slavery days. By describing past painful events, the speaker begins to move beyond them, while not denying that they occurred and inflicted scars. And telling is not a unidirectional process. Psychological research indicates that those who listen to such stories participate in the teller's evaluation of difficult events. The process of telling enacts change for the speaker/writer *and* for the listener/reader who empathizes with the narrator, affirming their experience through the mirror of feeling.[14] Through this process, the speaker confronts past difficulties in the company of another, gaining greater distance from the trauma and moving toward an interpretive synthesis that can bring emotional relief, even as the listener learns from the teller's experience in a rehearsal of life's potential challenges.

What is more, telling may have become a way for Ashley, as well as Ruth, to move beyond the constraining role of a victim and take up the empowering stance of a witness. Perhaps they felt, as the novelist Gayl Jones reflects through the eyes of her narrator, the lineal descendant of two generations of Black women enslaved and sexually abused by the same man, their master and master/father: "We got to burn out what they put in our minds, like you burn out a wound. Except we got to keep what we need to bear witness."[15] Novelists often display a knack for revealing the depths of interior life. Psychological studies indeed find that telling of traumatic experiences in repetitive fashion over time helps the speaker gain emotional and analytical control, decreasing the pain of the event in memory and yielding understanding that brings greater peace. As the teller repeats the story, a means of making sense of it, the traumatic tale becomes shorter and more succinct.[16] Bearing witness, then, may be the most effective way we know of carrying the weight of the past in order to arrive at generative resolutions.

We can imagine the process of transmission and transferal, of confrontation, evaluation, and gradual healing that the speech of a grandmother like Ashley to a grandchild like Ruth begins. And rather than a single moment, we should picture many such moments, as the story stitched onto the sack conveys a rhythm of familiarity as well as the compression of key events that often occurs as traumatic tales are retold over time. We can imagine that in telling and retelling the tale of past traumas to her granddaughter, Ashley became better equipped to process the pain for herself. We can anticipate that in receiving words from a relative with whom she empathized, Ruth was also strengthened and emboldened by the knowledge of her ancestors' willpower. For grandmother and grandchild both, "interpreting and reinterpreting the past [was] crucial for survival, strength, and carrying on."[17] How apt, how perfect, as if a fabrication of the story itself, that the "carrying on" enacted through Ashley and Ruth's exchanges is attached to an actual carrier in the form of the cotton seed sack? The bag held the memories of Ashley's tale until the time came when Ruth was ready to retell, interpret, and record it. Perhaps the very form of Ruth's inscription on Ashley's sack—the brevity and concision—is the result of many tellings across time that enabled a successful interpretive process.

Telling can be a cleansing, a clearing of the old wounds in preparation for the bandaging that can be found in relations of love. Telling is meditative, a process that slows time down, leads us into ourselves, and allows us to drag what we find out into the open. That motion of piercing into the inside, grasping what has been buried beneath, and circling back again to the outside has the shape of a loop, or a stitch. Is it any wonder, then, that sewers find stitching meditative, too? The inward and outward motion, the bringing together of loose ends, the making of something new in the process, heals. Such was the case for Ruth Middleton, we can suppose, when she decided, in a land far away from the South of her foremothers, to etch into the annals of history the story of Ashley and the sack.

Ruth's decision to tell this tale through needle and thread was a choice with significance. She could have selected a sheet of paper and written down the tale of the cotton sack, and perhaps she did sketch out a draft on some page long lost. But in the end, she chose to memorialize these family happenings in fabric, a medium used for millennia "as a vehicle for recording information, such as history or mythology."[18] Cloth is a particular kind of material for relating events of the past: it has traditionally been the craft of women across cultures, and it has held a special place in women's lives. "Textiles, homemade or store-bought, were a form of female inheritance," a particularly valued kind of movable property, as the celebrated scholar of women's material culture Laurel Thatcher Ulrich has explained.[19] For women, cloth also tended to represent the work of their hands, the female branches of family trees, and notions of the feminine ideal. Passing on a textile or inheriting a textile, then, symbolized women's ability, creativity, and continuance.

None of this would have been lost on Ruth Middleton, who must have had some degree of formal education, given her facility with the written word; who had evidently been exposed to the "feminine" art of embroidery; and who clearly possessed a keen mind. By inscribing her foremothers' story into cloth, Ruth made a series of strong assertions about her family and herself.[20] She stood as witness to the existence of the women in her family line, entering their plight and their intrinsic worth as human beings into the written record. She exposed the immorality of slavery and articulated her foremothers' implicit criticism of the inhumane system that had harmed them. She asserted the fact and perseverance of Black mother love and African American kinship even in a period when families were mercilessly separated. With cloth as surface and embroidery thread and needle as tools, she framed this survival tale as a *women's* story, claiming feminine space for her foremothers and for herself at a time— the early 1900s—when the value of Black womanhood was still widely denigrated in American society. She must have shared a sense of the cross-cultural symbolism that fabric carries as a metaphor for tying, weaving, knotting, and binding people together. Ruth united her own life and times with those of her foremothers through this craft project, "sewing together those [who] were torn asunder."[21]

Cloth can be magical, archaeologists have argued, in that textile makers around the world have adopted ritualistic processes to "weave" supernatural powers of protection, prosperity, or fertility into fabric through symbolic form or imagery. (The rose, as it happens, is a "very old . . . symbol of protection" dating back, some classicists argue, to ancient Greek mythology.)[22] Would it be too far a stretch for us to consider that Ruth cast her own spell, in a sense, when she metamorphized a tattered sack into a writing surface? Ruth invoked her female forebears, restoring the "(maternal) ancestral lines" made "near extinct" by slavery, and creating a "discursive alternative in which absences become presences in written form."[23] And by writing herself into it, Ruth claimed a place for herself as heir of the magic sack in a long line of women survivors. "To inscribe one's name on a material object assured some sort of immortality," writes Ulrich.[24] By affixing her version of a family story to the textile that was its subject, Ruth Middleton kept her foremothers alive in memory and linked herself to a living legacy that she could then bequeath.

MIGRATION, DISRUPTION, AND MEANING-MAKING

Ruth's tale conjures the life-affirming example of ancestors who survived dire times by marshaling love. These ancestors may have been especially important to Ruth as role models in the early 1900s, yet another dramatically low point in African American history. As Ruth would discover after leaving South Carolina in the 1910s, the urban North was no racial haven. Some white residents in the North vehemently objected to Black progress. They had expressed their animosity publicly in the 1800s when riots aimed at limiting the residency of free Blacks and curtailing their economic accomplishment erupted in cities like Cincinnati (1829) and Philadelphia (1846).[25] A preexisting anti-Black prejudice in northern cities and towns expanded and sharpened in the decades of Reconstruction and post-Reconstruction, exacerbated by the arrival of hundreds of thousands of poor Black southern migrants. White city dwellers felt threatened by this wave of newcomers, whose color, class, and mannerisms made them easy targets for discrimination in housing and hiring as well as ridicule in newspapers and stage performances. While Jim Crow segregation did not have the same legal bite and seamless structure in the North as in the South, an informal culture of segregation kept Blacks sequestered in poor and increasingly overcrowded neighborhoods and marginalized in public spaces.

The last two decades of the 1800s and first two decades of the 1900s brimmed with racial conflict even as World War I fed economic volatility and political repression at the national level. After the war's end, the anxiety and resentment felt by many European Americans toward African Americans living among them, competing for jobs, walking the streets, and changing the culture of urban areas trumped patriotic sentiment. Black soldiers who had fought overseas in the conflict faced vocal slurs and violent attacks in their own cities, perpetrated by whites angered at seeing African Americans in military uniform and pressing for equal rights. Twenty-six deadly race riots broke out across the country in the spring and summer of 1919 (in Charleston, South Carolina; Chicago, Illinois; East St. Louis, Illinois; Houston, Texas; Knoxville, Tennessee; Omaha, Nebraska; and other towns) and in 1921 (the devastating Greenwood Massacre in Tulsa, Oklahoma), during which white Americans injured and killed Black Americans and destroyed Black homes and businesses even as incidents of lynching reached record highs in the South.[26] "What are the stories one tells in dark times?" African American culture theorist Saidya Hartman asks in a pensive essay about girls on slave ships.[27] In the darkness of the late 1910s and early 1920s, Ruth Middleton chose to tell a story of women's separation, perseverance, and tenderness through an especially intimate material that was at once durable and delicate.[28] Her antidote to dark times was a story of time-toughened love, an inheritance from her great-grandmother, the family protector, Rose.

Three pivotal events occurred in Ruth Jones Middleton's life between her departure from South Carolina around 1918 and her embellishment of the cotton seed sack in 1921. She wed a man from Camden, South Carolina, named Arthur Middleton, gave birth to a baby girl within a year of marriage and during the deadly Spanish flu pandemic, and saw her husband depart for military service in World War I. This frenzy of change in just a few short years would surely have felt overwhelming, especially for a person so young. Ruth was around sixteen when she married Arthur Middleton in the summer of 1918 and when she gave birth to Dorothy Helen Middleton in January 1919. Perhaps the couple elected to marry because Ruth was already pregnant. Her husband was inducted into the military at the rank of private and served overseas between August 1918 and July 1919. Arthur would not have been in the country at the time of Dorothy's birth. After 1919, existing records do not show the couple sharing a residence. Ruth was a young mother who had given birth during a frightening flu epidemic that hit her new city hard. She was living without her partner against the backdrop of terrifying racially motivated violence across the country and wartime deaths in Europe when she picked up her needle and began embroidering her grandmother's bag.[29]

Why Ruth chose Philadelphia as her new place of residence (or why Arthur chose it, if they were together before the South Carolina exodus and if he made the decision) is not readily apparent. Neither Ruth nor Arthur seems to have had relatives already established in that city. But Philadelphia was certainly a destination for thousands of African Americans looking to shed southern economic and political injustice. In the nineteenth century, the city housed the largest free Black population in the country. Although Pennsylvania had only gradually abolished slavery in the late 1700s and early 1800s (a transition that took fifty years), Philadelphia proved a place where African Americans could hone and market skills, such that a healthy Black entrepreneurial class emerged. A critical mass of talented Black businessmen (mostly in the food-service sector), clergymen, educators, writers, and abolitionists made Philadelphia "arguably the most important community of free blacks" prior to the Civil War.[30] There even seemed to be an invisible road leading out of Charleston straight to Philadelphia in the antebellum period, as nearly eight hundred free Blacks facing harsher restrictions and frequent arrests in South Carolina's coastal metropolis fled to Philadelphia in the 1850s.[31] This trend continued in the last decades of the century, when Philadelphia still claimed the largest Black population in the North. By 1900, the number of Black residents there had reached sixty-three thousand.[32]

Ruth joined this substantial, vibrant, struggling mass, at first with her new husband and then with their child. We can only imagine how disorienting it must have been for her, starting this next chapter of life in a teeming, strange city. Along with other Black newcomers in the 1910s, Ruth faced limited employment options. Here, as was the case in every other American city, most African American women were employed as domestic servants in private homes or institutions. Nearly 90 percent of Black women did some form of domestic labor in 1890; that number had decreased only to 84 percent by 1910. And although northern wages were higher than in the South, they were still low, keeping most Black Philadelphia families in the working or lower middle class even as an educated and financially stable Black community with local roots persisted.[33] Opportunities for economic advancement were limited enough that the upper classes of Black society in Philadelphia, whom W.E.B. Du Bois called the "aristocracy," consisted of merchants, caterers, teachers, and clerks with far less financial security and capital than their white upper-class counterparts.[34] In a context in which schoolteachers measured among the elite, domestic servants with steady employment could be counted in the Black middle class.[35] Those with steady employment and strong moorings in organized community life enjoyed a kind of stability that contrasted greatly with the hand-to-mouth lifestyles of many unemployed and poverty-stricken Black Philadelphians.

Back in Columbia, South Carolina, Ruth had been the child of domestic workers who served in a university community when she was young. Perhaps her youthful experience in this cultured Euro-American context equipped her with skills and modes of comportment that impressed potential employers. Soon after her arrival, Ruth managed to find regular work as a domestic in elegant homes. She also possessed the marketable skill of sewing, an ability she probably learned in the South and developed in the North. Sewing work opened new opportunities for Black women in the early twentieth century, but only the most highly skilled could make careers as seamstresses and dressmakers.[36] Although Ruth did not labor with her needle full-time, it is possible that she took in piecework to supplement her income and thereby improved her skill. Ruth's first position in Philadelphia may have been as a live-in servant in the home of a chemical engineer and an organist, Edward and Mabel Linch.[37] Ruth and her husband seem to have lived apart for many of these years, which would not have been unusual for families with women employed as domestics. In 1930, nearly a decade after she had moved north and sewed the text on the sack, Ruth was still working as a "servant," then in the home of Samuel and Cordelia Castner, a prominent family of politicians and photographers who occupied a mansion just outside of Philadelphia near Bryn Mawr College. Ruth's professional designation had broadened within the decade, as she now claimed "waitress" as well as a "servant." The addition of waitressing to her responsibilities, and her identification of such specific work, represented professional progress or an advance in professional identity. She still resided on the premises of her employers, though, a condition that often contributed to feelings of social isolation and sexual vulnerability for Black women in domestic service.[38]

Although Ruth created a record of her foremothers' lives, she left no memoir that has yet been found of her own. Nevertheless, the steps she took to move north, reside in a city, start a family, work as a domestic, and take up sewing were shared by many Black women, some of whom left more traces behind. The biography of Boston activist Melnea Cass, a woman whose life unfolded similarly to Ruth's in the same time period, provides perspective on Ruth's decisions and experiences. Melnea Cass shared the story of her life in a detailed oral history collected in the 1970s. The trajectory of Melnea Cass's life—her northern migration, frequent changes of residence, marriage and young motherhood, and maturation into a respected figure in her Black urban community—illuminates Ruth's. Like Ruth, Melnea was born in the post-Reconstruction urban South, a time and place of intense racism and limited opportunities. Born to a struggling family in Richmond, Virginia, in 1896, Melnea relocated with her parents and sister to Boston as a child. Melnea's parents moved north because "they weren't getting any place . . . weren't making any progress there" and "didn't like the environment." In Boston, the family settled first in a large boardinghouse, where they resided with thirty to forty other migrants. After Melnea's mother died, she and her two sisters moved more than once, living with an aunt and then their aunt's friend. Melnea was sent back down south to a high school for underprivileged girls, where she learned domestic skills, before returning to Boston and working as a domestic in a Cape Cod hotel and in private homes. Melnea married young during World War I, as did Ruth. Describing herself as a "war bride," Melnea Cass shared with her interviewer that many Black women made this choice: "Quite a lot of us got married, you know; we were afraid this boy wouldn't come back . . . so we got married."[39] The wartime context, as well as her pregnancy, likely also pushed Ruth toward early marriage.

Just as Ruth's husband hailed from her own home state, Melnea's husband, Marshall Cass, had been born in Richmond, Virginia, and had migrated north with his family, first living in Philadelphia and then in Boston. Melnea gave birth to their first child, a daughter, in 1919 while Marshall was away in the military, as was the case with Ruth. Notably, Melnea took up residence with her mother-in-law, a domestic worker and active community member, and received the support of family members even as she helped keep house. Melnea's interdependence with her in-laws points toward the same possibility in Ruth's situation. A 1919 transport record from Arthur Middleton's military file lists his mother, Pink (or Pinkie) Middleton, as an emergency contact residing at North Broad Street in Philadelphia. Arthur's mother may have lived in Philadelphia only briefly, as census records place her in Kershaw, South Carolina, with her husband, Flander, in both 1910 and 1920. Perhaps she moved north to assist her son and his young family. While no census lists Ruth at this address, it is very possible, even likely, that Ruth received her mother-in-law's help or lived with her temporarily while Arthur was away in training and in Europe.[40]

After Melnea Cass's husband returned from the war, the couple moved into a house of their own. Melnea ceased working outside of the home because her husband, a skilled tradesman, did not want the children to be placed in someone else's care. "So I always took care of my family," Melnea said, "and cooked and sewed, and did all kinds of things in the house. I would do everything. Made all their clothes, and everything." She spent her children's young years as a homemaker and community builder. With her own mother-in-law as a role model, Melnea turned to civic engagement while raising a family in Boston. She read the local Black press, joined the NAACP, voted at her mother-in-law's urging, and concerned herself with the status of Blacks in the South. She co-founded and joined what she described as "community clubs" and "social clubs" run by African American women. The Friendship Club, which supported the kindergarten program in her Roxbury neighborhood; the Pansy Embroidery Club; and the Harriet Tubman Mothers' Club were among her chief preoccupations between World War I and World War II. In addition to long-term membership in the Pansy Embroidery Club, where she often performed secretarial duties, Melnea plied her needle to make her three children's garments. By the 1940s, Melnea Cass was a Boston Black community maven and an officeholder in numerous clubs dedicated to African American advancement. She had left the South a poor girl, moved frequently to and from various residences, raised a family in a home she took pride in, and had come into her own as a leader and role model known as the "First Lady of Roxbury."[41]

Ruth Middleton's circumstances and contributions had also transformed in the interwar period. She and her husband were by all evidences living life apart while she continued to carry the name "Mrs. Middleton." By 1940, Ruth and her daughter, now a young woman of twenty-one, were living as boarders in the house of a sixty-four-year-old associate named Martha Horsey. Ruth, at age thirty-eight, worked as a waitress in a tearoom, and Dorothy (affectionately known as Dot) labored as a domestic in private homes.[42] Although mother and daughter still did the same general kind of work their enslaved ancestor Rose once had—that is, household and service labor—they had achieved a life beyond the baseline of freedom in the City of Brotherly

Love. In the North, they had established a household by choice and formed a wide web of enriching social connections. Their social lives and domestic arrangements were significant and interrelated. In the South as well as the North, Black women longed for private domestic space away from the scrutiny and sexual overtures of white employers. Ruth and Dorothy may not have had a home of their own by mid-century, but their mother-daughter bond was intact, and they lived independently as "lodgers" in the home of a chosen companion.[43] Beyond the parameters of their work worlds, Ruth and Dorothy Middleton led vibrant social lives that interconnected with their personal domestic sphere. If their foremothers Rose and Ashley had suffered acute separation and isolation, this mother-and-daughter pair celebrated intense sociality, especially with other Black women.

Ruth and Dorothy fully embraced a Black middle-class social life in Philadelphia that extolled women's roles as homemakers and hostesses. They entered a cozy circle of women with connections fanning out across the Northeast and westward to Chicago, likely with the help of a few key initial contacts. Martha Horsey, who rented rooms to Ruth and Dorothy in the 1940s, had entered their lives by 1929, and likely earlier, when Dorothy was not yet ten years old. Martha operated an employment agency and may have helped Ruth find work in the 1930s; perhaps this is how the two women met and formed a bond.[44] Sometimes in the company of Martha, Ruth soon joined the ranks of a rich social network made up mostly of middle-class Black migrants from the South. With these friends, Ruth adopted a mobile and enmeshed social life punctuated by parties and vacations. The social pages of *The Philadelphia Tribune*, a Black newspaper, covered Ruth's trip to Atlantic City with friends in 1932, where she sported "baby blue organdic [organdie]" beach-

EUBANK, MILDRED JEANETTE
"Mil"
2220 CHRISTIAN STREET, PHILADELPHIA, PA.
PRIMARY
Day Students' Club.

Mildred Eubanks (also spelled Eubank), niece to Martha Horsey and friend of Ruth Middleton, is pictured here in her yearbook. Eubanks's style of hair, dress, and accessorizing was likely shared by Ruth Middleton, a noted fashion trendsetter in her set. West Chester University *Serpentine*, 1931. Special Collections, University Libraries, West Chester University, West Chester, Pennsylvania.

wear. Community media coverage extended to her attendance at various dinner parties in Philadelphia as well as in New York City. In the 1930s, Ruth intensified her social activities, attending and hosting a flurry of bridge parties, tea parties, and cocktail parties with members of a Black professional elite, including doctors and financiers, that stretched across multiple states. Among her recurring destinations was the Brooklyn, New York, home of Helen Stebo, her sister-in-law, an indication that although Ruth lived apart from Arthur, she kept in close contact with his family. Strikingly, Ruth seems to have named her only known daughter, Dorothy Helen, after this paternal aunt.[45]

At home in Philadelphia, Ruth Middleton joined, and possibly helped organize, a series of Black women's social clubs in an era when clubs were central to community life. She was actively involved with the Rotators Bridge Club, the Philedona Club, and the Conochie Club; in 1935 the Conochie Club met in the "spacious home" of a Black associate to celebrate St. Patrick's Day amid green decor.[46] Ruth became a regular figure in the Black society pages, where her colorful style and witty personality emerge. She donned a "modish" aesthetic and was fond of fashionable dress. Her "blue taffeta pajamas topped by a shimmering silver lamé jacket" made a splash at a dinner party in April 1938, while her "gray wool three piece suit with a finger tip jacket and black accessories" set a "charming example" three weeks later. Ruth professed herself to be a progressive and devoted hostess. When asked by a peer in 1939 what she would like to receive as a Christmas gift, Ruth responded with a remark that inspired this line in the Black society pages: "any new gadget with which to delight her guests when she entertains, would warm the cockles of this lovely hostesses heart." When quoted about her pet peeves in 1938, Ruth exclaimed that she was "irritated by people who chewed gum incessantly."[47]

By 1940, when she and her daughter were ensconced in the home of Martha Horsey, Ruth Middleton had secured her place among the Black upper crust. Described as an "Attractive South Philadelphia Matron" in January of that year, Ruth took one more crucial step in her social ascent.[48] She joined a large Black congregation where she had surely been attending as a visitor for years. Black churches towered as central institutions for longtime residents as well as new arrivals in Philadelphia and other Great Migration destination cities. The Episcopal congregation Ruth chose, St. Simon the Cyrenian Church, had been assembling since 1894. In 1897, its founding members had purchased land on Twenty-second and Reed streets in South Philadelphia. Ruth's formal admission to the church in February was followed by a laying on of hands ceremony in March. Dorothy had formally joined the church as a teen, several years before her mother, a further indication that Ruth had long been attending there.[49] Dorothy, like her mother, began to appear in the social pages as a vivacious club and church member. In the spring of 1940, Dorothy authored installments of the youth section of the society pages, noting "all sorts of parties and dances" in celebration of Easter and a "whirlwind of formals."[50] But all of this buzzing social activity had yet to unfold when Ruth arrived in Philadelphia around the year 1918, possibly pregnant, probably afraid of the multiple risks surrounding her, and certainly carrying her formerly enslaved grandmother's sack.

54 Receive "Laying On Of Hands"

"54 Receive 'Laying On Of Hands.'" This grainy newspaper photograph records Ruth Middleton's confirmation at St. Simon the Cyrenian Church, Philadelphia, in February 1940. Ruth J. Middleton is listed in the article as a member of this group; however, specific individuals are not identified by face. The newspaper print preceding the list that contains her name reads: "The following persons were confirmed at the same time for the Mission of the Holy Spirit." *The Philadelphia Tribune*, March 7, 1940.

On Wednesday evening, February 28, the Rt. Rev. Charles Fiske, D.D., acting for the Bishop of Pennsylvania, the Rt. Rev. Francis M. Taitt, D.D., visited the Chapel of St. Simon the Cyrenian, 22nd and Reed streets where he preached an excellent sermon and was greeted by a large congregation.

The following persons, presented by the Rev. John R. Logan, Sr., Vicar were confirmed:

The following persons were confirmed at the same time for the Mission of the Holy Spirit, presented by the Rev. John R. Logan, Jr., Curate of St. Simon's and minister in charge of the Mission: Edward Armster, Earl Mosley, Dorothy Meeley, St. Julian Jamison, and Joseph Smallwood.

John Brant, Isaac Briscoe, Mrs. Dorothy L. Carter, Eugene B. Coursey, Mabel M. Dorsey, William H. Dorse, Norman J. Edwards, John R. Exum, Irene R. Harmon, Mary R. Hawkins, Leslie P. Hill, 2nd, Mrs. Laura S. Hinson, Selena R. Howard, Mrs. Thelma A. Hodgin, Katherine Jackson, Mrs. Eva M. Johnson, Isaac F. Johnson, Alvin W. King, Kathryn A. King, Lenwood L. Langston, Easton P. Ledgister, Mrs. Mary A. Matthews, Edwin R. Matthews, Mrs. Ruth J. Middleton, Clarice V. Ransome, Mrs. Elizabeth S. Reid, Mrs. Ella M. Ridgway, Charles W. Scott, Mrs. Ruby S. Seamon, Edwin G. Simmons, Junius B. Simmons, Mrs. Margaret Smith, Kenneth S. Stokes, Mrs. Edith B. Taylor, Hester N. Taylor, Martha L. Thompson, David R. Thompson, Elizabeth J. Tripp, Walter M. Tripp, Mary G. Ward, Jean V. Webb, Robert H. Webb, Jr., Lewis H. White, Cynthia A. Whittaker, Mrs. Rose J. Williams, John N. Williams, Leslie R. Willis, Mrs. Minnie H. Wills, Isaac M. Wilson.

———A Colored Judge———

What made Ruth record her family story during those first few years in the city? Had the disruption of relocation brought to mind a longing for home? Did isolation in a new place lead her to dwell on separation from family? Had the birth of a child inspired reflection about her own role as a mother and the plight of the foremothers who had preceded her? Did she wish to shape her family story into a concrete anchor of identity—as a Black woman, a southerner, a survivor—for herself and for her daughter? Had she become keenly aware, in the disorienting North, of the need for a tangible heritage to hold fast to and pass down? Perhaps if Ruth had never experienced the trial of having to make life anew that was the chief test of the Great Migration generations, she would not have sewn on the sack, and we would not be contemplating this rare artifact of multigenerational Black women's experience.

And why did Ruth, a few years into her Philadelphia sojourn, choose embroidery as the method for preserving her family's story? How did that choice relate to the woman she would become by the 1940s—a respected hostess, fashion exemplar, and church member? By the time Ruth occupied living quarters in the posh homes of Philadelphia elites while working as a domestic servant, embroidery had long been associated with the feminine sphere. In eighteenth-century Europe and the United States, writers, artists, and cultural connoisseurs had come to define the pastime exclusively as a women's craft that soon stood "entirely as the expression of femininity."[51] Women who diligently and skillfully embroidered text and images onto fabric properly fulfilled the gender ideology of their society and time, performing a task that met the growing cultural expectations of women as the submissive, quiet, pious, and domestic sex. As we saw in a previous chapter, white women of the antebellum upper-class South sewed as a matter of duty and embroidered as a feature of gender decorum. In the Victorian era, the idealization of embroidery work as evidence of femininity, domesticity, and gentility skyrocketed. Girls and women of the elite classes embroidered alphabet samplers, Bible verses, floral still-life arrangements, forest animals, and bucolic scenes of peopled landscapes and calming interiors, and women of the aspiring middle and working classes did the same, straining toward the higher status associated with feminine drawing room culture and, increasingly, middle-class style.[52] Because women produced embroidery in domestic spaces for the purpose of bringing comfort to the home, which had taken on greater importance for the Victorian-era middle class, embroidery came to "evoke the home" and to signal the space of the family, "specifically mothers and daughters," explains the author of a classic book on embroidery, *The Subversive Stitch*.[53]

Needlework picture. African American student Rachel Ann Lee fashioned this canvas-work scene, an example of the needlework some Black girls did in northern schools in the mid-nineteenth century. Rachel Ann Lee, Oblate Sisters of Providence School, Baltimore, Maryland, 1846, wool, linen, and metallic thread, 2009.0013 A, B, museum purchase with funds drawn from the Centenary Fund, courtesy of Winterthur Museum.

While enslaved Black women in the United States were forced to sew clothing and textiles for plantation enterprises, they were rarely trained in the ornamental needlework of embroidery, marking an invisible line of status between feminized sewing ladies of the big house and defeminized sewing laborers of the slave quarters. White women of the elite classes and the aspiring middle classes embroidered to be (and be viewed as) feminine women, a category from which Black women were almost universally barred. Enslaved Black women who were exposed to "cultured" dress and manners sometimes had access to training in embroidery prior to the Civil War. Following emancipation, formerly enslaved African American women of the aspiring working and middle classes took up a range of needle crafts associated with the feminine ideal, such as crocheting and embroidery.

In the pages of the St. Simon the Cyrenian Church monthly newsletter in 1917–18, for instance, a sewer identified only as "Jane," presumably a Black woman seeking a like clientele, advertised "Art Needlework," "Infants' Wear," and "Lessons in Knitting and Crocheting" on Fifty-second Street.[54] Melnea Cass, as we know, fashioned her children's clothing by hand in Boston. In another example, a Black woman named Beatrice Jeanette Whiting, who grew up and remained in Cass's hometown of Richmond, Virginia, studied embroidery as a teen or young woman. Born in 1890, of the same generation as Ruth and Melnea, Beatrice Whiting hailed from an educated family and became a high school home economics teacher remembered by students for introducing them to sewing. Whiting's sewing exercise book from her own time learning to embroider in the early 1900s features twenty-seven practice pages sewn in white and red thread. The accession record for Whiting's sample book, housed at the Schlesinger Library at the Harvard Rad-

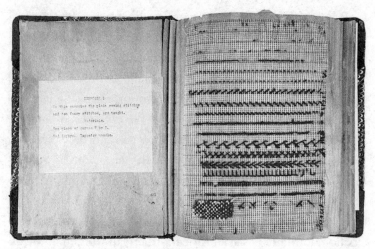

Beatrice Jeanette Whiting's sewing exercise book, front inside cover and first page, ca. 1915. African American sewer Beatrice Whiting completed these sewing exercises in the early 1900s, in Richmond, Virginia. From *75 Stories, 75 Years: Documenting the Lives of American Women at the Schlesinger Library*, exhibition, 2018. Photograph by Kevin Grady/ Harvard Radcliffe Institute. Courtesy of the Schlesinger Library, Harvard Radcliffe Institute.

cliffe Institute, notes her improvement in skill and "excellent" stitching by the final exercise. Whiting may have treasured this evidence of her youthful effort featuring all manner of sophisticated hems and stitch patterns, for it was saved together with her "embossed leather" memory book, filled with inscriptions from students and colleagues upon her retirement in 1960.[55]

Black women's enthusiasm for adopting the fine needle arts was also evident in public exhibits of the late nineteenth and early twentieth centuries, like the cotton and craft fairs where prize-winning quilter Harriet Powers displayed her work in the 1880s. At an annual African American fair held in Powers's hometown of Athens, Georgia, a local newspaper reported on the wares of the "women's department," describing "a great many very pretty quilts and home-made bed coverings . . . a white knit quilt that is quite pretty . . . some nice fancy work, conspicuous among which we noticed silk pillows and cushions." The reporter noted, in addition, that students from the Atlanta Baptist Female Seminary (now Spelman College) had submitted "credible specimens of crayon work, embroidery and sewing."[56]

Attaining these comparatively rarefied skills common to white women of certain classes was a source of pride for Black women who were striving to gain ground in an arena that white women across the class spectrum had long claimed: the ability to maintain domestic spaces of their own for their families. For "Black Victorians," especially in northeastern cities like Philadelphia, where Ruth Middleton resided, the appearance of the "decorous" home was paramount to the respectability of the family, and women's textile and lace work was instrumental to the achievement of this aesthetic.[57] St. Simon the Cyrenian Church in Philadelphia hosted sewing and knitting classes, among other activities, for local youths and exhibited articles of clothing made by the participants. Among the "Pages of Interest to Women" printed by *The Philadelphia Tribune* were meeting announcements for the Willow Green Embroidery Club, the Friendly Sewing Club, and the Fireside Sewing Club, each of which would meet in a private home.

Indeed, much of this social sewing took place inside the home and would eventually enhance home decor, even as members of the Black intelligentsia, like W.E.B. Du Bois, urged "the mass of Negro people" to "sacredly guard the home, to make it the centre of social life and moral guardianship."[58] Anna Julia Cooper, a contemporary of Du Bois's and a scholar, teacher, and principal in Washington, D.C., likewise praised the Black domestic endeavor in her treatise *A Voice from the South*, noting that "this hope for our country primarily and fundamentally rests . . . on the homelife and on the influence of good women in those homes."[59]

In the decades spanning the nineteenth and twentieth centuries when Melnea Cass did club work and Anna Julia Cooper praised home life, educated Black women in northern, southern, midwestern, and western cities formed local associations that embraced and linked both. Among the major goals of these women was advancing the progress of Black women in society and strengthening the Black family unit, which suffered from persistent poverty, a lack of economic and educational opportunity, and the cloud of everyday racial prejudice. They shared the sense that they were duty-bound, as African American women, to bear the burdens of their race, of their sex, and of the nation. Those burdens were understood to be contemporary as well as historical, consisting of the weight of past wrongs and present urgencies.

In keeping with the gender sensibility of their times, clubwomen believed that the role of the Black wife and mother stood central to the improvement of Black family life and the advancement of the race as a whole. They also aimed to defend Black women against defamation in American public culture, where journalists and correspondents routinely accused them of sexual immorality, impropriety, and vice. The impetus for connecting scores and then hundreds of local Black women's clubs into a formalized national network, the National Association of Colored Women (NACW), in 1896, had taken shape in response to a flagrant incident of politically motivated public shaming. After a group of Black women in Boston, led by *Woman's Era* magazine editor Josephine St. Pierre Ruffin, saw antilynching activist Ida B. Wells pilloried as "having no sense of virtue and . . . being altogether without character" in a southern newspaper, they called a meeting for Black women to come together and act.[60] As club organizer and intellectual Fannie Barrier Williams put it at the World's Columbian Exposition in Chicago in 1893: "The morality of our home life has been commented on so disparagingly and meanly that we are placed in the unfortunate position of being defenders of our name."[61]

Black women organizers issued a vehement self-defense in print and in speeches, referring to Christian theology, royal women in antiquity, and the accomplishments of contemporary Black women in order to ground their claims of propriety and moral standing.[62] Mary Church Terrell, the first president of the expanded NACW, stressed this advance in her 1896 speech titled "The Progress of Colored Women": "So gloomy were their prospects, so fatal the laws, so pernicious the customs, only fifty years ago. But, from the day their fetters were broken . . . colored women have forged steadily ahead in the acquisition of knowledge and in the cultivation of those virtues which make for good."[63] Their strategy of using personal comportment as a weapon of defense was just as important to clubwomen as eloquent rebuttal. For many of these women, standing against public disparagement meant the constant demonstration of high moral character and proper feminine attributes reflective of Victorian mores.[64]

As a Black clubwoman, Mamie Garvin Fields participated in this major social movement at the local level in Charleston, South Carolina. In her memoir, Fields depicts a Black southern family striving to achieve and maintain middle-class standing in the post-Reconstruction South, a quest in which domestic life was central. Her family defined status as having a financial position secure enough for men to work in a profession or at a skilled trade, earning enough so that the women could work in their own homes rather than in the homes of white families, while their children could regularly attend school rather than laboring for wages. The space of the private home beyond white supervision was paramount, even if it was a home shared with extended kin. Mamie Garvin Fields grew up in this kind of relatively privileged social world. Her uncle, in whose home Mamie's mother lived from a young age, served as a Methodist minister. Mamie's parents disdained the thought of Black women in the family performing domestic work in white people's homes or "carrying around anybody's white baby."[65] Instead, Mamie's mother worked as a dressmaker until she married, at which point she became a full-time homemaker. Mamie's father labored as a skilled carpenter. Mamie became an educator and a community organizer in mutual aid societies and Black women's clubs. A twentieth-century resident of Charleston, Mamie Garvin Fields came to exemplify the middle-class values her family upheld, despite her grandparents' history of enslavement on a farm in the Barnwell District (the same county where Ashley was enslaved in 1853).

As Mamie Garvin Fields tells her story to her granddaughter (and co-author) in the book *Lemon Swamp*, she connects sacrosanct domestic space with women's fiber arts and care for heirloom fabrics. Embroidery and well-wrought cloth represent the attainment of middle-class respectability and the opportunity for Black women to be "ladies" rather than "field hands," "wenches," or "fancies" (in the pejorative terms of the slave auction block). Mamie Fields's grandmother kept a trunk "full of soft linen and handmade finery from the West Indies" and "dried petal flowers, which she had sewed into little silk bags." This captivating grandmother "entertained the girls, showing [them] her wedding dress and veil, the hemstitched petticoats, the scarves and antimacassars to put on the furniture," while making promises about which of her "beautiful things" she would pass on to each young relative when she died. In this elaborate ritual of opening and examining the contents of the trunk, Mamie Fields's grandmother was demonstrating for the children what it meant to be a properly feminized Black woman through the language of textiles, and enveloping them in a fantasy of grand inheritance and maternal lineage.[66]

Although Mamie confessed that she "never got so much as a doily out of that trunk!," she became expert at "needlework." After she attended college and began working as an elementary school teacher, Mamie Fields, along with some close friends, formed a group dedicated to "uplifting" the race. In 1927, they founded a Charleston organization called the Modern Priscilla, which joined with the NACW, the umbrella organization of Black women's clubs dedicated to improving living conditions and opportunities for African Americans. The work of the NACW was national and regional, as well as local.

Northward of Mamie Garvin Fields, in Boston, Melnea Cass became president of the NACW's northeastern region. The Charleston club, which took its name from a Boston ladies' art magazine (suggesting the transregional shape of Black women's club consciousness), "dressed fine because needlework was our forte," Mamie Fields recalled. The Black women of Charleston's Modern Priscilla "published directions to make everything for the home and for yourself, from crocheted tablecloths to the crocheted yoke for your shirtwaist, and from old-fashioned flounce curtains to the newest type of skirt."[67] In addition to promoting her social club's dedication to sewing and yarn art and passing these skills along to her students in the classroom, Mamie ensured that her own granddaughters learned the feminine craft of embroidery that African American women had long been dissociated from. Mamie Fields, who refers to herself and her friends as "ladies" in the memoir, made it a point to teach her granddaughters "crocheting, embroidering, and the like."[68]

For Mamie Fields's generation, which was also Ruth Middleton's generation, sophisticated sewing was a sign of feminine, middle-class refinement and a simultaneous projection of Black women's dignity. After living through the insidious racial environment of the early twentieth century, Fields was "determined to pass on a heritage" to her granddaughters, which she did through telling stories about the struggles and accomplishments of their family and teaching sewing skills that exemplified African American women's virtue and their essential contributions in the home and in society.[69]

Given what we know of Ruth Middleton's slow shift into a more specialized level of domestic service, her exposure to the domestic spaces of highly educated white people's homes, and her eventual acceptance into the ranks of the Philadelphia Black middle class, her choice to embroider, rather than write, her family story suggests cultural as well as political motives. Through this artistic medium, Ruth demonstrated her skill in a craft that signified her class aspirations and her identity as a refined Black woman who embraced the domestic arts of the feminine "sphere." In addition to claiming this elevated space for herself, she simultaneously claimed it for her foremothers. Ashley, who had little more to her name than a battered sack, and Rose, who possessed scarcely more than a tattered dress, would be memorialized through an art form that showcased feminine worth, propriety, and delicacy, a posthumous display of respect withheld from them during their lifetimes.

There is, of course, a complicating aspect to Black as well as white women's embrace of a craft that was so closely wedded to fixed ideas of what "proper" womanhood entailed. In the 1700s and 1800s, women were relegated to the endeavor of embroidery, which was defined as a craft rather than a fine art, an indication of its relatively low cultural value when compared to masculine-associated activities like painting or sculpture. Embroidery gained even greater social importance in the nineteenth century when women of means were banished into the domestic sphere, where their lives were tightly regulated. Embroidery, often taken up in the feminine spaces of drawing rooms and requiring quiet diligence, represented a sequestering of women's lives in the home and signified "absolute innocence and subservience." No artistic act is ever without nuance. Even as embroidery work was encouraged to "still and silence" privileged women, it could serve as a vehicle for circumventing societal rules. In Victorian novels, embroidery played the symbolic role of representing lost speech for women characters, serving as a "loophole" for "what they were unable to say openly," writes a foundational scholar of embroidery.[70] Despite the constraints of the form, women did use needlework as a way of expressing personal feelings and wishes.[71]

Embroidery was a flexible art in its ability to convey meaning. It was also a slighted form because of its association with women. In the 1960s and 1970s, feminists seized on the possibilities presented by these competing characteristics. Artists in the studio and activists in the streets took up embroidery to satirize cultural convention and invest typically feminized imagery (such as embroidered floral bouquets) with double meanings that exposed and criticized the confinements of domesticity. Feminist fiber artists brought a cottage pastime out into the public arena, reinvesting fabric imagery with the rhetorical message that the personal is political. A form that implied "impotence" could be turned against cultural expectation to slyly imply a refusal to cede power.[72]

The clever, creative, sometimes quiet, and often tongue-in-cheek reclamation of the needle arts among women has seen a resurgence since the 1970s. Around the year 2000, women began to reclaim knitting and sewing circles as spaces of solidarity, to use handiwork as a social connector and form of giving, and to make political commentary through craft in a movement termed "craftivism."[73] A knitting wave gave rise to the "pussy hat" following the 2016 presidential election (in which Hillary Clinton won the popular vote but Donald Trump won the presidency) and continues in the form of knit-bombed urban landscapes that force a reexamination of common objects and community values. The current resurgence of arts and crafts traditionally associated with women extends to embroidery. The journalist E. Tammy Kim explained in a story about her admiration for her Korean grandmother's embroidery work from the 1940s that her own return to the "hoop and thread" came in a "moment of anger and news overload." The political upheaval of the Trump presidency pushed her practice, and, she observed, "the fabric arts tick upward in times such as these, when women feel particularly indignant."[74]

As a young African American woman facing the daily task of cleaning her wealthy employers' home while looking out at a segregated world where Blacks could be killed just for occupying urban spaces, Ruth may have taken up her needle as an expression of gender identity as well as familial remembrance. Her chosen medium mirrored the gender and class ideals of dominant society even as it undercut that very society's exclusion of Black women from those ideals. Perhaps the darkened crease line still apparent across the upper edge of the sack indicates how the textile may have once been folded for tabletop display or set behind a frame as part of a domestic statement. Perhaps Ruth felt, as E. Tammy Kim speculated about her grandmother, that embroidery "lent her a quiet, fleeting freedom."[75] Sewing has been oppressive work, but it has also been healing work. Sewing, like telling, is meditative. A suture is a stitch.

SCARLET LETTERS

It is difficult to tell, by peering at the thread on the sack, exactly what Ruth's capacities were in the art of sewing. She confines her use of embroidery to letters only, electing to omit pictorial imagery. She worked with "three strand-cotton embroidery floss," and employed a basic "back-stitch."[76] The anthropologist Mark Auslander has observed that the "final three lines of the embroidery (in blue or green thread) are in a somewhat more mature or skilled hand," leading him to wonder if Ruth began the work at one period in time and finished it in another.[77] Perhaps Ruth did not yet possess the skill required to fashion the "hair-fine embroidery" akin to realistic painting described by E. Tammy Kim in homage to her grandmother's handiwork. Or perhaps Ruth opted to omit pictures in favor of the specificity of language and purposefully retained only the vague impression of a heart shape in the spatial arrangement of her indented lines. Whatever her level of skill, Ruth seems to have been interested in the kind of telling in which words were worth more than pictures.

Ruth's needlework is in many ways a singular creation. It does carry hints and imprints of other forms, such as the controlled, regulated, verselike lines of the middle-class schoolgirl sampler. At the same time, Ruth's sewing veers off into distinctive terrain that suggests a personal purpose. In contrast to the nineteenth-century sampler, which typically contains alphabetic lines; biblical, moral, or poetic verse; local scenes, houses, or landmarks; autobiographical sketches; or genealogical information such as birth and death dates, Ruth's embroidery chronicles an intergenerational family history in original language and with intense focus.[78]

By choosing to write through stitches, Ruth transformed her fabric canvas into a document, a written record of past events.

This decision, similar to her election to work in a "feminine" form, elevated the cultural resonance of her creation. By scripting a family history onto the bag that was core to the story, Ruth accomplished two crucial feats: she succeeded in attaching a special story to a precious object, permanently joining them together so that neither would be forgotten, and she entered her family's humble sack into the written record from which histories of the nation are made. Ruth turned the story she had heard through the years into a remarkable document, a written record with the cultural power to augment history. She created a form of what the grandmother character in Gayl Jones's novel *Corregidora* insists upon when she passes down the family story of surviving slavery to her granddaughter: evidence. "They didn't want to leave no evidence of what they done—so it couldn't be held against them," the grandmother insists. "And I'm leaving evidence. And you got to leave evidence too."[79] In her act of retelling a story she had been told in order to fix it in permanent form, Ruth Middleton, a domestic laborer, became an oral historian—a collector and interpreter of evidence, a preserver of knowledge about the past.

Ruth's investment in history-making through written documentation and the preservation of a fragile artifact is apparent in her care for the sack (patched, folded, and stored over time) and the details she chose to inscribe. She offers, first, an orientation for the reader that includes historical context and key facts: her relationship to her subject matter, the names of the main actors in the narrative, the location of the action, the context of slavery. She shifts into narrative when recounting events unfolding in time: Rose giving Ashley a sack when a dramatic change befell them. She lists what the sack held with purposeful precision. She quotes the mother's parting words ("Told her"), employing a space break rather than quotation marks to differentiate this direct speech, and using the color red, perhaps in keeping with the rendering of Jesus's words in Bible translations.[80] She moves to close the text by underscoring her relational tie to Ashley. Finally, Ruth documents her name and the date, lending this textile the feel of an official report equal to any document and standing as a poetic rebuttal to the anonymizing archives of slavery.

More than a recorder of events, Ruth offers an artistic interpretation of these historical happenings, too. Her moral indictment of slavery is clear in the final line of her narrative: "She never saw her again." And alongside this charge, she concludes that love and family triumphed over immorality, suffusing the text with an enduring emotive tone through the stress she places on particular words. Ruth conveys this emotional emphasis directly. The word "Love" dominates her fabric page, declaring itself her major theme in the enlarged line: "It be filled with my Love always." This choice to visually highlight feeling suggests what the poet Elizabeth Alexander has called the artist's capacity to "envision what we are not meant to envision: complex black selves, real and enactable black power, rampant and unfetishized black beauty."[81]

Ruth's use of the color red combined with an emphasis on emotion taps into shared human associations with archetypal tropes. Cloth work, Ruth's medium, gathers its communicative power through broad symbolic imitation and association on a relatively permanent material. Although cultural differences certainly exist in the use of fabrics, people associate pattern and color with aspects of shared human experience in order to make meaning. Think especially of culturally significant textiles such as the robe of a queen, the vestments of a priest, the flag of a nation, the dress of a bride, or the shroud of the dead, which all communicate meaning beyond their home cultures. Colored thread, invented between 3000 and 4000 B.C., was an important innovation in conveying such meaning. Red, one of the first dyes developed from plants, is among the most primal of textile color communicators, long representing vitality "in the imitation of blood."[82] In eliciting associations with blood, Ruth's stitchery signifies at once the pain of slavery and the vibrancy of the beating heart.

She may also have been aware of old meanings the color red carried from slavery days in the coastal South. In the practice of magical folk religion by enslaved people, red flannel was preferred for the bundling of sacred objects, such as roots, graveyard dust, or animal bones, invested with supernatural power. These conjure bags or gris-gris bags held either protective or destructive properties, depending on the kind of magic the conjurer had locked into it through ritual.[83] Ruth uses this red line in her record—the brightest and biggest of them all—to emphasize the culturally layered meanings in her narrative palimpsest. We can imagine her hope that her reader (herself at a later point in life, or her daughter, or a descendant she could not yet imagine) would sense these rich reverberations when they encountered the object.

Like miners with our headlamps on, we could continue to dig for Ruth's interpretations as conveyed by the lines of the sack. We might or might not be in keeping with Ruth's intentions in our haul of subterranean meanings. Ruth chooses to name her foremothers but not her forefathers, suggesting a particular investment in women's history and a rejection of a paternal line that might include enslavers. While she names unfree forebears, she refuses to name the people who owned them, limiting their centrality in her record. In offering an inventory of all that Rose packed, including love, Ruth produces a ledger of what enslaved people, counted as possessions, themselves possessed: the hard-won material things that could cushion bruised spirits and the strength of character as well as feeling that could carry generations through adversity.[84]

Did Ruth take a writer's license in the order of the items she named on the sack: a dress, pecans, a braid, love? Did she intend to shape a narrative that moves incrementally into an interior space of Black experience, beginning with the external covering of clothing, shifting to the ingested matter of food, noting an outgrowth of the body itself, and ending at a center of feeling? Is this how she understood the story of her ancestors' sack, as a journey inward to the self that is at heart relational? And did she seek to preserve that experience in her craft, steadily leading the reader from an outer material state to an inner emotional sphere, perhaps maintaining a trace of how her grandmother had told it? In place of the cold slave list, Ruth gives us a family recipe, the life-sustaining ingredients a mother passes on to a daughter. And chief among these ingredients of clothing, food, and lineage is the emotional driver of love. *Told her*—Rose said, Ashley recalled, and Ruth stitched—*It be filled with my Love always.*

The many ways we can interpret these sparse yet pregnant lines reveal Ruth's inscription as more than evidence, more than an inventory, more than a record, more than a history. The sewing on Ashley's sack relies on an immediacy of form, a crispness of diction, and an emotional shimmer reminiscent of literary poetry. Some might even feel that this inscription reads like haiku, a form of poetry characterized by its brief numbers of lines, a seasonal tag, implicit references to a preexisting body of like poems, the recounting of an event, and a tone of openness or "welcome."[85] In this swatch of sentences read as poetry, Ruth is greeting her ancestors, welcoming them into her memory and into reunion with one another.[86] Similarly to haiku, this sack embroidered by busy hands has zero extra words to spare. It reduces down to steam in the pot, a ghost in our peripheral vision, the essential yet ephemeral thing all human beings need. Here, at the bottom of the sack, we find unburied the gift of love, which, as the poet Nicole Sealey has said, is the satisfying sound of a poem "click[ing] shut."[87]

Ruth Middleton stood toward the end of a long line of women survivors. She was clearly conscious, even reverent, of this lineage and her special place in it, and she used fabric, as women had for centuries, in a process not only of "memorializing their families," but also of "creating" those families.[88] Perhaps this sensibility of family-making by passing down objects inspired Ruth's use of varied earth tones in her embroidery. The brown thread of the opening lines gives way to green thread by the close, mimicking the loose form of an inverted family tree, with roots reaching back into the past and shoots fanning out into the future, where the written record of known time ends.[89] A daughter, mother, embroiderer, storyteller, and historian of her family's past, Ruth died of tuberculosis while in her mature youth, not yet forty. She had been ill for months and under the care of her friend Martha Horsey, who also provided data for the death certificate. Ruth succumbed to the disease at Frederick Douglass Memorial Hospital in the winter of 1942, just under a century since her grandmother Ashley had been taken from her great-grandmother Rose in an undocumented slave sale. Ruth's own daughter, Dorothy, who would have inherited the sack, passed on in 1988 with no known lineal descendants.[90] Afterward, the textile was lost, perhaps boxed, donated, or sold with other items once attached to these lives as ephemeral as our own.[91] But the bag Rose packed, the cloth Ashley kept, and the tale Ruth told live on to declare the staying power of love's ties and women's stories.

CONCLUSION

IT BE FILLED

Well now, what about us, the women who were sitting here in
Mt. Zion Church, the women coming after our great ances-
tresses? WHO OF YOU KNOW HOW TO CARRY YOUR
BURDEN IN THE HEAT OF THE DAY?

— MAMIE GARVIN FIELDS recalling a speech by
Mary Church Terrell, president, National Association
of Colored Women, in Charleston, 1916

Still there are seeds to be gathered, and room in the bag of
stars.

—URSULA K. LE GUIN,
Dancing at the Edge of the World, 1989

AFRICAN AMERICAN THINGS HAD LITTLE CHANCE
to last. This is a painful lesson learned by family historians and
museum curators. How could people who *were* property acquire
and pass down property? How could families auctioned like
cattle hold on to a Bible or a bead? An excess of trauma, a glut
of disruption, and a surfeit of sudden migration severely limited
the chances for enslaved people to maintain troves. Cast into a
faulty freedom following the Civil War, without the benefit of
savings or stockpiles, formerly enslaved parents and children

often lived hand to mouth, desperate to fend off crushing debt peonage. They lacked land, animals to work it, and tools to aid in their labor. They could claim few personal items beyond "the clothes on their backs."[1] The modicum of things Black families did manage to acquire and hold on to were accorded little value by outsiders. Compared to other groups with a stability afforded by earnings, wealth, or racial privilege, Black people's possessions were more likely to wind up in dump pits and rag bins as families lost elder members, moved on, or were pushed out during the height of Jim Crow segregation and racially motivated violence.[2] "There are so many stories about the objects that were lost," the family historian Kendra Field has noted, "lost letters, lost photographs, lost objects of meaning."[3] When African American things are lost, the stories once joined to them weaken, memories of the past fray, historical evidence shrinks, and intergenerational wisdom fades.

This loss of the material traces of history, which stands alongside a multitude of other losses in African American experience, has grave ramifications for well-being. Human values and human relations have been expressed and revealed through things for as long as we have been painting on cave walls and making tools. We come to know ourselves through things, cement community ties through things, think with things, and remember what is important to us with the aid of objects.[4] Beyond the critical role of communicating information, things function as tokens and repositories, as staples in the fabric of time, as a means to effect psychological, emotional, and existential transport or to "convey viewers to another world or state of being."[5] This quality allows people to use things in the service of compassion and communal life. When we see, touch, and consider another person's cherished object, we come to appreciate their experience and their group's experience that much more. In this

Interior page of the Morton family Bible. Aaron and Gardenia Morton used this family Bible as an archive, storing inside its pages hair clippings, lists of births and deaths, and funeral announcements. The parents of seven children (two boys and five girls), they passed the Bible down across generations. It remains a family keepsake today. Family story shared by Jessica D. Moorman. Photograph by Tiya Miles. Used by permission of Jessica D. Moorman.

way, the physical materials that we find, preserve, or make (from rocks and shells to books, blankets, and buildings) can function like social glue, adhering individuals to one another through felt relationship.

Beyond connecting people, things contain their own vitality, profusion of spirit, or even, we could say, personality. We recognize how many things in our daily lives were once (and are still?) alive when we consider the way in which materials (building supplies, clothing, glass bottles, and so on) are harvested from the living earth. We sense this strange quality of seeming aliveness when certain things capture our notice (a pearlescent button winking in the sunlight, a porcelain doll with perceptive eyes, a sculptural acorn poised like a dancer, a four-leaf clover lying in wait). Particular things can affect our thoughts, moods, and movements, as if they are acting in the world.[6] Enlivened things can call us into recognition of a material world that exists independently of the human sphere of action but also intersects with our lives. Cultivating a consciousness of this vibrant physical realm and a recognition of the ethical and primal implications of our interdependence with it may "chasten fantasies of human mastery" over nature and other people. It could help us find ways to live differently than we have since the industrial revolution, which has so badly damaged this physical planet.[7]

Having been treated as possessions and deprived of ownership of themselves, their families, crops they nurtured, and objects they made and maintained, African American survivors of slavery recognized the world of things. They lived each day in haunted awareness of the thin boundary line between human and non-human, a thinness daily exposed and abused by slave societies. Despite the prominence of a Cartesian duality in Western philosophy that proposed a clear split between spirit and matter, enslaved Blacks knew that people could be treated like things and things prized over people. Awash in this awful knowledge, African Americans may have been early theorists of the mercurial nature of things. In this understanding, they would have joined Native Americans, the first thing-thinkers on this continent who affirmed in their stories and lived through their actions a belief that many things have a kind of spirit and are capable of relationship. In their everyday lives, Indigenous North Americans recognized the animated nature of things as well as the innate relationality of people, non-human animals, and plants, all of which, scientists now confirm, share common fundamental elements (such as cell structure, chemical makeup, and DNA).[8]

In addition to enslaved people's knowing all too well the metaphysical quality of things that went deeper than the bare necessity of what was needed for survival, comfort, honor, and social connection, their understanding of the role of possession and possessions in their own subjugation motivated their desperate attempts to acquire and retain things of value. Objects became "weapons" in the ongoing struggle for dignity and liberty. Enslaved people used "coins, cloth, drams of liquor, [and] battered top hats" in pursuit of freedom and purpose. For them, things amounted to a real world of provision and beyond that, to "'dream worlds' of material possibility."[9] Material objects performed many functions in the lives of Black people and, indeed, all people, from the practical and economic uses of items to the mental and emotional meanings of things.

A heart-rending letter written by a man sold away from his family reflects this understanding of the material, social, and psychological importance of things. "My Dear," Abream Scriven penned to his wife, Dinah Jones, in the fall of 1858, "I want to Send you some things but I donot know who to Send them by but I will thry to get them to you and my children. . . . My Dear wife for you and my children my pen cannot Express the griffe I feel to be parted from you all."[10] Abream hoped that these things he possessed and touched, when received and held by his family members, could help fill the gulf of sadness that separated them. In another missive, dictated by an enslaved woman in Missouri named Ann to her husband, Andrew Valentine, a soldier in the Civil War, things represented remembered ties and a vision of freedom. "You do not know how bad I am treated," she related. "They are treating me worse and worse every day. Our child cries for you. Send me some money as soon as you can for me and my child are almost naked. My cloth is yet in the loom and there is no telling when it will be out. . . . Do not fret too much for me for it wont be long before I will be free and then all we make will be ours." Ann concluded the message to her husband with this postscript: "P.S. Send our little girl a string of beads in your next letter to remember you by."[11]

Elizabeth Keckley, the formerly enslaved dressmaker to Mary Todd Lincoln, emphasized the relationship between memory and things at the close of her memoir: "Every chair looks like an old friend. In memory I have travelled through the shadows and the sunshine of the past, and the bare walls are associated with the visions that have come to me from the long-ago. As I love the children of memory, so I love every article in this room, for each has become a part of memory itself."[12] For Keckley, the things she owns and lives with seem to store her memories, releasing them to her when she seeks them out while triggering emotions of affection, melancholy, and determination. This may, in fact, have been similar to the ensemble of emotions that flooded Ruth Middleton's chest when she touched and inscribed her grandmother's sack. Things awakened memory and inspired feeling as well as action. Keckley felt moved to recall and write with the aid of the things in her room. Ruth felt moved to stitch the sack and list the things once packed inside it. For each of these survivors of slavery or its legacies (and, indeed, for all of us), things possess the ability to house and communicate "the incorporeal": emotions like love, values like family, states of being like freedom.[13] And more than that, Elizabeth's walls and Ashley's sack may have felt alive and actively present to their caretakers. There is a sense in these women's reminiscences of a "spiritual imaginary of matter," a mental and even metaphysical space in which things incorporate, maintain, and release a psychic or spiritual quality.[14]

In their writings quoted above, formerly enslaved people mention hard, relatively durable things such as chairs, walls, and beads (the last item being a recurrent one that Black as well as Indigenous enslaved people sought and gifted to one another), but they also touch on textiles, as did many of the enslaved in interviews and narratives published from the 1840s to the 1930s.[15] Fabric—like the cloth still unfinished in the rungs of Ann Valentine's loom—stands out for its symbolic resonance in the history of African American women, enslaved or free, and women across boundaries of race and class.[16] Ann chose this cloth, and the process she undertook in making it, to convey to her husband the poverty of her domestic circumstances and also to lift his spirits with a vision of hope for their future. The cloth she wove was as fragile as their lives and stretched thin like their familial connections. Yet one day that cloth would be complete and counted as the family's property, softening the financial hardship they endured. And we can imagine, if that day came and Ann Valentine did finish her cloth, that she may have handed it down to the child she mentions in her letter. That child, and that child's children, might have used the cloth from Ann's loom as a table or bed covering into the 1900s, recalling through the object, through its warmth and its worn-in softness, the story of their family's love and persistence.

As a pliable and fragile type of thing, fabric uniquely conveys psychic meanings hinted at in Ann Valentine's desperate correspondence. The constituent parts of a textile—filaments woven, knitted, or fused—are countless elements made into one. Fabric therefore represents the connectedness of many threads that together create a whole cloth. It weakens over time through repeated use, washing, and sun exposure, lending it a quality of delicacy requiring care. Because of this innate multiplicity and natural fragility, cloth has stood for people across time and cultures. It symbolically represents our own bodies, our temporal lifelines, and our social ties to one another. The association between fabric and human life is only strengthened by our propensity to drape our days and nights in this material. At birth, in death, during sickness, and through religious ritual, we coexist with fabric. We wrap our bodies and our most intimate moments inside textiles, which accounts for the emotional effectiveness of projects like the 1980s collaborative AIDS Quilt. Requiring caretaking and at the same time providing solace, "textiles are often mobilized in the face of trauma, and not just to provide needed garments or coverings but also as a therapeutic means of comfort, a safe outlet for worried hands, a productive channel for the obsessive working through of loss," explains one art historian.[17]

Fabric is a special category of thing to people—tender, damageable, weak at its edges, and yet life-sustaining. In these dis-

Beatrice Jeanette Whiting's sewing exercise book, ca. 1915.
"Exercise 25: A Piece of Checked Gingham." Here the young sewer,
who would later become a home economics teacher, practiced
working a piece of gingham into the form of a small sack. Courtesy
of the Schlesinger Library, Harvard Radcliffe Institute.

tinctive features, cloth begins to sound like this singular planet we call home. Cloth operates as a "convincing analogue for the regenerative and degenerative processes of life, and as a great connector, binding humans not only to each other but to the ancestors of their past and the progeny of their future," fiber artist Ann Hamilton has written. "Held by cloth's hand," she continues, "we are swaddled at birth, covered in sleep, and shrouded in death. A single thread spins a myth of origin and a tale of adventure and interweaves people and webs of communication."[18] For women in particular, the primary weavers in many (though not all) traditional as well as modern societies, cloth has evoked all of this and more as a manifestation of "female power."[19]

In the basement gallery at the NMAAHC, at the time of this writing, an old cloth sack hangs in a hallway of the unfathomable: scenes and sounds of human sales on American streets. The fabric unfurls in a weighty cascade encased in a chest-high, vertical box beside a boulder once used as an auction block, a video rendition of the poem "The Slave Mother," by Frances Ellen Watkins Harper, and words stenciled onto the wall listing the monetary value of individuals long dead. This is a portal of horrors, almost too much for the modern-day viewer to bear. Visitors who encounter the sack tend to linger here, perhaps allowing Ruth's spare words to penetrate their invisible shells. "Sometimes you have to be quiet with it," Mary Elliott, co-curator of the slavery exhibition advised as she led me through the buried channel one cold winter day in 2017. "And you may hear voices."[20]

We have Rose, Ashley, Rosa, Ruth, and Dorothy to thank for allowing us to listen in on their family's story, and we have a host of caretakers to thank for an incredible rescue of African American material culture evident in the preservation of this sack. We can see in this enigmatic relic dense wrongs of injustice and a deep well of human resilience. Ashley's sack, and other "shards, wrecks, [and] rags" of Black material culture possess what NMAAHC curator Paul Gardullo has called "transformational power" to convey "the most important meanings for us and our nation."[21] Those meanings will surely differ in my mind and yours, but perhaps we can agree that this sack marks a spot in our national story where great wrongs were committed, deep sufferings were felt, love was sustained against all odds, and a vision of survival for future generations persisted. This is knowledge worth preserving. Even as the sack itself belongs to Rose and her descendants, the "custody of the memory" should be borne by all of us.[22] As we near the end of our journey, we hold a bag both empty and full, around which our many hands find the space for joining.

Rose and Ashley surely knew the value and weight of the burden they carried: the responsibility to envision a future and bear it forward through harrowing times. By assembling the bag and its contents, Rose turned fear into love, committing herself to a fight for life. In toting the sack and its story, Ashley realized Rose's radical vision of Black persistence. In embellishing the cloth with her foremothers' tale, Ruth committed this episode to family history and American history. And now that the sack is in our hands, we cannot forget its layered lessons. Horrible things take place. Nevertheless, survival is possible. Hope can gain ground, and generations can be sustained. When we bear into the future the full knowledge of our past, we walk with hearts unfolded. We recognize the brutality of our species and as well the light in our spirits. We see that nothing is preserved, and no child or grandchild is saved, without brash acts of love and wild visions of continuance.

"The greatest threat that slaves faced was separation from their families," wrote the maverick Black feminist scholar Barbara Christian, more than thirty years ago.[23] This "specter of separation," known intimately by our unfree forebears, plagues us now in qualitatively different but no less important ways as hatred and discontinuity shadow our present social and political worlds.[24] We agonize as immigrant children are torn from parents by government agents, as politicians and the public toss aside common civilities, and as our species quickly peels away the climatic constancies of the Pleistocene epoch on our home planet. Separation, distance, enmity, and loss seem to be hallmarks of our time. What is our answer to this threat, at once immediate and existential? Will we throw in the towel? Or will we pack an emergency sack and make every effort we can dream up to save our children and right our wrongs?

In the tear of humanity that was chattel slavery, Rose made an old thing new and passed it on to Ashley. Rose's creation was fashioned of fabric, echoing women's histories dating back to ancient times. Her crafted object consisted mainly of fibrous materials (a dress, plant matter, braided hair) and was later embroidered with colored thread in keeping with a story-cloth tradition. Even more deeply rooted and resonant of women's handiwork is Rose seizing upon a bag as her response to slavery's claim. The sack, even before cloth, was most likely a woman's invention, created for the essential and everyday tasks of carrying life: toting seeds, foodstuffs, tools, and newborn babes, the articles of existence that fell most readily into women's domain for our ancient ancestors.[25] Rose's sack was made of cotton grown by unfree people, produced by a poor and possibly enslaved working class in a factory, secured by a chain stitch eerily symbolic of the forced-labor ethos of the era, and intended to serve a mammoth agricultural industry that enriched an elite master class at the expense of those who made the sacks. That Rose took all of this in hand and renewed the sack's original purpose feels mystically fitting.

Ashley, the inheritor, then became a standard-bearer for the survival of her kin. We might even see Ashley as a mythic heroine: the seed carrier who totes a sack and plants new story lines. Much of our cultural lore lionizes male heroes wielding weapons of death, but an alternative archetype exists in history and myth the world over. The novelist Ursula Le Guin describes this second sort of protagonist as a gatherer instead of a hunter, a collector of wild plants rather than a shaker of spears. This alternative figure totes a bag as her principal object and tells stories as her primary mode of communication. While traversing the long, golden land, she "carries a sack, a bag, a sling, something to collect and carry home oats or potatoes from the field." When she returns to her people, she tells the story of her journey to encourage their own walks on the land in a cyclical fashion that has no end. As a gatherer of things, the seed carrier provides for the sustenance of physical life; as a teller of tales, she sustains emotional and spiritual resilience. She invests in continuation—of the person, family, fields, and planet. Her stories, like seed bags, carry on.[26] The sack carrier is the conveyor of new possibilities, but the sack, Le Guin reveals, a "thing that holds something else," is the actual hero of human ascent. She reminds us that a book is a sack; a medicine bundle is a sack; a house is a sack; a church is a sack; even a museum is a sack. We must add, too, that the earth is a sack. All are containers for carrying.[27]

Elizabeth Keckley was adept at telling colorful anecdotes that unveiled the intimacies and politics of life in the Lincoln-era White House. Among these stories is her account of Abraham Lincoln's first encounter with a colloquial term familiar to Blacks but unfamiliar to him. The Civil War was raging when this curious exchange took place. The president and his traveling party, including Mrs. Lincoln and Elizabeth Keckley, had arrived at Petersburg, Virginia, soon after the fall of Richmond in 1865. A little Black boy in the crowd, "ragged" in personal appearance, offered to "tote" the president's belongings. When Lincoln asked the meaning of the word, the boy replied, "To tote um on your back," leading Lincoln to understand that "when you tote a thing, you carry it." Confused about this usage, Lincoln turned to Senator Charles Sumner of Massachusetts to ascertain the etymology of the word. Sumner replied, according to Keckley, "Its origin is said to be African. The Latin word *totum*, from *totus*, means all—an entire body—the whole." Befuddled and maybe a bit annoyed, Lincoln objected to the disjuncture that he perceived between the two meanings his friend imparted. Sumner supported Lincoln's view, agreeing that there was a conflict between the Latin root meaning "whole" and the African usage "to carry, to bear." The European and African sources, these great men decided, were at odds.[28]

This earnest exchange between the elder statesmen on the meaning of "tote" in Black culture struck Elizabeth Keckley as humorous. The men saw two definitions standing in opposition, but perhaps the dressmaker appreciated an inner resemblance. Containers hold any and all things together in place and over time, instantiating whole, new, unexpected creations. Carrying a sack of these laden things, despite the weight of the burden, means bringing this hidden potential for new kinds of wholeness with us. "Tote" is, remarkably, a noun and a verb, a thing and an action. Can we commit our imaginations—like Rose, Ashley, and Ruth once did—to packing the sacks, carrying the seeds, and stitching the story cloths of tomorrow? All of our past, what we have valued and what we have undervalued, must be brought along this way, tucked and pressed inside the shelters of our story sacks. For, in our collective quest to survive with peoples and planet held intact—nothing is immaterial.

Ashley's sack, back. The rear view of the sack packed by Rose, carried by Ashley, and embellished by Ruth shows the care invested in the family keepsake over time. Notice the many meticulous patches in the form of tight geometric shapes: squares, rectangles, and a small circle. Courtesy of the Middleton Place Foundation.

ACKNOWLEDGMENTS

MY LIFE IS RICHER FOR HAVING ENCOUNTERED THE bottomless sack that was handled and fashioned by Rose, Ashley, and Ruth. I am grateful to the National Endowment for the Humanities Public Scholars program and its officers for making this journey possible. I have had the opportunity to learn from and work with many giving people as I wrote. Conversation partners along the way fundamentally influenced the shape and tone of this book through their wise feedback and insights. For their dogged genealogical detective work, I thank genealogists Jesse Bustos-Nelson, a Charlestonian from birth and a librarian by training, and Hannah Scruggs, a public historian and specialist in enslaved descendants' research at the Robert Frederick Smith Explore Your Family History Center at the NMAAHC. For engrossing exchanges about textiles and writing, I am deeply grateful to literary scholar Megan Sweeney, at the University of Michigan. To Lisa Brooks, Lauret Savoy, and Sadada Jackson, I am appreciative of our conversations about places, things, and their spirits; your work is inspirational. To Emily Lavelle, you are a steadfast supporter of my writing life and a sensitive yet acute reader; thank you for being there. To Cathleen Cahill, Martha Few, and Lauren Feldman, I am thankful for our conversation during a Berkshire Conference meeting at Johns Hopkins University about the characteristics of archives. To Kendra Field, Sarah Pinto, and participants in the Tufts University Mellon Sawyer Seminar, "Defamiliarizing the Family: Genealogy and Kinship as Critical Method," I thank you for planning and joining a set of generative conversations that kept this project simmering even as the novel coronavirus terribly disrupted our year together. I gave early talks on this project at the University of Georgia and at Columbia University. I extend a heartfelt thanks to all of those who shared incredible ideas about the sack at UGA: my host Stephen Berry, Claudio Saunt, Reinaldo Román, James Brooks, and so many other members of that warm community. At Columbia, I am particularly grateful to Celia Naylor, Marisa Fuentes, Michelle Commander, Rashauna Johnson, Kellie Jones, Farah Jasmine Griffin, Karl Jacoby, and Robert Gooding-Williams.

Presentations at Harvard University's Mahindra Humanities Center, Environment Forum (housed in Mahindra), Environmental History Working Group, Hutchins Center, and History Department in 2019–20 afforded me crucial feedback and new challenges that tested and strengthened the work. I am grateful to everyone who attended these sessions and offered their thoughts, including (but not limited to) Ian Miller, Robin Kelsey, Joyce Chaplin, Andy Robichaud, Kate Brown, Michaela Thompson, Sidney Chalhoub, Dan Smail, Sunil Amrith, Ju Yon Kim, Susan Lively, Hannah Marcus, Liz Cohen, and the lifesaving woman who suggested that I reread *Parable of the Sower*. I am especially grateful to President Emerita Drew Gilpin Faust, who took the time to attend the Mahindra Center talk and kindly sent me a book (and made my new job possible). I was touched by the generosity of William (Ned) Friedman, director of the Arnold Arboretum at Harvard, who confirmed for me that pecan trees can be grown from the nut and planted pecan seeds for me. To Henry Louis Gates, Jr., and all of the 2019–20 Hutchins Center Fellows, especially Imani Uzuri, Bakari Kitwana, Mireille Miller-Young, and Traci Parker, I offer a special thanks for your affirmation of the invisible value of this book.

Without the welcome and openness of the staff at Middleton Place and the NMAAHC, I would still be at square one with this project. Thank you to Paul Gardullo for your early encouragement, to Mary Elliott for your personal tour, and to Mary Edna Sullivan and Jeff Neale for your gifts of time, access, and frankness. Thank you to curator Jennifer Swope at the Museum of Fine Arts in Boston and curator Sara Hume at the Kent State University Museum for teaching me about quilts. I am grateful, as well, to the staff at the American Antiquarian Society and to all of those who shared knowledge during our memorable Historic Charleston trip of spring 2018, especially the food historian David Shields and the garden writer Ruah Donnelly (who asked me this lightning bolt of a question: Had Rose given Ashley the pecans as food or as seeds?). Much of this research was conducted at historic sites, in the pages of slave narratives, and in digital archives. I spent most of my archival research time at the Addlestone Library at the College of Charleston and at the South Carolina Department of Archives and History. I am grateful to the archivists there who kindly welcomed and helped me: Harlan Greene, Dale Rosengarten, Mary Jo Fairchild, and Steve Tuttle; I am grateful as well to Grimké Sisters Tour co-founder and guide Lee Ann Bain for an engaging tour and helpful follow-up correspondence. I am likewise grateful to Tamar Gonen Brown at Radcliffe's Schlesinger Library for her attentive assistance with adjacent sources for the Ruth Middleton chapter. I am thankful, also, to the librarians and staff at the South Carolina Room of the Charleston County Public Library, the Charleston Library Society, the South Caroliniana Library at the University of South Carolina, the Avery Research Center, the Fabric Workshop and Museum, and the Schomburg Center for Research in Black Culture, who aided me as well as my research assistants. I am grateful for the close reading of a related essay by the editors and peer reviewer of Winterthur Museum's *Portfolio*, especially Catharine Dann Roeber, Jennifer Van Horn, and Amy Earls. MLA president Anne Ruggles Gere offered fruitful thoughts about my interpretations of the literary aspects of the sack; for that I am grateful.

I am lucky to have friends and mentors who remind me that what we create in this world we accomplish in many unspoken ways, together. I am grateful to Celia Naylor, Paulina Alberto, Kelly Cunningham, Beth James, Sharony Green, Magda Zaborowska (who introduced me to the work of John Michael Vlach many years ago), Earl Lewis (whose Mellon Foundation convening about slavery and public scholarship in 2016 was pivotal), and Evelyn Brooks Higginbotham (who should wear a superhero cape). I am grateful to the organizing team of the Berkshire Conference of Women Historians 2020, who always inspired with their fierce dedication to telling the stories of women's pasts: Jennifer Brier, Marisa Fuentes, Stephanie Richmond, Sandra Dawson, Martha Jones, Cathleen Cahill, Martha Few, Shani Mott, and Courtney Hobson. I owe a debt of gratitude to colleagues and friends who read chapters of the manuscript and offered invaluable critiques: Meg Sweeney, Marisa Fuentes, Martha Jones, Jallicia Jolly, Hannah Scruggs, and William (Ned) Friedman. Many individuals knowingly and unknowingly nursed this project along with their suggestions and presence; my thanks to Ben Goggins, Sean Halloran, Mary Kelley, Barbara

Savage, Rebecca Scott, Sonya Clark, LaKisha Simmons, Alison
Frank Johnson, Kirk Sides, Bobby Donaldson, Lisa McGirr,
David Blight, Walter Johnson, Anne Steinert, Rowena
McClinton, Annette Gordon-Reed, and Laurel Thatcher Ulrich. Several incredible graduate students conducted research
for chapters of this book; my thanks to Dylan Nelson, Michelle
May-Curry, and Mary McNeil. I am grateful to Kimberly
O'Hagan, Cory Paulsen, and Sylvie Papazian of Harvard's History Department, who managed my NEH grant funds and permissions payments with care and good cheer. I have been
fortunate to work with the skillful and supportive literary agent
Deirdre Mullane on three books, including this one, whose lives
she tended with care. I am now fortunate to be working with the
inspirational literary agent Tanya McKinnon, whose passion for
narrating Black experiences and midwifing voices of change re-
shaped and reinvigorated this book in its final year. My efferves-
cent editor at Random House, Molly Turpin, took a chance on
this unusual project, encouraged it with a patience of spirit and
clarity of editorial vision, and championed its value at her press.
Thank you, as well, to Bonnie Thompson, who copyedited this
manuscript with a sharp eye and intentional pen, and to Chris
Dodge, who always crafts meticulous and masterful indexes.

As always, my family cheered this project on from its incep-
tion. My father, Benny Miles, never failed to ask how things were
going with "Sarah's Satchel" (which, although it is not the subject of this book, fascinates me as a fictive possibility), and my
mother, Patricia Miles King, stayed with us during major transi-
tions and challenges over the last two years, helping to care for
the kids and making my writing possible. My love and thanks
always extend to the people who have to live with the intense
creature I become as I struggle with the pages: Joe, Sylvan, Noa,
and Nali; I send love and appreciation as well to those family

members who offer sustenance from all of the places where they are, especially (but not only) Erin, Erik, Aunt Vanessa, Aunt Deborah, Montroue (a crochet artiste), Sharon (an embroiderer extraordinaire), and, finally, my godfather, Joseph Porter (gifter of pens), and my father-in-law, Joe Azure (maker of prayers), both departed from this sphere in 2020, but not from our memories.

There are bound to be errors in this book, and they are mine. I regret that even with the help of two able genealogists, I was unable to identify living descendants of Rose. If I have offended the spirits of Rose, Ashley, Rosa, Ruth, Dorothy, or their descendants in any way, I offer my apology. If I have contributed to love and life in any way, I offer my gratitude for the opportunity. Thank you to the ancestors for their company and forbearance. Thank you to the descendants for carrying on.

Embroidered work bag. Unknown maker, England or United States, 1753, wool, linen, silk, and cotton, 1960.1123, bequest of Henry Francis du Pont, courtesy of Winterthur Museum. On the front of this eighteenth-century utilitarian bag, an unknown craftswoman embroidered a lush floral display. The exhibit note reads, "Large bags that held a variety of plain and ornamental needlework projects were often embellished with embroidered decoration. These could be taken on visits, when groups of friends gathered to chat and stitch." *The Diligent Needle: Instrument of Profit, Pleasure, and Ornament*, online exhibit, Winterthur, 2020.

SAMPLER:
A NOTE ON TERMS

OVER THE PAST DECADE, HISTORIANS OF SLAVERY have moved toward a shift in language propelled in part by community members' protest at references to ancestors as "slaves." This push by readers paralleled a reexamination by scholars seeking to more accurately name historical populations and processes. The term "slave," common in the literature as recently as five years ago, reduces unfree people to an external categorization that renders them subhuman and makes it difficult to imagine their full lives and subjectivities beyond this reductive classification. More recently, cognates of "slave," such as "slaveholder" and "slavery," as well as words that convey unassailed authority, such as "master" and "owner," and words that blur or romanticize historical roles, such as "planter," have also come under scrutiny for negating Black humanity and erasing the active violence of those who bought, sold, and legally possessed others. (These discussions have unfolded in a context of African diaspora slavery studies rather than Native American slavery studies, where "slave" and "slavery" are now often used in place of the formerly preferred and arguably softer terms "captive" and "captivity.") I write this note at the end of the summer of 2020, in which massive protests against anti-Black racism and police brutality shifted the axis of our public culture and set off new conversations about language and power that are still unfolding.

The terms preferred by many writers and readers of African diasporic history currently are "enslaved person," "enslaved people," "enslaver," and "enslavement." While I agree with the logic and politics behind these changes and often follow suit, I do not avoid the older terms uniformly. I find the words "slave" and "slavery" to be precisely what I mean when I am referring to categories defined and imposed by southern owners of people, to societal as well as legal dictates, and to racial systems of capture. In contrast, I try to select "enslaved" or "unfree" when I mean to designate a person from their perspective, the perspective of their community, or our perspective as researchers and readers. I use established terms from historical study such as "slave society," which points to places like South Carolina where slavery was the chief engine of the economy as well as the social structure, and "slave narrative," which points to a literary genre. I also retain the term "slave mother," which has a particular literary and historical valence, as seized upon by the African American poet, essayist, and suffragist Frances Ellen Watkins Harper in her anti-slavery poems of the same title, and as analyzed by Harriet Jacobs in her classic memoir, *Incidents in the Life of a Slave Girl.*

At times in this book, I select shorter words or word combinations for the sound or rhythm in the sentence rather than performing linguistic acrobatics to avoid using the word "slave" or "owner." Preferred racial and category terms change over time, and sometimes morph rapidly. While I fully support the evolution of preferred language regarding sensitive racial terms or other categories of identity, I also wish to reserve room to employ our full lexicon within the bounds of respect and settled discourse, to convey the full scope of my meaning as smoothly as my imperfect pen will allow. In this effort, I am practicing at my letters much like the maker of a needlepoint sampler. There will surely be spots that make you wish I had ripped out the stitches and started again, and for this I ask your forbearance.

LITTLE SACK OF SOMETHING: AN ESSAY ON PROCESS

THIS HAS BEEN A TALE OF A POWERFUL OBJECT touched by three women whose lives might have been lost to history: Rose, a visionary; Ashley, a survivor; and Ruth, a storyteller. Ordinary in their time among the roughly four million Americans caged by slavery, the women of this story are extraordinary in our time for their production and preservation of a rare object imbued with the memory of slavery's shadow. The story of the bag and of their family ripples out like salted waves off the coast of Lowcountry South Carolina, flowing into the histories of African America and the United States of America, a beleaguered race and a benighted nation both searching for ways to the light. Like no other artifact in African American material culture, this story cloth captures the emotional texture of Black women's lives during and after slavery and reveals the staying power of love across time—past, present, and unfolding.

While my journey with this story ended here—at a meditation on love and our carrying capacity as human beings for bearing the burdens of trauma as well as the gifts of fortitude—I entered the project serendipitously through the doorway of environmental history, which opened into still more doorways of material culture studies and cultural theories about how things function in human society. Once I began to see the layered shape of the project, I applied for funding from the Public Scholars program at the National Endowment for the Humanities. The award I received carried explicit expectations for public relevance and would add yet another layer to the project, compelling me to write with the interests of a public audience in mind and to strive toward translating the practices of scholars in the historical profession for that readership. The unusualness of the sack likewise pushed me to write an accounting of it that reaches for (but cannot attain) a parallelism with the object in form as well as spirit, which meant assembling and cinching together various kinds of source materials and attempting to craft history in a poetic mode that goes to the marrow of our human experience. The resulting book is many things at once: a public history, an object history, and a study of Black women's lives inspired by environmental understandings that all that we can trace and discover in human existence derives in some way from sources natural and material.

ECOLOGIES AND ROOTWORK

I did not see Ashley's sack coming in the winter of 2016. I certainly could not have predicted that I would first hear about it from a scientist in the Lowcountry South. I was attending a symposium about the environmental history of the Georgia coast held in Savannah and hosted by the Ossabaw Island Foundation (for the preservation of coastal nature), an event that attracted hundreds of teachers, researchers, and state employees. I just had shared my research on the spiritual role of water to the enslaved people of the Georgia coast, culminating in the tale of Igbo Landing at Dunbar Creek on St. Simons Island, where,

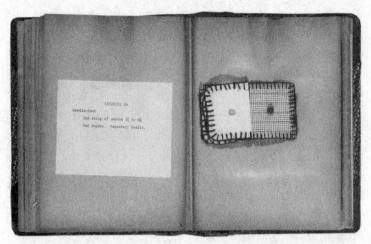

Beatrice Jeanette Whiting's sewing exercise book, ca. 1915.
"Exercise 24: Needle-book. One strip of canvas 21/4 by 41/2. Red
zephyr. Tapestry needle." For our consideration of the associations
between words and stitches, books and sacks. Courtesy of the
Schlesinger Library, Harvard Radcliffe Institute.

according to the narratives of formerly enslaved people interviewed by employees of the Georgia Writers Project of the
Works Progress Administration (or WPA), their ancestors leapt
off a slaving ship (or out of a rice field, or away from a whipping—
oral accounts vary) and flew back home to Africa. It was an unusual lecture for this gathering of science instructors, naturalists,
and environmental historians, given my focus on ghosts and oral
history, but the audience filled the auditorium and overflowed
into a secondary room, eager for a discussion about the meeting
grounds of nature and narrative. Many audience members embraced this story, standing to tell of their personal experiences at
Igbo Landing, where one woman said she used to hear murmurs, perhaps echoes of enslaved voices, rising from the deep-
water creek.[1] Among them was Ben Goggins, a retired marine
biologist and a local columnist for *Savannah Now*, who asked

me after the talk if I "knew" Ashley's sack. Before departing, he insisted that I had to see it.

That evening in my hotel room, I was surprised to find an email from Ben Goggins; it included a link to an article he had written a few weeks prior. Ashley's sack, his piece explained, was a cotton bag given by an enslaved mother, Rose, to her enslaved daughter, Ashley, on the eve of the daughter's sale in South Carolina. The Middleton Place Foundation of Charleston held the rights to the artifact, and a historical interpreter there, Jeff Neale, had recently traveled to Savannah to share news of the object's temporary loan to the new Smithsonian National Museum of African American History and Culture. Four days later, another missive appeared in my in-box. This time Ben reflected on the rising tides around his sea island home due to climate change and included a link to a CBS news story on Ashley's sack. The article included a photograph of the bag, a dingy white cloth discolored by patches of dirt or blood and seared with punctures. Sentences formed from scrupulous stitching trailed across the cotton weave, an embroidered story of the item's heartbreaking origins in a family's forced division. Below the last sewn line, the handiwork was signed in thread: "Ruth Middleton 1921."[2]

My unexpected interlocutor had been right. Seeing the sack, experiencing its material nature, changed everything. The image, haunting as any story about the people who could fly, stole a beat from my heart. This object was dazzling in its immediacy, devastating in its story, and stunning in the simultaneity of gut responses it elicited. I had been studying Black history for over twenty years. I had visited African American museums, stared unbelievingly at leg chains and neck irons, but no remnant from those dark times had arrested my spirit quite like this one. It was, as the senior curator at Middleton Place Foundation, Mary Edna Sullivan, would later tell me, "visceral." She described observing people bursting into tears while viewing the bag and mentioned her repeated offering of tissues. "I cry when I read it aloud," Tracey Todd, then vice president at the Middleton Place Foundation, confided to Ben Goggins.[3]

I did not cry at first while staring at the photograph that night. Perhaps I was too stunned. I had never before viewed a visual record of slavery so riveting, so disquieting, so gorgeous in its ghostly presence that it seemed to "hail" me, or call me to perform an action, as feminist theorist Robin Bernstein has said about the power of certain things. This unassuming sack on the screen in my hands was an invaluable heirloom, for the descendants of the Black Middleton family and for a composite African American family ceaselessly in search of its tangled roots. Invaluable—but vulnerable to the vagaries of circumstance. The sack's survival seemed miraculous, given the fragile nature of its organic material as well as "the diminutive value accorded the historical relics of black American Life." I understood why Goggins had led me here and felt a surge of gratitude for his opening of a door. The tale of the salvaged cotton sack combined nature, spirit, and transcendence, akin to the story of enslaved resistance at Igbo Landing. Floating across our email exchange was an implicit link about things of beauty under threat (oceans, islands, lives, families) and in need of rescue (human and perhaps divine). I enlarged the image on my screen, the better to absorb Ruth's words, and lost myself in their waves of grief and oceans of meaning.[4] My first reaction was some form of reverence, tempered later by research. Gradually, I attempted to uncover the meanings of the cloth by joining environmental studies, the means by which I had learned of it, to African American studies, slavery studies, women's history, and material culture studies. A primary way of connecting these fields that I seized on was positioning the story of this physical thing created and carried by Black women as a "parable of resilience," one of three approaches to aligning the work of public history with the spirit of restoration ecology articulated by the historian David Glassberg. By writing history as "collapse" parables, "sustainability" parables, or "resilience" parables, Glassberg suggests, scholars can "intervene responsibly in the memory streams of human communities" and thereby meaningfully contribute to a public reckoning with climate change. "Parables of resilience have the most value for public historians," he argues, "since properly told they neither romanticize the past nor imply that it's too late to avoid a pre-determined dystopian future."[5]

I began thinking about the sack in earnest during the spring of 2016, when I first traveled to Middleton Place plantation. Within a year, I got my first startling look at the object while visiting the recently opened Smithsonian National Museum of African American History and Culture. That visit and an awe-inspiring tour with curator Mary Elliott led me to apply for funding to write a book about the sack. The National Endowment for the Humanities granted me funding and moral support under the aegis of its (fairly new at the time) Public Scholars program, which aims to foster the production of scholarship intended for public audiences. Work created with grant funds are meant to serve the public good by presenting new questions for a public readership and by translating current ideas of scholarly inquiry for a range of readers beyond academia. It seemed to me that this special textile was the kind of object and subject that was capable of doing this work, and I am grateful to the staff members and reviewers of the NEH, whose support first signaled to me that I had a feasible project and buoyed my courage in pursuing it.

After receiving positive news about this grant, I contacted Mark Auslander, whose brilliant online articles about the sack were critically important to my research. I learned from Mark that he was also writing a book and planning a major event with descendants he had identified. Nevertheless, he was open to hearing about my plans, noting that he might have expected that more people would take up this compelling subject. I am grateful to Mark for his scholarship and also for his acceptance of an invitation from me, Megan Sweeney, and the University of Michigan Museum of Art, where he spoke not about the sack but about a moving contemporary textile project: his work, as the director of the Michigan State University Museum, with survivors of sexual violence and their parents, to preserve the teal ribbons they tied around campus trees to mark their experience and strength.

After my research was well under way in 2018, I moved with my family to a different town and started a new job. While I parted from treasured friends and colleagues at the University of Michigan, I entered a novel space that profoundly influenced this project. I joined the History Department at Harvard just as Laurel Thatcher Ulrich was retiring, and I inherited her cozy first-floor office (with a tall window looking out at a taller evergreen tree), as well as several books from her shelves and a heavy crate of inventories from a historic Massachusetts house museum. With the sack on my mind, I gravitated toward Laurel's books on textiles. I then reread her book *The Age of Homespun*, in my own collection. I am convinced that it was the silent surround of her books and her space that led me to think so consistently about the sack as a textile and about the role of the material in African American women's history.

This project took root at a southern environmental studies conference, and it has grown in light of a series of later public presentations and exchanges. I first presented the research at a Modern Language Association conference in 2019. As part of the "Presidential Plenary: Textual Transactions" panel, I was fortunate to hear thoughts on my project from Kim Hall, a quilter and a Black studies, feminist studies, and Shakespearean scholar. Hall's comment "I'm frustrated because I don't know how to talk about love" stuck with me, as did her speculation that Black scholars recovering "love in the archive" could allow for the recovery of love in Black lives. A visit to the History Department at the University of Georgia in Athens (quilter Harriet Powers's hometown) showered me with insights at a critical point in my thinking and allowed me to see, in a suggestion by the Civil War historian Stephen Berry, that the shape of Ruth's embroidered text may loosely resemble a heart. Participating in the Columbia University–Barnard College symposium "1619 and Its Legacies" also yielded incredible exchanges and brought me into generative contact with the art historian Kellie Jones, who urged me to think harder about artistic comparisons with the sack, an exercise that seeded the exhibit-like shape of the color images insert. Also at the Columbia event, Robert Gooding-Williams made a lasting impression on this project when he took me aside to offer the sharp observation that the name "Ashley's sack" narrows the scope of inquiry and suggests that this story is about just one person. His influence inspired my attempt at more inclusive language throughout the book, especially around the notion of collective and cultural descendants, rather than strictly lineal descendants.

Presenting this work for the Hutchins Center for African and African American Research transformed how I viewed the enterprise. While joking that I had clearly gone "deep into the textiles," Henry Louis Gates, Jr., suggested that I needed to tunnel my way back out because I had what I needed to finish the book. Hutchins Center fellows urged me to focus on the supernatural, spiritual, and creative aspects of the work, insisting that this project had the chance to revivify an inner calling in the field of African American studies to feed the soul, a calling that had been lost amid the pressures of the academy to adopt objectivist stances. Because of them, I am letting the book go in this difficult season when we are all facing traumatic change in the form of the novel coronavirus (and despite a canceled final research trip to South Carolina in the spring of 2020). I hope this story of women who creatively, actively, and courageously confronted the worst will help shore up our resolve as we reimagine what life can look like in the aftermath of the virus and political vitriol.

Also due to the Hutchins fellows' encouragement, I have allowed myself to thread this book through with references to the spiritual realm of life, which was, in fact, central to the survival of many enslaved African Americans, and still is to many of their descendants. The Hutchins fellows' comments brought back to mind poignant words spoken by Kim Hall at the 2019 MLA Conference—about how "conviviality and love take a back seat in Black studies." We want to change that. As I write these lines and reflect on her words, I am thinking about how historical work may in some way resemble rootwork, in its effort to gather meaningful materials for the purpose of revealing information about social relations that might yield results.

TRACES AND ARCHIVES

With this project, I sought to answer a series of questions: What is the story of this cloth? Who were the mothers and daughters that touched it? What compelled Black women to struggle in defense of life in a system that turned mere existence into hardship? How did they maintain their will across generations in bleak times? And what can Black women's creative response to the worst of circumstances teach us about the past and offer us for the future?

Pursuing the answers to these questions would depend on the availability of evidence. Every scholar of early Black or Native women's history, and the history of slavery, must confront the conundrum of the archives. Embarking on a search for evidence to verify the text of the sack compelled my turn to the traditional historical archive in these pages, notwithstanding its gruesomely violent episodes and unnervingly silent gaps. Where that archive of written documents offers distortion by rendering enslaved people as objects when they are even present at all, I attempted to see "the hidden truths of slavery," in the words of the historian Nell Irvin Painter, by peering between and beyond the lines of the written records.[6] Here I employed an interpretive method articulated by Marisa Fuentes that proposes reading archival documents "along the bias grain," which refers to the angled line across a swath of fabric where a natural give already exists. A diagonal reading of documents looks beyond what seems straightforward and feels for the stretch in the scholar's materials, the leeway that more likely reveals hidden interiors and obfuscated realities. I practiced this, for example, in my reading of Robert Martin's estate inventory, which I stretched to consider how his financial investments reverberated in the world of Black people until I began to imagine what a fugitive inventory might look like and realized that I had one in hand, in the form of Rose's gift list.[7] Evocatively, but perhaps not unexpectedly, this method devised by a woman historian takes up cloth as a metaphor, describing a practice of reading documents to access the lives of enslaved women as if these papers were bolts of fabric. In the stretch of the cloth exists a certain kind of gleaning, and, in that gleaning, a more capacious kind of knowledge.[8]

This confrontation with the archive and the call to stretch sources like textiles raises a narrative imperative that I borrow from the incisive theorist Saidiya Hartman: to write history "with

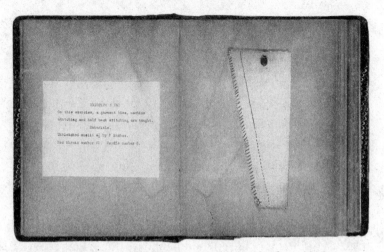

Beatrice Jeanette Whiting's sewing exercise book, ca 1915.
"Exercise 3(b): On this exercise, a garment bias, machine stitching
and half back stitching are taught. Materials: Unbleached muslin
4½ by 7 inches. Red thread number 50. Needle number 8." For our
consideration of the bias-grain method of archival research.
Courtesy of the Schlesinger Library, Harvard Radcliffe Institute.

and against the archive."[9] It also raises questions about where to
turn when the archival ground collapses beneath us. How do we
discover past lives for whom the historical record is abysmally
thin? What materials should we use as sources of information?
Should we attempt to interpret odd sources, particularly material things that deviate from the norm of traditional document-
driven historical scholarship?

Evidence, or the lack thereof, presents a particular challenge
for the study of Black women, women of color, and women on
the whole as groups that have been socially disempowered and
therefore often overlooked by the keepers of records and the intellectual architects of archives. Indeed, as the historian Jill
Lepore has encapsulated the problem in relation to the wide
scope of American history: the "archive of the past . . . is mad-

deningly uneven, asymmetrical, and unfair."[10] Researchers working in pre-twentieth-century records who care about Black lives are often left with the disparaging theorizations of slavery's apologists and the cold notations of plantation diarists. What we might call the blood documents generated by the life of a "slave"—birth notations, food rations, clothing and blanket distributions, physician bills, bills of sale, death data—routinely confront researchers in Black women's history and the history of slavery. Blood documents, like the blood diamonds on today's jewelry market, were produced at the expense of real lives.

Where written records leave gaps, we can look for material traces as historians of the environment have done. Lauret Savoy, a memoirist, environmental studies scholar, and descendant of enslaved and Indigenous people in Virginia, mourned how her enslaved "ancestors disappeared" into dull lists and anonymous graves. Rejecting the disciplinary expectation of reliance on written records, Savoy chose to follow the "trace," which she defines as memory and loss "inscribed in the land."[11] In order to reconstruct the experiences of her ancestors, she travels to the places where they lived and interprets the built environment (like plantation houses and slave quarters) and the natural environment (like waterways and rocks) in conjunction with personal and family memories. In this method that makes space for physical remnants and memories, Savoy joins with other historians, particularly of Native America and the environment. Traces, sometimes called echoes, are often unseen and untapped reserves that can provide us with deeper information.[12]

Endeavoring to reconstruct any history, but especially the histories of the marginalized, requires an attentiveness to absence as well as presence, to traces of the past as much as documentary evidence of events. A trace might be defined as a material, a memory, or even an artistic imagining, as the poet

Elizabeth Alexander suggests. "The historian," Alexander writes, "laments caesuras in the historical record; the artist can offer deeply informed imagining that, while not empirically verifiable, offers one of the only routes we may have to imagine a past whose records have not been kept precious." In the case of Ashley's sack, a hearsay seed sack is an imperfect historical record but also a valuable trace that can be prompted to reveal worthwhile information. The "artifact," Alexander finds, is another kind of "record," another route to "history."[13] We need to be mindful, the art historian John Michael Vlach concurs, "of the artifact's value as historical evidence."[14] In doing so, we join in the twenty-first-century revival of a vibrant interdisciplinary method of historical study from the 1970s and 1980s that turned to material objects, arts, and crafts as a means to fill out the woefully inadequate "archive" of slavery.[15]

To interpret this mixed bag of traces that is Ashley's sack, I have tried to identify aspects of the object's makeup as well as particular words in the text of the embroidery where focused thought might loosen the threads into larger meanings.[16] This approach is in play, for example, when I touch on what Ruth has stitched into remembrance and continuance (a family sustained by love) and stretch that material into the space she has left unspecified (a regional and national culture of human diminishment). Ashley's sack opens up in the light of this elasticized view. Having to burrow into the cloth, to make do with its evidentiary limits, pulled me toward a mode of associational thinking of the kind archaeologist Alexandra Chan suggested, in her study of an eighteenth-century New England plantation, when writing that "artifacts are metaphorical expressions of culture."[17] An object like Ashley's sack invites us to consider the interlaced cultural worlds of African American, Native American, and European American life, and of southern and northern experience, in the time periods when it was used. The artifact might also inspire, and did for me, invigorated ways of conceptualizing and communicating contemporary cultural efforts, from responding to the emergencies of our times to doing the work of history. We might, for instance, see this sack (or any sack) as a metaphor for vibrant historical research and writing. Packing a sack requires gathering and combining select items and then allowing those things to mix and mingle. New combinations and ideas emerge from that process, formed of the innate vitality of loosely composite parts now linked. Borrowing from philosopher Jane Bennett, we can think of these configurations—these histories—as assemblages, odds and ends that together produce a special kind of synergy.[18]

The account I have offered in this book, this "little sack of something," is not final.[19] Interpretations of the past never are nor can they be. While the past itself does not change, the production of history—our studied scrutiny and reconstruction of the past—always shifts over time, sometimes blooming with our discovery of new sources and formulation of fresh questions, and sometimes buckling from the weight of cultural transformations. Indeed, as these pages go to press, preparations are being made to transport Ashley's sack from the nation's capital back to Charleston. There, in the aged interiors of Middleton Place plantation, or in the modern galleries of the city's International African American Museum, this time-tested tote will grace more lives and make new histories. After only five years spent drawing near to this textile, I cannot claim to know Rose, Ashley, Ruth, or their families intimately. But I take heart from their example of an ethic of bequest, love made manifest in the preservation of things passed on.

NOTES

PROLOGUE: EMERGENCY PACKS

1. My thinking on love was influenced by Jonathan L. Walton, *A Lens of Love: Reading the Bible in Its World for Our World* (Louisville, Ky.: Westminster John Knox Press, 2018), 38, 42. In writing these prefatory pages, the notion of "love-craft" as fashioned and applied emotion in response to urgent trouble occurred to me as an oppositional kind of idea to statecraft and perhaps as a kindred idea of witchcraft, as in the making of something magical through belief, materials, and the spoken word.

2. This is the kind of hope philosopher Jonathan Lear articulated when writing about the destruction of traditional Crow Indian culture by U.S. military and colonial violence. A disposition such as this requires, Lear avows, "imaginative excellence" and a will to reach "toward a future goodness that transcends the current ability to understand what it is." Novelist Junot Díaz repurposed Lear's concept when writing about the election of Donald J. Trump to the U.S. presidency in 2016: "Radical hope is our best weapon against despair, even when despair seems justifiable; it makes the survival of the end of your world possible." Jonathan Lear, *Radical Hope: Ethics in the Face of Cultural Devastation* (Cambridge, Mass.: Harvard University Press, 2006), 117, 103. Junot Díaz, "Aftermath: Sixteen Writers on Trump's America," *New Yorker*, November 21, 2016.

INTRODUCTION: LOVE'S PRACTITIONERS

1. Zora Neale Hurston, *Their Eyes Were Watching God* (1937; repr., New York: HarperCollins Perennial Classics, 1998), 14. Hurston's precise quote, a line spoken from Grandma to Janie, is: "De nigger woman is de mule uh de world so fur as Ah can see. Ah been prayin' fuh it tuh be different wid you."

Abraham Lincoln, First Inaugural Address, March 4, 1861, Avalon Project, Yale Law School; avalon.law.yale.edu/19th_century/lincoln1.asp.

2. The story of the cow is a composite from my memory based on the many times my grandmother told it. One of those times, the summer after I had enrolled in a graduate program in women's studies in June 1993, I wrote it down. We were on her front porch, the perpetual stage for her storytelling. I asked her if she would tell me the story of her life. She started with her birth in 1914, described a move to a new home at age five, described each of her parents in turn, depicted their life on the farm, told the story of expulsion, described meeting her first husband and their early life together, told of the move to Cincinnati in 1941, and dwelled on their poverty in the city and leaving her first husband at the age of thirty-six or thirty-seven due to domestic abuse. The two events or phases of life she stressed most, as measured by the amount of time she spent narrating them, were: the eviction in Mississippi and the economic and social difficulty of life in urban Ohio.

3. Laurel Thatcher Ulrich, *The Age of Homespun: Objects and Stories in the Creation of an American Myth* (New York: Alfred A. Knopf, 2001), 149, 418.

4. For the sake of readerly ease and writerly fluidity, I will generally use the terms "thing" and "object" interchangeably, although a field of academic inquiry referred to as thing theory and new materialism studies differentiates between their definitions. I follow the lead of historians Laurel Thatcher Ulrich and Ivan Gaskell and their co-authors, museum studies scholars and practitioners Sara J. Schechner and Sarah Anne Carter, in adopting the wider use of the terms "object" and "thing" as interchangeable. However, as the gender studies and cultural studies scholar Robin Bernstein explains, the difference between an object and a thing is the thing's active ability to stand out in human awareness above and beyond the many objects that surround us. Bernstein also compellingly defines the special quality of the thing as its ability to "hail" people, or compel them into action. Literary critic Bill Brown was probably the first in that subfield to mark this distinction when he described things as possessing an assertiveness and "unspecificity" lacking in the object and explained that one cannot straightforwardly peer through a thing as through a window. Bill Brown, "Thing Theory," *Critical Inquiry* 28, no. 1 (Autumn 2001): 1–22, 3, 4. Philosopher Jane Bennett developed this difference, pointing to the strange vitality of the thing in relation to human experience and specifying that an object transforms into a thing "when the subject experiences the object as uncanny." The historian of science and Indigenous studies scholar Kim TallBear has pointed out that what she calls an "indigenous metaphysic"—a theory and orientation to the world that emphasizes human relationship to places and understands the interconnectedness of all things (animate and inanimate) and sees anything as potentially "vibrant material"—long pre-dates thing theory. Laurel Thatcher Ulrich, Ivan Gaskell, Sara J. Schechner, and Sarah Anne Carter, eds., *Tangible Things: Making History Through Objects* (New York: Oxford University Press, 2015), 2. Robin Bernstein, *Racial Innocence: Performing American Childhood from Slavery to Civil Rights* (New York: New York University

Press, 2011), 72, 73. Jane Bennett, *Vibrant Matter: A Political Ecology of Things* (Durham, N.C.: Duke University Press, 2010), 2. Also see Jane Bennett, "The Force of Things: Steps Toward an Ecology of Matter," *Political Theory* 32, no. 3 (June 2004): 347–72. Kim TallBear, "Beyond the Life/Not Life Binary: A Feminist-Indigenous Reading of Cryopreservation, Interspecies Thinking, and the New Materialisms," in *Cryopolitics: Frozen Life in a Melting World*, ed. Joanna Radin and Emma Kowal (Cambridge, Mass.: MIT Press, 2017), 191, 195, 199.

5. For an excellent analysis of ways in which the commemoration of women's needlework, especially pieces produced in the colonial period, have romanticized that past and covered over race and class differences, see Martha R. Miller, *The Needle's Eye: Women and Work in the Age of Revolution* (Amherst: University of Massachusetts Press, 2006), 3, 93–94, 216–22.

6. Elizabeth Wayland Barber, *Women's Work: The First 20,000 Years; Women, Cloth, and Society in Early Times* (New York: W. W. Norton, 1994), 149, 229, 230, 153, 154.

7. Barber, *Women's Work*, 299, 23.

8. Elsa Barkley Brown, "African-American Women's Quilting: A Framework for Conceptualizing and Teaching African-American Women's History," *Signs* 14, no. 4 (1989): 929.

9. For a discussion of the AIDS Quilt as an archive, see Julia Bryan-Wilson, *Fray: Art and Textile Politics* (Chicago: University of Chicago Press, 2017), 226.

10. Walter Johnson, *Soul by Soul: Life Inside the Antebellum Slave Market* (Cambridge, Mass.: Harvard University Press, 1999), 11.

11. This object history appreciates, as archaeologist Jane Spector spelled out, the necessity of building a narrative and at the same time offering alternative story lines of possibility. Jane D. Spector, *What This Awl Means: Feminist Archaeology at a Wahpeton Dakota Village* (St. Paul: Minnesota Historical Society Press, 1993), 18.

12. Marisa Fuentes, *Dispossessed Lives: Enslaved Women, Violence, and the Archive* (Philadelphia: University of Pennsylvania Press, 2016), 1, 4–7, 78. The terms "the bias" or "bias grain" refer to a line cutting diagonally across the horizontal and vertical grains of a piece of fabric.

13. Saidiya Hartman, "Venus in Two Acts," *Small Axe* 26 (June 2008): 1–14, 4, 12, 14. By "counter-histories," Hartman points to histories that oppose past dehumanizing or invisibilizing historical narratives. By "trans-temporal," I mean an interpretive positionality that crosses time periods when seeking to understand and render the rippling meanings of slavery. See also Saidiya Hartman's definition of "the time of slavery," as "the relation between the past and the present, the horizon of loss, the extant legacy of slavery, the antinomies of redemption . . . and irreparability," in "The Time of Slavery," *The South Atlantic Quarterly* 101, no. 4 (Fall 2002): 757–77, 759. The historian LaKisha Simmons offers another rich description of how time takes an alternative shape for Black women, a quality she calls "a Black sense of time." Simmons argues, in her study of Black mothers' loss of infants, that

Black women collapse "notions of time, space, and generation" in their understandings of self and family. She offers a definition of "Black feminist relationality as always in conversation with the dead and with the past." LaKisha Michelle Simmons, "Black Feminist Theories of Motherhood and Generation: Histories of Black Infant and Child Loss in the United States," *Signs: Journal of Women in Culture and Society* 46, no. 2 (2021): 311–35, 318, 319.

14. Michel-Rolph Trouillot, *Silencing the Past: Power and the Production of History* (1995; repr., Boston: Beacon Press, 2015), 29.

15. Jeff Neale, "Ashley's Sack: A Humble Object of Revelation," Davenport House Museum, Savannah, Ga., December 2016.

16. Human feelings and desires do change over time in expression, intensity, and cultural allowance, but many of these we share across time, circumstance, and status. For an intricate analysis of the social and psychological revelations afforded by the study of objects, see Jennifer Van Horn, *The Power of Objects in Eighteenth-Century British America* (Chapel Hill: University of North Carolina Press, published for the Omohundro Institute of Early American History and Culture, 2017). Also see the equally compelling Bernard L. Herman, *Town House: Architecture and Material Life in the Early American City, 1780–1830* (Chapel Hill: University of North Carolina Press, published for the Omohundro Institute of Early American History and Culture, 2005).

17. Timothy J. LeCain, *The Matter of History: How Things Create the Past* (New York: Cambridge University Press, 2017), 21.

18. The history of emotion is a field of historical studies that has seen greater emphasis in the past decade. Interdependent with psychological studies, this field explores human emotions of the past and whether they are transhistorical or transcultural ("universal"), specific to cultural moments and time periods ("contingent"), or, most convincingly, a combination of the two. Scholars in this field employ a range of sources, including written, visual, and sensory (i.e., smell). Jan Plamper, *The History of Emotions: An Introduction*, Emotions in History series (Oxford, UK: Oxford University Press, 2015), 5, 293–95. Heather Williams, the first academic to publish about Ashley's sack, is also one of the few historians to probe the emotions of slavery as a history of emotions. Heather Andrea Williams, *Help Me to Find My People: The African American Search for Family Lost in Slavery* (Chapel Hill: University of North Carolina Press, 2012). David Blight also closely considers feeling and psychology in his biography of abolitionist Frederick Douglass: *Frederick Douglass: Prophet of Freedom* (New York: Simon and Schuster, 2018). Martha Hodes's history of the nation's reaction to Abraham Lincoln's death focuses on the emotion and culture of mourning: Martha Hodes, *Mourning Lincoln* (New Haven: Yale University Press, 2016).

19. Ursula K. Le Guin, *Dancing at the Edge of the World: Thoughts on Words, Women, Places* (New York: Grove, 1989), 169. Le Guin writes: "A novel is a medicine bundle, holding things in a particular, powerful relation to one another and to us."

20. Harriet Jacobs, *Incidents in the Life of a Slave Girl* (1861; repr., Cambridge, Mass.: Harvard University Press, 1987). Elizabeth Keckley, *Behind the Scenes, or Thirty Years a Slave and Four Years in the White House* (1868; repr., New York: Oxford University Press, 1988). Louisa Picquet, *The Octoroon: A Tale of Southern Life* (New York: published by the author, 1861), 12, electronic ed., Documenting the American South, University of North Carolina, Chapel Hill, docsouth.unc.edu/neh/picquet/picquet.html. Eliza Potter, *A Hairdresser's Experience in High Life* (1859; repr., New York: Oxford University Press, 1991), 18, 27. Mamie Garvin Fields with Karen Fields, *Lemon Swamp and Other Places: A Carolina Memoir* (New York: Free Press, 1983). Melnea Cass, transcript, Black Women's Oral History Project, OH-31; T-32, Schlesinger Library, Harvard Radcliffe Institute. I am grateful to Sharony Green, a scholar of Black women's history in Cincinnati, who suggested that I consider Picquet's and Potter's narratives for this study.

21. My approach, a shared one in Black women's historical scholarship, takes Black women of 150 years ago not just as eyewitnesses but also as intellectuals. As Elsa Barkley Brown argues: "African-American women have indeed created their own lives, shaped their own meanings, and are the voices of authority of their own experience." Brown, "African-American Women's Quilting," 927. In addition, I draw this approach of centering Black women as intellectuals in and on the past from Mia E. Bay, Farah J. Griffin, Martha S. Jones, and Barbara D. Savage, *Toward an Intellectual History of Black Women* (Chapel Hill: University of North Carolina Press, 2015).

22. Darlene Clark Hine formulated the classic insight that African American women have made a practice of shielding their inner lives in an article turned book chapter, "Rape and the Inner Lives of Black Women: Thoughts on the Culture of Dissemblance." See Darlene Clark Hine, *Hine Sight: Black Women and the Re-Construction of American History* (Bloomington: Indiana University Press, 1994), 37–48. Additional written sources have aided in building a history of the sack. Even with the loss of records from General William Tecumseh Sherman's torching of Columbia, South Carolina, the state capital, in 1865, the ledgers, journals, inventory books, and recipe books of South Carolina's elite planter class overflow southern archive shelves. Anthropologist Mark Auslander pioneered research on the object and the family, and his work is meticulous. I conducted independent research, which included hiring genealogists Jesse Bustos-Nelson (based in Charleston) and Hannah Scruggs (at the NMAAHC). My inquiry, with their vital assistance, has yielded findings that corroborate the arguments and suppositions of Auslander's initial genealogical work. See Auslander, "Tracing Ashley's Sack," *Cultural Environments* blog, January 2016; his "Slavery's Traces: In Search of Ashley's Sack," *Southern Spaces* blog, November 29, 2016, southernspaces.org/2016/slaverys-traces-search-ashleys-sack; and his "Clifton Family and Ashley's Sack," *Cultural Environments* blog, December 30, 2016, culturalenvironments.blogspot.com/2016/.

23. The literary scholar Megan Sweeney shared this response with me during a series of conversations about both of our fabric-focused books in 2017–18.

CHAPTER 1: RUTH'S RECORD

1. Arthur Middleton and Ruth Jones, Application of Marriage 387059, June 25, 1918, Commonwealth of Pennsylvania, Marriage License Bureau, Philadelphia.

2. While scholars have reconstructed the demographic, social, economic, political, and cultural dimensions of this mass movement, they have not considered what we might make of a migration of things. Isabel Wilkerson's commentary in her chapter "The Things They Left Behind" contends beautifully with natural things (trees—including pecans—and flower gardens and birdcalls), cultural practices (cooking, language, music), ritual (communal gatherings), and relatives, but not as directly with material goods. Isabel Wilkerson, *The Warmth of Other Suns* (New York: Vintage, 2010), 9–10, 538; "Things" quote, 238–41. Tera W. Hunter, *To 'Joy My Freedom: Southern Black Women's Lives and Labors After the Civil War* (Cambridge, Mass.: Harvard University Press, 1997), 232, 217.

3. "Assert identities": Laurel Thatcher Ulrich, *The Age of Homespun: Objects and Stories in the Creation of an American Myth* (New York: Alfred A. Knopf, 2001), 133, 138. For more on how women passed down clothing as assets, see Martha R. Miller, *The Needle's Eye: Women and Work in the Age of Revolution* (Amherst: University of Massachusetts Press, 2006), 28.

4. Arlette Farge, *The Allure of the Archives* (1989; repr., New Haven: Yale University Press, 2013), 97.

5. Historical interpretations are always in motion. This statement refers to the current moment, as new discoveries may yet come to light about Rose, Ashley, Ruth, and the sack. DNA and polymer testing ("polymer" in this case refers to natural polymers such as silk, wool, and wood, rather than the more familiar definition signifying plastics only), in particular, have not yet been done on the sack and might yield illuminating results about its past contents and family linkages.

6. In its reliance on childhood memory and transgenerational memory, the sack is similar to the Federal Writers' Project interviews with formerly enslaved people (the Works Progress Administration, or WPA, Slave Narratives), which solicited memories of slavery several decades after the system had been abolished. Many of the interviewees were children when they experienced bondage, which cast their memories in a particular, often golden light; many also recounted memories of things that happened to their parents and grandparents and could not have been directly observed. Historians use these sources but often in batches (comparing, for instance, all of the narratives from a state or region rather than relying on just one) and with an admittance of the narratives' limitations.

7. David W. Blight, *Frederick Douglass: Prophet of Freedom* (New York: Simon and Schuster, 2018), 24. Memory is fallible and sifted through the biased filters of individual investment and psychological need. But written documents are faulty, too, which is why researchers gather as many records as possible pursuant to their topics for comparison. As Daniel Lord Smail points out, documents housed in archives are often themselves fashioned of the memo-

ries of those who created them in their time. Imagine, for instance, a diary in which the writer must recall her day or an interview in which an interviewee is called on to answer questions about the past. Smail, *On Deep History and the Human Brain* (Berkeley: University of California Press, 2008), 56.

8. "Archivally unknown": Julia Laite, "The Emmet's Inch: Small History in a Digital Age," *Journal of Social History* (2020): 1–27, 17. "Second death": Farge, *Allure*, 121.

9. Heather Andrea Williams, *Help Me to Find My People: The African American Search for Family Lost in Slavery* (Chapel Hill: University of North Carolina Press, 2012), 2.

10. Paul Gardullo, NMAAHC, email exchange with Tiya Miles, February 19, 2018.

11. In this popular Monday evening show on PBS, everyday people bring in personal treasures and extraordinary finds for evaluation by expert appraisers. Barry Garron, "'Antiques Roadshow' Tweaks Formula to Keep Viewers Watching," *Current*, December 5, 2018.

12. Ben Goggins, "Looking for Pearls: Ashley's Sack, Davenport Dolls Give Insight into Lives of Slaves," *Savannah Now*, January 28, 2016, savannahnow .com/article/20160128/LIFESTYLE/301289786. Mark Auslander, "Tracing Ashley's Sack," *Cultural Environments* blog, January 2016. The staff at the Middleton Place Foundation have conveyed to me that the donor wishes to remain anonymous. Tiya Miles, email exchange with Tracey Todd, Mary Edna Sullivan, and Jeff Neale, September 2018. Adam Parker, "Slave Child Torn from Mom Filled Sack with Love," Spartanburg *Herald-Journal*, April 16, 2007, C1, C3.

13. Miles, email exchange with Tracey Todd, Mary Edna Sullivan, and Jeff Neale, September 2018.

14. Laurel Thatcher Ulrich, Ivan Gaskell, Sara J. Schechner, and Sarah Anne Carter, eds., *Tangible Things: Making History Through Objects* (New York: Oxford University Press, 2015), 2. This is not the first time a precious fabric has been dumped into a rag box and later uncovered. In 1977, two museum curators found what was then the oldest surviving piece of clothing known to researchers while digging through "heaps of dirty 'funerary rags'" stored at the University College of London. They identified it as an Egyptian linen shirt dating back to 3000 B.C. Elizabeth Barber, *Women's Work: The First 20,000 Years; Women, Cloth, and Society in Early Times* (New York: W. W. Norton, 1994), 136.

15. Tiya Miles, email exchange with Mary Edna Sullivan, November 22, 2019.

16. Miles, email exchange with Tracey Todd, Mary Edna Sullivan, and Jeff Neale, September 2018. Miles, interview with Mary Edna Sullivan, November 13, 2018, Middleton Place. The first detailed description of Ashley's sack was written for the show *Grandeur Preserved: Masterworks Presented by Historic Charleston Foundation*, loan exhibition for the 57th Annual Winter Antiques Show, January 21–30, 2011. Catalog text draft for *Grandeur Preserved*, 2011, given to Tiya Miles by Mary Edna Sullivan, March 29, 2017.

17. Goggins, "Looking for Pearls." This early trajectory of the sack's movements

derives from Mark Auslander's work. Mark Auslander, "Tracing Ashley's Sack," *Cultural Environments* blog, January 7, 2016, culturalenvironments .blogspot.com/2016/01/; "Clifton Family and Ashley's Sack," December 30, 2016, culturalenvironments.blogspot.com/2016/. Mark Auslander, "Slavery's Traces: In Search of Ashley's Sack," *Southern Spaces* blog, November 29, 2016, southernspaces.org/2016/slaverys-traces-search-ashleys-sack. For more early media coverage of the sack, see the following stories: Leslie Cantu, "'Filled with My Love': Slave Artifact to Be Displayed in New Smithsonian Museum," *Summerville Journal Scene*, December 29, 2015, www .postandcourier.com/journal-scene/news/filled-with-my-love-slave -artifact-to-be-displayed-in-new-smithsonian-museum/article_f2a0eb 0b-2a8a-5a62-a9a9-78f626e0f6ba.html. Vera Bergengruen, "This Scrap of Cloth Is One of the Saddest Artifacts at New DC Museum," McClatchy .com, September 23, 2016, www.mcclatchydc.com/news/nation-world/ national/article103443792.html. Heath Ellison, "The Mystery Behind an Intriguing Lowcountry Slave Object, 'Ashley's Sack,' May Have Been Solved," *Charleston Observer*, December 12, 2016, charlestoncitypaper .com/TheBattery/archives/2016/12/12/the-mystery-behind-an-intriguing -lowcountry-slave-object-ashleys-sack-may-have-been-solved. Bo Peterson, "Mystery Remains in Haunting Slave Sack," *Post and Courier*, January 7, 2017, postandcourier.com/news/mystery-remains-in-haunting-slave-sack/ article_932f3362-d431-11e6-a96c-cbe5336e7237.html. Erin Blakemore, "Show and Tell: A Sack Filled with an Enslaved Mother's Love, *Mental Floss*, January 27, 2017, mentalfloss.com/article/91583/show-tell-sack-filled -enslaved-mothers-love. Melanie Eversley, "Slavery-Era Embroidery Excites Historians, Evokes Heartbreak of Its Time," *USA Today*, February 16, 2017, usatoday.com/story/news/2017/02/16/slavery-era-embroidery-excites -historians-invokes-heartbreak-its-time/96702424/. Sarah Taylor, "'Ashley's Sack' Gathers National Attention," Central Washington University *Observer*, March 1, 2017, cwuobserver.com/9449/news/ashleys-sack-gathers-national -attention/. Dionne Gleaton, "Ashley's Sack: 'National Treasure' of Slavery Era Has Local Ties," Orangeburg, S.C., *Times and Democrat*, June 20, 2017, thetandd.com/lifestyles/ashleys-sack-national-treasure-of-slavery-era-has -local-ties/article_1f7689d3-275b-5f1c-9841-20d7a74e420f.html. Tammy Ayer, "A Stitch in Time: CWU Professor Tracks History of Embroidered Seed Sack to People Held in Slavery on South Carolina Plantation," *Yakima Herald*, November 22, 2017, www.yakimaherald.com/news/local/a-stitch-in -time-cwu-professor-tracks-history-of-embroidered/article_9f2d8aba-c298 -11e6-8653-f7f4a912b32a.html.

Academic studies written about this artifact are few but valuable. University of Pennsylvania historian Heather Williams was the first to publish about the object when she highlighted Ashley's sack in the Epilogue of her wrenching book on the separation of Black families during slavery. Mark Auslander, a cultural anthropologist of Africa and former museum director at Central Washington University and then Michigan State University, was the first to track the genealogy of the family named on the sack and to interview descendants. He researched the sack intensively in 2016–17, served as a consultant to Smithsonian curators, and generously published his early findings online. Auslander brought the sack to national attention, and his work has been indispensable to my research. Williams, *Help Me to Find My People*, 196–97. Auslander, "Tracing Ashley's Sack," "Slavery's Traces," and "Clifton Family and Ashley's Sack." Art historian Jennifer Van Horn used the sack as an example of "affective objects" in her riveting article about enslaved people and artistic iconoclasm that took Civil War–era Charleston as its major site of investigation: Jennifer Van Horn, "'The Dark Iconoclast': African Americans' Artistic Resistance in the Civil War South," *Art Bulletin* 99, no. 4 (2017): 133–67, 157–58.

18. Tiya Miles, tour and interview with Mary Elliott, NMAAHC, Washington, D.C., February 10, 2017. It seems worth noting that Elliott is the only African American person in this preservation and interpretation chain. Miles, email exchange with Tracey Todd, Mary Edna Sullivan, and Jeff Neale, September 2018. While the sack was examined through a high-powered microscope by Mary Edna Sullivan, it has not been subjected to scientific testing, which might verify or disprove what items were packed inside and if there are bodily fluids in the material.

19. Mark Auslander has speculated that Arthur Middleton, Ruth Middleton's husband, may have been descended from enslaved people at Middleton Place through his father's line (Flander Middleton). Auslander traces this genealogy in his article "Slavery's Traces," note 18.

20. Miles, email exchange with Tracey Todd, Mary Edna Sullivan, and Jeff Neale, September 2018. Miles, interview with Mary Edna Sullivan, November 13, 2018, Middleton Place. *Grandeur Preserved* and catalog text draft for *Grandeur Preserved*, 2011, given to Tiya Miles by Mary Edna Sullivan, March 29, 2017.

21. On May 29, 2009, NMAAHC staffers visited Charleston as part of their search for objects for the new museum's collections. At the invitation of the Smithsonian, Middleton Place staff members attended and brought the sack with them, at Mary Edna Sullivan's suggestion. Miles, email exchange with Mary Edna Sullivan, November 22, 2020. Auslander, "Slavery's Traces." Miles, email exchange with Tracey Todd, Mary Edna Sullivan, and Jeff Neale, September 2018. The legal owner of Ashley's sack is the Middleton Place Foundation, a nonprofit organization.

22. Miles, interview with Mary Edna Sullivan, November 13, 2018, Middleton Place.

23. Stephen Berry sent me these thoughts via email after I visited the University of Georgia at his invitation to give the Gregory Lecture for the history department. In that talk I described the sack as sharing qualities in common with the as-told-to slave narrative form. Stephen Berry's note expanded that idea, stressing the way in which slave narratives encourage the reader's identification with the writer's subjective experience, and concluding with the sentence quoted here. Stephen Berry to Tiya Miles, email exchange, October 25, 2019.

24. I am borrowing this language of purity from a concept expressed by Elizabeth Keckley. Keckley, *Behind the Scenes, or Thirty Years a Slave and Four Years in the White House* (1868; repr., New York: Oxford University Press, 1988), xv. Marla Miller discusses the associations of sweetness and comfort often made with women's needlework from previous eras. Miller, *Needle's Eye*, 3.

25. Daina Ramey Berry, *The Price for Their Pound of Flesh: The Value of the Enslaved, from Womb to Grave, in the Building of a Nation* (Boston: Beacon Press, 2017), 128.

26. Quilter and quilt historian Kyra Hicks uncovered a short transcribed text in which Powers describes having made four distinctive quilts. Kyra E. Hicks, *This I Accomplish: Harriet Powers' Bible Quilt and Other Pieces* (N.p.: Black Threads, 2009), 38–40. Collector Jennie Smith is quoted here describing the transfer of what curators refer to as Powers's Bible quilt. Smith first saw Powers's Bible quilt on display at the Northeast Georgia Fair in 1886. Later, she tracked Powers down in an attempt to purchase it. Jennie Smith, handwritten essay, c. 1891, Textile Department, Smithsonian National Museum of American History, Washington, D.C., quoted in Hicks, *This I Accomplish*, 28. Hicks, *This I Accomplish*, 27. Smith's quote about buying the quilt is also reproduced in Gladys-Marie Fry, *Stitched from the Soul: Slave Quilts from the Antebellum South* (1990; repr., Chapel Hill: University of North Carolina Press, 2002), 86. I am grateful to textile curator Jennifer Swope for spending two engrossing hours with me in a private showing of Powers's Pictorial quilt, owned by the Museum of Fine Arts in Boston.

27. Laurel Thatcher Ulrich, "'A Quilt Unlike Any Other': Rediscovering the Work of Harriet Powers," in *Writing Women's History: A Tribute to Anne Firor Scott*, Elizabeth Anne Payne, ed. (Jackson: University Press of Mississippi, 2011), 86–90, 105. I first read the unpublished version of this paper in the Harriet Powers object files, Museum of Fine Arts, Boston. Fry, *Stitched*, 84–91. Marie Jeanne Adams, "The Harriet Powers Pictorial Quilts," *Black Art* 3, no. 4 (1979): 12–28. For further analysis of Harriet Powers's quilt in relation to the sack and slavery studies, see Tiya Miles, "Packed Sacks and Pieced Quilts: Sampling Slavery's Vast Materials," *Winterthur Portfolio* 54, no. 4 (Winter 2020).

28. Williams, *Help Me to Find My People*, 197.

29. I am borrowing and slightly adjusting the language of Sue Monk Kidd, who writes of an enslaved story quilter, Handful's mother, Mauma: "She would tell it in the cloth." Sue Monk Kidd, *The Invention of Wings* (New York: Penguin Books, 2014), 282.

30. Angelina E. Grimké, *Appeal to the Christian Women of the South*, 1836, in *The Public Years of Sarah and Angelina Grimké: Selected Writings 1835–1839*, ed. Larry Ceplair (New York: Columbia University Press, 1989), 53.

31. This statement was made by the journalist and descendant of slaveholders Edward Ball, quoting his cousin Elias Ball, in *Slaves in the Family* (New York: Ballantine Books, 1998), 47.

32. Unlike other southern colonies, Carolina had a Black majority population within two generations of European settlement, by around 1708. Peter H.

Wood, *Black Majority: Negroes in Colonial South Carolina from 1670 Through the Stono Rebellion* (New York: W. W. Norton, 1974), xiv, 143. By the 1720s, Carolina had reached a degree of wealth and concentration of wealth in the hands of an elite minority that would not be present in New York or Philadelphia until the 1760s or 1770s; the colony was also "the most inegalitarian." Stephanie McCurry, *Masters of Small Worlds: Yeoman Households, Gender Relations, and the Political Culture of the Antebellum South Carolina Low Country* (New York: Oxford University Press, 1995), 33.

33. Richard S. Dunn, *Sugar and Slaves: The Rise of the Planter Class in the English West Indies, 1624–1713* (1972; repr., Chapel Hill: University of North Carolina Press, 2000), 82, 84.

34. Dunn, *Sugar and Slaves*, 70.

35. Hilary Beckles, *The First Black Slave Society: Britain's "Barbarity Time" in Barbados, 1636–1876* (Jamaica: University of the West Indies Press, 2016), 160, 76.

36. Beckles, *First Black Slave Society*, 171.

37. Dunn, *Sugar and Slaves*, 71. Winthrop D. Jordan, *White over Black: American Attitudes Toward the Negro* (New York: W. W. Norton, 1968), 4–11, 89. Ibram X. Kendi, *Stamped from the Beginning: The Definitive History of Racist Ideas in America* (New York: Nation Books, 2016), 22–23, 36.

38. Alan Gallay, *The Indian Slave Trade: The Rise of the English Empire in the American South, 1670–1717* (New Haven: Yale University Press, 2002), 43. Cynthia M. Kennedy, *Braided Relations, Entwined Lives: The Women of Charleston's Urban Slave Society* (Bloomington: Indiana University Press, 2005), 18. Charles H. Lesser, "Lords Proprietors of South Carolina," *South Carolina Encyclopedia*, June 2016, scencyclopedia.org/sce/entries/lords-proprietors-of-carolina/.

39. Marisa Fuentes, *Dispossessed Lives: Enslaved Women, Violence, and the Archive* (Philadelphia: University of Pennsylvania Press, 2016), 16, 20, 35, 40–41, 102–3, 124–25.

40. "Desire to resemble": Joyce E. Chaplin, *An Anxious Pursuit: Agricultural Innovation and Modernity in the Lower South, 1730–1815* (Chapel Hill: University of North Carolina Press, 1993), 2, 4. Kennedy, *Braided Relations*, 18. Peter Wood points out that in addition to tensions over limited land availability, natural disasters pushed Anglo-Barbadians to emigrate. Wood, *Black Majority*, 8–9.

41. Taylor, *American Colonies: The Settling of North America* (New York: Penguin Books, 2001), 224. Dunn, *Sugar and Slaves*, 111, 112.

42. Wood, *Black Majority*, 19, 20. Taylor, *American Colonies*, 224, 225. Daniel C. Littlefield, "Slavery," *South Carolina Encyclopedia*, October 2016, 2, scencyclopedia.org/sce/entries/slavery/. Carolina B. Whitley, *North Carolina Head Rights: A List of Names, 1663–1744* (Chapel Hill: University of North Carolina Press, 2001).

43. Taylor, *American Colonies*, 225. The Fundamental Constitutions of Carolina: March 1, 1669, Avalon Project, Yale Law School, avalon.law.yale.edu/17th_century/nc05.asp, number 110. Lesser, "Lords Proprietors."

44. Fuentes, *Dispossessed Lives*, 19.

45. Dunn, *Sugar and Slaves*, 144, 115. Taylor, *American Colonies*, 225. Charles Duell, *Middleton Place: A Phoenix Still Rising* (2016 revision; Charleston: Middleton Place Foundation, 2011), 11. An influential group of early Barbadian planters, including the Middletons, settled on land around Goose Creek, just north of Charles Towne, and hence became known as the Goose Creek men.

46. Gregory O'Malley, *Final Passages: The Intercolonial Slave Trade of British America, 1619–1807* (Chapel Hill: University of North Carolina Press, 2014), 120.

47. Duell, *Middleton Place*, 12.

48. "Barbados style": Beckles, *First Black Slave Society*, 203. Dunn, *Sugar and Slaves*, 111.

49. Dunn, *Sugar and Slaves*, 17, 18.

50. Dunn, *Sugar and Slaves*, 73. Gallay, *Indian Slave Trade*, 300. Taylor, *American Colonies*, 231. Christine M. DeLucia, *Memory Lands: King Philip's War and the Place of Violence in the Northeast* (New Haven: Yale University Press, 2018), 289. O'Malley, *Final Passages*, 128. Wendy Warren, *New England Bound: Slavery and Colonization in Early America* (New York: Liveright, 2016), 6, 7, 34, 36.

51. Charles M. Hudson, *The Catawba Nation* (Athens: University of Georgia Press, 1970), 1–3, 6, 10. Douglas Summers Brown, *The Catawba Indians: The People of the River* (Columbia: University of South Carolina Press, 1966), 3. James Merrell, *The Indians' New World: Catawbas and Their Neighbors from European Contact Through the Era of Removal* (1989; repr., New York: W. W. Norton, 1991), 27, 45, 57, 93. Gallay, *Indian Slave Trade*, 10–17, 52. Ball, *Slaves*, 28–30. Lesser, "Lords Proprietors."

52. Gallay, *Indian Slave Trade*, 3, 5.

53. Hudson, *Catawba Nation*, 17, 22, 29, 30. Brown, *Catawba Indians*, 8–9. Hudson also notes that the Catawba location allowed them to hunt and store passenger pigeons for food, allowing them more time for winter hunting, which helped them secure their strong spot in the chain of trade (22).

54. Merrell, *Indians' New World*, 88. Hudson, *Catawba Nation*, 39, 43. Gallay, *Indian Slave Trade*, 43–44, 50, 94, on Westos, 53–61. Christina Snyder, *Slavery in Indian Country: The Changing Face of Captivity in Early America* (Cambridge, Mass.: Harvard University Press, 2010), 49, 76, 77. As the historian Hayley Negrin points out, these personal attacks included sexual assaults on Native women in their villages. Hayley Negrin, "Possessing Native Women and Children: Slavery, Gender and English Colonialism in the Early American South, 1670–1717" (PhD diss., New York University, 2018), 90–91, on Westos 41–42. Regarding attacks on Native women, also see Merrell, *Indians' New World*, 100. Robbie Ethridge, "Introduction: Mapping the Mississippian Shatter Zone," in *Mapping the Mississippian Shatter Zone: The Colonial Indian Slave Trade and Regional Instability in the American South*, Robbie Ethridge and Sheri M. Shuck-Hall, eds. (Lincoln: University of Nebraska Press, 2009), 14–15. Fundamental Constitutions of Carolina,

Avalon Project, number 112. Taylor, *American Colonies*, 226. Duell, *Middleton Place*, 11–12.

55. Hudson, *Catawba Nation*, 22. Gallay, *Indian Slave Trade*, 6.
56. Gallay, *Indian Slave Trade*, 49, on Kussoe Wars, 51–52. Negrin, "Possessing Native Women and Children," 76–88. Christina Snyder argues that a long-standing practice of taking Indigenous captives in the Southeast supported the development of English plantations by providing labor; Snyder, *Slavery in Indian Country*, 75. Ethridge, "Introduction: Mapping the Mississippian Shatter Zone," 25.
57. Wood, *Black Majority*, 38–40. Hudson, *Catawba Nation*, 39–40. Merrell, *Indians' New World*, 92–94. Gallay, *Indian Slave Trade*, 65, 299. Negrin, "Possessing Native Women and Children," 2, 5. Snyder, *Slavery in Indian Country*, 78.
58. Gallay, *Indian Slave Trade*, 47; also see "Afterword: Africans and Indians," 345–57. Richard Dunn calls this "noble savage" romanticization a "sentimental advantage" that Native slaves had over Africans; Dunn, *Sugar and Slaves*, 73.
59. Wood, *Black Majority*, 39.
60. Almon Wheeler Lauber, *Indian Slavery in Colonial Times Within the Present Limits of the United States* (New York: Columbia University Press, 1913), 315. Lauber cites a 1740 statute as the decision treated in South Carolina courts as the outlawing of Native enslavement. Hudson, *Catawba Nation*, 42–43. Kennedy, *Braided Relations*, 19. Wood, *Black Majority*, 38–40.
61. Alan Gallay argues that availability was the key feature that made African slaves more attractive to English settlers. Alan Gallay, "Indian Slavery in Historical Context," in *Indian Slavery in Colonial America*, Alan Gallay, ed. (Lincoln: University of Nebraska Press, 2009), 20. Local Native power diminished especially after the Yamassee War of 1715, a conflict that pitted Yamassees and like-minded fighters against Charlestonians and their Native allies, ending in a Yamassee defeat and a decisive blow to Indigenous strength. Wood, *Black Majority*, 80–81, 85. Merrell, *Indians' New World*, 101. Chaplin, *Anxious Pursuit*, 119. Lauber, *Indian Slavery*, 232. Sylviane Diouf writes that English settlers saw Native people, especially Catawbas, as effective hunters of Black maroons and as barriers to the growth of maroon communities. Sylviane A. Diouf, *Slavery's Exiles: The Story of the American Maroons* (New York: New York University Press, 2014), 31–32.
62. Chaplin, *Anxious Pursuit*, 134, 228. Judith A. Carney, *Black Rice: The Origins of Rice Cultivation in the Americas* (Cambridge, Mass.: Harvard University Press, 2001), 85, 89.
63. Kennedy, *Braided Relations*, 19.
64. Chaplin, *Anxious Pursuit*, 8.
65. Quoted in Maurie D. McInnis, *The Politics of Taste in Antebellum Charleston* (Chapel Hill: University of North Carolina Press, 2005), 5.
66. "Distinctive crop": Chaplin, *Anxious Pursuit*, 227.
67. Judith A. Carney and Richard Nicholas Rosomoff, *In the Shadow of Slavery: Africa's Botanical Legacy in the Atlantic World* (Berkeley: University of Cali-

fornia Press, 2009), 150–53. Wood, *Black Majority*, 59, 61, 119. Chaplin, *Anxious Pursuit*, 228. Philip Morgan disagrees that rice expertise was a significant factor in the valuation and organization of African labor in South Carolina. While noting that many (but not the majority) of the enslaved came from a ricing region, he points out that rice cultivators in Africa were women rather than the men preferred by planters, and that African rice cultivation took place in the drier uplands, using different techniques than South Carolina required; Philip D. Morgan, *Slave Counterpoint: Black Culture in the Eighteenth-Century Chesapeake and Lowcountry* (Chapel Hill: University of North Carolina Press, 1998), 66 (map), 182–83. Carney, a geographer, argues in her comparative study of African and U.S. mainland rice cultures that a wide range of ricing environments and practices were employed in West Africa. She suggests that African techniques are indeed evident in South Carolina wetland cultivation even as some technological modifications were made. She notes that women's role in rice production did continue in South Carolina slavery in the form of a "female knowledge system." Carney, *Black Rice*, 88, 92, 96, 104, 110, 117.

68. Amrita Chakrabarti Myers, *Forging Freedom: Black Women and the Pursuit of Liberty in Antebellum Charleston* (Chapel Hill: University of North Carolina Press, 2011), 28.

69. Dunn, *Sugar and Slaves*, 115.

70. Both McInnis and Myers emphasize the contrasts that marked the city's particular character; McInnis, *Politics of Taste*, 30. Myers, *Forging Freedom*, 26.

71. Brendan Clark, "Good Question: Who Coined Charleston as 'The Holy City,'" *Count on News* 2, WCBD-TV, Charleston, March 11, 2019. Interviewed for this piece is Grahame Long, curator of the Charleston Museum.

CHAPTER 2: SEARCHING FOR ROSE

1. Stephanie McCurry, *Masters of Small Worlds: Yeoman Households, Gender Relations, and the Political Culture of the Antebellum South Carolina Low Country* (New York: Oxford University Press, 1995), 37.

2. Alice Walker, Foreword, "Those Who Love Us Never Leave Us Alone with Our Grief," to *Barracoon: The Story of the Last "Black Cargo,"* by Zora Neale Hurston (New York: HarperCollins, 2018), ix.

3. Harriet Martineau, *Retrospect of Western Travel*, vol. 1 (1838; repr., Bedford, Mass.: Applewood), 227–28.

4. Some 55 percent of the Charleston peninsula was filled in over time to make way for building. Christina Shedlock, "'Prejudicial to the Public Health': Class, Race, and the History of Land Reclamation, Drainage, and Topographic Alteration in Charleston, South Carolina, 1836–1940" (master's thesis, Graduate School of the College of Charleston and the Citadel, April 2010), 6, 9, 24.

5. These findings reflect a search of federal, state (South Carolina), county (statewide), and city (Charleston) records. With the essential help of Charleston genealogist and trained librarian Jesse Bustos-Nelson, I searched hundreds of slaveholder records that have been preserved from the 1700s and

1800s and are publicly accessible. The process included a digital search of the online database of the South Carolina Department of Archives and History (SCDAH); an in-person search of property transfer books at SCDAH; review of the Slave Name database created by SCDAH and housed in the Charleston Public Library's South Carolina Room Special Collections; a search of plantation records of the South Carolina Historical Society and the College of Charleston Special Collections housed at the Addlestone Library; a search of published and unpublished records at Middleton Place plantation; a search of records in the Charleston Office of Records/Mesne Conveyance; a search of the WPA narratives for the state of South Carolina; and a search of the Freedmen's Bureau Records for the state. The process involved a direct review of 165 to 200 relevant sets of slaveholder records. These searches often revealed duplicate names and head counts for the most prominent slaveholding families, which I have tried to control for here. While it is impossible to conduct this search for Rose in a comprehensive fashion—due to the lack of genuine interest in enslaved people by record keepers of the time; the destruction of some records from that period, especially in the Civil War; the retention of some records in private hands; and the likely scattering of some records across the country and Europe that would take significant additional time to discover and access—the search was detailed and broad. I conducted this search independently with the aid of Jesse Bustos-Nelson and archivists in South Carolina, but I had the real benefit of not being the first scholar to search for Rose. My independent findings matched those published by Mark Auslander in 2016, suggesting that two researchers have pinpointed the family most likely to have been Rose's, based on the records that survive. See Auslander, "Tracing Ashley's Sack," *Cultural Environments* blog, January 7, 2016, culturalenvironments.blogspot.com/2016/01/; Auslander, "Slavery's Traces," Southern Spaces blog, November 2016, southernspaces.org/2016/slaverys-traces-search-ashleys-sack; and Auslander, "Rose's Gift: Slavery, Kinship, and the Fabric of Memory," *Present Pasts* 8, no. 1 (2017): 1, doi.org/10.5334/pp.78.

6. I have taken some license here in using the term "grandmother"; whether or not this old woman had children—biological or adoptive—is not recorded. For more on African day and seasonal names as well as naming ceremonies, see Peter H. Wood, *Black Majority: Negroes in Colonial South Carolina from 1670 Through the Stono Rebellion* (New York: W. W. Norton, 1974), 181; Ira Berlin, *Generations of Captivity: A History of African-American Slaves* (Cambridge, Mass.: Harvard University Press, 2003), 65; Sterling Stuckey, *Slave Culture: Nationalist Theory and the Foundations of Black America* (New York: Oxford University Press, 1987), 194–96. Middleton Family Papers, Middleton Place Foundation office, Charleston, S.C. Barbara Doyle, Mary Edna Sullivan, Tracey Todd, eds., *Beyond the Fields: Slavery at Middleton Place* (Charleston: Middleton Place Foundation, 2008). "Principal Middleton Family Properties," Eliza's House Exhibit, Middleton Place Plantation.

7. Middleton Family Papers, Middleton Place Foundation. *Beyond the Fields*, 44, 47, 55. Henry Middleton, Weehaw Plantation Journal, Addlestone Li-

brary. I am grateful to Mary Edna Sullivan, who pulled MP records for me and shared with me the story of the Middleton Place Foundation's decades-long history of compiling African American history and slavery history data. Sullivan credited a former president of the foundation, Charles Duell, with inaugurating a concerted effort to preserve Black history in the 1970s and with working with Black site staff members and volunteers Mary Sheppard, Anna Perry, Eliza Leach, and Martha DeWeese to do so. Middleton Place seems to have been decades ahead of the local and national curve of incorporating African American history into plantation site interpretation, although this incorporation has not been smooth or uncomplicated, as curators readily share.

8. For Drayton Hall architecture, see draytonhall.org/. Drayton Family Papers, Drayton Hall List for Negro Clothes and Blankets, 1860, Addlestone Library. Notably, in 2020 Drayton Hall staff members integrated enslaved people's names and stories into the historic site's audio tour narrative. Emily Williams, "Untold Stories and Names Now Part of Historic House Tour at Drayton Hall," *Post and Courier*, December 28, 2020.

9. Brown, Barnett H., "Petition for Compensation for the Execution of his Slave, Rose," November 23, 1853, Petitions, Series S165015, SCDAH. Treasurer of the Upper Division, Journal 1849–57 S108091, pp. 153–54, May 1855, Rosanna, slave of B. H. Brown, SCDAH. Report of the Committee on Claims, General Assembly, Committee Reports S165005 1853 No. 89 (House), H-B Brown, SCDAH. Treasury Office, Columbia, April 1855, Melton A. McLaurin, *Celia: A Slave* (Athens: University of Georgia Press, 1991), ix, 18, 20, 21, 22, 27–31. Daina Ramey Berry, *The Price for Their Pound of Flesh: The Value of the Enslaved, from Womb to Grave, in the Building of a Nation* (Boston: Beacon Press, 2017), 80–81. McLaurin's study is the classic text on Celia's ordeal. In the 2000s, a group of scholars began convening in an effort to inaugurate the Celia Project, a new investigation and interpretation of the *State of Missouri v. Celia* court case. This project is currently in progress and will result in a website and edited collection. One of the project founders, historian and attorney Martha S. Jones, has begun a process to appeal to the Missouri legislature to have Celia pardoned. For information on the Celia Project, see sites.lsa.umich.edu/celiaproject/ and c-span.org/video/?321554-1/female-slaves-law.

10. I borrow this language from Vincent Brown: Vincent Brown, *The Reaper's Garden: Death and Power in the World of Atlantic Slavery* (Cambridge, Mass.: Harvard University Press, 2008).

11. I have adopted an interpretive approach modeled by Marisa Fuentes, a historian of slavery in Barbados, the island from which many of Charleston's first white settlers and slavers emigrated. Fuentes exposes the "distortion" of Black women in the archives and offers a strategy of reading along the flexible "bias grain," as if documents were textiles. Marisa Fuentes, *Dispossessed Lives: Enslaved Women, Violence, and the Archive* (Philadelphia: University of Pennsylvania Press, 2016), 1, 78. For a discussion of knowledge gleaned beyond the archives in slavery studies, see Christina Sharpe, *In the*

Wake: On Blackness and Being (Durham, N.C.: Duke University Press, 2016), 12–13.

12. MES and KS, "Ashley's Sack" label and catalog, *Grandeur Preserved: Master-works Presented by Historic Charleston Foundation*, loan exhibition for the 57th Annual Winter Antiques Show, January 21–30, 2011. MES and KS, "Ashley's Sack" label and catalog, hard copy text used for *Grandeur Preserved* altered with deletion note, Middleton Place archives, no date.

13. It is difficult to say why the person named Ashley would vanish from the Bonneaus' estate records while a person named Rose appears in a related set of estate records years later. Because the second set of records detailed the holdings of children who had inherited slave property from Bonneau, there certainly could have been the mistaken inclusion of a woman who entered the children's property holdings at some point over the intervening years but had actually not been owned by their father. In addition, plantation records were not necessarily comprehensive. People could be present and not be recorded in every accounting, as in the informal freeing of slaves that sometimes took place in instances of sexual indiscretion. Thomas Jefferson, for example, left his enslaved partner, Sally Hemings, and children he had conceived with her out of his will in order to avoid further public exposure of the rumored relationship. Annette Gordon Reed, *The Hemingses of Monticello: An American Family* (New York: W. W. Norton, 2008), 657–58. Finally, in the case of the Bonneau family, only probate and sales records are filed in the South Carolina state archives, which means that the more detailed and regularly occurring lists of slave distribution are not available in this case.

14. Wilson, Samuel, as Atty. for Judith H. Wilson of Bordeaux, France, to John E. Bonneau, Bill of Sale for 3 Mullatto [*sic*] Slaves, Miscellaneous Records, S213003, V. 50, p. 920, SCDAH. John E. Bonneau, Inventory and Appraisement of Goods, Chattel, and Personal Estate, Dec. 1849, Inventories, Appraisements, & Sales, 1850–1853, vol. C, pp. 15–18, SCDAH. Eliza E. Bonneau, Sale of John Bonneau Villa, Feb. 18, 1850, SCDAH. Sales of Negroes of the Estate of John Bonneau, Feb. 20, 1850, Inventories, Appraisements, & Sales, 1850–1853, vol. C, SCDAH. Martha Bonneau, Bond, Jan. 25, 1841, BK 5S, p. 105, SCDAH. John E. Bonneau, Bills of Sale, 5G pp. 212, 246, 318, SCDAH. Peter and Martha Bonneau to William Bonneau, S213050, Charleston District, vol. 60, p. 403, November 9, 1855, SCDAH.

15. Inventory of All Goods and Chattels and Personal Estate in the District of Barnwell of Robert Martin, Inventories, Appraisements, & Sales, 1850–1853, vol. C, pp. 366–67. Appraisement of the Personal Property in the City of Charleston of the Late Robert Martin, Inventories, Appraisements, & Sales, 1850–1853, vol. C, pp. 358–59.

16. This statement refers to the records I could access—those that still exist and are in public collections or private collections made accessible to researchers. It is important to note again here that numerous records from the state were destroyed by incidental fire and also by the destruction of Sherman's March during the Civil War. There is always the possibility, as well, that sources now held by a private family or collector or buried in an as yet un-

identified cache will come to light in the future. There is agreement, though, on my reading of the extant sources in the findings of a scholar who traced the sack before me. In his published research on Ashley's sack, Mark Auslander writes: "Rose and Ashley almost certainly were owned by the wealthy Charleston merchant and planter Robert Martin." Auslander, "Rose's Gift," 2.

17. *Milberry S. Martin v. James B. Campbell*, Charleston District Court of Equity, Decree Books L 10092, 1858–1861, pp. 64–76.

18. Henry J. Martin, *Notices: Genealogical and Historical, of the Martin Family of New England* (Boston: Lee and Shepard, 1880), No. 34. David Martin, of Fairfield District, S.C., 236. Robert Martin, American Genealogical-Biographical Index, vol. 111, p. 158, Ancestry.com. Charleston City Directory, 1816, 1829, 1830, 1837, Addlestone Library. Note: the bound copy of the 1830 city directory differs from the digital copy posted at Ancestry.com; the records list Martin at two different locations: Kiddell's Wharf (bound) and Boyce's Wharf (digital). I expect that he operated out of both locations in this time period and may have reported differently from year to year. Maurie D. McInnis, *The Politics of Taste in Antebellum Charleston* (Chapel Hill: University of North Carolina Press, 2005), 49n23, 57.

19. An Inventory and Appraisement of the Goods and Chattels of William Daniel, March 1829, Kershaw County Probate Court Estate Papers Apartment 19, Package 625, William Daniel C9239, Charleston County Register of Deeds Office, Reproduced from Microfilm in South Carolina Department of Archives and History, Columbia, S.C. Will of William Daniel, August 25, 1828, Kershaw County Probate Court Estate Papers, William Daniel. For genealogical sources on Serena Daniel's family, see word document derived from the Martin Family Bible, taken from a narrative by Annie Elizabeth Miller dated 1934, posted by Lucy Gray, DANIEL-L@rootsweb.com, at rootsweb .com, January 22, 2003, rolodafile.com/williamodaniel/d3.htm#c905.

20. Martin R., Deed of Gift to Elizabeth Martin, Nov. 19, 1838, Bill of Sale Indexes, Book L, pp. 187–88, SCDAH. Martin, Robert, Miscellaneous Records, Bills of Sale, BS, 5A, pp. 280, 452; BS 5K, p. 455, SCDAH. Aiken: Martin, Robert, Miscellaneous Records, S213003, Book 5M, pp. 165, 194, SCDAH; Chalmers Gaston Davidson, *The Last Foray: The South Carolina Planters of 1860: A Sociological Study* (Columbia: University of South Carolina Press, 1971), 8, 171. Martin, Robert, Miscellaneous Records, S213003, Book 5I, p. 39; Book 5N, p. 270.

21. Robert Martin Will, Pinckney-Means Family Papers, 208.03, Folder E, Estate Records, 1795–1971, Will Book No. L 1851–1856, p. 126, Addlestone Library. McInnis, *Politics of Taste*, 338n18. Inflation rates for "today" in the text are calculated to 2019, using the Inflation Calculator (also linked through the Library of Congress website), westegg.com/inflation/infl.cgi. The exact figure for the $20,000 distribution calculation was $486,244.51. The detailed provision for daughters in the Robert Martin will is an example of what Stephanie Jones-Rogers has highlighted as slaveholding relatives' attempts to protect the property of white women even after marriage. Stepha-

nie E. Jones-Rogers, *They Were Her Property: White Women as Slave Owners in the American South* (New Haven: Yale University Press, 2019), Kindle loc. 885, 916. When Robert Martin named Milberry Martin as executor, the practice of propertied husbands assigning this managerial role to widows had been declining across the country. Married white women were increasingly defined as dependents (rather than as productive members of households) and saw their influence curtailed to the domestic sphere. Joan R. Gunderson, "Women and Inheritance in America: Virginia and New York City as a Case Study, 1700–1860," in *Inheritance and Wealth in America*, ed. Robert K. Miller, Jr. and Stephen J. McNamee (New York: Plenum, 1998), 103, 108.

22. Martin named his rural estate Milberry Place Plantation after his wife. J.L.P. Powell to Robert Martin, Bill of Sale, Barnwell County Deeds, Deed Book BB, p. 136, SCDAH. U. M. Robert to Robert Martin, 2,400 A. Savannah River, Deed Book BB, p. 400. See various Robert Martin land purchases between 1843 and 1849, Barnwell County Deeds, Books BB, DD, SCDAH. According to Joseph P. Madden, Erwinton was a distinctive, well-off community that used to have its own post office. The figures Madden names as prominent in the community were listed in the deed books as having sold land tracts and/or enslaved people to Robert Martin, including General Erwin, Captain Robert, and Mr. Powell. Joseph P. Madden, *A History of Old Barnwell District, SC to 1860* (Blackville, S.C.: Historical Business Ventures, 2001), 75–77, South Caroliniana Library, University of South Carolina, Columbia. *Milberry S. Martin v. James B. Campbell,* Charleston District Court of Equity, Decree Books L 10092, 1858–1861, pp. 64–76. In further evidence of the couple's rising status, Milberry Martin became a lifetime member of the City Mission Society of the prestigious St. Philip's Church in 1849. St. Philip's City Mission, St. Philip's Church Records, South Carolina Room, Charleston Public Library.

23. James Oakes, *The Ruling Race: A History of American Slaveholders* (New York: Vintage, 1982), 57. I extend my thanks to the genealogist Jesse Bustos-Nelson for tracking these church records down, and to Patricia Smith Moore, St. Philip's Archivist, for assisting him.

24. James Oakes discusses the disproportionate number and nature of planter records, often preserved as the papers of prominent families, noting that scholars have tended to rely on these narrowly prescribed sources to the detriment of understanding the diversity of slaveholders. Oakes, *Ruling Race*, xvi.

25. Robert Martin was already related to some branch of the Aikens through his mother, Mary Aiken; Martin, *Notices: Genealogical and Historical*, 236. U.S. Federal Census, 1840, Ancestry.com. Charleston City Directory, 1852. Ellen Martin married Joseph D. Aiken; Henrietta Martin married Edward B. Means; Barbara R. Langdon, *Barnwell County Marriages 1764–1859 Implied in Barnwell County South Carolina Deeds*, 12058, Reference Library, South Carolina Department of Archives and History, Henrietta Martin: Pinckney-Means Family Papers, Box 4, Correspondence, 1840s–1860s, Special Collections and South Carolina Historical Society, Addlestone Library.

26. Erskine Clarke, *Wrestlin' Jacob: A Portrait of Religion in Antebellum Georgia and the Carolina Low Country* (Tuscaloosa: University of Alabama Press, 2000), 90, 98.

27. McInnis, *Politics of Style*, 46, 49, 45. For a further description of Charleston's urban architectural styles, see Bernard L. Herman, *Town House: Architectural and Material Life in the Early American City* (Chapel Hill: University of North Carolina Press, published for the Omohundro Institute of Early American History and Culture, 2005), 65–70.

28. Martin, Robert House (SC-150), Historic American Building Survey South Carolina 10, Char, 141, Washington, D.C. McInnis, *Politics of Style*, 47. While the HABS describes the home as "Greek Revival," Maurie McInnis calls it a "suburban villa," referring to a rural-inflected twist on a traditional Charleston elite style that was often classical and Georgian. McInnis, *Politics of Taste*, 37, 46, 57–58.

29. Appraisement of the Personal Property in the City of Charleston of the Late Robert Martin, Inventories, Appraisements, & Sales, 1850–1853, vol. C, pp. 358–59, SCDAH. 1840 U.S. Federal Census, 1840.

30. Harriet Ann Jacobs, *Incidents in the Life of a Slave Girl, Written by Herself* (1861; repr., Cambridge, Mass.: Harvard University Press, 1987), 55.

31. Izard quoted in Maurie D. McInnis, *Politics of Taste*, 178. Glass shards, sounds of violence, and walls as control mechanisms: McInnis, *Politics of Taste*, 180, 181. The opening mood and language of this chapter was inspired by an enslaved woman's folk song that refers to Charleston's enclosed gardens and imposed curfew for enslaved people, which was signaled each night by a drum beat: "Oh! Dear! I can't get out, / For I'm in dis lady's garden. / Bell done ring and drum done beat, / And I'm in dis lady's garden"; quoted in McInnis, *Politics of Taste*, 264.

32. HABS, Robert Martin House.

33. Emily Burke, *Pleasure and Pain: Reminiscences of Georgia in the 1840s* (1850; repr., Savannah: Beehive Press, Library of Georgia, 1991), 9.

34. Jacobs, *Incidents*, 27.

35. Herman notes the placement of slaves in white-owned urban townhouses as "props," "fixtures," and "animated furnishings"; Herman, *Town House*, 148–49. McInnis notes the social significance of the Martin double parlors; McInnis, *Politics of Taste*, 47.

36. Robert Martin, Property Appraisement, Charleston, SCDAH. Karen Hampton, "African American Women: Plantation Textile Production from 1750 to 1830," *Approaching Textiles, Varying Viewpoints: Proceedings of the Seventh Biennial Symposium of the Textile Society of America*, Santa Fe, N.M., 2000, Digital Commons, University of Nebraska–Lincoln, digitalcommons.unl.edu/tsaconf/770, 266. Madelyn Shaw, "Slave Cloth and Clothing Slaves: Craftsmanship, Commerce, and Industry," *Journal of Early Southern Decorative Arts* 41 (2012), mesdajournal.org/2012/slave-cloth-clothing-slaves-craftsmanship-commerce-industry. Enslaved women were rarely afforded the opportunity to learn specialized skills beyond sewing; see Jacqueline

Jones, *Labor of Love, Labor of Sorrow: Black Women, Work, and the Family, From Slavery to the Present* (New York: Vintage, 1985), 18.

37. Gladys-Marie Fry, *Stitched from the Soul: Slave Quilts from the Antebellum South* (Chapel Hill: University of North Carolina Press, 1990), 14–15. Fry points out that while cloth-making was mainly the provenance of men in West and central African societies, the skilled work of spinning and weaving became the specialty of Black women enslaved in the United States. Enslaved Black women were, however, rare in the high-skilled artisanal category of dressmaker. An 1848 Charleston census of mantua-makers counted 38 white, 128 free Black, 4 enslaved; McInnis, *Politics of Style*, 362n8.

38. Quoted in McInnis, *Politics of Taste*, 28; Journal of G. F. Fox, Jr., November 5, 1834, Rubenstein Rare Book & Manuscript Library, Duke University, Durham, N.C.

39. Harlan Greene, Harry S. Hutchins, Jr., and Brian E. Hutchins, *Slave Badges and the Slave-Hire System in Charleston, South Carolina, 1783–1865* (Jefferson, N.C.: McFarland, 2004), 3, 4, 5, 6, 127, 128, 120–34; 1840–50 sales chart: 133–34, images A–H. Free people of color were required to pay for and wear badges in the 1780s, before the law pertaining to them was repealed; they later had to pay special taxes to the city as a class (23–24, 28). Greene, Hutchins, and Hutchins also note that only dogs were also required to wear badges regularly in this period (64). Charleston's curfew for the enslaved was nine P.M. in winter and ten P.M. in summer. Frances Anne Kemble, *Journal of a Residence on a Georgian Plantation in 1838–1839* (1961; repr., Athens: University of Georgia Press, 1984), 38; McInnis, *Politics of Taste*, 84–85.

40. Robert Martin and Serena Milberry Daniel were married by an Episcopal priest, the Reverend Mr. Davis. *Camden Journal*, September 27, 1828. Milberry Martin belonged to an Episcopalian charity society. St. Philip's City Mission, St. Philip's Church Records, South Carolina Room, Charleston Public Library.

41. Clarke, *Wrestlin' Jacob*, 104–6, 145. Ethan J. Kytle and Blain Roberts, *Denmark Vesey's Garden: Slavery and Memory in the Cradle of the Confederacy* (New York: New Press, 2017), 26. Philip D. Morgan, *Slave Counterpoint: Black Culture in the Eighteenth-Century Chesapeake and Lowcountry* (Chapel Hill: University of North Carolina Press, 1998), 284. Cynthia M. Kennedy, *Braided Relations, Entwined Lives: The Women of Charleston's Urban Slave Society* (Bloomington: Indiana University Press, 2005), 79. Tristan Stubbs, *Masters of Violence: The Plantation Overseers of Eighteenth-Century Virginia, South Carolina, and Georgia* (Columbia: University of South Carolina Press, 2018), 4, 6, 8. In a polite revision of the work of Eugene Genovese, James Oakes argues that the paternalist ethos recedes among southern slaveholders, replaced by a racial argument for Black subjugation, as the market economy and profit motive expand in the nineteenth century; Oakes, *The Ruling Race*, xii–xiii, 34. Also see Eugene D. Genovese, *Roll, Jordan, Roll: The World the Slaves Made* (New York: Vintage, 1972), 3–7.

42. Burke, *Pleasure and Pain*, 13. Emily Burke, a teacher from New Hampshire, was not a professed abolitionist. She enjoyed her decade-long sojourn in coastal Georgia even as she noted with alarm the cruel and violent treatment of enslaved people in a series of letters. Library of Georgia, Introduction, *Pleasure and Pain*, xi.

43. Drew Gilpin Faust, *Mothers of Invention: Women of the Slaveholding South in the American Civil War* (Chapel Hill: University of North Carolina Press, 1996), 6, 32, 59.

44. Burke, *Pleasure and Pain*, 14.

45. Jacobs, *Incidents*, 52.

46. U.S. Federal Census, 1840, Robert Martin, Charleston Neck, Charleston, S.C. These children in 1840 would have been Henrietta Aiken Martin, Ellen Daniel Martin, William Aiken Martin, and Robert Martin, Jr. All of these children, plus Serena Milbury Martin, born after this census was taken, were listed as recipients of the sale and partition of Robert Martin's property in 1853. James W. Gray to Mrs. M. S. Martin, Deeds Barnwell County Book HH, 1854, pp. 183–84. A sixth child, Charles Wentworth Martin, is listed in public genealogy sources: Robert Martin, www.findagrave.com/memorial/69820867/robert-martin.

47. The 1840 census lists two enslaved women in Martin's Charleston household between the ages of twenty-four and thirty-five, matching up with this age and date conclusion for Rose. Rose was probably born around 1818.

48. Deborah Gray White, *Ar'n't I a Woman? Female Slaves in the Plantation South* (New York: W. W. Norton, 1985), 97.

49. Slave marriage: Kennedy, *Braided Relations*, 95–97. Mark Auslander was the first to suggest that Robert Martin may have fathered Rose's child; Auslander, "Slavery's Traces," 2016. Over a decade ago an individual on Ancestry.com asserted the belief that an enslaved ancestor, a woman named Katie, had children fathered by Robert Martin. The creator of that post to a public Martin family tree seems to have been referring to a different Robert Martin from the man we are following, as more than one slaveholder with that name lived in South Carolina at the time. The post reads: "Katie was a slave owned by John Martin. She would have been born between 1803 and 1810. Her name could have possibly been spelled Catey. She gave birth to six (6) children (father was Robert Martin/slave owner and grandson of John Martin). She may have been married at least three (3) times, and gave birth to one (1) additional child. Husband—Morgan Latta?" This described sexual relationship between a white Martin man and an enslaved woman may, however, have taken place within an extended Martin slaveholding family, of which the Robert Martin we are tracing was a part. A recent newspaper article profiles the African American Martin family descended from this relationship. These family members trace their ancestry to Katie (daughter of an enslaved woman named Trasie) and John Martin, and to their descendants, Black community leaders in Fairfield County. The Robert Martin connected to Rose in our study was born in Fairfield District and was likely related to the John Martin noted above. While a family tree posted to Ancestry.com states

that Robert Martin of Charlotte Street was the grandson of said John Martin and the son of a John Martin and Margaret Elizabeth Aiken, a published genealogy of the Martin family gives Robert Martin of Charlotte Street's parents as David Martin and Margaret Aiken. Despite possible discrepancies about genealogical details, the case of Katie Martin indicates that there is at least one documented example of interracial sexual relations between an owner and owned person in the extended South Carolina Martin family. Ava Pearson, Martin Family Tree Post, 9 May 2008, ancestry.com/family-tree/tree/116756017/story/20?pgn=32912&usePUBJs=true&_phsrc=aPm3. Caitlin Byrd, "Slave's Legacy an Influential Family," *Post and Courier*, May 10, 2020. I am grateful to genealogist Jesse Bustos-Nelson, who found this Ancestry.com post and made the connection, as well as to Victoria Carey, who shared the recent news article on the Black Martin family with Mr. Bustos-Nelson. Martin, *Martin Family*, 1880. Jacobs, *Incidents*, 28.

50. Marise Bachand, "A Season in Town: Plantation Women and the Urban South, 1790–1877" (PhD diss., University of Western Ontario, 2011), 28. The letters by women in the Best and Hext families of Aiken, S.C., include numerous examples of this regular travel between Charleston and rural farm and plantation country for seasonal respites, shopping, and social occasions; Best and Hext Family Papers, Manuscripts Annex Box 1, South Caroliniana Library, University of South Carolina. Burke, *Pleasure and Pain*, 73. Although rural and urban zones were distant in a society dependent on horse-drawn conveyances, they were integrally linked by the movement of capital, people, and animals. As Edda Fields-Black has shown, relational networks connected enslaved people across the coast and the interior of the South Carolina and Georgia region. Edda L. Fields-Black, "Lowcountry Creoles: Coastal Georgia and South Carolina Environments and the Making of the Gullah Geechee," in *Coastal Nature, Coastal Culture: Environmental Histories of the Georgia Coast*, ed. Paul S. Sutter and Paul M. Pressly (Athens: University of Georgia Press, 2018), 141.

51. Here I borrow from notions of "abundant histories" and "symbolic truths" articulated by Walter Johnson, who points to truths that are recognizable even as they "exceed the facts of events that entered the historical record." Johnson cites his readings of scholars of divinity—Robert Orsi and Amy Hollywood—for his adoption of this idea. Walter Johnson, "Haunted by Slavery," in *Goodness and the Literary Imagination*, ed. Davíd Carrasco, Stephanie Paulsell, and Mara Willard (Charlottesville: University Press of Virginia, 2019), 32, 34.

52. This evocative phrasing comes from the novelist Gayl Jones and her classic fictional work on women in slavery; I will return to it periodically throughout this book. Gayl Jones, *Corregidora* (Boston: Beacon Press, 1975), 10, 22, 41, 90.

CHAPTER 3: PACKING THE SACK

1. Magnolia Cemetery, Lot 584 Old, Purchased 1854 -P/C F-23 March 31, 1955, by R. M. Means Trustee, Mrs. Milberry Serena Martin. Magnolia Led-

ger Sheet provided by Magnolia superintendent Beverly Donald to re-searcher Jesse Bustos-Nelson, January 2020. This grave plot diagram dates Robert Martin's death as December 12, 1852, at age sixty-two. His wife, Mil-berry Serena Martin, is buried next to him, with her death noted as Febru-ary 2, 1877, at age sixty-nine. Other members of the Martin, Aiken, Means, and Barnwell families are buried around the Martin grave. Robert Martin (1791–1852), Find a Grave memorial, findagrave.com/memorial/69820867/robert-martin.

2. Wilma King, *Stolen Childhood: Slave Youth in Nineteenth-Century America*, 2nd ed. (1995; repr., Bloomington: Indiana University Press, 2011), 59.

3. Return of Deaths within the City of Charleston, from the 12th to 18th De-cember 1852, South Carolina Death Records, South Carolina Data Collec-tions, Ancestry.com.

4. Edward Ball describes what he terms "the slave trail of tears" in detail, using, in the main, letters written to and from Virginia and Tennessee slave dealers. He also describes revealing interactions with descendants of dealers and the people once traded by them. He notes multiple times the attention paid to providing enslaved people with new clothing as part of their packaging for sale. He notes, as well, that Brooks Brothers was known for providing dressy clothing for enslaved people in high-level servant positions, such as coach drivers. Edward Ball, "Retracing Slavery's Trail of Tears," *Smithsonian Mag-azine*, November 2015.

5. Ophelia Settle Egypt et al., *Unwritten History of Slavery: Autobiographical Accounts of Negro Ex-Slaves* (Nashville, Tenn.: Fisk University, 1968), 41.

6. Edward E. Baptist, *The Half Has Never Been Told: Slavery and the Making of American Capitalism* (New York: Basic, 2014), xxi.

7. Quoted in Baptist, *The Half*, xxi.

8. Frances Ellen Watkins Harper, "The Slave Mother: A Tale of the Ohio," in *A Brighter Coming Day: A Frances Ellen Watkins Harper Reader*, ed. Frances Smith Foster (New York: Feminist Press, 1990), 84–86.

9. "Incapacitating uncertainty": Drew Gilpin Faust, *This Republic of Suffering: Death and the American Civil War* (New York: Vintage, 2008), 131. Faust uses this phrase to capture the social and cultural volatility that resulted from the Civil War and the common experience of widespread death and change. I use it to suggest that this was the state of the enslaved mother's existence.

10. Nell Painter has argued that familial support and religious beliefs were the two means by which Black people survived the psychological and physical damage of enslavement. Nell Irvin Painter, "Soul Murder and Slavery: Toward a Fully Loaded Cost Accounting," in *U.S. History as Women's His-tory: New Feminist Essays*, ed. Linda K. Kerber, Alice Kessler-Harris, and Kathryn Kish Sklar (Chapel Hill: University of North Carolina Press, 1995), 139–40.

11. Hortense Spillers, "Mama's Baby, Papa's Maybe: An American Grammar Book," *Diacritics* 17, no. 2 (1987): 64–81, 74.

12. Harriet Ann Jacobs, *Incidents in the Life of a Slave Girl, Written by Herself* (1861; repr., Cambridge, Mass.: Harvard University Press, 1987), 139, 62, 77.

13. Daina Ramey Berry, *The Price for Their Pound of Flesh: The Value of the Enslaved, from Womb to Grave, in the Building of a Nation* (Boston: Beacon Press, 2017), 28, 30.

14. Toni Morrison, *Beloved* (New York: Plume, 1987), 272.

15. Moses Grandy, "Life of Moses Grandy," in *North Carolina Slave Narratives: The Lives of Moses Roper, Lunsford Lane, Moses Grandy, and Thomas H. Jones*, ed. William L. Andrews (Chapel Hill: University of North Carolina Press, 2003), 159. Also cited in Berry, *The Price*, 27–28.

16. Mary White Ovington in John W. Blassingame, ed., *Slave Testimony: Two Centuries of Letters, Speeches, Interviews, and Autobiographies* (Baton Rouge: Louisiana State University Press, 1977), 537.

17. Egypt, *Unwritten History*, 145. "Puss" was a nickname for this elder daughter bestowed by her mother, Fannie. Puss was also called Cornelia. Egypt, *Unwritten History*, 143.

18. For a biography of Margaret Garner, see Nikki M. Taylor, *Driven Toward Madness: The Fugitive Slave Margaret Garner and Tragedy on the Ohio* (Athens: Ohio University Press, 2016). Garner was the model for Toni Morrison's character Sethe in *Beloved*.

19. This sold sister's name was Ellen. Egypt, *Unwritten History*, 53.

20. Lewis Hayden in Blassingame, *Slave Testimony*, 696. Hayden says he was seven or eight when his mother accosted him.

21. Egypt, *Unwritten History*, 99–100.

22. Egypt, *Unwritten History*, 143.

23. Nell Irvin Painter addresses the psychological damage of slavery and enslaved parents' beating of Black children to acclimate them to slavery. Painter, "Soul Murder and Slavery," 133, 141. For more on religion as support, consolation, and resistance, see Albert J. Raboteau, *Slave Religion: The "Invisible Institution" in the Antebellum South* (1978; repr., New York: Oxford University Press, 2004), 310–11. Erskine Clarke, *Wrestlin' Jacob: A Portrait of Religion in Antebellum Georgia and the Carolina Low Country* (Tuscaloosa: University of Alabama Press, 2000), xxvii.

24. "Rescue their families": Verena Theile and Marie Drews, "Introduction: African American and Afro-Caribbean Women Writers: Writing, Remembering, and 'Being Human in the World,'" in *Reclaiming Home, Remembering Motherhood, Rewriting History: African American and Afro-Caribbean Women's Literature in the Twentieth Century*, ed. Verena Theile and Marie Drews (Newcastle upon Tyne: Cambridge Scholars, 2009), xviii.

25. Charles Whiteside in Blassingame, *Slave Testimony*, 597–98.

26. In a circumstance of dread and fear, Harriet Jacobs refers to her children as "ties" and "links" to life. Jacobs, *Incidents*, 58, 76.

27. For a history and analysis of reproductive slavery, see Jennifer L. Morgan, *Laboring Women: Reproduction and Gender in New World Slavery* (Philadelphia: University of Pennsylvania Press, 2004).

28. Amrita Chakrabarti Myers, *Forging Freedom: Black Women and the Pursuit of Liberty in Antebellum Charleston* (Chapel Hill: University of North Carolina Press, 2011), 51.

29. Agent John William De Forest quoted by Heather Andrea Williams, *Help Me to Find My People: The African American Search for Family Lost in Slavery* (Chapel Hill: University of North Carolina Press, 2012), 146.

30. Vilet Lester letter to Miss Patsey Patterson, August 29, 1857, Bullock County, Georgia, Joseph Allred Papers, Special Collections Library, Duke University, scriptorium.lib.duke.edu/lester/.

31. Vilet Lester letter to Miss Patsey Patterson, August 29, 1857. The historian Jessica Milward writes that "enslaved women existed in a constant state of mourning," resulting in a field of Black women's history that has also been characterized by the study—and felt impact—of this emotion. Jessica Milward, "Black Women's History and the Labor of Mourning," *Souls* 18, no. 1 (2016): 161–65, 162.

32. For a discussion of the use of feeling in Indigenous feminist historical interpretive practice, see Dian Million, "Felt Theory: An Indigenous Feminist Approach to Affect and History," *Wicazo Sa Review* 24, no. 2 (Fall 2009): 53–76.

33. Dylan C. Penningroth, *The Claims of Kinfolk: African American Property and Community in the Nineteenth-Century South* (Chapel Hill: University of North Carolina Press, 2003), 54–55. Myers, *Forging Freedom*, 49.

34. Myers, *Forging Freedom*, 47, 61, 54–59.

35. Baptist, *The Half*, 168.

36. Spillers, "Mama's Baby," 74. As David Blight wrote in an analysis of Frederick Douglass's view of Black spirituals: "Slaves were always *making* their own balm in Gilead." Blight, *Frederick Douglass: Prophet of Freedom* (New York: Simon and Schuster, 2018), 33, italics in original. Saidiya Hartman points to the jeopardy Black mothers faced when they engaged in acts of care and provisioning. Saidiya Hartman, "The Belly of the World: A Note on Black Women's Labors," *Souls* 18, no. 1 (2016): 166–73, 171.

37. Alice Walker, *In Search of Our Mothers' Gardens* (New York: Harcourt Brace Jovanovich, 1983). Blood-relations quote: Spillers, "Mama's Baby," 74.

38. Egypt, *Unwritten History*, 133.

39. Jane Clark, narrative recorded by Julia C. Ferris, read at the banquet of the Cayuga County Historical Society, February 22, 1897. Jane Clark escaped in 1857, reached New York in 1859, and told her story to Julia Ferris in the 1890s. I am grateful to Robin Bernstein, who uncovered this narrative, transcribed it, and shared a copy with me before later publishing it in *Common-Place: The Journal of Early American Life*. Ira Berlin describes enslaved people who had acquired property attempting to sell items or give things away to kin when they learned they would be relocated westward; Berlin, *Generations of Captivity: A History of African-American Slaves* (Cambridge, Mass.: Harvard University Press, 2003), 218. Lauren Olamina, the protagonist of Octavia Butler's *Parable of the Sower*, also packs two pillowcases, "a pair of old pillowcases, one inside the other for strength," when she must escape an attack on her town. Octavia E. Butler, *Parable of the Sower* (New York: Warner Books, 1993), 71.

40. Legal historian Laura F. Edwards makes this point about clothing, identity,

and escape. She has demonstrated how women of various backgrounds and classes owned, loaned, and traded fabric as a store of wealth. Edwards, "Textiles: Popular Culture and the Law," *Buffalo Law Review* 64 (2016): 199, 196, 197. Also see Laura F. Edwards, "Sarah Allingham's Sheet and Other Lessons from Legal History," *Journal of the Early Republic* 38, no. 1 (Spring 2018): 121–47. For a discussion of wardrobe changes to mask or transmute gender in escapes, see C. Riley Snorton, *Black on Both Sides: A Racial History of Trans Identity* (Minneapolis: University of Minnesota Press, 2017), 55–84.

41. Mark Auslander based this intriguing interpretation, which he acknowledges is tentative, on seven interviews with Black residents from the coast. He considers Rose to have been part of a Black ethnic group extending down the ricing coast from southern North Carolina to northern Florida that retained African-derived cultural practices during slavery and in the decades following, due to its isolation. Auslander, "Rose's Gift: Slavery, Kinship, and the Fabric of Memory," *Present Pasts* 8, no. 1 (2017): 4. While African Americans in this region are often referred to generally as Gullah (associated with the Carolinas) or Geechee (associated with Georgia), this group was not as culturally coherent in the nineteenth century as contemporary understandings would suggest. For a recent study of how Gullah Geechee took shape as a cultural identity and identifier, see Edda L. Fields-Black, "Lowcountry Creoles: Coastal Georgia and South Carolina Environments and the Making of the Gullah Geechee," in *Coastal Nature, Coastal Culture: Environmental Histories of the Georgia Coast*, ed. Paul S. Sutter and Paul M. Pressly (Athens: University of Georgia Press, 2018). Fields-Black argues that "Gullah Geechee" is a twentieth-century term that names just one example and moment of creolization experienced by Blacks on the southeastern coast, pp. 129–31, 141. Albert Raboteau writes that hair, along with fingernails and other bodily fragments, was thought to have special power in "offensive charms"; Raboteau, *Slave Religion*, 34. Archaeologist Maude Wahlman has suggested that hair was viewed as a powerful element in charms because "it grows near the brain, and 'a hand made of hair can sure effect the brain'"; Maude Southwell Wahlman, "African Charm Traditions Remembered in the Arts of the Americas," *African Impact on the Material Culture of the Americas: Conference Proceedings* (Winston-Salem, N.C.: Museum of Early Southern Decorative Arts, 1996), 6.

42. Yvonne P. Chireau, *Black Magic: Religion and the African American Conjuring Tradition* (Berkeley: University of California Press, 2003), Kindle loc. 826. Sharla M. Fett, *Working Cures: Healing, Health, and Power on Southern Plantations* (Chapel Hill: University of North Carolina Press, 2002), 102, 104, 105. Raboteau, *Slave Religion*, 276, 278.

43. Chireau, *Black Magic*, Kindle loc. 807, 817. Fett, *Working Cures*, 102–3. Raboteau, *Slave Religion*, 237–38.

44. Sterling Stuckey, *Slave Culture: Nationalist Theory and the Foundations of Black America* (New York: Oxford University Press, 1987), 33, 35, 54–55; Raboteau, *Slave Religion*, 29–30, 45–46, 74, 212, 243.

45. Blight, *Frederick Douglass*, 64. Frederick Douglass, *Narrative of the Life of Frederick Douglass* (1845; repr., Google Books version), 62, 65–66. Like Douglass, Henry Bibb, a man born into slavery in Kentucky who plotted several escapes, reported the use of rootwork in enslaved communities; Bibb notes that he did not have faith in roots protecting him. Henry Bibb, *The Life and Adventures of Henry Bibb, an American Slave* (1850; repr., Madison: University of Wisconsin Press, 2001), 26–27. Raboteau, *Slave Religion*, 276–77. Fett, *Working Cures*, 102–3. Chireau, *Black Magic*, Kindle loc. 826, 107.

46. "Empowerment": Fett, *Working Cures*, 102.

47. James H. Sweet, *Domingo Álvares, African Healing, and the Intellectual History of the Atlantic World* (Chapel Hill: University of North Carolina Press, 2011), 182. Chireau, *Black Magic*, Kindle loc. 807.

48. Patricia Samford, "The Archaeology of African-American Slavery and Material Culture," *William and Mary Quarterly*, 3rd ser., 53, no. 1 (1996): 87–114, 107.

49. Fett, *Working Cures*, 103.

50. Stephanie Camp, *Closer to Freedom: Enslaved Women and Everyday Resistance in the Plantation South* (Chapel Hill: University of North Carolina Press, 2004), 84. Shane White and Graham White, "Slave Hair and African American Culture in the Eighteenth and Nineteenth Centuries," *Journal of Southern History* 61, no. 1 (1995): 45–76, 49, 50, 56, 69, 71, 72, 73.

51. White and White, "Slave Hair," 73.

52. White and White, "Slave Hair," 60.

53. See, for instance, Noliwe M. Rooks, *Hair Raising: Beauty, Culture, and African American Women* (New Brunswick, N.J.: Rutgers University Press, 1996), 5, 8, 9.

54. Deborah Gray White, *Ar'n't I a Woman? Female Slaves in the Plantation South* (New York: W. W. Norton, 1985), 42, 38–40. Also see Edward E. Baptist, " 'Cuffy,' 'Fancy Maids,' and 'One-Eyed Men': Rape, Commodification, and the Domestic Slave Trade in the United States," *American Historical Review* 106, no. 5 (2001): 1619–50.

55. Jacobs, *Incidents*, 77.

56. Louisa Picquet, *The Octoroon: A Tale of Southern Life* (New York: published by the author, 1861), 17, electronic ed., Documenting the American South, University of North Carolina, Chapel Hill, docsouth.unc.edu/neh/picquet/picquet.html.

57. Egypt, *Unwritten History*, 67.

58. Quoted in White and White, "Slave Hair," 58, 68.

59. Egypt, *Unwritten History*, 1.

60. Camp, *Closer to Freedom*, 84. White and White, "Slave Hair," 46, 48. Mark Auslander offers an intriguing interpretation of Ashley's sack as a religious ritual in which he notes the spiritual power of hair in African American protective bundles or conjure bags as influenced by West African faith practices. Auslander, "Rose's Gift," 4.

61. Ira Berlin, Steven F. Miller, and Leslie S. Rowland "Afro-American Families in the Transition from Slavery to Freedom," *Radical History Review* 42

(1988): 89–121, 105. I am grateful to Evelyn Brooks Higginbotham for informing me of this example. Helen Sheumaker found in her research on hair tokens of the dead that Black families separated by the slave trade in the antebellum era sometimes requested cuttings of a child's hair as proof that the child still lived. Though this hypothesis warrants corroboration through further research, Black families may have treasured severed hair as a sign of life rather than as a token of death. Helen Sheumaker, *Love Entwined: The Curious History of Hairwork in America* (Philadelphia: University of Pennsylvania Press, 2007), xiii, xii.

62. Phebe Brownrigg to Amy Nixon in Blassingame, *Slave Testimony*, 22.

63. Siri Hustvedt, "Notes Toward a Theory of Hair," *New Republic*, September 23, 2015, 2; also see her analysis of the Rapunzel story and "maternal love," 11–12.

64. Sheumaker, *Love Entwined*, x. Ellen Parker, "The Vogue of Hair Jewelry and Ornaments Made of Hair," opening lecture of the hair jewelry exhibit, Gibbes Gallery of Art, Charleston, S.C., 1945, Hinson Audio/Visual Collection: Hinson Clippings, Box 1, Arts and Crafts, Charleston Library Society.

65. Sheumaker, *Love Entwined*, ix.

66. Parker, "Vogue of Hair Jewelry," 1.

67. Sheumaker, *Love Entwined*, xiii, xii. Men also worked in this craft, but in smaller numbers. In Charleston, men advertised in local newspapers for hairwork business as early as the 1780s. Charleston also continued a hairwork trade into the early 1900s, longer than many locations; Parker, "Vogue of Hair Jewelry," 6.

68. Sonya Clark, *The Hair Craft Project*, exhibit catalog (Richmond, Va.: Sonya Clark, 2016).

69. Sonya Clark, email interview with Tiya Miles, October 21, 2018.

70. Potter, *A Hairdresser's Experience*, 27, 45.

71. Sharon G. Dean, "Introduction," Potter, *A Hairdresser's Experience*, xliii–xlv.

72. Potter, *A Hairdresser's Experience*, 145, 186.

73. Dean, "Introduction," Potter, *A Hairdresser's Experience*, xlvii.

74. Potter, *A Hairdresser's Experience*, 212, 64–65, 71, 151.

75. Potter, *A Hairdresser's Experience*, iv, 4. Potter uses this term for herself when describing the Palace of Versailles.

76. Myers, *Forging Freedom*, 53.

77. [John] Sella Martin, 1867 narrative, in Blassingame, *Slave Testimony*, 712–13. Heather Williams recounts this story in *Help Me to Find My People*, 124.

78. Many scholars of slavery note how enslaved people used the night; see, for instance, Camp, *Closer to Freedom*, 80; and Baptist, *The Half*, 144. "Part of the night": Kathleen Dean Moore, "The Gifts of Darkness," in *Let There Be Night: Testimony on Behalf of the Dark*, ed. Paul Bogard (Reno: University of Nevada Press, 2008), 12.

79. Walter Johnson, *Soul by Soul: Life Inside the Antebellum Slave Market* (Cambridge, Mass.: Harvard University Press, 1999), 2, 48, image inset, caption 1 below advertisement for slaves. Another typical time for the sale of enslaved people directly off plantations was New Year's Day, immediately

following the Christmas holiday, which enslaved people looked forward to as a highlight of the year. Jacobs, *Incidents*, 15–17.

80. My notion of Rose's statement as "last words" is inspired by Drew Gilpin Faust's work on emotion during the Civil War. Faust describes the culturally important role of the deathbed scene in Victorian America and the way in which soldiers in the field and in hospitals, and compatriots of dead soldiers in letters back to the families of the deceased, attempted to produce the sentiment and effect of last-words moments that suggested the person died in peace and with God. Drew Faust, *Republic of Suffering*, 10–13.

81. Jan Plamper, *The History of Emotions: An Introduction*, Emotions in History series (Oxford, UK: Oxford University Press, 2015), 56.

82. Certainly, there were many and complex ways that enslaved mothers behaved toward their children. Not all mothers saw enslaved persistence as a form of acceptable life. Daina Ramey Berry and Kali Nicole Gross point to the practice of infanticide as resistance in *A Black Women's History of the United States* (Boston: Beacon Press, 2020), 37, 53, 60, 61, 63. Mothers of living children engaged in distancing and violent behaviors. Like any relationship between two people, and all relationships between parents and children, an enslaved mother's reactions to a child were not predestined. See Maria Mårdberg, "'A Bleak, Black Wind': Motherlessness and Emotional Exile in Jamaica Kincaid's *The Autobiography of My Mother*," in Theile and Drews, eds., *Reclaiming Home*, 6. In this mode of mother love, Black enslaved women—and those who follow in their tradition of visionary love and radical hope—expand the act of mothering to a form of social action, building on what the feminist theorist Stanlie James has called "the indigenous African" foundation of motherhood characterized by "creativity and continuity." A term offered by James for this type of maternal action is "motherwork," a particular "model of resistance." Stanlie M. James, "Mothering: A Possible Black Feminist Link to Social Transformation?," in *Theorizing Black Feminisms*, ed. Stanlie M. James and Abena P. A. Busia (London: Routledge, 1993), 45. For a nuanced study of the many, and at times fraught, ways in which Black women strove to build and defend kin networks in the eighteenth century, see Jessica Marie Johnson, *Wicked Flesh: Black Women, Intimacy, and Freedom in the Atlantic World* (Philadelphia: University of Pennsylvania Press, 2020).

83. Saidiya Hartman, *Lose Your Mother* (New York: Farrar, Straus and Giroux, 2007), 155. Hartman writes, strikingly, that "the stamp of the commodity haunts the maternal line," 80.

84. Jones, *Corregidora*, 10, 22.

CHAPTER 4: ROSE'S INVENTORY

1. Robert Martin, Property Appraisement, Charleston, South Carolina Department of Archives and History (SCDAH). The commas in brackets have been added for clarity in the list.

2. Hortense Spillers takes careful stock of this moment in documents of slavery—in her example, a Maryland slave code—when "slave" appears in a

list with animals and "a virtually endless profusion of domestic content." Spillers, "Mama's Baby, Papa's Maybe: An American Grammar Book," *Diacritics* 17, no. 2 (1987): 79.

3. Daina Ramey Berry and Stephanie Jones-Rogers make the point that unfree people knew what they were "worth" in the marketplace of slavery and reacted to these assigned values. Ramey Berry, *The Price for Their Pound of Flesh: The Value of the Enslaved, from Womb to Grave, in the Building of a Nation* (Boston: Beacon Press, 2017), 2; Stephanie E. Jones-Rogers, *They Were Her Property: White Women as Slave Owners in the American South* (New Haven: Yale University Press, 2019), Kindle loc. 1095. Berry proposes that enslaved people and their families countered these commercial values with the understanding of a "soul value," 6.

4. Enslaved people could not legally write wills or pass on possessions. Joan R. Gundersen, "Women and Inheritance in America: Virginia and New York City as a Case Study, 1700–1860," in *Inheritance and Wealth in America*, ed. Robert K. Miller, Jr., and Stephen J. McNamee (New York: Plenum, 1998), 100.

5. Dylan C. Penningroth, *The Claims of Kinfolk: African American Property and Community in the Nineteenth-Century South* (Chapel Hill: University of North Carolina Press, 2003), 12, 61, 76, 77, 86, 90, 91.

6. Quoted in Penningroth, *Claims of Kinfolk*, 79, 223. Maria Perkins to Richard Perkins, October 8, 1852, quoted in Ulrich B. Phillips, *Life and Labor in the Old South* (Boston: Little, Brown and Company, 1929), 212. Penningroth writes in interpreting this letter: "Both family and property mattered to enslaved people" (79). Noting the emotional dimension of property ownership, Philip Morgan quotes a formerly enslaved woman who says she cried when Union soldiers took her property; Philip D. Morgan, "The Ownership of Property by Slaves in the Mid-Nineteenth-Century Low Country," *Journal of Southern History* 49, no. 3 (1983): 399–420, 409.

7. Philip Morgan notes the personal responsibility and pride in one's accomplishments and the accomplishments of ancestors that stemmed from the Lowcountry task system of labor that allowed enslaved people to save time and acquire property; Morgan, "Ownership of Property," 401, 403. Morgan also notes ways in which kin groups pooled resources and bequeathed property after deaths; Morgan, "Ownership of Property," 403, 416–17. He argues that the federal government's recognition of some property claims by formerly enslaved people after the Civil War indicates that they were recognized property holders; at the same time, he recognizes that during slavery, individual masters had the power to determine whether unfree people could hold property. The extent to which slaveholders exercised that power varied; Morgan, "Ownership of Property," 409–10. Twenty years after Morgan, Dylan Penningroth discusses the illegality of property ownership among the enslaved, while also acknowledging that enslaved people practiced a de facto kind of ownership that was often recognized in local contexts and in direct interactions; Penningroth, *Claims of Kinfolk*, 7, 11, 45.

8. This interviewee is not named in the record, which is the case for most of

these interviews conducted by researchers at Fisk University in 1929 and 1930 in Kentucky and Tennessee. Notably, the head of this research team was an African American woman, which would have affected the dynamics of the interviews she conducted, likely leading to greater (though, of course, not total) comfort and disclosure on the part of the African American interviewees. In contrast, most interviews conducted by the WPA Federal Writers' Project in this same period were recorded by whites. Ophelia Settle Egypt et al., *Unwritten History of Slavery: Autobiographical Accounts of Negro Ex-Slaves* (Nashville, Tenn.: Fisk University, 1968), 108.

9. Penningroth, *Claims of Kinfolk*, 90, 91.

10. Egypt, *Unwritten History*, 124.

11. As Dylan Penningroth notes, things could also "make family," drawing people who might not have been blood-related into close and enduring connection as they worked together to acquire and share possessions. Penningroth, *Claims of Kinfolk*, 86, 87.

12. Elizabeth Wayland Barber, *Women's Work: The First 20,000 Years; Women, Cloth, and Society in Early Times* (New York: W. W. Norton, 1994), 128.

13. Women have been the primary makers of cloth across time, a product and art shaped out of the interlacing of fibers. A fiber is any kind of minute strand that can be used to make thread or yarn. These strands (derived from animals or plants in the past, but now often from synthetic materials) can be twined around themselves, or spun, to create thread. Thread of various thicknesses and lengths are then woven into and through one another to create cloth. The loom, an ancient and effective weaving tool, is made up of a vertical set of thick strands (called a warp) and a horizontal set of thick strands (called a weft). Four kinds of natural fibers have predominated in cloth-making: wool (sheared from sheep), flax (a plant woven into linen), and silk (spun by silkworms), and cotton. Wool and linen are the world's oldest fabric types. Cotton has been the most commonly worn fabric since the nineteenth century, a direct result of increased production in the U.S. South through slave labor and the industrialization of cotton production. Jane Schneider and Annette B. Weiner, "Introduction," in *Cloth and the Human Experience*, Annette B. Weiner and Jane Schneider, eds. (Washington, D.C.: Smithsonian Institution Press, 1989), 1. Barber, *Women's Work*, 34, 35, 39. Ellsworth Newcomb and Hugh Kenny, *Miracle Fabrics* (New York: G. P. Putnams Sons, 1957), 13, 38–39, 60. Sven Beckert, *Empire of Cotton: A Global History* (New York: Vintage, 2014), xvi, xix, 100, 119, 431.

14. This full quote reads: "Dress became a language and scholars can turn to clothing as revealing materials akin to documents." Drew Gilpin Faust, *Mothers of Invention: Women of the Slaveholding South in the American Civil War* (Chapel Hill: University of North Carolina Press, 1996), 221. Viewing clothes like documents: Celia Naylor, " 'Born and Raised Among These People, I Don't Want to Know Any Other': Slaves' Acculturation in Nineteenth-Century Indian Territory," in *Confounding the Color Line: The Indian-Black Experience in North America*, ed. James F. Brooks (Lincoln: University of Nebraska Press, 2002), 166.

15. An Act for the Better Ordering and Governing of Negroes, No. 57, 1690, David J. McCord, ed., *The Statutes at Large of South Carolina*, vol. 7, *Containing the Acts Relating to Charleston, Courts, Slaves, and Rivers* (Columbia, S.C.: A. S. Johnston, 1840), 343–47, Addlestone Library. An Act for the Better Ordering and Governing of Negroes, No. 586, 1735, McCord, ed., *Statutes at Large*, 385–97. An Act for the Better Ordering and Governing of Negroes, No. 670, 1740, McCord, ed., *Statutes at Large*, 397–416. The 1740 law repeated the language of the 1735 text.

16. Michael Zakim argues, for instance, that homespun clothing represented a particular kind of American "political imagination" in the pre-Revolutionary and Revolutionary War period. Notions of simplicity, frugality, industriousness, and democracy were associated with this homemade cloth, which was set in opposition to British luxury. Michael Zakim, "Sartorial Ideologies: From Homespun to Ready-Made," *American Historical Review* 106, no. 5 (2001): 1553–85, 1554, 1562, 1564, 1570. Elite Charlestonians, however, embraced a notion of European elegance rather than simplicity in apparel. The lavish quality of women's dress in particular gained special notice from critical northern observers. Julia Bryan-Wilson uses the term "textile politics" as an indication of "how textiles have been used to advance political agendas" as well as "a procedure of making politics material." Her first example in support of this argument is women in New England in, again, the pre–Revolutionary War moment who gathered in spinning bees as a way to express anti-British sentiment as well as produce practical necessities. Julia Bryan-Wilson, *Fray: Art and Textile Politics* (Chicago: University of Chicago Press, 2017), 7. Bryan-Wilson cites Laurel Thatcher Ulrich on this point, as Ulrich was the first to explore in detail the politics and myth of women's production of homespun in early America; see Laurel Thatcher Ulrich, *The Age of Homespun: Objects and Stories in the Creation of an American Myth* (New York: Alfred A. Knopf, 2001).

17. For more on the use of secondhand shops to acquire cloth by women who were Black or white, enslaved or free, see Laura F. Edwards, "Textiles: Popular Culture and the Law," *Buffalo Law Review* 64 (2016): 193–214, 202.

18. Emily Burke, *Pleasure and Pain: Reminiscences of Georgia in the 1840s* (1850; repr., Savannah: Beehive Press, Library of Georgia, 1991), 24, 33.

19. Faust, *Mothers of Invention*, 221.

20. For fascinating readings of gender, social power, and material culture among merchant elites, see Jennifer Van Horn, *The Power of Objects in Eighteenth-Century British America* (Chapel Hill: University of North Carolina Press, published for the Omohundro Institute of Early American History and Culture, 2017). The Stranger, "Mr. Fowell," *South-Carolina Gazette*, August 27, 1772, Addlestone Library.

21. The Stranger, "Mr. Fowell." Faust, *Mothers of Invention*, 226. "Defensive costume": Alison Lurie, *The Language of Clothes* (1981; repr., New York: Henry Holt, 2000), xiv.

22. The Stranger, "Mr. Fowell." Lurie, *Language of Clothes*. "An Ordinance to Amend 'An Ordinance for the Government of Negroes and Other Persons of

Color, Within the City of Charleston,'" in *A Digest of the Ordinances of the City Council of Charleston from the Year 1783 to Oct. 1844*, ed. George B. Eckhard (Charleston: Walker & Burke, 1844), Addlestone Library.

23. Robert Martin, who recognized the riches involved in cotton processing, bought $1,000 worth of stock in an early South Carolina cotton manufacturer called Graniteville that mainly employed poor white children. Ernest McPherson Lander, Jr., *The Textile Industry in Antebellum South Carolina* (Baton Rouge: Louisiana State University Press, 1969), 63. Robert Martin, Property Appraisement, Charleston, SCDAH.

24. Madelyn Shaw, "Slave Cloth and Clothing Slaves: Craftsmanship, Commerce, and Industry," *Journal of Early Southern Decorative Arts* 41 (2012): 1, 3, 4, 5. Eulanda A. Sanders, "The Politics of Textiles Used in African American Slave Clothing," Textile Society of America Symposium Proceedings, 740 (2012), Digital Commons, University of Nebraska–Lincoln, digitalcommons.unl.edu/tsaconf/740, 1, 2, charts pp. 3–4. Joyce E. Chaplin, *An Anxious Pursuit: Agricultural Innovation and Modernity in the Lower South, 1730–1815* (Chapel Hill: University of North Carolina Press, 1993), 215. Louis Harmuth, *Dictionary of Textiles* (New York: Fairchild Publishing Company, 1915), 93. Mary Madison, *Plantation Slave Weavers Remember: An Oral History* (Middletown, Del.: Create Space Independent Publishing Platform, 2015), 133. Alison Kinney, *Hood*, Object Lessons Series (New York: Bloomsbury, 2016), Kindle loc. 433, 758. Kinney notes that even as forced hooding is used to hide the individuality and suffering of the wearer, voluntary hooding, such as that employed by the Ku Klux Klan, is used to anonymize perpetrators of violence and to project a sense of mysterious and frightening power (loc. 758). I am grateful to Megan Sweeney for informing me of this Object Lessons Series and for making this connection between slave dress and prison garb.

25. Florence M. Montgomery, *Textiles in America, 1650–1870* (New York: W. W. Norton, 1984), 309. Shaw, "Slave Cloth," 3. Edward E. Baptist, *The Half Has Never Been Told: Slavery and the Making of American Capitalism* (New York: Basic Books, 2014), 81.

26. As Ed Baptist writes: "Lowell consumed 100,000 days of enslaved people's labor every year"; Baptist, *The Half*, 319. Sven Beckert notes that the term "Lowell Cloth" became a generic term for coarse fabric among enslaved people; Beckert, *Empire of Cotton*, 147. Chaplin, *Anxious Pursuit*, 215.

27. In her study of textile use among enslaved Blacks, Eulanda A. Sanders finds that in enslaved people's descriptions of how slave clothing made them feel, joint themes of conspicuousness and inconspicuousness prevailed. I am referring to the same idea as hypervisibility and invisibility. Sanders, "Politics of Textiles," 740.

28. Shaw, "Slave Cloth," 1. "Sort of sack": quoted in Shaw, "Slave Cloth," 2.

29. Baptist, *The Half*, 114, 122.

30. Louisa Picquet, *The Octoroon: A Tale of Southern Life* (New York: published by the author, 1861), 12, electronic ed., Documenting the American South,

University of North Carolina, Chapel Hill, docsouth.unc.edu/neh/picquet/picquet.html. Edward Ball, *Slaves in the Family* (New York: Ballantine Books, 1998), 97. Shaw, "Slave Cloth." Henry Middleton, Clothing Lists, Weehaw Plantation Journal, Addlestone Library.

31. Egypt, *Unwritten History*, 3, 24.

32. Wilma King discusses the uncomfortable texture and fit of clothing for unfree children as well as the negative commentary about these children's clothes by observers visiting the South. Wilma King, *Stolen Childhood: Slave Youth in Nineteenth-Century America*, 2nd ed. (1995; repr., Bloomington: Indiana University Press, 2011), 64–65.

33. Eliza Potter, *A Hairdresser's Experience in High Life* (1859; repr., New York: Oxford University Press, 1991), 18–19, 182, 192.

34. Frederick Law Olmsted, *A Journey in the Seaboard Slave States* (New York: Mason Brothers, 1861), 432.

35. Harriet Martineau, *Retrospect of Western Travel*, vol. 1 (1838; repr., Bedford, Mass.: Applewood), 218.

36. Shaw, "Slave Cloth," 3. In contrast to plantation labor relations in the old coastal Southeast, characterized by a task system of organization and at times a paternalistic ethos, planters of the westward-expanding cotton kingdom of Alabama, Louisiana, Mississippi, and so on, would reach new degrees of brutality as a mechanism for labor extraction. For more on this see Baptist, *The Half*; also see Walter Johnson, *River of Dark Dreams: Slavery and Empire in the Cotton Kingdom* (Cambridge, Mass.: Harvard University Press, 2013).

37. "Cheap calico": quoted in Shaw, "Slave Cloth," 2. Elizabeth Keckley, *Behind the Scenes, or Thirty Years a Slave and Four Years in the White House* (1868; repr., New York: Oxford University Press, 1988), 255–56. South Carolina slaveholder and statesman James Hammond distributed extra clothes to mothers of infants as an incentive for "fecundity"; see Drew Gilpin Faust, *James Henry Hammond and the Old South: A Design for Mastery* (Baton Rouge: Louisiana State University Press, 1982), 88.

38. Harriet Ann Jacobs, *Incidents in the Life of a Slave Girl, Written by Herself* (1861; repr., Cambridge, Mass.: Harvard University Press, 1987), 11.

39. Keckley, *Behind the Scenes*, 20–21.

40. James Hammond's private diary indicates that he also had sexual relations with a mother and a daughter he owned, Sally and Louisa Johnson, and that he may have impregnated both of them. Faust, *James Henry Hammond*, 314–17, 319.

41. Picquet, *The Octoroon*, 9, 12. Gayl Jones, *Corregidora* (Boston: Beacon Press, 1975). Deborah Gray White, *Ar'n't I A Woman? Female Slaves in the Plantation South* (New York: W. W. Norton, 1985), 32–34. Wilma King makes important observations about the physical exposure of enslaved teenaged boys, who were given only long shirts to wear even as they developed physically. Exposure of these boys' genitals was noted by some visitors as well as slaveholders, and most certainly contributed to these boys' public humili-

ation and sexual vulnerability. King, *Stolen Childhood*, 65–66. For the cloth-ing excerpt transcript of the Morris Sheppard narrative that King analyzes here, see Madison, *Plantation Slave Weavers*, 83–84.

42. Emily Thornwell, *The Lady's Guide to Perfect Gentility in Manner, Dress, and Conversation* (New York: Derby & Jackson, 1856), 119–20.

43. White, *Ar'n't I A Woman*, 29, 32–34.

44. Shaw, "Slave Cloth,". 5. Kathleen M. Hilliard, *Masters, Slaves, and Exchange: Power's Purchase in the Old South* (New York: Cambridge University Press, 2014), 71.

45. Egypt, *Unwritten History of Slavery*, 22, 20, 24, 27. Madison, *Plantation Slave Weavers*, head weavers: 31, 73, 98; sounds of weaving: 3, 21, 24, 49–50, 69, 101; night work: 9, 11, 79; nursing weavers: 17 (Cato Carter); falling asleep: 19. In her classic study of Black women's labor, Jacqueline Jones notes that some women were released from fieldwork before the day was done in order to make preparations for cloth-making. She also points out that Saturdays were sometimes reserved for cloth production on plantations. Jacqueline Jones, *Labor of Love, Labor of Sorrow: Black Women, Work, and the Family, From Slavery to the Present* (New York: Vintage, 1985), 30–31.

46. Karen Hampton, "African American Women: Plantation Textile Production from 1750 to 1830," *Approaching Textiles, Varying Viewpoints: Proceedings of the Seventh Biennial Symposium of the Textile Society of America*, Santa Fe, N.M., 2000, Digital Commons, University of Nebraska–Lincoln, digital commons.unl.edu/tsaconf/770, 266. Weaving houses were usually small, plain buildings; their size, materials, and capacity varied from plantation to plantation. John Michael Vlach, *Back of Big House: The Architecture of Plantation Slavery* (Chapel Hill: University of North Carolina Press, 1993), 84 , 100, 101. Elise Pinckney, "Pinckney, Eliza Lucas," *South Carolina Encyclopedia*, scencyclopedia.org/sce/entries/pinckney-eliza-lucas/.

47. Madison, *Plantation Slave Weavers*, dyes: 35, 37, 47, 61, 76, 103; artistry: 53, 61 (Susie King), 89, 99, 103. Hampton, "African American Women," 262, 265.

48. Faust, *Mothers of Invention*, 47, 48.

49. Hampton, "African American Women," 266. Hampton spells this surname "Izad," a typographical error. For examples of enslaved women trained in weaving, see Madison, *Plantation Slave Weavers*, 33, 57.

50. Keckley, *Behind the Scenes*, 20.

51. Chaplin, *Anxious Pursuit*, 215. Maurie D. McInnis, *The Politics of Taste in Antebellum Charleston* (Chapel Hill: University of North Carolina Press, 2005), 261–62. Hilliard, *Masters, Slaves, and Exchange*, 71. Stephanie M. H. Camp, *Closer to Freedom: Enslaved Women and Everyday Resistance in the Plantation South* (Chapel Hill: University of North Carolina Press, 2004), 81–82.

52. "Hidden world": Shaw, "Slave Cloth," 7.

53. Language in this paragraph was inspired by the Bible: "For every trampling boot of battle and every garment rolled in blood will be burned as fuel for the fire," Isaiah 9:5, Berean Study Bible Translation. Some readers will notice

that here I am borrowing language from Harriet Jacobs, who used this phrasing to describe her choice of a lesser of evils. Jacobs, *Incidents*, 54.

54. Hilliard, *Masters, Slaves, and Exchange*, 62, 83, 127.

55. Narrative of James Curry in John W. Blassingame, ed., *Slave Testimony: Two Centuries of Letters, Speeches, Interviews, and Autobiographies* (Baton Rouge: Louisiana State University Press, 1977), 128–29.

56. Stephanie Camp was the first scholar to capture the depth of ingenuity and creativity of enslaved women's self-made apparel. Camp, *Closer to Freedom*, 79, 69–78, 82–83. Drew Gilpin Faust discusses the rise of the hoopskirt as well as the difficulty white women faced in acquiring hoops during the Civil War; see Faust, *Mothers of Invention*, 223–25. Sharla Fett describes enslaved women making dried berries into jewelry and wearing mulberry bark for belts; see Sharla M. Fett, *Working Cures: Healing, Health, and Power on Southern Plantations* (Chapel Hill: University of North Carolina Press, 2002), 70.

57. Faust, *Mothers of Invention*, 226, 223.

58. Egypt, *Unwritten History*, 134.

59. Egypt, *Unwritten History*, 144–45.

60. "Shape of their own form": Camp, *Closer to Freedom*, 79, 121–22. Faust, *Mothers of Invention*, 223.

61. Keckley, *Behind the Scenes*, 20, 141–42. Shaw, "Slave Cloth," 5. Hilliard, *Masters, Slaves, and Exchange*, 71.

62. Picquet, *The Octoroon*, 13–14.

63. Potter, *A Hairdresser's Experience*, 15.

64. Picquet, *The Octoroon*, 16–19.

65. Picquet, *The Octoroon*, 18–22. Sharony Green offers a detailed interpretation of Picquet's abuse by Cook and Randolph in her *Remember Me to Miss Louisa: Hidden Black-White Intimacies in Antebellum America* (DeKalb: Northern Illinois University Press, 2015), 72, 62–63.

66. Keckley, *Behind the Scenes*, 39–42.

67. Keckley, *Behind the Scenes*, 39–42, 31–36. For a rich analysis of this period of Keckley's life when she was owned by the Burwells and likely hired out to William Bingham, see Jennifer Fleischner, *Mrs. Lincoln and Mrs. Keckley* (New York: Broadway Books, 2003), 65–88. These scars upon the body, symbolized in a shredded dress, are an archive of their own, and transform over time into "enslaved women's stories." I derive this notion of scars as archives and this quote from Marisa Fuentes, *Dispossessed Lives: Enslaved Women, Violence, and the Archive* (Philadelphia: University of Pennsylvania Press, 2016), 14. The translation for Louisa Picquet's price was dated from 1840, the approximate year of her sale, using the Inflation Calculator at westegg.com. The precise figure came out to $38,920.32.

68. Keckley, *Behind the Scenes*, 42, 43, 45. Toni Morrison, *Beloved* (New York: Plume, 1987), 257.

69. Erskine Clarke, *Wrestlin' Jacob: A Portrait of Religion in Antebellum Georgia and the Carolina Low Country* (Tuscaloosa: University of Alabama Press, 2000), 88, 89, 90, 91, 99.

70. Sam Aleckson, *Before the War and After the Union: An Autobiography* (Boston: Gold Mind, 1929), 51–53. Maurie McInnis interprets this scene somewhat differently; see McInnis, *Politics of Taste*, 240–41. Thornwell, *Lady's Guide*, 125.

71. Frances Anne Kemble, *Journal of a Residence on a Georgian Plantation in 1838–1839* (1961; repr., Athens: University of Georgia Press, 1984), 93. This passage from Kemble is quoted in Camp, *Closer to Freedom*, 84. Camp analyzes the clothing that Kemble reported as having "roots in African visual arts."

72. Mary Boykin Chesnut, *A Diary from Dixie*, ed. Isabella D. Martin and Myrta Avary (New York: D. Appleton and Company, 1906), 250 (November 30, 1861).

73. Egypt, *Unwritten History*, 77.

74. I refer here again to the sewer and memoirist Megan Sweeney, with whom I had many exchanges about clothes. Put another way by an art historian, there is a "capacity of textiles to mean in multiple directions." Bryan-Wilson, *Fray*, 9.

CHAPTER 5: THE AUCTION BLOCK

1. Peter H. Wood, *Black Majority: Negroes in Colonial South Carolina from 1670 Through the Stono Rebellion* (New York: W. W. Norton, 1974), xiv, 25; Wood cites 1708 as the likely year that Black slaves overtook free whites in population numbers, 143. Judith A. Carney and Richard Nicholas Rosomoff, *In the Shadow of Slavery: Africa's Botanical Legacy in the Atlantic World* (Berkeley: University of California Press, 2009), 151. Amrita Chakrabarti Myers, *Forging Freedom: Black Women and the Pursuit of Liberty in Antebellum Charleston* (Chapel Hill: University of North Carolina Press, 2011), 30–32. Stephanie McCurry, *Masters of Small Worlds: Yeoman Households, Gender Relations, and the Political Culture of the Antebellum South Carolina Low Country* (New York: Oxford University Press, 1995), 33–34. Manisha Sinha, *The Counter-Revolution of Slavery: Politics and Ideology in Antebellum South Carolina* (Chapel Hill: University of North Carolina Press, 2000), 12.

2. Sinha, *Counter-Revolution of Slavery*, 13.

3. Adam Hodgson, *Letters from North America*, vol. 1 (1824; repr., Bedford, Mass.: Applewood), 55–58. Harriet Martineau, *Retrospect of Western Travel*, vol. 1 (1838; repr., Bedford, Mass.: Applewood, 2007), 234–36.

4. Ethan J. Kytle and Blain Roberts, *Denmark Vesey's Garden: Slavery and Memory in the Cradle of the Confederacy* (New York: New Press, 2017), 12, 16–17. Myers, *Forging Freedom*, 28. Walter Johnson, *Soul by Soul: Life Inside the Antebellum Slave Market* (Cambridge, Mass.: Harvard University Press, 1999), 7. Edward E. Baptist, *The Half Has Never Been Told: Slavery and the Making of American Capitalism* (New York: Basic Books, 2014), 181–82.

5. Maurie D. McInnis, *The Politics of Taste in Antebellum Charleston* (Chapel Hill: University of North Carolina Press, 2005), 28. Sven Beckert, *Empire of Cotton: A Global History* (New York: Vintage, 2014), 114.

6. McInnis, *Politics of Taste*, 5, 35–36, 79.

7. Cynthia M. Kennedy, *Braided Relations, Entwined Lives: The Women of Charleston's Urban Slave Society* (Bloomington: Indiana University Press, 2005), 15.

8. Frances Anne Kemble, *Journal of a Residence on a Georgian Plantation in 1838–1839* (1961; repr., Athens: University of Georgia Press, 1984), 37.

9. Frederick Law Olmsted, *A Journey in the Seaboard Slave States* (New York: Mason Brothers, 1861), 404.

10. Beckert, *Empire of Cotton*, 102–6, xvi–xvii, 60. Baptist, *The Half*, 350. Joyce E. Chaplin, *An Anxious Pursuit: Agricultural Innovation and Modernity in the Lower South, 1730–1815* (Chapel Hill: University of North Carolina Press, 1993), 220–21, 278–80; Chaplin points out that the first cotton seed grown in Carolina came from the West Indies, 153–54. McCurry, *Masters of Small Worlds*, 33–34. See, for example, Drew Gilpin Faust, *James Henry Hammond and the Old South: A Design for Mastery* (Baton Rouge: Louisiana State University Press, 1982).

11. Angelina E. Grimké, diary entry, February 6, 1829, Charleston, in *The Public Years of Sarah and Angelina Grimké: Selected Writings 1835–1839*, ed. Larry Ceplair (New York: Columbia University Press, 1989), 16.

12. Martineau, *Retrospect of Western Travel*, 236, 238–39.

13. On anxiety: Leslie A. Schwalm, *A Hard Fight for We: Women's Transition from Slavery to Freedom in South Carolina* (Urbana: University of Illinois Press, 1997), 13. "Architecture": Kytle and Roberts, *Denmark Vesey's Garden*, 21.

14. Myers, *Forging Freedom*, 25.

15. Olmsted, *Journey in the Seaboard Slave States*, 404.

16. Samantha Quantrellis Smalls, "Behind Workhouse Walls: The Public Regulation of Slavery in Charleston, 1730–1850" (PhD diss., Duke University, 2015), 7, 8, 15, 16, 22, 23. Michael D. Byrd, "The First Charles Town Workhouse, 1738–1775: A Deterrent to White Pauperism?," *South Carolina Historical Magazine* 110, nos. 1–2 (2009): 35–52.

17. John J. Navin, "A New England Yankee Discovers Southern History," in *Becoming Southern Writers*, ed. Orville Vernon Burton and Eldred E. Prince, Jr. (Columbia: University of South Carolina Press, 2016), 186–87. Brenda Thompson Schoolfield, "Charleston Poorhouse and Hospital 1770–1856," *South Carolina Encyclopedia*, https://www.scencyclopedia.org/sce/entries/charleston-poorhouse-and-hospital. In 1780, an explosion of a powder magazine in the area during the Siege of Charleston damaged the workhouse building and injured or killed two to three hundred people inside. The city moved the operation to a rented sugar loaf (or cube) factory building following the incident; Navin, "New England Yankee," 187; Smalls, "Behind Workhouse Walls," 27–28. *The Statutes at Large of South Carolina*, vol. 1 (Columbia, 1836), 432, quoted in Smalls, "Behind Workhouse Walls," 63. The term "fugitive seamen" referred to criminals at sea.

18. Smalls, "Behind Workhouse Walls," 28, 29, 32. McInnis, *Politics of Taste*, 22, 225, 226.

19. McInnis, *Politics of Taste*, 22, 225, 226. Navin, "New England Yankee," 188.

20. Navin, "New England Yankee," 187. The novelist Sue Monk Kidd repeats this "sugar" phrase in her moving novel about the Grimké sisters as slave-holders; see Sue Monk Kidd, *The Invention of Wings* (New York: Penguin Books, 2014), 215.

21. Terror quote: Maria Fuentes, *Dispossessed Lives: Enslaved Women, Violence, and the Archive* (Philadelphia: University of Pennsylvania Press, 2016), 8. Fitzhugh Brundage implicitly links practices of European religious and state tortures designed to elicit confessions with the tortures of American slavery. See W. Fitzhugh Brundage, *Civilizing Torture: An American Tradition* (Cambridge, Mass.: Harvard University Press, 2018), 24–30, 88–117.

22. Sinha, *Counter-Revolution of Slavery*, 5, 13, 14, 2. The state legislature was elected by propertied white men until 1810, when pressure by an expanding white middle- and upper-country population pushed the state to adopt suffrage for most adult white men. Even after this limited expansion of suffrage, slaveholders dominated state offices. Sinha, *Counter-Revolution of Slavery*, 13. Erskine Clarke, *Wrestlin' Jacob: A Portrait of Religion in Antebellum Georgia and the Carolina Low Country* (Tuscaloosa: University of Alabama Press, 2000), 85.

23. As recounted in chapter 2, Ashley appears as the name of an enslaved girl or woman only three times in the public South Carolina slave records. I am grateful to the historian and academic administrator Susan Lively, whose interest in this project led her to search the Social Security Administration database for the name Ashley. She found that Ashley was used for boys especially after 1900 (when data collection began) but not very often for girls until the 1960s. These data are not specific about race, but it seems a fair assumption that whiteness was assumed, at least for the early years of the record; see ssa.gov/cgi-bin/babyname.cgi. Charles H. Lesser, "Lords Proprietors of South Carolina," *South Carolina Encyclopedia*, June 2016, scencyclopedia.org/sce/entries/lords-proprietors-of-carolina/, 2.

24. My description of slaveholder naming practices is drawn from Ira Berlin's analysis; Berlin, *Generations of Captivity: A History of African-American Slaves* (Cambridge, Mass.: Harvard University Press, 2003), 54. The specific examples are all drawn from the slave lists of the Middleton plantations, which are representative, in this regard, of slave lists across the state. Barbara Doyle, Mary Edna Sullivan, and Tracey Todd, eds., *Beyond the Fields: Slavery at Middleton Place* (Charleston: Middleton Place Foundation, 2008). For lists of slaves owned by the Middletons, see 43–59.

25. "Contempt": Berlin, *Generations of Captivity*, 54. On names bestowed in secret, see Berlin, *Generations of Captivity*, 65; also see Sterling Stuckey, *Slave Culture: Nationalist Theory and the Foundations of Black America* (New York: Oxford University Press, 1987), 196. Wilma King offers a sustained analysis of Black family names during slavery that I have drawn from for this account; see her *Stolen Childhood: Slave Youth in Nineteenth-Century America*, 2nd ed. (1995; repr., Bloomington: Indiana University

Press, 2011), 47–50. Day and seasonal names in this example are, again, drawn from Middleton Place lists; Doyle, Sullivan, and Todd, *Beyond the Fields*, lists of slaves owned by the Middletons, 43–59.

26. On place-names see King, *Stolen Childhood*, 49; Charles Joyner, *Down by the Riverside: A South Carolina Slave Community* (Urbana: University of Illinois Press, 1984), 217–21. We should note that some place-names given as personal names were the work of slave owners, given the specificity of certain European cities with which enslaved people were less likely to have had a sense of aspirational connection. The Middleton Place slave lists include, for example, a Glasgow, Bristol, London, Belfast, Sheffield, and York. For more on African American naming ceremonies and theories of African connections, see Stuckey, *Slave Culture*, 194–98.

27. Harriet Ann Jacobs, *Incidents in the Life of a Slave Girl, Written by Herself* (1861; repr., Cambridge, Mass.: Harvard University Press, 1987), 78.

28. A survey of places and natural features named Ashley in the state of South Carolina yielded few results besides the Ashley River; however, it did reveal a town called Ashley in the Barnwell District (or County) where the Martins had a plantation. I do not see this town being of the size or stature that would inspire either a slave owner or a Black family member to take it as a namesake. I am grateful to my research assistant Dylan Nelson for conducting this survey.

29. Mark Auslander, "Slavery's Traces: In Search of Ashley's Sack," *Southern Spaces* blog, November 29, 2016, southernspaces.org/2016/slaverys-traces -search-ashleys-sack, 4–5. The overseer of Milberry Place Plantation was Robert Harper; Auslander, "Slavery's Traces," 4.

30. Schwalm, *A Hard Fight for We*, 51. Also see p. 54.

31. Mark Auslander first made this argument about Ashley's possible grandparents; Auslander, "Slavery's Traces," 4.

32. Katherine McKittrick originated the ideas I am presenting here about the spatial nature of the auction block and the social and economic work such use of space performed. Katherine McKittrick, *Demonic Grounds: Black Women and the Cartographies of Struggle* (Minneapolis: University of Minnesota Press, 2006), 72, 73, 75.

33. Walter Johnson has argued the point I am borrowing here about the psychological and social dimensions of buying people, including the feeling slave buyers had that their purchases could present opportunities to act out the principles of paternalism; Johnson, *Soul by Soul*, 78–79, 108, 113.

34. For a study of plantation soil depletion, see Drew Swanson, *A Golden Weed: Tobacco and Environment in the Piedmont South* (New Haven: Yale University Press, 2014). Beckert, *Empire of Cotton*, 102–3, 107–8. Johnson, *Soul by Soul*, 6, 8. Walter Johnson, *River of Dark Dreams: Slavery and Empire in the Cotton Kingdom* (Cambridge, Mass.: Harvard University Press, 2013), 40–45. Baptist, *The Half*, 112–13, 116–17, 119–22.

35. Johnson, *Soul by Soul*, 23, 7.

36. Thomas More Downey, "Planting a Capitalist South: The Transformation of

Western South Carolina, 1790–1860" (PhD diss., University of South Carolina, 2000), South Caroliniana Library, University of South Carolina, Columbia, 16–17.

37. Ruffin, quoted in Joseph P. Madden, *A History of Old Barnwell District, SC, to 1860* (Blackville, S.C.: Historical Business Ventures, 2001), 11, 10 ("pine barren"), South Caroliniana Library, University of South Carolina, Columbia. Downey, "Planting a Capitalist South," 17.

38. James W. Gray (Master in Equity) to James Carroll, 414(1), pp. 263–64, Charleston County Register of Mesne Conveyance. Property disputes engaged in by M. Martin after R. Martin's death: *Milberry S. Martin v. James B. Campbell*, Charleston District, Court of Equity Decree Books L 1092, 1858–61 pp. 64–76, 183H06. *M. S. Martin v. E. W. Pettit, et al.*, Charleston District, Court of Equity Decree Books L 1092, 1858–61, pp. 223–27, 183H06. *Mrs. M. S. Martin v. E. W. & L. F. Petit*, Charleston District, Court of Equity Bills, 1858, No. 65, L10090. *Milberry S. Martin, executrix of Robert Martin v. James B. Campbell*, Charleston District, Court of Equity Bills, 1858, No. 65, L10090.

39. Examples of several land transactions carried out by Milberry Martin in the 1850s: Milberry Serena Martin, lessor to City Council of Charleston, lessee, July 22, 1855, Book Q13, p. 389; M. S. Martin to Jos Aiken, August 2, 1858, Book E14, p. 198; MSM to Thomas Gadsden, July 6, 1854, Book V12, p. 209; MSM to James Gadsden, March 18, 1857, Book XB, p. 158; MSM to James Doolan, June 22, 1859, Book L14, p. 23; MSM to R. G. Stone, June 3, 1854, Book L13, p. 26. Js Bee, May 19, 1854, Book HB, p. 193, Charleston County Register of Mesne Conveyance. Milberry Martin continued to conduct various transactions into the 1860s. Announcement for Barnwell plantation sale: Under Decree in Equity, *Martin v. Aiken et al.*, *Charleston Courier*, February 6, 1854.

40. Elizabeth Keckley, *Behind the Scenes, or Thirty Years a Slave and Four Years in the White House* (1868; repr., New York: Oxford University Press, 1988), 23–34.

41. The historian Heather Williams makes this argument about the psychological toll of loved ones being sold away into ambiguous futures in comparison to the finality of death; Heather Andrea Williams, *Help Me to Find My People: The African American Search for Family Lost in Slavery* (Chapel Hill: University of North Carolina Press, 2012), 122. For a detailed account of one enslaved mother's long-term emotional distress at separation from her children, see Sydney Nathans, *To Free a Family: The Journey of Mary Walker* (Cambridge, Mass.: Harvard University Press, 2012).

42. Picquet, *The Octoroon*, 18.

43. Johnson, *Soul by Soul*, 22. Daina Ramey Berry, *The Price for Their Pound of Flesh: The Value of the Enslaved, from Womb to Grave, in the Building of a Nation* (Boston: Beacon Press, 2017), 61. Kemble, *Journal of a Residence on a Georgia Plantation*, 133.

44. Berry, *The Price*, 35–36. "A person with a price": Johnson, *Soul by Soul*, 1, 2.

45. Johnson, *Soul by Soul*, 113–15; Berry, *The Price*, 72.

46. Johnson, *Soul by Soul*, 2.

47. Kytle and Roberts, *Denmark Vesey's Garden*, 19, 176, 246. Robert Behre, "80 Years After Opening, Charleston's Old Slave Mart Museum Adds New Layers of History," *Post and Courier*, February 23, 2018. Edward Rothstein, "Emancipating History," *The New York Times*, March 11, 2011. The open exhibition of partially nude Blacks in public was to some unseemly, especially as visitors to the state observed these scenes and published accounts that fed northern radicals' call for abolition in the 1830s. Concerned with outward appearances, Charleston officials mandated in 1856 that slave sales be moved off the public streets.

48. Hodgson, *Letters from North America*, 55–58; italics in original. McInnis, *Politics of Taste*, 15–16.

49. Quoted in Berry, *The Price*, 10–11.

50. "Helped them to": Baptist, *The Half*, 108–9. Pamela Newkirk, *A Love No Less: More Than Two Centuries of African American Love Letters* (New York: Doubleday, 2003), 9. Beads, especially in the color blue, seem to have been used to convey spiritual protection. Buttons could be used in the fashioning of rattle-like instruments out of gourds. For more on archaeological excavations that have uncovered beads and buttons in slave quarters, and on the range of spiritual and creative uses for these items, see Patricia Samford, "The Archaeology of African-American Slavery and Material Culture," *William and Mary Quarterly*, 3rd ser., 53, no. 1 (1996): 102, 111.

51. Picquet, *The Octoroon*, 18, 30–31, 25.

52. Picquet, *The Octoroon*, 25, 23, 24, 20, 31.

53. Ulrich, *Age of Homespun*, 111, 133.

54. Downey, "Planting a Capitalist South," 23–24.

55. Auslander, "Slavery's Traces," 6.

56. Josephine St. Pierre Ruffin quoted in Madden, *A History of Old Barnwell District, SC, to 1860* (Blackville, S.C.: Historical Business Ventures, 2001), 11.

57. Barnwell, S.C., Record of Deeds, Vols. AA–BB, 1842–47, Box 11, BW 18, Deed Book BB, pp. 6, 75, 136, 215, 400, South Carolina Department of Archives and History (SCDAH); Deed Book HH, pp. 183, 184, 543, 544, SCDAH. The Rose listed in Thomas Gadsden's holdings was not explicitly tied to the Martins in the records. Thomas Gadsden's firm was located at No. 2 Chalmers Street. The death of an enslaved woman named Rose is listed in the City of Charleston Health Department Death Records, January 1853–December 1857, p. 40. Thomas Gadsden's incomplete set of papers at the South Carolina Historical Society do not include a bill of sale for Ashley or Rose; however, such records could have been lost. While it is clear that Milberry Martin sold the bulk of her property in 1854, none of these transactions (as recorded in the Charleston Mesne Conveyance records and Barnwell District deeds) mention enslaved people. Thomas Gadsden, Slave Bills of Sale; Gadsden Family, Gadsden Family Papers, 1701-ca.–1955, South Carolina Historical Society, Addlestone Library. I am grateful to genealogist Jesse Bustos-Nelson, who realized the Martins' proximity to this major slave-

trading family, identified a Rose in the traders' holdings as well as names that overlapped with other slaves formerly owned by the Martins, and arrived at the supposition that Rose was sold and died in the pen. Jesse Bustos-Nelson surmises that at thirty-five, this woman is the right age to have been the Rose we first picked out among so many others in slavery's garden. This Rose may have been sold soon after Ashley. She might have contracted a fatal illness in the cell overcrowded with other chattel-people, or she may have been sold because she exhibited prior symptoms of smallpox, an epidemic of which swept through Charleston in 1854.

58. King, *Stolen Childhood*, 234–35. Ball, "Retracing Slavery's Trail of Tears." The documents referred to here that identify children's ages consist mainly of ship manifests for the domestic trade that list enslaved people being transported.

59. "Statement of APA President Regarding the Traumatic Effects of Separating Immigrant Families," press release, American Psychological Association, May 29, 2018, apa.org/news/press/releases/2018/05/separating-immigrant-families. "Immigrant Family Separations Must End, Psychologist Tells Congressional Panel," press release, American Psychological Association, February 7, 2019, apa.org/news/press/releases/2019/02/immigrant-family-separations. "Beating and torture" quote: Heather Stringer, "Psychologists Respond to a Mental Health Crisis at the Border," APA *Monitor on Psychology* (September 2018), apa.org/news/2018/border-family-separation.

CHAPTER 6: ASHLEY'S SEEDS

1. Stanlie M. James, "Introduction," in *Theorizing Black Feminisms*, eds. Stanlie M. James and Abena P. A. Busia (London: Routledge, 1993), 4. James suggests that Black motherhood, as influenced by African cultural roots, was characterized by the qualities of "creativity and continuity." See also, in the same volume, James, "Mothering," 45.

2. For discussions of enslaved people and ecological resistance, see J. T. Roane, "Plotting the Black Commons," *Souls: A Critical Journal of Black Politics, Culture and Society* 20, no. 3 (2019): 239–66. Tiffany Lethabo King, "Racial Ecologies: Black Landscapes in Flux," in *Racial Ecologies*, ed. Leilani Nishime and Kim D. Hester Williams (Seattle: University of Washington Press, 2018). Tiffany Lethabo King, "The Labor of (Re)reading Plantation Landscapes Fungible(ly)," *Antipode*, 2016.

3. I am grateful to the members of the environmental history workshop at Harvard University, who shared feedback on this chapter in the fall of 2019. In this discussion, Andy Robichaud, a professor of history at Boston University, suggested that the handfuls here sounded like a measurement for cooking. Others suggested that the pecans might have been tradeable as a nonperishable luxury items, or, if they were actually another variety of nut that included natural toxins, they might have been taken like cyanide pills.

4. David S. Shields, "The Pecan (*Carya illinoinensis*)," unpublished paper, shared with Tiya Miles, April 22, 2019.

5. Texas pecans were transported in barrels to the Charleston harbor and would

have required smaller storage containers for carrying back to private homes. References to and quotes from antebellum Charleston menus are taken from Shields, "The Pecan (*Carya illinoinensis*)."

6. Shields, "The Pecan (*Carya illinoinensis*)."

7. The Boone Hall Avenue of the Oaks had been planted around fifteen years before the pecan cuttings, in 1843. David S. Shields, "Major John Horl-beck's Pecan Grove at Boone Hall Plantation," paper shared with Tiya Miles, April 22, 2019. Also published as "Going Nuts," *Charleston Magazine*, October 2018, charlestonmag.com/features/going_nuts.

8. Shields, "The Pecan (*Carya illinoinensis*)." David Shields emphasizes that the pecan pie, famously associated with Charleston and the broader South, was not invented until the 1880s—in Texas. David S. Shields, untitled, unpublished paper on pecan pie, shared with Tiya Miles, April 22, 2019. Shields notes that his argument about the origins of the pecan pie confirmed the finding of Andrew F. Smith, stated in a Charleston lecture titled "The Pecan: A Culinary History," February 21, 2012.

9. Joyce E. Chaplin, *An Anxious Pursuit: Agricultural Innovation and Modernity in the Lower South, 1730–1815* (Chapel Hill: University of North Carolina Press, 1993), 10. Lenny Wells, *Pecan: America's Native Nut Tree* (Tuscaloosa: University of Alabama Press, 2017), 34.

10. Abner Landrum quoted in Wells, *Pecan*, 37.

11. Abner Landrum, "Fruit Trees," *American Farmer*, February 28, 1822, 8.

12. Wells, *Pecan*, 37. A prototypical Renaissance man, Landrum worked in numerous fields of endeavor; he was a physician, newspaper editor, natural scientist, and artist. His innovative pottery manufacturing plant in central South Carolina made use of both enslaved and free Black labor. Abner Landrum's nephew and pottery-manufacturing business partner, Harvey Drake, owned Dave Drake. Thomas More Downey, "Planting a Capitalist South: The Transformation of Western South Carolina, 1790–1860" (PhD diss., University of South Carolina, 2000), 147, South Caroliniana Library, University of South Carolina, Columbia. Leonard Todd, *Carolina Clay: The Life and Legend of the Slave Potter Dave* (New York: W. W. Norton, 2008), 16, 30–31, 36–37, 95, 262n14. Mark Newell, "Lives in Clay: Lewis Miles," Tag Archives: Lewis Miles, February 3, 2019, The Archaelogy Hour Podcast Blog, archaeologyhour.com.

13. Whitehead writes of the character Terrance Randall, the brutal owner of a plantation split with his brother, James Randall: "Content to leer at his brother's women, he grazed heartily upon the women of his own half. 'I like to taste my plums,' Terrance said, prowling the rows of cabins to see what struck his fancy. He violated the bonds of affection, sometimes visiting slaves on their wedding night to show the husband the proper way to discharge his marital duty. He tasted his plums, and broke the skin, and left his mark." Colson Whitehead, *The Underground Railroad* (New York: Doubleday, 2016), 30.

14. Landrum, "Fruit Trees," *American Farmer*, 6, 7, 8.

15. The doctor who attempted to grow pecans was A. E. Colomb; the owner of

Oak Alley Plantation who received the cuttings was J. T. Roman. Wells, *Pecan*, 38–40. James McWilliams, *The Pecan: A History of America's Native Nut* (Austin: University of Texas Press, 2013), 61–62. Lenny Wells, "The Slave Gardener Who Turned the Pecan into a Cash Crop," What It Means to Be American: A National Conversation Hosted by the Smithsonian and Arizona State University, December 14, 2017, whatitmeanstobeamerican .org/ideas/the-slave-gardener-who-turned-the-pecan-into-a-cash-crop. David S. Shields, "The Big Four Pecans & 3 Others of Note," unpublished paper, shared with Tiya Miles, April 22, 2019.

16. Frederic Rosengarten, Jr., *The Book of Edible Nuts* (New York: Walker, 1984), 182. Quoted in Wells, *Pecan*, 34.
17. Wells, *Pecan*, 39, 40, 46. The Yale scientist was William H. Brewer; Brewer quoted in Wells, *Pecan*, 40.
18. "Much longer": McWilliams, *The Pecan*, 52. McWilliams, *The Pecan*, 69–70, Rosengarten, *Book of Edible Nuts*, 177.
19. McWilliams, *The Pecan*, 4.
20. Lauret Savoy, *Trace: Memory, History, Race, and the American Landscape* (Berkeley: Counterpoint, 2015), 29.
21. "The Old Woman Who Kept All the Pecans," George A. Dorsey, *Traditions of the Caddo* (Washington, D.C.: Carnegie Institution of Washington, 1905), 27, accessed at Louisiana Anthology, www2.latech.edu/~bmagee/louisiana _anthology/texts/dorsey/dorsey–caddo_traditions.html. Wells, *Pecan*, 17.
22. McWilliams, *The Pecan*, 18. Grant D. Hall, "Pecan Food Potential in Prehistoric North America," *Economic Botany* 54, no. 1 (2000): 105. "An Act to Amend the Law Passed 24th September, 1839, Regulating the Public Domain," Cherokee Executive Committee, *Constitution and Laws of the Cherokee Nation: Passed at Tahlequah, Cherokee Nation, 1839–51* (Tahlequah, Okla.: Cherokee Nation, 1852), 48. "An Act Against Destroying Pecan and Other Trees," Davis A. Homer, published by the Authority of the Chickasaw Legislature, *Constitution and Laws of the Chickasaw Nation, Together with the Treaties of 1832, 1833, 1834, 1837, 1852, 1855, 1856* (Parsons, Kans.: Foley Railway Printing Company, 1899), 91. A similar Seminole law is quoted in McWilliams, *The Pecan*, 18.
23. Kay Shaw Nelson, "A Paean to the Popular Pecan: Saga of an American Native," Special to *The Washington Post*, F14.
24. Susan Tucker, "Not Forgotten: Twenty-five Years Out from *Telling Memories*: Conversations Between Mary Yelling and Susan Tucker," *Southern Cultures* (Spring 2014): 93–101, 97.
25. Tiya Miles, "The Black Gun Owner Next Door," *The New York Times*, March 9, 2019.
26. A Google search for "survival foods" in 2019 turned up 123,000 results, especially of disaster preparedness and prepper websites, such as: skilled survival.com/5-things-to-consider-for-the-best-survival-foods/, primalsurvivor .net/survival-foods-list/, and "Plan Ahead for Disasters: Food," ready.gov/ food. Jackie Mansky, "Food Historian Reckons with the Black Roots of Southern Food," Smithsonian.com, August 1, 2017. See also Michael W.

Twitty, *The Cooking Gene: A Journey Through African American Culinary History in the Old South* (New York: HarperCollins, 2017).

27. Jill Radsken, "Second Life for Slave Narrative," *Harvard Gazette*, August 8, 2018.

28. Leslie A. Schwalm, *A Hard Fight for We: Women's Transition from Slavery to Freedom in South Carolina* (Urbana: University of Illinois Press, 1997), 35.

29. "Dangerous": Maurie D. McInnis, *The Politics of Taste in Antebellum Charleston* (Chapel Hill: University of North Carolina Press, 2005), 253. David S. Shields, *Southern Provisions: The Creation and Revival of a Southern Cuisine* (Chicago: University of Chicago Press, 2015), 27. Rebecca Sharpless, *Cooking in Other Women's Kitchens: Domestic Workers in the South, 1865–1960* (Chapel Hill: University of North Carolina Press, 2010), 4, 25.

30. Jane Clark, narrative recorded by Julia C. Ferris, read at the banquet of the Cayuga County Historical Society, February 22, 1897. Wilma King, *Stolen Childhood: Slave Youth in Nineteenth-Century America*, 2nd ed. (1995; repr., Bloomington: Indiana University Press, 2011), 59.

31. Jane Clark, by Julia Ferris.

32. Charles Joyner, *Down by the Riverside: A South Carolina Slave Community* (Urbana: University of Illinois Press, 1984), 100. Philip Morgan's study of enslaved people's property ownership in the Lowcountry lists foodstuffs as the most common kinds of possessions claimed in the Southern Claims Commission post–Civil War testimony. Items included, in order of prevalence: hogs, corn, rice, and fowls; Philip D. Morgan, "The Ownership of Property by Slaves in the Mid-Nineteenth-Century Low Country," *Journal of Southern History* 49, no. 3 (1983): 409. This dietary variety also seems to have been the case for coastal Virginia; see Patricia Samford, "The Archaeology of African-American Slavery and Material Culture," *William and Mary Quarterly*, 3rd ser., 53, no. 1 (1996): 95–96. Although the task system is often held up as a preferable labor arrangement for the enslaved (and it was, with regard to personal time management and property acquisition), Leslie Shwalm points out that task assignments were sometimes made without concern for ability, despite the special needs of pregnant and postpartum women, and, more nefariously, to put Black women on work details in places that made them sexually vulnerable to white men. Schwalm, *A Hard Fight for We*, 41–44.

33. Schwalm, *A Hard Fight for We*, 14.

34. King, *Stolen Childhood*, 67.

35. Henry Brown, Federal Writers' Project: Slave Narrative Project, vol. 14, South Carolina, Part 1, Abrams-Durant, 1936, pp. 120–21, loc.gov/item/mesn141/. Ed McCrorey, Federal Writers' Project: Slave Narrative Project, vol. 14, South Carolina, Part 3, 1936, p. 147, loc.gov/item/mesn143/.

36. Mamie Garvin Fields with Karen Fields, *Lemon Swamp and Other Places: A Carolina Memoir* (New York: Free Press, 1983), 59.

37. Fields, *Lemon Swamp*, 59.

38. Adrian Miller, *Soul Food: The Surprising Story of an American Cuisine One*

Plate at a Time (Chapel Hill: University of North Carolina Press, 2013), 26. Miller does not provide a source for the "oversized shoes" rice-collection method. For an overview of his sources, which included historical documents, Federal Writers' Project ex-slave interviews, historical cookbooks, soul food restaurant visits, and consultations with cooks, see p. 5.

39. Drew Swanson describes a "fusion" diet on a coastal Georgian plantation, made up of "Native American, African, and European Influences." Drew Swanson, *Remaking Wormsloe Plantation: The Environmental History of a Lowcountry Landscape* (Athens: University of Georgia Press, 2012), 74. Adrian Miller describes soul food as "a cuisine 400 years in the making, melding African, European, and Native American influences," which was claimed as "Black" in the 1960s as part of the cultural solidarity ethos inspired by the Black Power political movement. Miller, *Soul Food*, 45. Shields, *Southern Provisions*, 7, 30, 31. Judith A. Carney and Richard Nicholas Rosomoff, *In the Shadow of Slavery: Africa's Botanical Legacy in the Atlantic World* (Berkeley: University of California Press, 2009), 17, 24, 112–13, 149, 180. Rayna Green, "Mother Corn and the Dixie Pig: Native Food in the Native South," *Southern Cultures* 14, no. 4 (2008): 114–26, 117. Miller, *Soul Food*, 113, 150, 188, 259. Francis Lam, "Edna Lewis and the Black Roots of American Cooking," *The New York Times Magazine*, October 28, 2015.

40. Walter Johnson has asserted that the narratives of the formerly enslaved "contain more information about food than any other topic other than beatings and escapes." Walter Johnson, *River of Dark Dreams: Slavery and Empire in the Cotton Kingdom* (Cambridge, Mass.: Harvard University Press, 2013), 178.

41. Kathleen M. Hilliard, *Masters, Slaves, and Exchange: Power's Purchase in the Old South* (New York: Cambridge University Press, 2014), 48–49. Shields, *Southern Provisions*, 7–8.

42. Drew Faust discusses this dialectic between labor and comfort on James Henry Hammond's South Carolina cotton plantation. Faust, *James Henry Hammond and the Old South: A Design for Mastery* (Baton Rouge: Louisiana State University Press, 1982), 75.

43. Thomas Andrews, "Beasts of the Southern Wild: Slaveholders, Slaves, and Other Animals in Charles Ball's *Slavery in the United States*," in *Rendering Nature: Animals, Bodies, Places, Politics*, ed. Marguerite S. Shaffer and Phoebe S. K. Young (Philadelphia: University of Pennsylvania Press, 2015), 26, 24, 27.

44. Hilliard, *Masters, Slaves, and Exchange*, 116, 127.

45. Schwalm, *A Hard Fight for We*, 34.

46. Johnson, *River of Dark Dreams*, 179. Miller, *Soul Food*, 26–27.

47. Joyner, *Down by the Riverside*, 102. Daughter of Robert F. W. Allston quoted on p. 101.

48. Miller, *Soul Food*, 19, 22, 24. Jessie Sparrow, Federal Writers' Project: Slave Narrative Project, vol. 14, South Carolina, Part 4, Raines-Young, 1936, pp. 138–39, 194, loc.gov/item/mesn144.

49. Sarah Byrd, Federal Writers' Project: Slave Narrative Project, vol. 4, Georgia, Part 1, Adams-Furr, p. 2, image 174, loc.gov/resource/mesn041. Also quoted in Hilliard, *Masters, Slaves and Exchange*, 47.

50. Eliza Potter, *A Hairdresser's Experience in High Life* (1859; repr., New York: Oxford University Press, 1991), 187–88.

51. As environmental historian Drew Swanson notes: "Food sheds light on the shaping power of local environments"; Swanson, *Remaking Wormsloe*, 75. Sharpless, *Cooking in Other Women's Kitchens*, 2, 63.

52. Jim Henry, Federal Writers' Project: Slave Narrative Project, vol. 14, South Carolina, Part 2, 1936, pp. 266–67, loc.gov/item/mesn142/. Anderson Bates, Federal Writers' Project: Slave Narrative Project, vol. 14, South Carolina, Part 1, 1936, p. 42, loc.gov/item/mesn141/. Ed McCrorey, Federal Writers' Project: Slave Narrative Project, vol. 14, South Carolina, Part 3, p. 147.

53. Potter, *A Hairdresser's Experience*, 182.

54. "Protein": Wells, *Pecan*, xxiv. McWilliams, *The Pecan*, 7. "Designed": Robin Wall Kimmerer, *Braiding Sweetgrass: Indigenous Wisdom, Scientific Knowledge, and the Teachings of Plants* (Minneapolis: Milkweed Editions, 2013), 14.

55. Pecans grew wild around the Mississippi River and the Guadalupe River and its rivulets. Although wild pecans did not originate in the Southeast, the trees are prevalent now in the region where Ashley and Rose lived. McWilliams, *The Pecan*, 3. Wells, *Pecan*, 1, xiv, 9. Shields, "The Big Four Pecans & 3 Others of Note."

56. "Natural food": Grant D. Hall, "Pecan Food Potential in Prehistoric North America," *Economic Botany* 54, no. 1 (2000): 103–12, 110. Thomas R. Hester, Stephen L. Black, D. Gentry Steele, Ben W. Olive, and Anne A. Fox, *From the Gulf to the Rio Grande: Human Adaptation in Central, South, and Lower Pecos Texas*, Karl Reinhard Papers/Publications 59 (1989), chapter 6, Digital Commons, University of Nebraska–Lincoln. This archaeological survey submitted to the U.S. Army Corps of Engineers quotes from Thomas N. Campbell, *The Payaya Indians of Southern Texas* (1975) on Payaya encampments near streams where pecans grew.

57. Bruce W. Wood, Jerry A. Payne, and Larry J. Grauke, "The Rise of the U.S. Pecan Industry," *HortScience* 25, no. 6 (June 1990): 594, 721–23. McWilliams, *The Pecan*, 8, 10.

58. Wells, *Pecan*, 16, 20.

59. Wells, *Pecan*, 3, 4. McWilliams, *The Pecan*, 7. Hall, "Pecan Food Potential," 106–7. Rosengarten, *Book of Edible Nuts*, 171. See also Art Slemering, "Palate-Pleasing Pecans Are a Versatile, Native American Food," *Kansas City Star*, November 28, 1986, F1. "Native Americans Used Pecans Well," *Philadelphia Tribune*, December 3, 1991, 2C. For a poetic discussion of Native place-names and national memory, see Savoy, *Trace*, 69–87.

60. Hall, "Pecan Food Potential," 107–8. McWilliams, *The Pecan*, 16–17.

61. Rosengarten, *Book of Edible Nuts*, 189. Nelson, "A Paean to the Popular Pecan," F1, F14.

62. "Cushion": King, *Stolen Children*, 70.

63. As strangers coming into already deprived and stressed populations, enslaved children were not necessarily and automatically welcomed into new plantation communities. Integration and acceptance took time and was often preceded by long periods of loneliness. See, for instance, Dylan C. Penningroth, *The Claims of Kinfolk: African American Property and Community in the Nineteenth-Century South* (Chapel Hill: University of North Carolina Press, 2003), 88. Dylan C. Penningroth, "My People, My People: The Dynamics of Community in Southern Slavery," in *New Studies in the History of American Slavery*, ed Edward E. Baptist and Stephanie M. H. Camp (Athens: University of Georgia Press, 2006), 168. Edward E. Baptist, "'Stol' and Fetched Here': Enslaved Migration, Ex-Slave Narratives, and Vernacular History," in Baptist and Camp eds., *New Studies*, 250.

64. Alice Walker, Foreword, *Barracoon: The Story of the Last "Black Cargo,"* by Zora Neale Hurston (New York: HarperCollins, 2018), ix. Ruth Gaskins, *A Good Heart and a Light Hand: Ruth L. Gaskins' Collection of Traditional Negro Recipes* (New York: Simon and Schuster, 1968), vii.

65. Edna Lewis's recipe includes this direction for making vanilla sugar: "Just bury a split vanilla bean in a cannister of granulated sugar. It needs to ripen at least 1 week before using." Edna Lewis, *In Pursuit of Flavor* (New York: Alfred A. Knopf, 1988), 304.

66. Recipes: Vertamae Smart-Grosvenor, *Vibration Cooking, or The Travel Notes of a Geechee Girl* (New York: Ballantine, 1970), 91, 94. National Council of Negro Women, *The Historical Cookbook of the American Negro* (1958; repr., Boston: Beacon, 2000), 119. Carolyn Quick Tillery, *The African-American Heritage Cookbook: Traditional Recipes and Fond Remembrances from Alabama's Renowned Tuskegee Institute* (Secaucus, N.J.: Carol Publishing Group, 1997), 200–201. Ruth L. Gaskins, *A Good Heart*, 77. Lewis, *In Pursuit of Flavor*, 304.

CHAPTER 7: THE BRIGHT UNSPOOLING

1. Based on his tracing of Rosa Clifton's family, working backward, Mark Auslander speculates that Ashley's name may have become Sarah Clifton (in Orangeburg County, S.C., in 1880) or Dosky/Dasky Clifton (in Columbia, S.C., in 1870 or 1880). Although this linkage between Ashley and these two named women is tentative, it further suggests that Ashley remained in central South Carolina. Using census records, Auslander found that the extended Black Clifton family was spread out across Barnwell County and Orangeburg County, about fifty miles away from the Martins' Milberry Place Plantation. Mark Auslander, "Clifton Family and Ashley's Sack," *Cultural Environments* blog, December 30, 2016, culturalenvironments.blogspot .com/2016/. Auslander, "Slavery's Traces: In Search of Ashley's Sack," *Southern Spaces* blog, November 29, 2016, 12–13, southernspaces.org/2016/ slaverys-traces-search-ashleys-sack. In 2017, Auslander announced a search for descendants through the Clifton family line in local Orangeburg County media; Dionne Gleaton, "Ashley's Sack: 'National Treasure' of Slavery Era Has Local Ties," Orangeburg, S.C., *Times and Democrat*, June 20, 2017.

2. "Fragile": Erica Armstrong Dunbar, A Fragile Freedom: African American Women and Emancipation in the Antebellum City (New Haven: Yale University Press, 2008), 3.

3. Richard Zuczek, State of Rebellion: Reconstruction in South Carolina (Columbia: University of South Carolina Press, 1996), 15–16. Richard Mark Gergel, "Wade Hampton and the Rise of One-Party Racial Orthodoxy in South Carolina," in South Carolina in the Civil War and Reconstruction Eras, ed. Michael Brem Bonner and Fritz Hamer (Columbia: University of South Carolina Press, 2016), 198.

4. Zuczek, State of Rebellion, 17–18; Edgefield Appeal quoted in Zuczek, 18. Dan T. Carter, "Fateful Legacy: White Southerners and the Dilemma of Emancipation," in Bonner and Hamer, eds., South Carolina in the Civil War, 142, 145, 149. Martin Abbott, "The Freedmen's Bureau and Its Carolina Critics," in Bonner and Hamer, eds., South Carolina in the Civil War, 153, 154.

5. "Armed bands": Zuczek, State of Rebellion, 12–13, 19, 30, 34, 55, 79, 138. Eric Foner, Reconstruction: America's Unfinished Revolution, 1863–1877 (New York: Harper & Row, 1988), 342–43. Edward L. Ayers, The Thin Light of Freedom: The Civil War and Emancipation in the Heart of America (New York: W. W. Norton, 2017), 371–72. Steven Hahn, A Nation Under Our Feet: Black Political Struggles in the Rural South from Slavery to the Great Migration (Cambridge, Mass.: Harvard University Press, 2003), 267–72.

6. Fields, Lemon Swamp, 200.

7. Fields, Lemon Swamp, 200–202.

8. On her marriage license application, Ruth gives her mother's name as "Rose." She also gives her birth year as 1897. Census records indicate circa 1902 for her year of birth. Although 1897 and ca. 1902 are within the same range and could easily reflect minor mistakes in memory or recording, it might also be the case that Ruth purposefully aged herself by five years for the marriage application. Arthur Middleton and Ruth Jones Application of Marriage 387059, June 25, 1918, Commonwealth of Pennsylvania, Marriage License Bureau, Philadelphia. Through the "naming of offspring for beloved kin," as Tera Hunter observed, African Americans in this period of tumult made clear "the significance of family." Tera W. Hunter, To 'Joy My Freedom: Southern Black Women's Lives and Labors After the Civil War (Cambridge, Mass.: Harvard University Press, 1997), 38.

9. John Hope Franklin, Sidney Hillman Lectures, 1961, quoted in Kendra Taira Field, Growing Up with the Country: Family, Race, and Nation After the Civil War (New Haven: Yale University Press, 2018), 2. Franklin dates this period, also referred to as the "nadir," from the end of Reconstruction to 1923. Rayford Whittingham Logan, The Negro in American Life and Thought: The Nadir, 1877–1901 (New York: Dial, 1954). Field, Growing Up, 176.

10. Hunter, To 'Joy My Freedom, 111, 217, 232.

11. City Directories, Columbia, S.C,. 1906, 1909, 1910, 1911, 1912, 1913, 1915, 1917, 1922, digital.tcl.sc.edu/digital/collection/sccitydirec/search. Ancestry .com. 1910 United States Federal Census, Lehi, Utah, USA: Ancestry.com

Operations, 20060. Ancestry.com. 1900 United States Federal Census. Provo, Utah, USA: Ancestry.com Operations, 2004. I am grateful to genealogist Jesse Bustos-Nelson, who identified Rosa and Austin in the Columbia city directories. For a sense of the kind of work, often exploitative, that Blacks might do on university campuses in this period, see the Universities Studying Slavery Roundtable, *Public Historian* 42, no. 4 (2020).

12. Auslander, "Slavery's Traces," 6. Arthur Middleton and Ruth Jones Application of Marriage 387059, June 25, 1918, indicates that both of Ruth Middleton's parents were dead by 1918. After 1912, Austin Jones no longer appears in the Columbia city directories.

13. Italics added for emphasis.

14. Storytelling or personal narrative is often used today as a therapeutic tool in the treatment of trauma and emotional distress. Jan Plamper, *The History of Emotions: An Introduction*, Emotions in History series (Oxford: Oxford University Press, 2015), 201. The impact of storytelling on processes of healing is also suggested by the power of testimony in social repair work such as the Truth and Reconciliation Commission that followed the end of South African racial apartheid and the Truth and Reconciliation Commission that stemmed from Canada's reckoning with its abuse of First Nations (Indigenous) children in state-run residential schools. The synergistic relationship between telling and healing may stem from the "structural similarity between emotion and narrative"—that is, the parallelism between how we experience feelings and how we experience stories. Scholars of cognition explain that we respond with emotion when we experience a rise of feeling in reaction to change—the disruption of our expectations or momentary state of being. Similarly, the form of a narrative follows a set of reactions or events unwinding over time in response to a "break with normality." Upon recognizing this shift (the "complication" of the regular flow of events), the protagonist of a narrative begins journeying toward a desired restoration of normalcy but instead finds herself changed, and her life changed, as a result of how the narrative has unfolded. Tilmann Habermas and Verena Diel, "The Emotional Impact of Loss Narratives: Event Severity and Narrative Perspectives," *Emotion* 10, no. 3 (2010) 312–23. The momentum of narration mirrors the motion of emotion, then, which makes storytelling an effective means of examining and reorienting feelings. This effect operates in the processing of past traumatic happenings. Habermas and Diel found in two studies on the impact of oral stories of emotional loss on listeners that women tended to be more sympathetic and empathetic listeners to the emotional plight of storytellers. (Study 1 included 162 participants; study 2 included 216 participants.)

15. Gayl Jones, *Corregidora* (Boston: Beacon Press, 1975), 72.

16. Tilmann Habermas and Nadine Berger found that the way people tell stories about emotional events changes over time. As the same event is retold by the speaker, and as the speaker moves toward greater distance and approaches closure, stories become more compressed—shorter, less descriptive—and at the same time more evaluative—distant and impersonal. In the middle of

this process (after the first telling but before the story has been told multiple times), the story is narrated at greater length, as the teller struggles to interpret and integrate it. Tilmann Habermas and Nadine Berger, "Retelling Everyday Emotional Events: Condensation, Distancing, and Closure," *Cognition and Emotion* 25, no. 2 (2011): 206–19.

17. Susan Tucker, *Telling Memories Among Southern Women: Domestic Workers and Their Employers in the Segregated South* (Baton Rouge: Louisiana State University Press, 1988), 4.

18. Elizabeth Wayland Barber, *Women's Work: The First 20,000 Years; Women, Cloth, and Society in Early Times* (New York: W. W. Norton, 1994), 153.

19. Laurel Thatcher Ulrich, *The Age of Homespun: Objects and Stories in the Creation of an American Myth* (New York: Alfred A. Knopf, 2001), 40. In the eighteenth and nineteenth centuries, household items and clothing were considered movable property or "paraphernalia" (small-scale personal property), both of which were counted among the kinds of property free white, married women could legally own. These were the items women tended to hand down, especially to daughters. Importantly, enslaved people were also defined as movable property in some colonies and states, making them another category of property that free white women could own and inherit. Joan R. Gundersen, "Women and Inheritance in America: Virginia and New York City as a Case Study, 1700–1860," in *Inheritance and Wealth in America*, ed. Robert K. Miller, Jr., and Stephen J. McNamee (New York: Plenum, 1998), 94, 96, 104, 110. See also Stephanie E. Jones-Rogers, *They Were Her Property: White Women as Slave Owners in the American South* (New Haven: Yale University Press, 2019), chapter 2.

20. Julia Bryan-Wilson argues that fabric stands out as a material in its ability to convey different meanings at once, as well as in its tensile quality—a capacity to be stretched and stressed while maintaining its physical coherence. Bryan-Wilson, *Fray: Art and Textile Politics* (Chicago: University of Chicago Press, 2017), 4, 5, 28.

21. "Sewing together": Mark Auslander, "Rose's Gift: Slavery, Kinship, and the Fabric of Memory," *Present Pasts* 8, no. 1 (2017): 6, doi.org/10.5334/pp.78. Auslander's full quote about this dimension of the sack in the cited article offers a beautiful analysis: "She has created, out of this valued family textile, the fabric of their female lineage. The finished sack, while a lamentation of long ago injustice, is also a tangible family reunion, sewing together those [who] were torn asunder, and recreating the lines of descent that the slavery system had sought to annihilate." Anthropologists Jane Schneider and Annette B. Weiner point to cloth "as a common metaphor for society, thread for social relations" and note "how readily its appearance and that of its constituent fibers can evoke ideas of connectedness or tying." Jane Schneider and Annette B. Weiner, "Introduction," in *Cloth and Human Experience*, Annette B. Weiner and Jane Schneider, eds. (Washington D.C.: Smithsonian Institution Press, 1989), 2.

22. The archaeologist Elizabeth Wayland Barber has explored how "cloth and clothing invoke magic in their encoding." Barber, *Women's Work*, 155,

155n4. Barber notes that not all scholars of Greek mythology agree with the linguistic interpretation advanced by George Bolling about the role of the rose in Homer's *Iliad*.

23. The literary scholar Maria Mårdberg uses this phrasing in an analysis of how the African American author Jamaica Kincaid employs narrative to reconnect a maternal line severed through slavery in one of her books. Maria Mårdberg, "'A Bleak, Black Wind': Motherlessness and Emotional Exile in Jamaica Kincaid's *The Autobiography of My Mother*," in *Reclaiming Home, Remembering Motherhood, Rewriting History: African American and Afro-Caribbean Women's Literature in the Twentieth Century*, ed. Verena Theile and Marie Drews (Newcastle upon Tyne: Cambridge Scholars, 2009), 28. Auslander, "Rose's Gift."

24. "To inscribe": Ulrich, *Age of Homespun*, 141.

25. Nikki M. Taylor, *Frontiers of Freedom: Cincinnati's Black Community, 1802–1868* (Athens: Ohio University Press, 2005), 64. Jeffrey C. Stewart, *The New Negro: The Life of Alain Locke* (New York: Oxford University Press, 2018), 17.

26. James R. Grossman, "A Chance to Make Good: 1900–1929," in *To Make Our World Anew*, vol. 2, *A History of African Americans from 1880*, ed. Robin D. G. Kelley and Earl Lewis (New York: Oxford University Press, 2000), 119, 122.

27. Saidiya Hartman, "Venus in Two Acts," *Small Axe* 26 (June 2008): 14.

28. On the intimacy of fabric see Bryan-Wilson, *Fray*, 12–13.

29. Arthur Middleton was drafted in June 1917, prior to his marriage to Ruth. His registration card lists him as a laborer in Philadelphia. Ruth Jones, Pennsylvania Marriages, 1852–1968, Lehi, Utah, Ancestry.com Operations, 2016. Dorothy Middleton Page (Dorothy Helen Middleton), Ancestry.com. U.S., Social Security Applications and Claims Index, 1936–2007. Provo, Utah: Ancestry.com Operations, 2015. Arthur Middleton served from August 26, 1918, to July 18, 1919, and was honorably discharged on July 24, 1919. Arthur Middleton, Application, Ancestry.com. Pennsylvania, World War I Veterans Service and Compensation Files, 1917–1919, 1934–1948, Provo, Utah: Ancestry.com Operations, 2015. Women in domestic service had a variety of living situations (including sleeping on their employers' premises, away from their own children). Rebecca Sharpless, *Cooking in Other Women's Kitchens: Domestic Workers in the South, 1865–1960* (Chapel Hill: University of North Carolina Press, 2010), 113. Also see W.E.B. DuBois, *The Philadelphia Negro: A Social Study* (1899; repr.: Philadelphia: University of Pennsylvania Press, 1996), on Black women as heads of households, Kindle loc. 1445, 1808.

30. "The most important": Dunbar, *Fragile Freedom*, 4; Dunbar, *Fragile Freedom*, 34, 44. For descriptions of the early Black business class, also see DuBois, *Philadelphia Negro*, Kindle loc. 622, 630, 631, 999, 1001. Sharon Harley notes that most Black women who lived in Philadelphia in the antebellum period labored as domestic workers and washerwomen. A smaller percentage worked in the needle trades, for lower wages than their white

counterparts. Sharon Harley, "Northern Black Female Workers: Jacksonian Era," in *The Afro-American Woman: Struggles and Images*, ed. Sharon Harley and Rosalyn Terborg-Penn (1978; repr., Baltimore: Black Classic Press, 1997), 10–11.

31. Amrita Chakrabarti Myers, *Forging Freedom: Black Women and the Pursuit of Liberty in Antebellum Charleston* (Chapel Hill: University of North Carolina Press, 2011), 208, 206. For a description of the first waves of Black migration following emancipation, see DuBois, *Philadelphia Negro*, chapter 12.

32. Barbara Blair, "Though Justice Sleeps: 1880–1900," in Kelley and Lewis, eds., *To Make Our World Anew*, 10, 11.

33. Hunter, *To 'Joy My Freedom*, 111, 234. The historian Evelyn Brooks Higginbotham points out that only 1 percent of Black women had attained middle-class status in the 1890s. The vast majority were still limited to low-wage agricultural and domestic service labor. Higginbotham, *Righteous Discontent: The Women's Movement in the Black Baptist Church, 1880–1920* (1993; repr., Cambridge, Mass.: Harvard University Press, 2003), 40.

34. DuBois, *Philadelphia Negro*, Kindle loc. 631, 2586.

35. DuBois, *Philadelphia Negro*, Kindle loc. 621, 630, 2583.

36. Hunter, *To 'Joy My Freedom*, 111. The grandmother and mother of Philadelphia-born Black intellectual Alain Locke ran a dressmaking business and through that work helped maintain their family's place in the Black middle class. Stewart, *New Negro*, 22, 14.

37. Auslander, "Slavery's Traces," 8–9. The couple's marriage application lists Ruth's address as 501 Woodland and Arthur's address as 1731 Uber in June 1918. Arthur gave this same address on his military service application in July 1918. Middleton and Jones marriage application, June 25, 1918. Arthur Middleton, Military Service Application No. 272507, Pennsylvania (draft card): Ancestry.com. *Pennsylvania, World War I Veterans Service and Compensation Files, 1917–1919, 1934–1948*, Lehi, Utah: Ancestry.com Operations, 2015. Arthur Middleton, World War I veteran's compensation: Ancestry.com. Pennsylvania, World War I Veterans Service and Compensation Files, 1917–1919, 1934–1948, Lehi, Utah: Ancestry.com Operations, 2015. Pa.

38. U.S. Federal Census, 1930, Provo, Utah: Ancestry.com Operations, 2010. Images produced by Family Search; page 10B; Enumeration District: 0060; FHL microfilm: 2341816. Lawrence F. Flick, "Samuel Castner, Jr." *Records of the American Catholic Historical Society of Philadelphia* 40, no. 3 (1929): 193–225. George Eastman Museum, "Samuel Castner Papers, Louis Walton Sipley/American Museum of Photography Collection," George Eastman Museum, September 5, 2018, eastman.org/samuel-castner-papers -louis-walton-sipleyamerican-museum-photography-collection. Township of Lower Merion, Building and Planning Committee, November 8, 2017, lowermerion.org/Home/ShowDocument?id=17724. Sharpless, *Cooking in Other Women's Kitchens*, xiii. Hartman, "The Belly of the World," 170. I am grateful to the public historian and descendant coordinator Hannah Scruggs, whose research assistance on Ruth and Dorothy Middleton was invaluable.

39. Melnea Cass, transcript, Digital, Black Women's Oral History Project, OH-

31; T-32, Schlesinger Library, Harvard Radcliffe Institute, 3, 5, 20. Quoted with permission from the Schlesinger Library.

40. Middleton family (Pink, Flander, Arthur) in the censuses of 1910 and 1920: Ancestry.com, 1910 United States Federal Census, Lehi, Utah, USA: Ancestry.com Operations, 2006. Ancestry.com, 1920 United States Federal Census, Provo, Utah, USA: Ancestry.com Operations, 2010. Arthur Middleton's Transport record: Outgoing and Incoming, U.S. Army World War I Transport Service, Passenger Lists 1910–1939, pp. 92/60. National Archives, fold3.com/image/604049037?rec=621933109&xid=1945. U.S. Army World War I Transport Service, Passenger Lists, National Archives, 1910–39, USA. Arthur Middleton is listed as a member of the 856th Company Colored with a port of sail from Brest, France, in July 1919. After his discharge, census records do not list him at the same address as Ruth Middleton.

41. Melnea Cass, transcript, 21, 25, 27, 64–66, 70–71, 107, 40–41, iv.

42. Trummel Valdera, "Younger Set Activities," *Philadelphia Tribune*, January 13, 1938, 6–7. The author of this youth-oriented social page refers to "Dot Middleton."

43. U.S. Federal Census, 1940, Provo, Utah: Ancestry.com Operations, 2012, provided in association with National Archives and Records Administration.

44. Martha Horsey's employment agency: Philadelphia City Directory, 1924. Ancestry.com. *U.S. City Directories, 1822–1995* [database online]. Philadelphia City Directory 1924. Provo, Utah: Ancestry.com Operations, 2011.

45. Helen Middleton, Arthur Middleton's sister, married a Dutch Caribbean man named Louis Stebo (or Steba) in 1935; they lived in Brooklyn. Helen Middleton Delayed Birth Certificate: Ancestry.com, South Carolina, Delayed Birth Records, 1766–1900 and City of Charleston, South Carolina, Birth Records, 1877–1901, Provo, Utah: Ancestry.com Operations, 2007. Helen and Louis Marriage index: Ancestry.com, New York, New York, Extracted Marriage Index, 1866–1937, Provo, Utah: Ancestry.com Operations, 2014. Louis and Helen Stebo in the 1940 census: U.S. Federal Census, 1940; Census Place: Kings County, New York; roll: m-t0627-02578; page: 9B; Enumeration District: 24–1244. United States of America, Bureau of the Census. *Sixteenth Census of the United States, 1940* (Washington, D.C.: National Archives and Records Administration, 1940). T627, 4,643 rolls. "Virginian: A Dinner Guest Here," *Philadelphia Tribune*, June 6, 1929, 6. "Baby blue" quote: social pages, *Philadelphia Tribune*, December 8, 1927, 4. Visits with sister-in-law: "Gad-Abouts," April 21, 1938, *Philadelphia Tribune*, 5; "Newsy Nibbles," *Philadelphia Tribune*, January 4, 1940, 8. Additional social occasion mentions from the 1920s and 1930s: *Philadelphia Tribune*, July 25, 1929, 4; August 13, 1931, 4, February 18, 1932, 5, June 30, 1932, 5; September 8, 1932, 5; October 19, 1933, 6; December 21, 1933, 6; March 28, 1935, 9; December 30, 1937, 6; "Newsy Nibbles," *Philadelphia Tribune*, February 24, 1938, 6.

46. "Spacious home": "Club Parties," *Philadelphia Tribune*, March 28, 1935, 9. *Philadelphia Tribune*, October 19, 1933, 6. "Society at a Glance," *Philadelphia Tribune*, March 3, 1938, 5.

47. Modish: Trummell Valdera, "Younger Set Activities," *Philadelphia Tribune*, December 10, 1937, 6. "Blue taffeta": "Younger Set," *Philadelphia Tribune*, April 7, 1938, 6. "Gray wool": Trummell Valdera, "Younger Set Activities," *Philadelphia Tribune*, April 21, 1938. "New gadget": Trummell Valdera, "Younger Set Activities," *Philadelphia Tribune*, December 14, 1939, 9. "Annoyed": Trummell Valdera, "Younger Set Activities," *Philadelphia Tribune*, February 3, 1938, 6.

48. "Matron": *Philadelphia Tribune*, January 18, 1940.

49. Study of the Episcopal Diocese of Pennsylvania: St. Simon the Cyrenian Church (1964), "St. Simon the Cyrenian Church, Diocese of Pennsylvania, Philadelphia, Pennsylvania," p. 13, https://philadelphiastudies.org/2018/04/07/study-of-the-episcopal-diocese-of-pennsylvania-st-simon-the-cyrenian-church-1964/. Ruth Middleton was confirmed at St. Simon the Cyrenian Church in 1940. Ruth J. Middleton is pictured and listed among people receiving the laying on of hands; she is not identified individually in the photograph. *Philadelphia Tribune*, January 18, 1940; *Philadelphia Tribune*, March 7, 1940, 18. Auslander, "Slavery's Traces," 10. After a three-month preparation, Dorothy Middleton was confirmed in March; she was a young teenager at the time; "Seventy-eight Confirmed at St. Simon's Chapel," *Philadelphia Tribune*, April 6, 1933, 14. According to the Archdiocese of Pennsylvania, many of the St. Simon records have been lost due to asbestos. Reports of the church in 1917–18 can be found in *The Monthly Message of the Parish of the Holy Apostles*, digitized at philadelphiastudies.org.

50. "Parties": Dorothy Middleton, "Younger Set Activities," *Philadelphia Tribune*, April 4, 1940, 9. "Formals": Dorothy Middleton, "Younger Set Activities," *Philadelphia Tribune*, April 4, 1940, 8. In the April 4 issue, Middleton notes that Trummell Valdera, the regular author of this column, had moved to Washington.

51. Rozsika Parker, *The Subversive Stitch: Embroidery and the Making of the Feminine* (1984; repr., London: I. B. Tauris, 2016), 5.

52. Jennifer Van Horn's analysis of school samplers created in early-nineteenth-century Pennsylvania demonstrates that middle-class white girls forged social capital for their families by embroidering samplers that would hang on the walls of the home. Such samplers showed off the family's ability to relinquish girls from manual domestic labor for the purposes of finer work. Van Horn also argues that middle-class families, through girls' embroidery, were forging a class-based culture of their own that was not simply a mimicking of upper-class aesthetics and values. Jennifer Van Horn, "Samplers, Gentility, and the Middling Sort," *Winterthur Portfolio* 40, no. 4 (2005): 219–48. Middle-class African American girls in the North also studied embroidery via the sampler form, though in much smaller numbers. For more on Black girls and sampler work, see the research blog of Kelli Coles, a designer and scholar of Black girlhood and textiles. Kelli Coles, *Made in the African Diaspora*, kellicoles.tumblr.com/tagged/blackgirlneedlework.

53. Parker, *Subversive Stitch*, 148, 151, 152; "Evoke the home": 2.

54. *Monthly Message of the Parish of the Holy Apostles*, December 1917, p. 30;

November 1917, p. 31; January, 1918, p. 33; February 1918, p. 30; and March 1918, p. 30, digitized at philadelphiastudies.org.

55. African American Child's Sewing Exercise Book with 20 Hand-Sewn Sample Pieces, accession record, Schlesinger Library, Harvard Radcliffe Institute, Cambridge, Mass. Beatrice Jeanette Whiting Papers, Sewing Exercise Book, ca. 1915, MC897, folder 1.1, Schlesinger Library. Beatrice Jeanette Whiting Papers, Retirement Gift Album, 1960, MC897, folder 1.2v, Schlesinger Library. The accession record notes a Richmond oral history that quotes a sewing student of Whiting's; also see a reference by a sewing student in the Retirement Album, sequence 90. The estimated date range of Whiting's sewing exercise book is broad, from the bookseller's estimate of 1900–1905 to a Schlesinger librarian's estimate after acquisition of circa 1915 (which indicates a range of plus or minus five years). Because books like this were more commonly made by children, my discussion assumes a date in the middle of this range, when Whiting would have been a teenager. It is also possible that Whiting created this book as a model for her students to follow when she first began teaching (by 1916), in her twenties.

56. *Weekly Banner-Watchman* (Athens, Ga.), November 30, 1886, quoted in Kyra E. Hicks, *This I Accomplish: Harriet Powers' Bible Quilt and Other Pieces* (N.p.: Black Threads, 2009), 25–26.

57. "Black Victorians": Jeffrey Stewart uses this richly descriptive term in his biography of Alain Locke, a Philadelphian. Stewart, *New Negro*, 17. Women's sewing and decorating with textiles are prevalent in the Black Victorian culture of domesticity that Stewart describes (pp. 7, 15, 16, 17, 19, 25, 29). To see an example of this Black middle-class style from the period, visit Cedar Hill, Frederick Douglass's family home outside Washington, D.C., which is today a national historic site.

58. "Mass of Negro people": DuBois, *Philadelphia Negro*, Kindle loc. 2767. Du Bois also expressed concern that Blacks were spending more than they could afford on clothing and "extravagantly furnished parlors, dining rooms, guest chambers, and other visible parts of the homes" (Kindle loc. 2601).

59. Anna Julia Cooper, "Womanhood a Vital Element in the Regeneration of a Race," in *A Voice from the South* (1892; repr., New York: Oxford University Press, 1988), 12.

60. Paula Giddings, *When and Where I Enter: The Impact of Black Women on Race and Sex in America* (New York: Bantam, 1984), 93. Higginbotham, *Righteous Discontent*, 152. Also see Martha S. Jones, *Vanguard: How Black Women Broke Barriers, Won the Vote, and Insisted on Equality for All* (New York: Basic Books, 2020), 149, 152–53.

61. "The morality": Quoted in Giddings, *When and Where I Enter*, 86.

62. Higginbotham, *Righteous Discontent*, 137–44. See also Cooper, *A Voice from the South*, 62–63, 140–41.

63. Mary Church Terrell, *The Progress of Colored Women* (Adansonia Publishing, 2018), 9. See also Cooper, *A Voice from the South*, 9–47.

64. Evelyn Brooks Higginbotham made the now-classic argument that the politics of respectability served as a weapon for these women organizers in their

bid for community defense and racial betterment. Higginbotham, *Righteous Discontent*, 192, 227. See also Darlene Clark Hine, *Hine Sight: Black Women and the Re-Construction of American History* (Bloomington: Indiana University Press, 1994), 109–28. For a rereading of clubwomen's engagement with respectability among other political tactics, see Brittney C. Cooper, *Beyond Respectability: The Intellectual Thought of Race Women* (Urbana: University of Illinois Press, 2017).

65. Mamie Garvin Fields with Karen Fields, *Lemon Swamp and Other Places: A Carolina Memoir* (New York: Free Press, 1983), 9.

66. Fields, *Lemon Swamp*, 21. Fields explains that this woman she called "Grandma" was actually her maternal step-grandmother. She never knew her maternal birth grandmother, who was deceased.

67. Fields, *Lemon Swamp*, 199. Melnea Cass, transcript, Black Women's Oral History Project, OH-31; T-32, Schlesinger Library, Harvard Radcliffe Institute, 68–69.

68. Fields, *Lemon Swamp*, xvi.

69. Fields, *Lemon Swamp*, xx. The historian Michele Mitchell demonstrates how aspiring and middle-class Black women of this time period used domestic material culture such as Black dolls, books about racial improvement, and photographs of Black families to reinforce an intertwined ideology of acceptable gender roles and racial uplift. While she does not discuss embroidery or textiles passed down between mothers and daughters, objects like these would have fit into this domestic material ideal. Dolls, of course, also had fabric elements. Michele Mitchell, *Righteous Propagation: African Americans and the Politics of Racial Destiny After Reconstruction* (Chapel Hill: University of North Carolina Press, 2004), 178, 179, 194.

70. Parker, *Subversive Stitch*, 151; "absolute innocence": 166; "still and silence": 167; "loophole": 167.

71. Ulrich, *Age of Homespun*, 40.

72. Parker, *Subversive Stitch*, 205. Bryan-Wilson, *Fray*, 14, 1. Julia Bryan-Wilson also notes the use of embroidered banners by British suffragists in the early 1900s as a means of broadcasting women's dignity and making their demand for the vote seem less threatening; *Fray*, 9.

73. Betsy Greer, a knitter, coined the term "craftivism" in 2003 or 2004 (sources differ). Bryan-Wilson, *Fray*, 25. Stephanie Buck, "Women Craftivists Are Reclaiming Domesticity as a Quiet Form of Protest, *Timeline*, November 22, 2016, timeline.com/craftivism-art-women-82cf1d7067c8.

74. E. Tammy Kim, "The Feminist Power of Embroidery," *The New York Times*, May 27, 2019. See also the Instagram project Tiny Pricks, curated by Diana Weymar. In this project, started as a response to Donald Trump's presidency, artists stitch lines of cultural and political commentary onto vintage fabrics, signifying, Weymar writes, "warmth, craft, permanence, civility, and a shared history" in a "tumultuous political climate." See Instagram.com/tinypricks project/.

75. Kim, "Feminist Power of Embroidery." Julia Bryan-Wilson offers an interesting and similar analysis of the iconic photograph in which Sojourner Truth

is shown sitting and knitting with white yarn: "Truth might have so carefully deployed knitting *because* it could have been seen in several ways, as a non-threatening demonstration of her aptitude for domestic work, a reassuring sign of her femininity, *and* as an assertion of her strident activism and creative self-production"; *Fray*, 8.

76. *Grandeur Preserved: Masterworks Presented by Historic Charleston Foundation*, loan exhibition for the 57th Annual Winter Antiques Show, January 21–30, 2011.

77. Mark Auslander, "Tracing Ashley's Sack," *Cultural Environments* blog, January 7, 2016, note 3, culturalenvironments.blogspot.com/2016/01/.

78. Sampler scholars Jennifer Van Horn and David Stinebeck note the collaborative nature of embroidery samplers—between girls and teachers, as well as between girls and female relatives. In this way, in addition to her tight, verse-like lines, Ruth's inscription echoes the sampler. For detailed readings of several girls' samplers, see Van Horn, "Samplers." David Stinebeck argues that samplers showcasing poetic verse should be examined as part of the tradition of American literature. Sampler poems range from popular to original verse but, he says, were "rarely individually conceived." David Stinebeck, "Understanding the Forgotten Poetry of American Samplers," *Journal of Popular Culture* 52, no. 5 (2019): 1183–99, 1184, 1186. Also see the NEH-funded Sampler Archive project, a collaboration between the University of Oregon, the University of Delaware, and the Sampler Consortium; http://sampler archive.org/about.php. Ruth's attention to a "complex set of relations" inclusive of ancestors and even the unborn (given that she may have been pregnant when she began the craft project) suggests an alignment of her sense of identity with that of other Black women of the early twentieth century, as detailed by LaKisha Simmons in her study of oral histories from the 1930s. Simmons, "Black Feminist Theories of Motherood and Generation," 319.

79. Jones, *Corregidora*, 14.

80. The parallelism between Ruth's use of red for her quotation and Jesus's words printed in red in the Bible has been noted by academics from different fields. Mark Auslander was the first to publish this observation, in his article "Rose's Gift." The historian of Native America James Brooks raised this point in a public comment following a lecture I delivered: Tiya Miles, "'This Sack': Reconstructing Enslaved Women's Lives Through Objects," University of Georgia, Athens, October 24, 2019. And the African American studies scholar Henry Louis Gates, Jr., noted the same when he served as facilitator for another lecture of mine: Tiya Miles, "'A Tattered Dress': Reconstructing Enslaved Women's Lives Through Objects," Hutchins Center, Harvard University, Cambridge, Mass., February 19, 2020. Auslander makes note of the sense of Black English in Ruth's writing, a readily apparent feature in this line's use of the verb "be"; Auslander, "Rose's Gift."

81. Elizabeth Alexander, *The Black Interior: Essays* (Minneapolis: Graywolf, 2004), x.

82. Elizabeth Wayland Barber, *Women's Work: The First 20,000 Years; Women,*

Cloth, and Society in Early Times (New York: W. W. Norton, 1994), 127, 91, 114, 161, 162.

83. Albert J. Raboteau, *Slave Religion: The "Invisible Institution" in the Antebellum South* (New York: Oxford University Press, 2004), 276–78. Michael A. Gomez, *Exchanging Our Country Marks: The Transformation of African Identities in the Colonial and Antebellum South* (Chapel Hill: University of North Carolina Press), 206. Yvonne P. Chireau, *Black Magic: Religion and the African American Conjuring Tradition* (Berkeley: University of California Press, 2003), Kindle loc. 823. Another striking use of red fabric in African American folk culture is more uniformly menacing. The historian Michael Gomez recounts how formerly enslaved people on the South Carolina coast retold stories handed down about the capture of their ancestors for the slave trade in West Africa. In these tales, slave catchers used red cloth in the form of a handkerchief to lure unwitting victims onto slave ships; thus red was the color of warning and trickery. Gomez also notes, importantly, that textiles were the major item of value exchanged for captive Africans during the transatlantic slave trade (that is, Africans were usually sold for cloth). Gomez, *Exchanging Our Country Marks*, 202, 200, 205.

84. It is interesting to consider Ruth's inclusion of this list in relation to an argument that the women's studies scholar Brittney Cooper makes about what she calls the practice of "listing" among Black women intellectuals and activists of the late 1800s and early 1900s. "Listing" in Cooper's formulation is "a long practice . . . in which African American women created lists of prominent, qualified Black women for public consumption." Cooper then uses a fabric metaphor to explain the purpose of this practice: "to constitute a critical edge, without which the broader history of African American knowledge production would unravel." Cooper, *Beyond Respectability*, 26.

85. I am grateful for a casual conversation with Keith Vincent, a literary scholar, a haiku expert, and the chair of the Department of World Languages and Literature at Boston University, in which I learned these elements of the haiku and made a connection to the sack in the fall of 2018.

86. Keith Vincent gave me the idea that Ruth is welcoming Rose through these words, resulting in a metaphysical kind of reunion. Mark Auslander also uses "reunion" to describe the joining of the women on the surface of the cloth. Auslander, "Rose's Gift."

87. Nicole Sealey, *Ordinary Beast* (New York: HarperCollins, 2017), 55.

88. Ulrich, *Age of Homespun*, 141.

89. Mark Auslander also notes this shift of colors in the thread on the sack and offers a moving reading, including the green at the end as a representation of "enduring and regenerative connectedness" and of "spring after the death of winter." Auslander, "Rose's Gift."

90. Ruth Middleton, Certificate of Death, File No. 9389, Registered No. 1352, Commonwealth of Pennsylvania, Department of Health Bureau of Vital Statistics. Census and death certificate records give slightly varying birth dates for Ruth Middleton: 1902, 1903, and 1905. Her birth date in this reconstruc-

tion is approximal. She passed away on January 20, 1942. The death certificate gives her age as thirty-five. She was buried in Eden Cemetery. I have tried to identify lineal descendants of Dorothy with the help of a genealogist. If I have overlooked any evidence or missed the existence of descendants, I extend my heartfelt apology.

91. Mark Auslander states that Dorothy Middleton, Ruth Middleton's daughter, may have died in a nursing home in a suburb of Philadelphia (Wyncote), where her things would have been packed up and disposed of. Auslander, "Rose's Gift."

CONCLUSION: IT BE FILLED

1. Ira Berlin, Steven F. Miller, and Leslie S. Rowland, "Afro-American Families in the Transition from Slavery to Freedom," *Radical History Review* 42 (1988): 90, 110.

2. Pamela Newkirk, *A Love No Less: More Than Two Centuries of African American Love Letters* (New York: Doubleday, 2003), 3.

3. Kendra Field, "Things to Be Forgotten: Time, Place, and Silence in African American Family Histories," Q & A response following her lecture, Little Berks symposium, Berkshire Conference of Women Historians, Harvard Radcliffe Institute, Cambridge, Mass., June 7, 2019. For a thoughtful exploration of one Black family's incredible collection of photographs that did survive, see Evelyn Brooks Higginbotham, "History in the Face of Slavery: A Family Portrait," in Ilisa Barbash, Molly Rogers, and Deborah Willis, *To Make Their Way in the World: The Enduring Legacy of the Zealy Daguerreotypes* (Cambridge, Mass.: Peabody Museum Press, 2020).

4. Laurel Thatcher Ulrich, Ivan Gaskell, Sara M. Schechner, and Sarah Anne Carter, eds., "Introduction: Thinking with Things," *Tangible Things: Making History Through Objects* (New York: Oxford University Press, 2015), 2, 5, 8. Also see Robin Bernstein, *Racial Innocence: Performing American Childhood from Slavery to Civil Rights* (New York: New York University Press, 2011), 73.

5. Sarah Anne Carter, "Objects as Portals," in Ulrich et al., eds., *Tangible Things*, 164.

6. Robin Bernstein defines the special quality of certain things as an ability to "hail" people, get their attention, or call them into action. The actions she most explores are various kinds of performances. Bernstein, *Racial Innocence*, 73. Jane Bennett discusses the ability of things to act on people, especially as parts of assemblages. She calls this quality "thing power" and suggests that it is most easily realized or felt during childhood. Jane Bennett, *Vibrant Matter: A Political Ecology of Things* (Durham, N.C.: Duke University Press, 2010), 6, 21. Jane Bennett, "The Force of Things: Steps Toward an Ecology of Matter," *Political Theory* 32, no. 3 (June 2004): 348, 351, 353, 358. Bill Brown differentiates between an object and a thing in his essay introducing "thing theory," noting that things behave in distinctive ways: "lurk[ing]" in shadows, occupying liminal and "excessive" positions, and

suddenly "assert[ing] their presence and power." Bill Brown, "Thing Theory," *Critical Inquiry* 28, no. 1, *Things* (2001): 1–22, 3, 5.

7. Bennett, *Vibrant Matter*, 13, 112, 122.

8. See Kim TallBear's definition of an "indigenous metaphysic" that pre-dates Euro-American theories of new materialism. TallBear, "Beyond the Life/Not Life Binary: A Feminist-Indigenous Reading of Cryopreservation, Interspecies Thinking, and the New Materialisms," in *Cryopolitics: Frozen Life in a Melting World*, ed. Joanna Radin and Emma Kowal (Cambridge, Mass.: MIT Press, 2017), 191. Also see Robin Wall Kimmerer, "The Intelligence of Plants," *On Being*, National Public Radio, February 25, 2016, onbeing.org/programs/robin-wall-kimmerer-the-intelligence-of-plants/.

9. Kathleen M. Hilliard, *Masters, Slaves and Exchange: Power's Purchase in the Old South* (New York: Cambridge University Press, 2014), 7, 14.

10. Newkirk, *A Love No Less*, 7.

11. Newkirk, *A Love No Less*, 9.

12. Elizabeth Keckley, *Behind the Scenes, or Thirty Years a Slave and Four Years in the White House* (1868; repr., New York: Oxford University Press, 1988), 330.

13. Sarah Anne Carter, "Objects as Portals," in Ulrich et al., eds., *Tangible Things*, 165.

14. Davíd Carrasco, "The Ghost of Love and Goodness," in *Goodness and the Literary Imagination*, ed. Davíd Carrasco, Stephanie Paulsell, and Mara Willard (Charlottesville: University Press of Virginia, 2019), 121. In this statement, Carrasco is describing Toni Morrison's literature and the way in which she "infuses nature with the supernatural."

15. Beads carried symbolic importance for African Americans and Native Americans as religious charms, artistic materials, and modes of communication. For examples of enslaved people's desire to obtain and gift beads, see John Sella Martin's account discussed in chapter 4. See Rashauna Johnson, *Slavery's Metropolis: Unfree Labor in New Orleans During the Age of Revolutions* (New York: Cambridge University Press, 2016), 221. Also see Hayley Negrin's dissertation, "Possessing Native Women and Children: Slavery, Gender and English Colonialism in the Early American South, 1670–1717" (PhD diss., New York University, 2018), 102; here Negrin summarizes an eighteenth-century account of a white Carolina trader, Phillip Gilliard, who captured a Native woman for sexual slavery and "whipped her and her brother for accepting a few beades from her." For more on beads as protective charms, see Maude Southwell Wahlman, "African Charm Traditions Remembered in the Arts of the Americas," in *African Impact on the Material Culture of the Americas: Conference Proceedings* (Winston-Salem, N.C.: Museum of Early Southern Decorative Arts, 1996), 5. Also see Amy L. Young, "Religion and Ritual Among African American Slaves During the Antebellum Period in Kentucky: An Archaeological Perspective," in *African Impact on the Material Culture of the Americas*, 3–4. Young notes the prevalence of beads—particularly blue beads—recovered at multiple archaeologi-

cal sites of slave dwellings; Wahlman points out that blue beads were thought to have especially protective properties.

16. Laura F. Edwards, "Textiles: Popular Culture and the Law," *Buffalo Law Review* 64 (2016): 195, 207.

17. Julia Bryan-Wilson, *Fray: Art and Textile Politics* (Chicago: University of Chicago Press, 2017), 215, 217. Also see Julia Bryan-Wilson's analysis of the quilt as archive, *Fray*, 226.

18. Ann Hamilton, *Habitus* (Philadelphia: The Fabric Workshop and Museum, 2017), 5.

19. Jane Schneider and Annette B. Weiner, "Introduction," in *Cloth and Human Experience*, Annette B. Weiner and Jane Schneider, eds. (Washington, D.C.: Smithsonian Institution Press, 1989), 3, 21.

20. The historian Nancy Bercaw was co-curator, with Mary Elliott, of this exhibition.

21. Paul Gardullo, NMAAHC, email exchange with Tiya Miles, February 19, 2018.

22. W. Fitzhugh Brundage, *Civilizing Torture: An American Tradition* (Cambridge, Mass.: Harvard University Press, 2018), 153.

23. Barbara Christian, introduction to Dorothy Sterling, *Black Foremothers: Three Lives*, 2nd ed. (New York: Feminist Press, 1988), xxiv.

24. Heather Andrea Williams, *Help Me to Find My People: The African American Search for Family Lost in Slavery* (Chapel Hill: University of North Carolina Press, 2012), 13.

25. Drawing on the work of archaeologists and anthropologists, women's studies scholar Elizabeth Fisher argues that the carrier bag was an early and essential human tool likely developed by women, who used it in gathering and carrying infants. Elizabeth Fisher, *Woman's Creation: Sexual Evolution and the Shaping of Society* (1979; repr., New York, McGraw-Hill, 1980), chapter 7: "The Carrier Bag Theory of Evolution," 56–61. Ursula Le Guin describes the sack as "the tool that brings energy home"; see "The Carrier Bag Theory of Fiction" in her *Dancing at the Edge of the World: Thoughts on Words, Women, Places* (New York: Grove Press, 1989), 167.

26. I owe my introduction to this concept of the seed carrier as alternative hero to literary and film scholar Kirk Sides, and my introduction to Kirk Sides's work to environmental historian Martha Few. Kirk Sides discusses the seed bag carrier figure, borrowing from Ursula K. Le Guin, who borrows from Elizabeth Fisher. Sides argues that the adoption of ways of storytelling capable of narrating crisis is a necessity, as these stories carry the seeds for Afrofuturist visions in an apocalyptic age of "planet-death." Kirk Bryan Sides, "Seed Bags and Storytelling: Modes of Living and Writing After the End in Wanuri Kahiu's *Pumzi*," *Critical Philosophy of Race* 7, no. 1 (2019): 107–23. Sides also gives workshops on this topic with his collaborator, the poet and literary critic Tjawangwa Dema. Kirk B. Sides, "Seed Bags and Storytelling: Modes of Living and Writing in the African Anthropocene," Anthropocene Storytelling: Ecological Writing and Pedagogies of Planetary Change, Penn-

sylvania State University, University Park, April 18–19, 2019. Ursula K. Le Guin, "Carrier Bag Theory of Fiction."

27. Le Guin, "Carrier Bag Theory of Fiction," 168.

28. Keckley, *Behind the Scenes*, 167–68.

LITTLE SACK OF SOMETHING: AN ESSAY ON PROCESS

1. Tiya Miles, "The Spirits of Dunbar Creek: Stories of Slavery in Coastal Ghost Tourism," Coastal Nature, Coastal Culture: Environmental Histories of the Georgia Coast, February 18–20, 2016, Coastal Georgia Center, Savannah. The revised presentations from the symposium have been published. See Tiya Miles, "Haunted Waters: Stories of Slavery, Coastal Ghosts, and Environmental Consciousness," in *Coastal Nature, Coastal Culture*, ed. Paul S. Sutter and Paul M. Pressly (Athens: University of Georgia Press, 2017).

2. Ben Goggins, "Looking for Pearls: Ashley's Sack, Davenport Dolls Give Insight into Lives of Slaves," *Savannah Now*, January 28, 2016, savannahnow.com/article/20160128/LIFESTYLE/301289786. "Artifacts That Will Send a Chill Down Your Spine: A CBS Team Shows the Most Moving Artifacts of African-American History Collected for a New Museum in Washington," February 28, 2016, cbsnews.com/news/60-minutes-presents-preserving-the-past/. Jeff Neale, "Ashley's Sack: A Humble Object of Revelation," Davenport House Museum, Savannah, Ga., December 2016.

3. Tiya Miles, interview with Mary Edna Sullivan, November 13, 2018, Middleton Place, Charleston, S.C. Robin Bernstein, *Racial Innocence: Performing American Childhood from Slavery to Civil Rights* (New York: New York University Press, 2011), 73. Todd quoted in Goggins, "Looking for Pearls."

4. "Diminutive value" quote: Pamela Newkirk, *A Love No Less: More Than Two Centuries of African American Love Letters* (New York: Doubleday, 2003), 3.

5. David Glassberg, "Place, Memory, and Climate Change," *The Public Historian*, Vol. 36, No. 3 (August 2014): 17–30, 25–26.

6. Nell Irvin Painter, "Soul Murder and Slavery: Toward a Fully Loaded Cost Accounting," in *U.S. History as Women's History: New Feminist Essays*, ed. Linda K. Kerber, Alice Kessler-Harris, and Kathryn Kish Sklar (Chapel Hill: University of North Carolina Press, 1995), 146.

7. By "fugitive inventory," I am referring to the lists of things and values—written on the page, or cloth, or heart—by unfree people seeking to repel the will of the master class through mobile or transitory acts of creative resistance.

8. Marisa Fuentes, *Dispossessed Lives: Enslaved Women, Violence, and the Archive* (Philadelphia: University of Pennsylvania Press, 2016), 1, 78.

9. Saidiya Hartman, "Venus in Two Acts," *Small Axe* 26 (June 2008): 12.

10. Jill Lepore, *These Truths: A History of the United States* (New York: W. W. Norton: 2018), 38.

11. Lauret Savoy, *Trace: Memory, History, Race, and the American Landscape*

(Berkeley: Counterpoint, 2015), 1, 2. It is worth noting that Savoy is an environmental historian as well as a creative-nonfiction writer. Historians of the environment are experienced at enlisting a material historical method that allows for hunting and gathering sources beyond the page. I embraced this approach in my exploration of the sack, turning to physical things in the world, like textiles, foodstuffs, buildings, needles, and landscapes, in addition to written pages (which are also material things, but rarely treated as such). Environmental historian Hayley Brazier has ably articulated the way in which, "as logophiles, historians understand the past through documents that tell us a story of the human experience. But we often forget the physicality and tangibility of our ancestors." "Documents," she continues, "cannot provide scale and sensation." Hayley Brazier, "Practicing in Place," *Environmental History* Field Notes 1, April 8, 2016, environmentalhistory.net/field-notes/2016-brazier/.

12. In his study of the Haitian Revolution, which doubles as a theory of history, Caribbean anthropologist Michel-Rolph Trouillot describes the remaining "facts" of the past as traces and notes that "the production of traces is always also the production of silences." Michel-Rolph Trouillot, *Silencing the Past: Power and the Production of History* (1995; repr., Boston: Beacon, 2015), 29. In his use of "traces" and "echoes," deep historian Daniel Lord Smail refers to any items that lend information about the past. He emphasizes natural and material things like fossils and pollen because these have often been devalued, but he also includes memory and manuscripts, noting that some traces are more instructive than others. Daniel Lord Smail, *On Deep History and the Human Brain* (Berkeley: University of California Press, 2008), 6, 49, 48, 52, 59. Christine DeLucia, a historian of Native America and colonial America, uses the term and concept of "trace" frequently in her study of King Philip's War. While she searches for and analyzes traces of past lives and events on the landscape, she also cautions against an overreliance on material traces at the expense of memory. She reminds readers that material traces are not self-evidentiarily factual; they, like memories, are filtered through layers of interpretation. She suggests, as well, that physical traces can ignite "memory-sparks" that are just as valuable for historical interpretation. Christine M. DeLucia, *Memory Lands: King Philip's War and the Place of Violence in the Northeast* (New Haven: Yale University Press, 2018), 17–18, 40, 146. The phrasing that came to my mind here, "ghostly matter," is surely influenced by Avery Gordon's book *Ghostly Matters: Haunting and the Sociological Imagination* (1997; repr., Minneapolis: University of Minnesota Press, 2008). For a discussion of historical texts as traces, see Amy J. Elias, "Metahistorical Romance, the Historical Sublime, and Dialogic History," *Rethinking History* 9, nos. 2–3 (2005): 159–72, 168.

13. Elizabeth Alexander, *Black Interior: Essays* (Minneapolis: Graywolf, 2004), x.

14. John Michael Vlach, *The Afro-American Tradition in Decorative Arts* (Athens: University of Georgia Press, 1990), ix. Vlach's book is based on a 1978 exhibition held at the Cleveland Museum of Art that later traveled to several

museums. The major categories of craft exhibited and discussed included basketry, musical instruments, wood carving, quilting, pottery, boat building, blacksmithing, architecture, and graveyard decoration.

15. See Vlach, *Afro-American Tradition*. I am referring here to what seems to be a resurgence in interest in material history among historians of slavery. For instance, see Amy Murrell Taylor's *Embattled Freedom*, in which she emphasizes "material reality" as a major thematic. Amy Murrell Taylor, *Embattled Freedom: Journeys Through the Civil War's Slave Refugee Camps* (Chapel Hill: University of North Carolina Press, 2018), 12, 18. See also a forthcoming special issue titled "Enslavement and Material Culture" in the Winterthur Museum journal, *Winterthur Portfolio* 54, no. 4 (Winter 2020). As I note elsewhere, Stephanie Camp is to be credited with revealing the richness of various materialities, including embodiment, geography, and cultures of personal adornment, in the study of enslaved women's lives; Stephanie Camp, *Closer to Freedom: Enslaved Women and Everyday Resistance in the Plantation South* (Chapel Hill: University of North Carolina Press, 2004).

16. Fuentes, *Dispossessed Lives*, 1, 78.

17. Alexandra A. Chan, *Slavery in the Age of Reason: Archaeology at a New England Farm* (Knoxville: University of Tennessee Press, 2007), 4.

18. I was influenced in this notion by science fiction writer Ursula Le Guin's discussion of the novel being like a sack. Ursula K. Le Guin, *Dancing at the Edge of the World: Thoughts on Words, Women, Places* (New York: Grove Press, 1989), 169. Le Guin writes: "A novel is a medicine bundle, holding things in a particular, powerful relation to one another and to us." For a definition of assemblage in new materialist theory, see Jane Bennett, *Vibrant Matter: A Political Ecology of Things* (Durham, N.C.: Duke University Press, 2010), 23–24. For a description of "vibrant material" with cultural and spiritual energy, see Kim TallBear, "Beyond the Life/Not Life Binary: A Feminist-Indigenous Reading of Cryopreservation, Interspecies Thinking, and the New Materialisms," in *Cryopolitics: Frozen Life in a Melting World*, ed. Joanna Radin and Emma Kowal (Cambridge, Mass.: MIT Press, 2017), 195, 197.

19. I am quoting Sharla Fett, quoting a woman describing her conjure bag in a WPA interview transcript. Fett, *Working Cures: Healing, Health, and Power on Southern Plantations* (Chapel Hill: University of North Carolina Press, 2002), 102, 229.

PERMISSIONS
ACKNOWLEDGMENTS

Simon & Schuster, Inc.: "Pecan Wafers" recipe from *A Good Heart and A Light Hand: Ruth L. Gaskin's Collection of Traditional Negro Recipes* by Rusk L. Gaskins, copyright © 1968 by Fund for Alexandria, Virginia. Reprinted by permission of Simon & Schuster, Inc. All rights reserved.

University of California, Berkeley Art Museum and Pacific Film Archive (BAMPFA) and the Estate of Rosie Lee Tompkins: Image of quilt on the sixth page of the insert, Rosie Lee Tompkins: Untitled, c. 2004, quilted by Irene Bankhead (2007), printed cotton, polyester, woven wool, velour, cotton flannel, wool, cotton embroidery, and other fabrics with cotton muslin backing, 40-½ x 53 inches. Bequest of The Eli Leon Living Trust, 2019.72.55. Photographed for the University of California, Berkeley Art Museum and Pacific Film Archive by Benjamin Blackwell. Reprinted by permission of University of California, Berkeley Art Museum and Pacific Film Archive (BAMPFA) and the Estate of Rosie Lee Tompkins.

INDEX

Page numbers in *italic* refer to illustrations.

Tiya Miles is a professor of history, a Radcliffe Alumnae Professor at the Harvard Radcliffe Institute for Advanced Study, and director of the Charles Warren Center for Studies in American History at Harvard University. She is a recipient of a MacArthur Foundation fellowship and the Hiett Prize in the Humanities from the Dallas Institute of Humanities and Culture. Her book *The Dawn of Detroit* received the Merle Curti Award in Social History, the James A. Rawley Prize in race relations, the James Bradford Biography Prize, the Hurston/Wright Legacy Award in Nonfiction, an American Book Award, and a Frederick Douglass Book Prize. Miles is also the author of *Ties That Bind*, *The House on Diamond Hill*, *The Cherokee Rose: A Novel of Gardens and Ghosts*, and *Tales from the Haunted South*, a published lecture series.